American Studies
Encounters the
Middle East

American Studies Encounters the Middle East

EDITED BY

Alex Lubin and Marwan M. Kraidy

University of North Carolina Press CHAPEL HILL

This book was published with support from the Center for American Studies and Research at the American University of Beirut.

Manufactured in the United States of America
Set in Espinosa Nova by Westchester Publishing Services

The University of North Carolina Press has been a member
of the Green Press Initiative since 2003.

Cover illustration: © iStockphoto.com/Richard Sharrocks

Library of Congress Cataloging-in-Publication Data
Names: Lubin, Alex, editor. | Kraidy, Marwan M., 1972– editor.
Title: American studies encounters the Middle East / edited by
    Alex Lubin and Marwan M. Kraidy.
Description: Chapel Hill: University of North Carolina Press, [2016] |
    Includes bibliographical references and index.
Identifiers: LCCN 2015042378| ISBN 9781469628844 (pbk: alk. paper) |
    ISBN 9781469630137 (hardback: alk. paper) | ISBN 9781469628851 (ebook)
Subjects: LCSH: United States—Relations—Middle East. |
Middle East—Relations—United States. | East and West.
Classification: LCC DS63.2.U5 A8225 2016 | DDC 303.48/273056—dc23
    LC record available at http://lccn.loc.gov/2015042378

Contents

Illustrations

Acknowledgments

The chapters in this collection came out of conversations held at the 2012 international conference of the Center for American Studies and Research (CASAR) at the American University of Beirut (AUB). That conference was titled "Shifting Borders: America and the Middle East/North Africa." At the time, Alex Lubin was director of CASAR and Marwan Kraidy was the visiting Edward Said Chair of American Studies. We owe a tremendous amount of gratitude to AUB. We especially want to thank AUB's administration for supporting the conference and our scholarship: former AUB president Peter Dorman; Provost Ahmad Dallal; and dean of the faculty of Arts and Sciences Patrick McGreevy. Each attended and addressed the conference. We are grateful for their visionary leadership at AUB and support for the work of transnational American Studies in Lebanon.

Anybody who has come in contact with CASAR at the AUB has likely interacted with Nancy Batakji-Sanyoura, the assistant to the director of CASAR. Nancy was a great help in organizing the "Shifting Borders" conference, and it was a pleasure for both of us to work with her in organizing the conference and working at AUB in general. We also wish to thank the work of colleagues at AUB who helped organize the conference, including Adam Waterman, Waleed Hazbun, Sirene Harb, Karim Makdisi, and Robert Meyers.

The entire editorial team at University of North Carolina Press has been excellent. Mark Simpson-Vos saw something important in this project, even when it was not well organized and lacked a coherent thread. Mark's smart feedback and tactful translation of editorial feedback has been most welcome. Elspeth Iralu, a graduate student at University of New Mexico, provided helpful editorial assistance in the final stages of the project.

We are also grateful for the patience of all of the authors in this collection. It took longer than expected to see this project to the end, and we are thankful that authors were willing to revise, wait, and revise again, as we asked for further information and as events across the United States and Middle East changed.

And, finally, we would both like to thank our partners and kids who traveled with us during our year together in Lebanon; they put up with far too much shop-talk during our collective outings.

American Studies
Encounters the
Middle East

Introduction

American Studies Encounters the Middle East

ALEX LUBIN AND MARWAN M. KRAIDY

In the hills above the Casino du Liban, in the predominantly Maronite Catholic Keserwan district of Lebanon, sits El Rancho, a Texas-style dude ranch that hosts the Cedar Stampede Rodeo, a Sunday Texas barbeque, evening campfires, and deluxe lodging in "genuine" Sioux Indian tepees. El Rancho is a tourist destination in which visitors, some of whom may be both Lebanese and American, recreate a mythic U.S. frontier, a landscape populated by images of cowboys and American Indians made popular in globalized U.S. culture. El Rancho promises visitors "an authentic Tex-Mex experience," where they can "set off on a dude ranch escape." For Lebanese and regional visitors who may not know the meaning of the term "dude ranch," the El Rancho website provides ample definition and examples. According to its advertising, "El Rancho Lebanon is modeled on the history of ranching in the United States, a history that can be accessed through the iconography of the 'wild west' made popular in the Hollywood Western." Visitors can go to El Rancho to indulge in Angus beef hamburgers imported from the United States in a restaurant that recreates a western saloon, with John Wayne paraphernalia. Moreover, visitors can walk through a recreated western town filled with wooden statues of cowboys and forlorn images of defeated, but noble, Indians.[1]

El Rancho is a private venture owned by a Lebanese businessperson, but the U.S. consulate and several U.S.-based corporations such as Baskin-Robbins and Krispy Kreme sponsor some of its activities, including the annual Cedar Stampede Rodeo. In this sense, although El Rancho is a private Lebanese venture, it is connected to the United States not only because it features a version of U.S.—Tex-Mex—culture but also because it receives authenticity through occasional sponsorship of the U.S. consulate.

Although El Rancho promises an authentic Tex-Mex experience, its symbols and icons have been reorganized and shuffled so that various particularities of western U.S. expansion are confused. The advertised

1

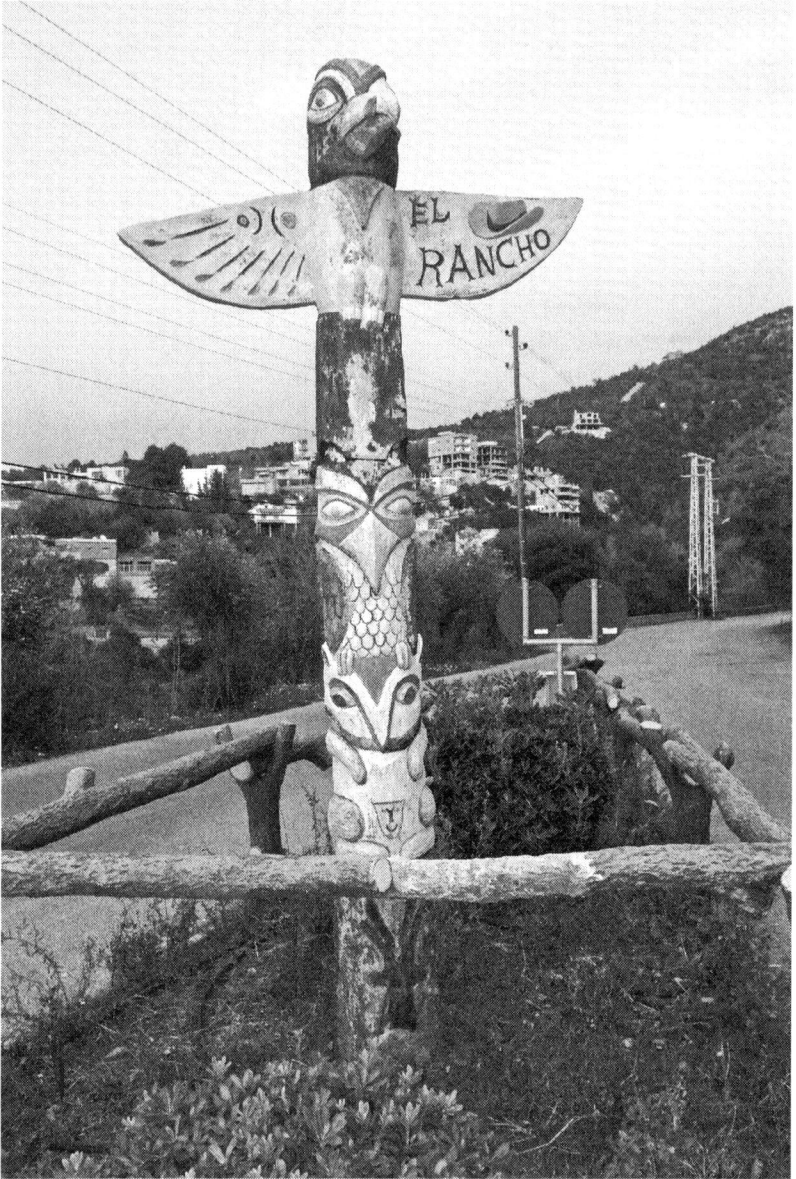

Totem pole with cowboy hat announcing the turn-off to El Rancho, Ghodras, Lebanon. Photo taken by Alex Lubin.

Photos of John Wayne and Johnny Cash on the wall at El Rancho's "western" saloon, where Angus beef hamburgers are imported from the United States. Photo taken by Alex Lubin.

"Sioux Indian Teepees," for example, might be found in the Northern Plains of the United States, but not in the U.S.–Mexico borderlands. Moreover, the activities available at El Rancho are not exclusively related to the mythical U.S. west. Among the activities advertised on the El Rancho website are "Espionage Wars" or "Roman Games." This mish-mash of seemingly random cultural activities presents a mediated vision of American culture, inaccurate in its history and geography but compelling in its iconography, disassociated from its original referent.

What makes El Rancho so fascinating is not only how U.S. culture travels internationally and is received in non-U.S. destinations but also how American culture circulates between and within complex geopolitical realities. The United States relationship with Lebanon is currently tense, as Hezbollah—a political party the United States regards as a terrorist organization—controls many areas of the Lebanese government. Moreover, Lebanon's capitol, Beirut, was the scene of a major U.S. military defeat, as U.S. forces intending to intervene in Lebanon's bloody civil war came under attack in 1983. Following the bombing of the U.S. marine barracks in Beirut, in which 299 American and French soldiers died, President Ronald Reagan prevented all direct, nonstop flights from Lebanon to the United States, a ban that continues to this day. Moreover, U.S. support for successive Israeli military occupations and attacks in Lebanon has only escalated Lebanese criticism of U.S. foreign policy. During the last two decades of the twentieth century Lebanon had been the scene of covert U.S. military intervention as well as kidnappings and assassinations of U.S. diplomats and American citizens. Given the thorny realities of U.S.–Lebanese geopolitics, it is even more curious why American culture circulates so prominently in Lebanon at places like El Rancho. Why would the American frontier play such a prominent role in a Lebanese tourist venue at a time when U.S. foreign policy is under intense Lebanese scrutiny?

Within the United States, the western frontier mythology thrives as well. It sutures together stories of cowboys and Indians in sparsely populated western landscapes with an imagined past—one that is used to explain who Americans are (or are not) as "a people" and often to hide the way this past is tied to a legacy of settler violence that underwrites much of the United States' national development. But what might these things mean in Lebanon? Perhaps the U.S. west represents something altogether different. It might signify how icons of American culture circulate in the Arab world, but it might also mean something about the borders and

Stereotypical American Indian statue holding cedar branch (the symbol of Lebanon) inside El Rancho, Lebanon. Photo taken by Alex Lubin.

frontiers of Lebanon or about the location of colonized "reservations"—Palestinian refugee camps—within Lebanon's borders.

Perhaps El Rancho is rooted to a genealogy of American exceptionalism intended to elide the legacy of conquest in the making of American culture *and* to a Lebanese desire for a (translated) version of American frontiers. Beyond the influence of the United States, El Rancho assumes many meanings as American culture gets reconstituted in ways that make tenuous its cultural and material referents. Hence, there is both something especially American and something foreign to America that El Rancho Lebanon is attempting to market and that the U.S. embassy is occasionally willing to sponsor. The seeming chaotic pastiche of El Rancho Lebanon might expose the contradictions inherent to both states and in this way becomes something that resides beyond any one nation. In its travels, American culture gets translated in ways that reveal the political unconscious of both its location of origin and its arrival destination.

American Studies Encounters the Middle East attempts to understand the dense and overlapping global cultural processes that make El Rancho intelligible as well as the complex narratives El Rancho tells about the United States and about globalized American culture. We are interested in how U.S. culture travels and the curious ways that notions of "America" transform in the process of international and global circulation. Moreover, in this collection, we are interested in how American culture circulates in the Middle East and North Africa within changing geopolitical contexts. We therefore focus our analysis on the historical encounters, especially of the Middle East *in* America in the making of early American culture as well as the contemporary encounter as it is shaped in the context of changing U.S. global prestige and political realities across the Arab world. These are topics that have renewed currency in the present moment given the changing geopolitical relationship of United States to the Middle East in particular.

El Rancho is but one example of the ways that cultural meanings are produced through movement, travel, and media—the Hollywood western being a relevant and familiar example in this case—as the idea of America is translated by and for Lebanese audiences. Yet, like all travel, cultural flows move within particular and shifting geopolitical topographies. It was the great contribution of Birmingham cultural studies scholars to illustrate how culture and material conditions are dialectically related in ways that suggest culture as a site of negotiation of material politics and not merely a reflection of representation. And yet, despite the important influence of Birmingham cultural studies over the discipline of American cultural studies, and despite the internationalist bent and transnational approach of leading figures like Stuart Hall and Paul Gilroy, questions of international geopolitics and U.S. foreign relations—in the Middle East, especially—have been largely overlooked by the discipline (and were sometimes relegated to postcolonial theory, a formation that U.S. cultural studies has tended to keep at an arm's length). As a result, and despite the avowedly anti-exceptionalist bent of American studies since at least the 1970s, the field remains largely rooted to an exceptionalist framework in which knowledge about the United States produced within the United States remains a privileged vantage point.[2]

Our goal with this collection is not merely to continue the ongoing process of internationalizing American studies approaches by including non-U.S. scholars and viewpoints but rather, by featuring multidisciplinary perspectives on the Arab–U.S. relation from scholars based in both the Middle East and the United States, we aim to place the discipline in transit in order to explore how cultural forms circulate transnationally and are shaped by and contribute to international geopolitical contexts. In particular, we seek to understand the possibilities of American studies during a moment of profound geopolitical transformation and during a historical conjuncture we identify by the end of the "American Century" and the ongoing social upheaval of the so-called Arab Spring. This is a conjuncture dominated by global economic and political crises that have momentous implications for the Middle East and pose unique challenges to scholars attempting to understand the meaning of U.S. economic, military, and cultural power.

The internationalization of the discipline of American studies is not new, having its roots in the earliest years of the institutionalization of the field. Throughout the 1950s as American studies programs were forming across the American academy, similar programs were formed in allied European countries. American studies institutes at Salzburg and Bologna led to the formation of a European American studies center in the mid-1950s. By 1964 the Fulbright-Hayes Act instituted an American studies international exchange program that helped foster university exchanges and American studies lecturers abroad, especially in allied Western European countries. Alongside the Fulbright program, the United States Information Agency (USIA) spread American history and culture as cultural diplomacy, and in this way the spread of the discipline of American studies would be carefully managed alongside efforts to spread an image of American power. American studies programs emerged in allied countries as a means to consolidate U.S. power over "the West," even as scholars within international American studies centers brought their own interests and agendas to the project.[3]

The internationalization of the field of American studies did not include the Middle East until 1998, however, when the first American studies program was launched at the University of Bahrain. By this time, the Cold War was over and the U.S. military presence across the Middle East was escalating. American studies programs once again were seen as useful platforms for cultural diplomacy, but the context for the post–Cold War internationalization of the field was significantly different than it was during the Cold War for a couple reasons. First, American studies entered the Middle East at a time when it was difficult to export an exceptionalist vision of American benevolence. The American studies program in Bahrain, for example, opened just two years following the formation of a permanent military base in Bahrain, and in this way American studies programs in the region would always be shadowed by the presence of the U.S. military.

Moreover, American studies programs emerged in the Middle East in places where an increasing popular and intellectual skepticism about the primacy of American power went hand-in-hand with official closeness to U.S. foreign policy. Following the formation of the State Department–sponsored program for American studies in Bahrain were the formation of programs at the University of Jordan and in East Jerusalem, at Al-Quds University. These programs, like the one at Bahrain, would have a specific mandate to educate a moderate leadership favorable to U.S. interests, including the interests of such U.S. allies as Israel, Jordan, and the Gulf monarchies. Still, it would be increasingly difficult to exert the tutelary power of American empire in these geographies given how American support for Israel would increasingly be identified as a key culprit in the instability of the region, especially in places where there were large numbers of Palestinian refugees.

While the Palestine question was largely taboo within American studies in the United States, at least until very recently, across the Arab region the question of Palestine was formative of regional understandings of American culture and power. As a result of the preeminent role of the Palestine question across the Middle East and its relative absence within the State Department vision of the field, a widening chasm divided the vision of the discipline from the U.S. State Department and regional practitioners across the Middle East. Like the folklore of the Hollywood western depicted in El Rancho Lebanon, American studies across the Middle East would be its own discipline, sometimes working in opposition to the State Department mandate of its donors.[4]

The particularities of the internationalization of American studies into the Middle East in conjunction with the changing fortunes and preeminence of the United States in the region raises important questions about the relationship of knowledge production to geopolitical power as well as about the possibilities of American studies as an intellectual project that can be distinct from U.S. empire. Popular protest against economic inequality, social discrimination, and political repression have swept the globe from Wisconsin to Greece, from Israel to Russia, from Spain to New York, culminating with the Arab uprisings that have radically transformed Arab politics. In the United States, fierce battles over the social contract enacted during the New Deal, intense struggles over immigration and ethnic studies, and organized protest movements to resist neoliberal labor and social relations focus attention on new subjects with new social imaginaries. In the Arab world, unlikely alliances of Islamist and secular activists have dislodged autocrats entrenched in power for decades while new fault lines emerge in the spaces made unlivable by decades of foreign intervention and military invasions. Though oceans apart, these struggles have in common the search for human dignity in political and economic contexts that put power and resources in the hands of the few.

In the wake of the Arab uprisings and at the twilight of the American Century, *American Studies Encounters the Middle East* contributes to a deeper understanding of the ways that geopolitical and academic borders of all kinds are malleable, socially constructed, and historically contingent. The primary subjects of the collection, America and the Middle East–North Africa (MENA), are themselves shifting imaginaries. Historically, culturally, politically, economically, and demographically, America is in MENA and MENA is in America. Moreover, social movements and struggles shaking America and MENA (including the Tea Party formation, the Occupy movement, and the Arab uprisings) have global ramifications; therefore, it is intellectually productive to shift the analytical borders of America and MENA by integrating the "Americas" or the Islamic "worlds" in a broader terrain that includes Africa, Asia, Europe, and Latin America. The transnational American studies conjured up in our book explicates the multiple and mutual entanglements of "America" and the "Middle East."

American Studies Encounters the Middle East addresses two related areas of American Studies scholarship: First, the collection aims to historicize the political, social, and cultural encounters that have taken place between the United States and MENA. Modalities of interaction including missionary work, "public diplomacy," lethal drones, and hip-hop reflect a historically deep, politically unsettled, and culturally complicated encounter between the United States and the Arab world. Second, by counterposing the Arab Spring to the American Century, this volume pushes for critical engagement with the trope of the "American Century" and attendant notions. It is well known that the discipline of American studies emerged within the context of the Cold War and the ascendancy of U.S. global supremacy. Since the fall of the Soviet system, however, the discipline finds itself confronting an American empire without a geopolitical rival, with declining geopolitical influence globally yet enduring economic, military, and cultural supremacy. The American Century has come to an end as the United States finds itself in a debilitating condition of permanent war (against terrorism) and declining economic futures. Since the Middle East is a primary locus of the exercise of American warfare, examining the Arab–U.S. encounter promises to shed critical light on how both sides of the relationship view themselves and one another.

What scholarly interventions might the end of the American Century require? This volume argues for a continued push by American studies toward a transnational approach that is not merely "postnationalist" as John Carlos Rowe advocated, but that is truly global, in this case, by a full inclusion of the voices and approaches of scholars writing from North America, the Middle East, and elsewhere.[5] *American Studies Encounters the Middle East* therefore takes as its subject the complex history and present of U.S. engagement with MENA in order to exemplify a different sort of American studies committed equally to the study of the transnational circulation of American culture outside the United States and to the circulation of other cultures in the American cultural imaginary.

The American Century

Before tracing the possibilities of American studies in the post–American Century, it is necessary to review how the American Century helped establish the current conjecture at the beginning of the second decade of the twenty-first century. In 1941 Henry Luce, the prolific owner of *Life* magazine, published his influential essay, "The American Century," in which he defined the contours of the post–World War II era. Writing before U.S. entry into World War II, Luce argued that the United States was poised to become a global leader within the West and that the nation had an indispensable, if not providential, role to play in global affairs. Luce sought to sway the U.S. government into joining World War II and to argue against the perceived isolationism of the Roosevelt administration. Were the United States to enter the war and replace European allies within the Atlantic world for economic and geopolitical primacy, it would be poised to assume the mantle of global leadership through America's unique ability to combine free markets with free peoples.

> It is for America and for America alone to determine whether a system of free economic enterprise—an economic order compatible with freedom and progress—shall or shall not prevail in this century. . . . We have to decide whether or not we shall have for ourselves and our friends freedom of the seas—the right to go with our ships and our ocean-going airplanes where we wish, when we wish and as we wish. The vision of America as the principal guarantor of the freedom of the seas, the vision of America as the dynamic leader of world trade, has within it the possibilities of such enormous human progress as to stagger the imagination. Let us not be staggered by it. Let us rise to its tremendous possibilities.[6]

Combined with the United States' ability to protect and spread the free market and, hence, global freedom, according to Luce, was the United States' exceptional ability to value self-determination in the international sphere and to respect the rule of law.

Although the values of free markets and free societies were promoted in Luce's popular magazines, the geopolitical realities of the American Century were articulated in the halls of Washington, where the federal government developed a road map to realize Luce's vision of an American Century. Following World War II, with the ascendance of the United States as a global power and the start of the Cold War and its bipolar world order, U.S. State Department officials sought to realize a vision for the American Century. The National Security Council issued policy document NSC-68 in April 1950, in which it formulated the parameters of the policy of containment as both a foreign policy to limit the spread of the Soviet Union beyond the borders outlined in the "Big Three" conferences that ended World War II and as a domestic policy to contain the threat of communism within the borders of the United States; indeed, containment was both a domestic and a foreign policy that required investments in warfare abroad and political repression at home.

Yet the American Century was shaped by a central contradiction, one that was identified by the important diplomatic historian from the University of Wisconsin, William Appleman Williams. In *The Tragedy of American Diplomacy*, Williams argued that the Cold War was merely a new phase in a long history of American imperial expansion. Throughout its history, Williams argued, three sometimes complementary but more often-contradictory currents characterized American power. "In the realm of ideas and ideals," he argued,

> American policy is guided by three conceptions. One is the warm, generous, humanitarian impulse to help other people solve their problems. A second is the principle of self-determination applied at the international level, which asserts the right of every society to establish its own goals or objectives, and then to realize them internally through the means it decides are appropriate. These two ideas can be reconciled; indeed, they complement each other to an extensive degree. But the third idea entertained by many Americans is one that insists that other people cannot *really* solve their problems and improve their lives unless they go about it the same way as the United States.[7]

In this way Williams argued that U.S. foreign relations were always framed through the language of benevolence and self-determination yet were actually guided by a desire to ensure the reproduction of the American way—its system of government and economy—in non-American places. Williams traced this impulse to the founding of the United States, when he argued that the United States committed to an idea of freedom tied to free enterprise, and American futurity tied to expanding markets and control of trade routes and infrastructure. Therefore, according to Williams, the Cold War was not a new formation but rather a continuation of American foreign relations that were characterized by a central contradiction. The United States would be committed to a bounded national landscape and a boundless marketplace; these commitments, argued Williams, would inevitably produce turmoil and eventually undermine the American Century.[8] "Seen in an historical perspective, therefore, what we are accustomed to call the Cold War," Williams argued, "is in reality only the most recent phase of a more general conflict between the established system of western capitalism and its internal and external opponents."[9]

Following World War II the United States gained economic and military control of the Atlantic world, including a seat at the head of the economic order established in the Bretton Woods agreements as well as a preeminent role in the newly formed international system enshrined by the United Nations and its Security Council. The 1945 Bretton Woods agreement that tied the global economy to gold and to U.S. notes helped the United States secure economic control within the West over European redevelopment plans. Japan and Europe rebuilt, often using dollars and purchasing U.S. goods. Moreover, the United States owned over half of the world's official gold reserves—574 million ounces at the end of World War II—ensuring that an international economic system would orbit around the United States.[10]

Throughout the first three decades of the Cold War and following the Korean War, the United States wielded its military supremacy over the developing world by waging proxy wars, secret wars, and counterinsurgency wars across the Third World in an effort both to push back the gains of socialist and communist organization and to expand existing, and to open new, American markets. Yet by the 1970s the Atlantic project was wearing thin; the United States was embroiled in Vietnam, and there was an overvaluation of the U.S. dollar—the bedrock exchange currency of the international monetary system. American president Richard Nixon broke the Bretton Woods agreement in the so-called Nixon Shock and brought on the era of deregulations and floating currencies. Here Nixon acted unilaterally, eschewing the internationalism that had initially established the Bretton Woods system. Nixon's brazen move to terminate the Bretton Woods system was one of a series of events that led to the increasing concentration of monetary and geopolitical power in the hands of the United States.

The United States further wielded the international economic system and the institutions of international governance to its benefit by using the International Monetary Fund and World Bank to enact political changes in foreign markets through coercive lending strategies. The use of so-called economic shocks in places like Chile in the mid-1970s to coerce political change that favored U.S. economic interests demonstrated a concentration of economic and military power in the United States.

Perhaps the most significant move toward the making of American hegemony took place in 1985, when Secretary of State Henry Kissinger helped the United States move important deliberations of the United Nations into the exclusive club of the UN Security Council that was then controlled by the three permanent members—the United States, the United Kingdom, and France (the P3).[11]

The end of the Cold War signaled the realization of American hegemony in economic, geopolitical, and military terms. By 1997 policymakers who had been an integral part of Reagan's Latin America policy, including illegally funding Nicaraguan contras, began to articulate a project for a new American Century built around the idea that "American leadership is good both for America and for the world."[12] The Project for the New American Century was established to advocate within the administration the expansion American militarism, but it had to do so in new ways given that the twentieth century's major threat, the Soviet Union, was no longer available. Hence, the project argued the need for significant increases in defense spending, including funds to modernize existing armed forces. It also argued that the United States' role in foreign affairs must revolve around the promotion of political and economic freedom abroad. And, finally, the Project for the New American Century revised for the twenty-first century Henry Luce's vision of American leadership in the world by arguing, "we need to accept responsibility for America's unique role in preserving and extending an international order friendly to our security, our prosperity, and our principles."[13] From the outset, the Project for the New American Century's leadership recommended regime change in Iraq as a means to assert American control of the Middle East, its oil, and, most importantly, the global price of oil. The Bush administration realized that goal following 9/11 through a series of domestic and international actions that asserted American hegemony over the world. And yet, as we will see, the fundamental contradiction of American power identified by William Appleman Williams endures as the movement of global capitalism would come to eclipse the power of the United States to maintain national borders during a global war on terror.

After the American Century

The end of the American Century and the ascendance of the global war on terror has produced new subject formations and subjectivities that require new scholarly approaches. As George Lipsitz argues in *American Studies in a Moment of Danger*, our ways of thinking about the past and present are shaped in profound ways by the historical conjunctures that produce our scholarly approaches. American studies scholarship has transformed as the Cold War state that produced the field has also transformed. As Lipsitz argues, "We see now, if only in retrospect, that industrialization, nationalism, and the cold war were not just historical processes and events—they were also ways of knowing and being. They had their own logics and optics; they encouraged us to see some things and prevented us from seeing others."[14] It is in the spirit of Lipsitz's observations about the relationship of historical context and knowledge production that *American Studies Encounters the Middle East* asks how the present conjunctures, including the end of the American Century, the ascendance of the global war on terror, and the rise of the Arab uprisings produce new ways of "knowing and being."

Against the backdrop of profound political, economic, environmental, and social local and global transformations by grounding itself in Arab–U.S. relations, this volume seeks to deepen the expansion of American studies in a global context that Giovanni Arrighi has called a "post-American" world.[15] Scholars in various disciplines have noted the relative decline in America's global power,[16] and in recent years the debate spilled over to public debate, pitting North American pundits like Fareed Zakaria and Robert Kagan against each other.[17] International relations scholars have, for some time, argued that the American empire is losing global influence.[18] The question of America's place in the world remains hotly contested in public discourse and academic circles.

Political economists and world system theories have argued that the contradictions William Appleman Williams identified at the outset of the Cold War are not only the contradiction of political liberalism but are more fundamentally contradictions applicable to capitalism. Giovanni Arrighi and Immanuel Wallerstein, to take just two examples, have argued that the American Century is merely the name for a stage in capitalist development—a cycle of accumulation and surplus—that would inevitably decline or transform as a result of the flexibility of capital. They argue that beginning in the 1970s global capital has eclipsed the nation form as the most important unit of global power. For example, in his forecast of the end of American hegemony, Immanuel Wallerstein argues that while the United States remains economically and militarily dominant, it no longer maintains its global prestige or its ability to dictate global events as it did during the Cold War. For Wallerstein, the end of the American empire is partly due to replacement of the nation with the global financial system as well as the emergence of new economic and geopolitical rivals, particularly Japan and Germany.[19]

Similarly, Arrighi has argued that the end of the American Century marks the decline of the American global hegemony. Arrighi reminds us that Antonio Gramsci's concept of hegemony relies not only on a notion of top-down dominance but also the production of consent from below. While the United States was hegemonic during the Cold War, Arrighi argues that this status has changed, particularly in the wake of the U.S. war on terror. Now, Arrighi argues, the United States is merely globally dominant while lacking the sort of global consent of U.S. rule that dominated during the Cold War. Importantly, Arrighi's diagnosis of American geopolitical power is tied to his understanding of global and transnational capitalist development.

As he argued in *The Long Twentieth Century*, U.S. geopolitical power was merely a phase of capitalist development rooted to the territory of the United States. Overaccumulation, argues Arrighi, has led the United States to expand territorially through war and geopolitical power. Yet the ability of the United States to expend its surplus is waning as it becomes more difficult for it to dictate world events in ways that favor its economic wishes. Moreover, Arrighi forecasts a "re-centering of the global political economy on East Asia" that will further characterizes the U.S. "dominance without hegemony."[20]

Published in 2002, a decade before the argument moved to English-language outlets, Emmanuel Todd's *Après l'empire: Essai sur la décomposition du système américain* harnessed a wealth of demographic, cultural, economic, industrial, and military data to argue that "America is a great nation whose power has been incontestable, but whose decline appears irreversible."[21] Similarly, Stephen Walt, in his article "The End of the American Era," argues that "when a state stands alone at the pinnacle of power . . . there is nowhere to go but down."[22] Walt argues that the "American era" of the Cold War decades was characterized by an inflated sense of peril and bipolarity. In reality, argues Walt, U.S. hegemony was secure throughout the Cold War as the United States operated without a serious military or economic rival. The fall of the Soviet Union, however, coupled with the decline in the U.S. economy has brought the American era to an end. There are new emerging areas of geopolitical power, most prominently in Asia. Moreover, for Walt, the Arab Spring most clearly demonstrates the decline of the American era, as the United States has been a marginal influence in developments across the MENA. However, Walt notes that while the American era is coming to a close, American power is still hegemonic; it is merely less influential. Hence, according to Walt,

> the real question was always whether what one might term the "American Era" was nearing its end. Specifically might the United States remain the strongest global power but be unable to exercise the same influence it once enjoyed? If that is the case—and I believe it is—then Washington must devise a grand strategy that acknowledges this new reality but still uses America's enduring assets to advance the national interest.[23]

Despite forecasts of geopolitical decline, we do not underestimate the enduring hegemony of U.S. military power globally. In 2012–13, the United States had special operations forces (military personal who operate beyond the reach of international law) covering 60 percent of the globe. The United States currently has no military rival. Yet, for the purposes of our argument, we suggest that the ability of the United States to shape the course of the future in its vision of the world order is over. The United States cannot speak of a "new world order" because it cannot shape events as it once could, or at least as it thought it could.

Moreover, the U.S. economy is no longer globally supreme, as China has recently surpassed the United States for the world's largest economy. Perhaps most significantly, American influence is in decline—it can no longer dictate events across the globe in ways that it once did, and this is in part due to the renewed economic strength of new multilateral coalitions of state that emerge from the global south, such as the BRICS countries (Brazil, Russia, India, China, South Africa), which have established trade and other economic policy beyond the networks of U.S.-led neoliberal economic policy. Nowhere, we argue, is the declining influence of the U.S. empire more visible than in the events of 2011–13 in the Arab world, the so-called Arab uprisings or spring.

Transnational American Studies in These Times

Transnational American studies is not merely the study of global flows of culture, people, economies, and resources across national boundaries but also of complex geopolitical relations that inform the infrastructure of circulation and the reception of America beyond the United States. Transnational American culture is enabled by the transnationalization of U.S.-led global economies and hegemony. Yet, as American culture travels, it becomes unmoored from its origin and can signify something entirely different in and for a non-U.S. audience. In this way the transnational flow of American culture enables a critical view of American culture that is often occluded within the United States. To take the case of El Rancho Lebanon, we can see how, in the flow of the U.S. "Wild West" to Lebanon, we witness the unmooring of western iconography from the state project of U.S. settler colonial expansion and its reinscription in Lebanese national culture.

In this volume, we are interested in American studies in transit during a geopolitical moment characterized by declining U.S. global influence and ubiquitous American cultural global circulation worldwide. The presidency of George W. Bush and his administration's handling of the September 11, 2001, attacks and their aftermath has been disastrous for perceptions of the United States in the Arab world. After what appeared to be a promising start, the Obama administration has failed to convince public opinion in the Middle East that there have been any fundamental changes to U.S. policy toward the region, and, if anything, drone strikes and support for the violence of regional allies like Saudi Arabia and Israel have only made life across MENA more precarious. The United States, it seems, is set on a path in its relation to the Arab world that is difficult to reverse. And yet, despite the enduring power of the United States, American prestige across the Middle East seems to be in decline.

The Arab uprisings of 2011 made starkly visible the declining geopolitical influence of the United States in the Arab world. This is a decline that began before the Arab uprisings, throughout the Cold War, with the unconditional aid the United States provided to Israel in the face of Israeli aggression in the Arab world. This support has endured even beyond the utility, it could be argued, of Israel as a strategic ally in the region.[24] Moreover, decades of U.S.-driven World Bank neoliberal lending has created vast problems of poverty and hopelessness across much of the Arab region well before the January 25, 2011, protests. Although the uprisings are directed against authoritarian regimes and not the United States, there is evidence that protesters saw the struggle against authoritarian rule as a means to reject the U.S.-dominated economic and military order.[25]

If U.S. prestige in MENA has been in decline since 1948, but especially since Oslo neoliberalism,[26] it was arguably the recent United States votes against recognizing Palestinian statehood in the United Nations that signaled the end of an American-dominated era in the region. The United States recently voted for the second time in two years against recognition of a Palestinian state in the United Nations. It stood with nine other countries over which it has economic and military control. Striking in the vote is that the United States can no longer count on European allies to stand against the Arab world—although some European allies chose to abstain from the vote. Moreover, while the European Union has begun to consider a boycott of Israeli settlement-produced goods, the United States remains firmly committed to its Israel policy, even after the alarming devastation brought on by successive invasions of Gaza.

After the U.S.-orchestrated and -led invasions of Iraq and Afghanistan and the many scandals of the George W. Bush presidency—Abu Ghraib, Guantanamo, torture, rendition—the Obama presidency was initially perceived as a radical shift in U.S. policy toward the Middle East. Obama's famous June 4, 2009, Cairo speech raised expectations that a fundamentally new U.S. approach to the MENA region was afoot. Within months, however, the Arab press began echoing rising public sentiments that the change was one of style, not substance. The Obama administration's calculated response to the Arab uprisings, however cautious, angered both revolutionary forces, who lamented U.S. hypocrisy on democracy and human rights, and counterrevolutionary rollback led by Saudi Arabia, irate at Obama's abandonment of longtime U.S. and Saudi ally Hosni Mubarak. Continued U.S. support for Israeli policies, Obama's escalation of drone warfare, and the administrations flagrant disregard for the Bahraini uprising dashed any remaining illusions about changes in U.S.–Middle East policies. The U.S. administration's initially timid rapprochement with Iran and rumors of a pending nuclear deal, in addition to Obama's not-so-red "red line" on chemical weapons use in Syria, transformed disappointment with U.S. policies to anger and opposition among steadfast allies in the Gulf Cooperation Council, led by Saudi Arabia. Columns with titles such "America's Weakness and Its Crisis" and "Who Is Responsible for Decline in U.S. Influence in the World?" have proliferated in the Arab—and even Israeli—press.[27]

If the 2003 invasion of Iraq signaled the apex of U.S. power, the Arab uprisings have since their onset in late 2010 confirmed the decline of

American global might. The United States government appeared more blindsided by the swift toppling of Zine El Abidine Ben Ali in Tunisia than embarrassed by a WikiLeaks document revealing the chumminess of Ben Ali's autocracy with Western governments. After much dithering in Egypt over Mubarak, the Obama administration announced it was ceasing its support to longtime U.S. ally Hosni Mubarak and has since then followed a road of inconsistency and ambiguity in dealing with Mubarak's successors, Mohamed Morsi of the Muslim Brotherhood and Abdel Fattah El-Sisi of the military. On Libya, the administration "led from behind," essentially assisting while the French and British took the lead in North Atlantic Treaty Organization efforts to help rebels against Muammar Gaddafi, but in the wake of Gaddafi's deposition, violence and political instability in Libya has only escalated. In Syria, rhetorical condemnation of Bashar al-Assad and lukewarm support of the rebels fueled a narrative that the United States, alongside Israel, was interested in seeing the two sides of the Syrian conflict bleed each other out. In Bahrain, the administration gave lip service to the rhetoric of human rights while supporting Saudi-led repression of dissent. Reactive and seemingly ad hoc, the U.S. response to the Arab uprisings has been consistently inconsistent.

It is perhaps paradoxical, then, that cultural forms developed in the United States, such as rap, free-style graffiti, and others explored in various chapters of this volume, have flourished as modalities of protest in the Arab uprisings. Although rap, graffiti, and others have received a fair share of attention, this pales in comparison to the hype that surrounded the use of social media such as Facebook, YouTube, and Twitter during the Arab uprisings. As Frank Rich wrote in the *New York Times*, "The talking-head invocations of Twitter and Facebook instead take the form of implicit, simplistic Western chauvinism. How fabulous that two great American digital innovations can rescue the downtrodden, unwashed masses."[28] The discourse privileging American technology in positive Arab political change has a long history in U.S. public discourse and harks back to Daniel Lerner's influential book *The Passing of Traditional Society* (1958), which was foundational to the modernization paradigm in international relations and comparative politics and to the development communication paradigm in international communication studies.[29]

The Passing of Traditional Modernity is a heuristic site to examine the imbrication of the Middle East, global media research, and American empire. The book is based on approximately three hundred surveys conducted in the early 1950s in Egypt, Iran, Jordan, Lebanon, Turkey, and Syria. Lerner identified three types of persons—the traditionalist, transitionalist, and modernist—and argued that people moved from the first to the third category through empathy. The media, which depicted a world larger than the traditionalists', created a desire for social mobility, what Lerner dubbed "psychic mobility." As Shah writes, the book was a product of its time, shaped by the forces of Cold War geopolitics (the book was funded by the Voice of America to learn more about Arab media audiences to better counter Soviet broadcasting); the rise of behavioral science at U.S. research universities, which encouraged the systematic study of social-cultural dynamics; and the advent of racial liberalism, which located social change in cultural patters rather than immutable racial characteristics, which was progressive thinking for the 1950s.[30] *The Passing of Traditional Modernity* has had an enduring influence on American perceptions of the Arab world, finding its most amplified manifestation in George W. Bush's Greater Middle East initiative—"Modernizing the Middle East," the subtitle of Lerner's book, echoes the Bush administration's "Reforming the Middle East."

In ensuing years, the field of communication research as an academic discipline, like the discipline of American studies, developed a social scientific epistemology adequate for its closeness to American government policymakers. It was made policy relevant but not intellectually autonomous. As Hanno Hardt wrote in a landmark essay critiquing the U.S. tradition in media research:

> This tradition fails to consider historical growth as an indissoluble process that cannot be dissected into empirical parts or facts and prefers to treat communication and media studies in terms of a series of specific, isolated social phenomena. In this context, it seems that the field suffers not only from a cultural bias but also from a social scientific bias toward searching for laws governing the relationship of media and society. As a result, empirical research techniques obscure cultural differences.[31]

But global media research underwent a momentous shift in the 1970s. The United States—state, economics, and culture—has historically had an enormous impact on global popular culture and has featured prominently in academic and public debates about cultural power and globalization. Influenced by a handful of radical U.S. intellectuals like Herbert

Schiller, whose books *Mass Communication and American Empire* (1971) and *Communication and Cultural Domination* (1976) were foundational to developing a globally oriented political economy of media and information, the "media imperialism" perspective dominated the study of global media and cultural flows in the 1970s.[32] This approach focused on the politico-economic and cultural inequalities between what were then known as "First," where the United States was a dominant country, and "Third" Worlds. In those years countries opposed to global U.S. media and cultural hegemony used meetings of the United Nations Educational, Scientific and Cultural Organization (UNESCO) to coordinate and publicize their grievances against Western dominance, especially against the United States. This led to the New World Information Order (later known as the New World Information and Communication Order) resolution against the neoliberal "free flow of information" doctrine, which UNESCO's 1976 General Conference endorsed in Nairobi, Kenya.[33]

Cold War geopolitics undergirded the New World Information Order debate as it influenced Lerner's work a few decades earlier: the Reagan administration and U.S. media bitterly fought UNESCO and opponents of the "free flow" doctrine. U.S. officials attacked UNESCO for its attempts to "control press freedom," and Elliott Abrams, then assistant secretary of state, called on UNESCO to consider the First Amendment of the U.S. Constitution as a template for a global policy regime.[34] The *New York Times* editorialized that "if it turns out to be impossible to reject this attempt to tamper with our basic principles, there is always the alternative of rejecting UNESCO itself," and soon the United States and United Kingdom suspended their memberships in UNESCO.[35] This led to the slow decline of the debate over global U.S. cultural influence in UNESCO, which the United States rejoined, of all times, during George W. Bush's infamous "Axis of Evil" speech.

Outline of the Book

American Studies Encounters the Middle East captures an important yet fleeting moment in the encounter between America and the Arab world. The book's focus on this time of widespread popular discontent, normative fragmentation, and economic uncertainty, in addition to adding historical depth to current problematics, casts the American–Arab encounter as the nexus for a new, transnational, global American studies capable of shedding light on the momentous ongoing transformations. The book is organized in two sections.

The first section of the book, "The Arab–U.S. Encounter: Entangled Histories and Contemporary Flows," features chapters on historical linkages and transborder exchanges between the United States and the Arab world from the eighteenth to the twenty-first centuries. The six chapters in this section demonstrate the breadth and depth of America's historical Arab entanglements. From the place of Islam in eighteenth-century American literature, the fascinating journey of an Algerian in colonial Virginia, together the chapters show that the U.S.–Arab encounter has for long haunted reading, writing, travel, politics, media and popular culture. In "Diabolical Enterprises and Abominable Superstitions: Islam and the Conceptualization of Finance in Early American Literature," Adam John Waterman explores how "Islam" operated as an important fount of cultural imagination for the early United States, through close readings of several early American writings focusing on finance, notably speculation. In so doing, he questions the dominant narrative that compares a long-standing European interaction with the Middle East and Islam against a putatively and relatively recent encounter between the worlds of Islam and the United States. In the same vein, Judith E. Tucker explores an Appalachian legend in "Salim the Algerine: The Muslim Who Strayed into Colonial Virginia." The character at the heart of the chapter was captured in turn by Spanish pirates who took him to America and sold him as a slave, then was captured by Shawnee Native Americans after he escaped. Through this engrossing story, Tucker explores the role of Islam in the changing meanings of dislocation, religion, and identity in the early American–Arab/Ottoman encounter. In " 'Race' and 'Blackness' in Moroccan Rap: Voicing Local Experiences of Marginality," Christina Moreno Almeida explores the specific dynamics of connection between Moroccan and United States rap scenes, looking at how Moroccan rappers recruit the U.S. civil rights movement to explore the intricacies of their own marginality. Finding U.S. culture to be a source for the cultural imaginations of young Moroccan rappers, Almeida concludes that "blackness" in Morocco goes beyond race to signal poverty and exclusion. In turn, Rayya El Zein's "Call and Response, Radical Belonging and Arabic Hip-Hop in 'the West,' " develops the notion of radical belonging as a "co-construction of community and identity" that she unravels via studying Arab hip-hop concerts in the West, identifying the kinds of politics produced in these performance. Focusing on how U.S. rhetoric was received and critiques in Egypt, Mounira Soliman, in "The Reception of U.S. Discourse on the Egyptian Revolution: Between the Popular and the Official," aims at understanding how U.S. popular culture and satire, with an interesting discussion of U.S. fast food, shaped Egyptian perceptions of American agendas in the uprisings. Finally, in "Arab Spring, American Autumn," Brian T. Edwards reflects on his own experience with American studies as a globalizing formation, concluding with thoughts on how the decline of U.S. influence in the Arab world is intertwined with the rise of Arab cultural production redolent with fragments of America.

The second section of the book, "Infrastructures of Control: From Mythmaking to Drone Warfare" moves the discussion to a techno-politico-economic plane while examining the discourses underlying transnational infrastructures of control and warfare. Waleed Hazbun's "The Uses of Modernization Theory: American Foreign Policy and Mythmaking in the Arab World," elaborates a "strategic logic of modernization" that, among other things, recruited the U.S. military as an agent in the modernization of the Arab world. Hazbun concludes with political and epistemological insights on how to better manage the Arab–American relation, with a note on the special role that the American University of Beirut can play in that process. Craig Jones, in "Traveling Law: Targeted Killing, Lawfare, and the Deconstruction of the Battlefield," explores the circulation of the notion of targeted killing between Israel and the United States and deploys the concept of "lawfare" to explore both the "weaponization of the law" and the way law has acted as a discursive naturalizer of targeted killing. When one thinks of tactics of extra- or parajudicial assassination, drones come to mind. Ashley Dawson, in "Drone Executions, Urban Surveillance, and the Imperial Gaze," offers a transnational and transhistorical study of imperial visuality beginning with the British Raj in Calcutta in the nineteenth century, Algiers under French control in the twentieth century, and U.S. war videogames in the twenty-first century, concluding that "drones are part of a long history of sanitizing imperial violence." Finally, moving to the contemporary Middle East, Helga Tawil-Souri, argues, in "Technology's Borders: The U.S., Palestine, and Egypt's Digital Connection," that U.S.-developed and -funded technology plays a contradictory role in both Egypt and Palestine, underscoring the fragility of notions of "opening" and "borderlessness" and asserting the lingering importance of space in global geopolitics. In "The Counterrevolutionary Year: The Arab Spring, the Gulf Cooperation Council, and U.S. Foreign Policy in the Middle East," Osamah Khalil identifies and analyzes a gap between U.S. rhetoric, which supported the emancipatory forces of revolution, with actual U.S. actions, which supported reactionary players in counterrevolutions aiming to bury the Arab uprisings. He concludes with thoughts on American hegemony in the age of Obama.

Collectively, the chapters in *American Studies Encounters the Middle East* are intended to provoke new questions about the futures of American studies as well as the future of American political and military engagement in the Middle East. Rethinking past cultural encounters may suggest examples of conviviality and cohabitation across the United States and Middle East that seem impossible, if not unfathomable in the present. Moreover, taking stock of the changing nature of the United States in the world at the end of the American Century and during the revolutions within the Arab world may suggest new possibilities for the location and subject of American studies.

Notes

1. www.elrancholebanon.com (accessed January 21, 2013).

2. Amy Kaplan made the observation in her introduction to her 1994 coedited volume with Donald Pease that the study of culture often lacks an analysis and accounting of imperialism. While much has changed in fields of cultural studies since the publication of *Cultures of United State Imperialism*, it remains the case that the Middle East is something of an absence in studies of U.S. imperialism. Moreover, Donald Pease has argued that as American studies has criticized American exceptionalism, it has regularly reinscribed another sort of exceptionalism whereby the America becomes the world, or American always signifies the U.S. State. See, for examples, Amy Kaplan, " 'Left Alone with America': The Absence of Empire in the Study of American Culture," in *Cultures of United States Imperialism*, ed. Amy Kaplan and Donald Pease (Durham, N.C.: Duke University Press, 1993); and Donald Pease, "Re-thinking 'American Studies' after U.S. Exceptionalism," *American Literary History*, September 29, 2008, 19–27.

3. For an analysis of the history of American studies in the Middle East, see Alex Lubin, "American Studies, the Middle East, and the Question of Palestine," *American Quarterly* 68, no. 1 (March 2016).

4. Ibid.; and Alex Lubin, "Breaking 'America's Last Taboo,' " *Middle East Research and Information Project*, November 27, 2013, http://www.merip.org/breaking -"america's-last-taboo" (August 27, 2015).

5. John Carlos Rowe, *Post-Nationalist American Studies*, Berkeley: University of California Press. 2000.

6. Henry R. Luce, "The American Century," *Life*, February 17, 1941, http://www.informationclearinghouse.info/article6139.htm (August 11, 2015).

7. William Appleman Williams, *The Tragedy of American Diplomacy*, (Cleveland: World Publishing Co. 1959), 13.

8. Echoes of Williams's thesis can be found in the scholarship of David W. Noble, especially in *The End of American History* (Minneapolis: University of Minnesota Press, 1985).

9. Williams, *The Tragedy of American Diplomacy*, 13.

10. See, for example, Vijay Prashad, *The Poorer Nations: A Possible History of the Global South* (New York: Verso Press, 2014).

11. Ibid.

12. See, for example, Greg Grandin, *Empire's Workshop: Latin America, the United States, and the Rise of the New Imperialism* (New York: Holt, 2007).

13. Project for the New American Century, "Rebuilding America's Defenses: Strategy, Forces and Resources for a New Century," September 2000, http://www .informationclearinghouse.info/pdf/RebuildingAmericasDefenses.pdf (August 11, 2015).

14. George Lipsitz, *American Studies in a Moment of Danger* (Minneapolis: University of Minnesota Press, 2001), 4.

15. Giovanni Arrighi, "Hegemony Unraveling—I," *New Left Review* 32 (March–April 2005), http://www.newleftreview.org/A2552. See also Beverly J. Silver and Giovanni Arrighi, "The End of the Long Twentieth Century," in *Business as Usual: The Roots of the Global Financial Meltdown*, ed. Craig Calhoun and Georgi Derluguian (New York: Social Science Research Council / New York University Press, 2011), 53–68.

16. Oliver Todd, *Après l'Empire: Essai sur la décomposition du système américain* (Paris: Gallimard, 2002). See also Joseph Straubhaar's doctoral dissertation about the U.S. influence over Brazilian television, summarized in an article published in 1984: J. Straubhaar, "Brazilian Television: The Decline of American Influence," *Communication Research* 11, no. 2 (1984): 221–40.

17. See, for example, Fareed Zakaria, *The Post American World* (New York: W. W. Norton, 2008); and Robert Kagan, *The World America Made* (New York: Knopf, 2012).

18. On the end of the American Century or era, see Giovanni Arrighi, interviewed by David Harvey, "The Winding Paths of Capital," *New Left Review* 56 (March–April 2009), http://newleftreview.org/II/56/giovanni-arrighi-the-winding-paths-of-capital (January 22, 2013); Richard Haas, "The New Middle East," *Foreign Affairs* (November/December 2006), https://www.foreignaffairs .com/articles/middle-east/2006-11-01/new-middle-east; Stephen M. Walt, "The End of the American Era," *National Interest* (November–December 2011), http:// nationalinterest.org/article/the-end-the-american-era-6037; Charles A. Kupchan, "America's Place in the New World," *New York Times*, April 7, 2012; Aaron David Miller, "For America, An Arab Winter," *Wilson Quarterly* (Summer 2011): 36–42; and Christopher Layne, "The Waning of U.S. Hegemony—Myth or Reality?," *International Security* 34, no. 1 (Summer 2009): 147–72.

19. Immanuel Wallerstein, "The Curve of American Power," *New Left Review*, 40 (July–August 2006): 77–94.

20. Giovanni Arrighi, *The Long Twentieth Century: Money, Power, and the Origins of Our Times*, new ed. (New York: Verso Press, 2010).

21. Emmanuel Todd, *Après l'empire: Essai sur la décomposition du système américain* (Paris: Gallimard, 2002).

22. Walt, "End of the American Era," 2.

23. Ibid.

24. See, for example, Anthony H. Cordesman, "Israel as a Strategic Liability?," Center for Strategic and International Studies, June 2, 2010, http://csis.org /publication/israel-strategic-liability (January 22, 2013).

25. On coercive lending programs in Egypt under Mubarak, see Bruce K. Rutherford, *Egypt after Mubarak: Liberalism, Islam, and Democracy in the Arab World* (Princeton, N.J.: Princeton University Press, 2008); and Vicki Langohr, "Too Much Civil Society, Too Little Politics: Egypt and Liberalizing Arab Regimes," *Comparative Politics* 36, no. 2 (January 2004): 181–204.

26. For an analysis of the Oslo Accords as neoliberal, see Joel Beinin and Rebecca Stein, eds., *The Struggle for Sovereignty: Palestine and Israel, 1993–2005* (Palo Alto, Calif.: Stanford University Press, 2006), 21–37; Joel Beinin, "Palestine and Israel: Perils of a Neoliberal, Repressive 'Pax Americana,'" *Social Justice* 25, no. 4 (Winter 1998): 20–39; and Ronnie D. Lipschutz, "Beyond the Neoliberal Peace: From Conflict Resolution to Social Reconciliation," *Social Justice* 25, no. 4 (Winter 1998): 5–19.

27. For example, Salama Keyla, "America's Weakness and Its Crisis," *Al-Ahram* (Egypt), June 3, 2014; Jamil Matar, "Who Is Responsible for Decline in US Influence in the World?" *Al-Hayat* (Saudi Arabia, published in Beirut and London), January 20, 2014; and Zvi Bar'el, "As U.S. Influence Wanes, Its Only Choice Is Mideast Compromise," *Haaretz* (Israel), June 10, 2014.

28. Frank Rich, "Wallflowers at the Revolution," *New York Times*, February 5, 2011, http://www.nytimes.com/2011/02/06/opinion/06rich.html?_r=o.

29. Daniel Lerner, *The Passing of Traditional Society: Modernizing the Middle East* (New York: Macmillan, 1958).

30. H. Shah, *The Production of Modernization: Daniel Lerner, Mass Media and the Passing of Traditional Society* (Philadelphia: Temple University Press, 2011). Also see Rohan Samarajiwa, "The Murky Beginnings of the Communication and Development Field: Voice of America and the Passing of Traditional Society," in *Rethinking Development Communication*, ed. Newille Jayaweera and Sarath Amunugama (Singapore: Asian Media Information and Communication Centre, 1987), 3–19.

31. H. Hardt, "Comparative Media Research: The World according to America," *Critical Studies in Mass Communication* 5, no. 2 (1988): 129–46, at 138.

32. H. Schiller, *Mass Communication and American Empire* (New York: Beacon Press, 1971); and H. Schiller, *Communication and Cultural Domination* (New York: Sharpe, 1976).

33. For a detailed critical explanation of the debate, see Marwan M. Kraidy, *Hybridity, or the Cultural Logic of Globalization* (Philadelphia: Temple University Press, 1995).

34. W. Kleinwachter, "Three Waves of the Debate," in *The Global Media Debate: Its Rise, Fall, and Renewal*, ed. G. Gerbner, H. Mowlana, and K. Nordenstreng (Norwood, N.J.: Ablex, 1994), 13–20.

35. G. Gerbner, "UNESCO in the U.S. Press," in *The Global Media Debate: Its Rise, Fall, and Renewal*, ed. G. Gerbner, H. Mowlana, and K. Nordenstreng (Norwood, N.J.: Ablex, 1994), 111–22, at 114.

PART I | The Arab–U.S. Encounter

Entangled Histories and
Contemporary Flows

Diabolical Enterprises and Abominable Superstitions

Islam and the Conceptualization of Finance in Early American Literature

ADAM JOHN WATERMAN

Edward Said once suggested that, before the end of the Second World War, Islam occupied no place in the American imagination.[1] In contrast to Europe, where direct social, economic, and military encounters with Muslims had given rise to a range of prejudicial constructions of Islamic difference—many with direct bearing upon the emergence of "Europe" as a cultural entity—American engagements with Islam were, in Said's estimation, "restricted," lacking in substance. "One thinks of occasional travelers like Mark Twain and Herman Melville, or of missionaries here and there, or of short-lived military expeditions to North Africa," Said wrote. "Academic experts did their work on Islam usually in quiet corners of schools of divinity, not in the glamorous limelight of Orientalism nor in the pages of leading journals."[2] Consequently, contemporary American perceptions of Islam, Said argued, were almost entirely overdetermined by the politics of the Arab–Israeli war, with Zionist institutions in both Palestine and the United States presenting the most egregious misrepresentations of the faith as part of a campaign to disqualify Palestinian claims to sovereignty and the right of self-defense. Absent a clear understanding of the faith, Islam could be figuratively manipulated to any variety of purposes, ultimately casting Arab resistance to the Zionist occupation of Palestine as an atavistic outgrowth of a revanchist civilizational discourse deeply at odds with the ostensibly inherent modernity of post-Reformation Judeo-Christianity.

While politically incisive with respect to the study of Islam and its representation in early American literature, Said's points require some qualification. In the years since Said's *Covering Islam: How the Media and the Experts Determine How We See the Rest of the World* was first published, scholars have gone on to locate numerous instances in which Islam "served as a vital source of cultural imagination" for the early United States, from the still controversial image of the Prophet Mohammed at the U.S. Supreme Court to the mischaracterization of Muslim piety in pursuit of temperance reform, the nineteenth-century campaign against the "false revelation" of Mormonism, and the development of a range of antebellum U.S. literatures.[3] In *The Cultural Roots of American Islamicism*, Timothy Marr has identified Islam as part of the transcultural matrix that subtends American culture, effectively revealing American culture's identity with those "multiplicities [that] are integrally enmeshed in the planetary commons."[4] For Marr, Islam has served the United States as a sort of prosthesis, a form upon which early Americans sought to erect a globally significant national culture. Wai Chee Dimock largely concurs, naming a range of antebellum American writers who were influenced— more or less directly—by Islamic world texts.[5] Calling for the plotting of American literary history within a planetary scene of cultural exchange, with Marr, Dimock suggests that attention to American engagements with the greater Islamic world offers a means by which critics might reconsider the performativity of terms like "hemispheric" and "transnational," thus rendering all projections of literary history as provisional and—ostensibly—political. Most recently, Jacob Rama Berman has complicated Said's notion of an American Orientalism that emerges in the absence of any immediate experience of the Islamic world, exploring myriad scenes of American and Muslim encounter and the transcultural consequences of such exchanges.[6]

Despite the wealth of their archives, what is immediately striking about these many instances of cultural "contact"—direct or indirect—is precisely how much they resonate with Said's characterization of American understandings of Islam as "peculiar . . . abstract . . . [and] second-hand."[7] For Marr, the American engagement with Islam constitutes a heterogeneous national cultural tradition, one that, in distinction to Orientalism, he has designated "Islamicist."[8] Where Orientalism proper emerged in relation to concrete imperial situations through which Europe sought to impose itself upon the greater Islamic world, within the terms of Marr's analysis, "Islamicism" evokes little more than an ungrounded funhouse-mirror vision of the faith. As a cultural tradition, it is less engaged by Islam as a sociohistorical formation or a political adversary than as a projection of anxieties endemic to early American society. Despite his emphasis on specific contact zones as sites of transcultural exchange, much the same could be said of Berman's analysis, which specifically foregrounds the relationship between Islam and the figurative topography of the American imaginary. For her part, Dimock's analysis tells us less about the representation of Islam in American literature than it does about the handful of medieval Islamic literary figures with whom nineteenth-century American writers were reasonably familiar.[9] In both instances, we learn less about how Americans have constructed or understood Islam than about how Americans have used Islam to construct provisional understandings of themselves. In attempting to dissolve the national insularity of American culture through a consideration of its relationship with a thoroughly global cultural formation, these works demonstrate some measure of the parochialism of the American imaginary, its curiosity little more than an undisciplined consumer sensibility.

From this perspective, the archives under consideration might be more properly understood as participating in what Saree Makdisi has recently termed "Occidentalism," the cultural process by which "the West," through the invocation of an Arab-Islamic other, posits itself as a discrete—if polymorphous—spatial entity, one identical with the autological subject of Enlightenment, liberalism, and modernity. As he notes in his discussion of Mary Wollstonecraft's *Vindication of the Rights of Woman*, Wollstonecraft and other bourgeois intellectuals regularly invoked "Mohametanism" as a signifier for both tyrannical despotism and unbridled licentiousness, charges Wollstonecraft leveled at British aristocrats and proletarians, respectively. Nonetheless, the writing of this class of intellectuals does not, as a rule, reveal any particular interest in, or engagement with, the sociohistorical reality of the greater Muslim world. Instead, in Wollstonecraft's treatise "Islam" appears as a wholly imaginary construct, a bit player in the cultural politics of class and racial formation in late-eighteenth-century England. Makdisi refers to such constructions as Occidentalist inasmuch as they retroactively posit the moral and economic superiority of the specifically English bourgeoisie and its Utilitarianism against the pretentions of the aristocracy and the intemperance of the working class. Within this tradition of Occidentalist literature, then, Islam emerges as a floating signifier, one capacious enough to allow for the coexistence of the most contrary representations, and one that constitutes a discursive formation that participates in the reproduction of bourgeois hegemony.[10]

What is at stake here would seem to be the doubling of Orientalism between its imperial and imaginative manifestations. On the one hand, Orientalism appears as a knowledge project, one that is, for all its misrepresentativeness and corruption by power, pragmatically engaged with an object in the world that knows itself as Islam; on the other, Orientalism appears as a cultural fantasy, one that takes the-thing-itself as a medium for the elaboration of self-reflective fictions. Within European forms of Orientalism, the imperial and the imaginative cross circuit, reinforcing and—in certain instances—disrupting one another. Within the United States, however, before 1948, Orientalism was largely confined to the realm of the fantastic, such that the American image of the Oriental, the Arab, or the Muslim was little more than a projection of the imaginary dimensions of the national subject, caught in the throes of infantile self-fashioning. Drawing on close readings of Peter Markoe's *The Algerine Spy in Pennsylvania*, Royall Tyler's *The Algerine Captive*, and Washington Irving's *Tales of the Alhambra*, this essay explores the use of Islam as a figure through which to route a range of anxieties characteristic of the immediate postrevolutionary moment. It argues that, within the literary culture of the early United States, Islam served as a figure for the social and cultural mutability enabled by the liberal invalidation of genealogical fictions, a process abetted by the near-simultaneous emergence of finance as a vehicle for capital accumulation. In these works, evocations of a figurative Islam work to modulate an emergent, anti-Semitic critique of capitalism such that Islam becomes a proxy for the propulsively abstractive dimensions of capital that—within European culture—were typically identified with the character of "the Jew." Absent a concept of capitalism as a systemically inequitable and exploitative socioeconomic formation, the culture of American Islamicism provided a set of racialized tropes through which early American literature registered the injuriousness of fictitious capital with respect to social relations in the early republic. In these works, Islam emerges as a means of interrogating finance as an abject mode of economic practice, one that was necessary for, but alien to, the political economy of early industrial capitalism.

While the analysis of finance capital has provided one of the optics through which scholars have attempted to grapple with the socioeconomic and cultural torsions of late capitalism, the question of speculation and its relationship to American culture has a far longer currency. In his analysis of antebellum sentimental literature, David Anthony has argued that, "by the mid-nineteenth century, America had become a kind of fiscal neurotic, given over to insecurity, anxiety, depression, and irrational fears" over the vexed relationship between fictitious capital and social formation.[11] Jennifer Baker and Bruce Mann have traced this anxiety through earlier colonial and postrevolutionary American literatures, arguing that questions of debt, credit, and speculation were integral to the formation of early American culture.[12] Having financed its revolution on credit, the United States was born a debtor nation, making questions of debt, credit, speculation, and solvency extraordinarily practical matters at all levels of society. At the same time, finance provided a metaphorical framework through which to construct the possibilities and perils inherent to the culture of American independence. Citing Founding Father Benjamin Rush, Cathy Davidson notes a homology between economic speculation, literary production, and self-making, each field indicating the possibility of "monstrous fictions" enabled by the erosion if not outright collapse of late feudal class structures. The critique of these modes of speculation, Davidson suggests, provided a language through which to confront anxieties over America's emancipation from the British political system and the attendant loss of traditional markers of class and status. Speculation, in this sense, named a quasi-Burkean anxiety about the potentialities inherent in Enlightenment notions of liberty and equality as well as their attendant impact upon those structures that mediate social identity. The critique of economic speculation from this perspective provided early American writers with a language through which to think the revolution as a transformation of social identity, one with deleterious consequences for social and political life. Although the works in question do not thematize questions of debt, credit, and speculation, finance makes an appearance in each, setting characters in motion, underlying crucial plot developments, or manifesting itself as material excess. Insofar as the texts evoke through repetition and metalepsis the formal characteristics of the commodity-structure, they register finance as the unconscious of early industrial capital, rendering their commentary on religious and social identity and their inchoate desire for a transcendental subject that might anchor the social field instances of a repetitive working through and working toward moments in an abortive movement for theoretical self-actualization.

The methodological apparatus that underwrites this argument owes a great debt to Georg Lukács, whose analysis of the categories of knowledge production under capitalism supposes their identity with the structure of the commodity as described by Marx. Lukács referred to the fetishization of objectivity characteristic of bourgeois thought as reification, and he upheld finance capital as its prototypical form. In his estimation, finance presented the face of reification at its most chillingly abstract. "In the minds of the people in bourgeois society," Lukács wrote, the forms of merchant or finance capital "constitute the pure, authentic, unadulterated forms of capital. In them the relations between men that lie hidden in the immediate commodity relation, as well as the relations between men and the objects that should really gratify their needs, have faded to the point where they can be neither recognized nor even perceived."[13] Historically, reification could only emerge after "all fixed, fast-frozen relations, with their train of ancient and venerable prejudices and opinions" were on the wane, replaced by an increasingly rationalized society whose principle of organization was not some metaphysical sense of mutual obligation but the naked interest of the profit motive.[14] Finance, within this milieu, became unmoored from the specific religious and racial formations through which it had emerged in premodern Europe, taking on the objective character of a thing, one independent of any overriding human agency. "For that reason," Lukács wrote, "the reified mind has come to regard [finance and money capital] as the true representatives of his societal existence. The commodity character of the commodity, the abstract, quantitative mode of calculability shows itself here in its purest form: the reified mind necessarily sees it as the form in which its own authentic immediacy becomes manifest and—as reified consciousness—does not even attempt to transcend it."[15]

The Lukácsian approach to materialist dialectics has also provided an important frame of reference for the theoretical work of Moishe Postone, whose analysis of the relationship between European anti-Semitism and the structure of capital underwrites much of what follows. For Postone, modern anti-Semitism, which achieves theoretical coherence only in the latter half of the nineteenth century, is distinguished from earlier forms of antipathy toward Jewish people in that it identifies the figure of "the Jew" with the abstracted dimensions of alienated social relations under capitalism—finance capital being perhaps the most insidiously significant. Modern anti-Semitism in this sense amplifies through codification certain latent tendencies within late medieval European culture, where attitudes toward Jewish people almost invariably concerned Jewish merchants' relationships to the reproduction of feudal power structures. Ostensibly liberated from the political half-life that had afforded Jewish merchants a social position as financiers, in the nineteenth century the figural "Jew" could emerge as a synecdoche for finance because Jewish difference was no longer enclosed within a comfortable feudal hierarchy. The uncertain social position of Jewish communities with respect to emergent nations as well as historical associations between Jewish communities, finance, and the sphere of circulation combined to render the figural "Jew" the uncanny image of all that was objectionable in early capitalism, a projection of all that was "foreign, dangerous, [and] destructive."[16] The elimination of the Jewish people, from this perspective, becomes what Postone characterizes as a "foreshortened course toward socialism," a misguided attempt at abrogating the injuriousness of capital by destroying its supposedly ideal representatives.[17]

Although Postone articulates this argument as a rebuttal to those who claim that anti-Semitism was epiphenomenal to National Socialism, it should be noted that the anti-Semitic identification of Jews with finance was contingent. It was also, given a long history of Jewish and Muslim co-racialization—a history rooted in the colonial culture that emerged from the Catholic conquest of Al-Andalus—transferrable.[18] As Postone notes, "What characterizes the power imputed to the Jews in modern anti-Semitism is that it is mysteriously intangible, abstract, and universal. It is considered to be a form of power that does not manifest itself directly, but must find another mode of expression. It seeks a concrete carrier, whether political, social, or cultural, through which it can work."[19] The works under consideration bear this out. In them, Muslim agents serve as the conduits of an abstractive, speculative potentiality that passes, more often than not, through the medium of Jewish merchants. Islam appears at different points as a monstrously tyrannical political order, one based upon a deeply entrenched sense of hierarchical distinctions and thus, in certain respects, concrete; at others, it appears as an ephemera, a shadow, its complete lack of substance a consequence of the "falsehood" of its founding revelation and a figure for the abstractive potentiality it entails. It becomes, in other words, a figure for the seemingly impossible simultaneity of the abstract and the concrete, value and use-value. Islamic values are, at one moment, considered to be real values because they are an expression of a divinely given hierarchy; at another, however, that hierarchy is revealed to be erected upon the most diabolical speculations, such that it has no social or cultural substance.

The works under consideration are held up for scrutiny insofar as they help to constellate a particular moment in the cultural politics of early American capitalism. Both *The Algerine Spy in Pennsylvania* and *The Algerine Captive* emerge in the first flush of postrevolutionary American literature. While many critics have examined them in this light, few have considered their relationship to the underlying debt crisis that drove political and party conflict in the early republic. Published in 1787 and 1797, respectively, *The Algerine Spy* and *The Algerine Captive* provide distinctly opposed cultural articulations of a widespread political economic anxiety, one that played out in the struggle between Federalists and Republicans over the distribution of power in the political and monetary system of the postrevolutionary United States. Significantly, the ten-year period framed by the books sees the redrafting and ratification of the Constitution, the emergence of the First Bank of the United States, the establishment of the national mint, the emergence of a Wall Street derivatives market based upon the circulation of government debt, and—after Alexander Hamilton's resignation as treasury secretary in 1795—the sale of government shares in the Bank by a revenue-strapped Congress. Along similar lines, *Tales of the Alhambra* was first published in 1832, after Irving's nearly fifteen-year absence from the United States and in the context of trans-Atlantic debates over centralized banking taking place in both Washington and London, the city in which it was initially composed. In 1832 President Andrew Jackson moved to "veto" the Second Bank of the United States and to devolve financial power back to state and local banks; at nearly the same moment, the British Parliament agreed to recharter of the Bank of England as a hedge against inflation, thus implicitly crediting, as Anna Kornbluh has indicated, the long-debased notion that money begets money.[20] Taken into consideration alongside his long-standing suspicions regarding financial speculation, Irving's tales of philosopher stone-like signets and secret caches of Moorish gold read as ornate, "arabesque" parables on the cultural politics of the early-nineteenth-century credit market.

Identity on Credit: Islam as a Figure for the Pleasures and Perils of Postrevolutionary Liberalism

While *The Algerine Spy in Pennsylvania* is often cited as one of the first American novels, its decidedly nonnovelistic character has typically barred it from consideration as a signal part of America's literary heritage.[21] The book was one of many texts that responded to the first Barbary crisis, a diplomatic standoff between the United States and the regencies of Tripoli and Algiers that was prompted by threats to American merchant shipping in the greater Mediterranean. Beginning in 1784, after the Treaty of Paris formally abrogated American rights of protection under treaties governing British maritime trade relations, Barbary corsairs began attacking American vessels, capturing well over one hundred sailors and demanding exorbitant ransoms as tribute.[22] Hamstrung by the relative weakness of the government established under the Articles of Confederation, U.S. officials were not capable of mounting a military opposition to the Barbary states, nor were they in a position to allocate the money to secure the captives' release. For the American public, the Barbary crisis became an enduring obsession, cutting through the vaunted rhetoric of postrevolutionary independence and exposing the practical limits to American power.

While Markoe's novel modulated anxieties around American vulnerability vis-à-vis the Barbary states, its subject was not the Barbary crisis but the domestic political reorganization that it occasioned. With the 1786–87 Shays' Rebellion, American impotence in the face of Barbary predations became one of the most compelling arguments for the creation of a stronger central government, one with greater powers over commerce, taxation, and defense. A dedicated anti-Federalist, Markoe offered in his novel a staunch critique of the nationalist movement through its celebration of the culture of liberty and liberality that had emerged from the American Revolution. As Timothy Marr has indicated, Markoe's portrait of the "Algerine spy," Mehemet, and the Algerian society from which he hails, reflected prevailing American understandings of Islamic government—the Ottoman state, in particular—as the embodiment of tyranny, and it was meant to comment upon the "tyrannical" expansion of centralized authority being formulated behind closed doors at the Constitutional Convention in Philadelphia.[23] As the agent of a Muslim power, Mehemet was an embodied prediction of what the future might hold should the Federalists prevail. From this perspective, Mehemet's gradual seduction by the United States and its culture of liberties stood as a counter claim, an evocation of the utopian promise of the postrevolutionary nation-state in the face of pragmatic considerations about its political and economic future.

Marr's reading of the text is supported by the circumstances of the book's initial publication. Largely set in Philadelphia, *The Algerine Spy* was released by a Philadelphia printer in 1787, while the Constitutional Convention was in session at Liberty Hall. There is little doubt that Markoe intended it as an intervention upon the political conversation of the time. What Marr's argument fails to take into account, however, is the specific nature of the crisis that prompted the constitutional delegations. At heart, the movement to redraft the Articles of Confederation was animated by concerns over the long-term impact of the Revolutionary War debt and the utter inability of the United States government to effectively manage its obligations to its creditors. Having financed the Revolution on credit, the United States entered the postrevolutionary era mired in debt; lacking the legal power necessary to levy taxes, the Congress of the Confederation struggled to find the resources whereby it might amortize its loans. Already under pressure from France, whose government was increasingly destabilized by a fiscal crisis brought on by American intransigence on the question of repayment, the Shays' Rebellion and the Barbary crisis only compounded a long-standing problem. Whether the question was annuities due Revolution-era soldiers, securing the release of Barbary captives, or propping up the French government, the United States was incapable of taking decisive action. For many of the Federalists with whom Markoe clashed, the greatest threat to American independence was not the elaboration of a stronger central authority but the largely invisible ties that bound the exercise of American liberty to financial actors whose interest in the United States was not conditioned by patriotic attachment.

An epistolary novel, *The Algerine Spy* unfolds over twenty-four chapters, each constructed as a single letter. The majority of these are written by the main character—the titular "Algerine spy," Mehemet—to his comrade Solayman; Mehemet's wife, Fatima; or his fellow conspirators in Algiers. The letters track Mehemet's movements from Algeria, through Gibraltar and then Portugal, and finally to the United States, where he takes up residence in Philadelphia. Commissioned by the Algerian government to report on the commercial prospects of this upstart nation, Mehemet's letters compose the bulk of that dossier, and they are overwhelmingly descriptive. Wherever he lands, Mehemet offers detailed accounts of social mores and economic relations; yet his portrait of late-eighteenth-century custom does little to advance the plot, nor does it provide particular insight into his character. Instead, Mehemet takes the measure of America as socioeconomic and cultural terrain, judging local practices against his own highly conservative sense of Islamic propriety. Throughout, Mehemet's identity as a Muslim provides Markoe's readers with an instrument through which to alienate their perspective and become—with him—an observer of their society, even as Mehemet's various disguises threaten to overwhelm the pillars of his faith. The story, such as it is, emerges only at the end of the novel, when Mehemet's former comrades turn on him, accuse him of apostasy, and declare him an enemy of the Dey. Mehemet's property in Algiers is seized, his wife leaves him, and Mehemet chooses exile and conversion, retiring in Philadelphia as an American Christian.

In *The Algerine Spy*, questions of finance first come into focus around the figure of the Jewish merchant who Mehemet first encounters while traveling into Europe. "The Jews are, I think, the principle merchants in Gibraltar; but may it not be asked, in what part of the world, where they are not the most industrious and wealthy part of the community? Wholly employed in commerce, they always educate their children for the mercantile profession."[24] As David Anthony has suggested, in early American culture, the identification of finance capitalism with "the Jew" served to deny any relationship between that culture and the "excesses" of finance capitalism insofar as it posited finance—like "the Jew"—as a foreign body.[25] Within Markoe's novel, however, the identification of "the Jew" with finance evokes the ominous specter of a more thoroughly modern anti-Semitic sensibility—one that prescribes the excision of Jews from the social body as a "foreshortened" course toward the amelioration of social ills brought on by the advent of industrial capitalism—in that this identification is underscored by the liminality of the characters' social identity as residents of an incoherent political space.[26] Headquartered in Gibraltar, the first Jewish merchant that Mehemet encounters, Solomon Mendez, exists in a realm that is at once hyperliminal with respect to Europe and Africa, Christianity and Islam, Britain and Spain, yet absolutely central to those myriad socioeconomic formations that found their anchor in the greater Mediterranean. As his name suggests, Mendez is split between these social and cultural formations, the seemingly unlikely pairing of "Solomon" with "Mendez" evoking overlapping histories of diaspora and legacies of displacement, just as Gibraltar's multiple toponyms evoke conflicting legacies of empire. Positioned between worlds, Mendez is the embodiment of the "rootless, the international, [and] the abstract," even as his liminality is critical to the proper function of the socioeconomic formations in which he is embedded. A perennial outsider, Mendez is nonetheless at the center of the action; throughout the novel, he remains peripheral to the unfolding of the narrative yet absolutely central to its eventual denouement.

Mendez's liminality with respect to conventional registers of class and status provides an optic through which to read the transformation of

Mehemet's identity over the course of the narrative. By providing Mehemet with the letters of introduction that facilitate his introduction to Philadelphia society and with the credentials that enable him to draw bills of exchange on American banks, Mendez transfers his liminality, with his financial capital, to Mehemet, rendering Mehemet the vehicle through which both find their expression. In the passage from Jew to Muslim, the potentiality of Mendez's uncertain social position is realized, enabling Mehemet to make manifest the "train of ideas, at once melancholy and pleasing" that he has entertained concerning his mission since the opening scene of the novel.[27] The transformation of Mehemet from Algerian to Frenchman, French to American, Muslim to Christian is, in this sense, underwritten by and evocative of the circulation of fictitious value, with each permutation of the self indicating another moment in a circuit of exchange. By positing its identity with racial-religious others, the novel attempts to isolate finance on the far side of a temporal divide from the emergent culture of American liberalism; nonetheless, Mehemet ultimately finds his identity as an American through exchange, comporting himself in emulation of the documentary culture that mediates his access to financial capital. Inscribed within this documentary culture, Mehemet surrenders the certainty of his life as an Algerian and a Muslim, embracing identity with finance itself.

This contradiction renders Markoe's polemic increasingly illegible. While attempting to valorize the notional openness of the liberal subject in opposition to the tyrannical other sustained by fictions of value, the novel continually collapses the two, consistently undermining its critique. Keeping with the convention of late-eighteenth-century American fiction, *The Algerine Spy* opens with a note from Mehemet's translator that addresses questions relating to the authenticity of Mehemet's dossier. "As the publication of the herewith enclosed letters will probably excite some degree of curiosity concerning Mehemet, the Spy, I wish it were in my power to gratify it."[28] Mehemet's identification with finance reflects back upon this frame narrative, rendering it a commentary on Mehemet's creditworthiness and the effective value of the text as an endorsement of the potentiality of early American liberalism. The translator's introduction asks readers to credit Mehemet's account insofar as Mehemet insists that translation and publication of the letters will serve the interests of the United States. "The letters," he writes, "were delivered into my hands with a note, which contained a request that I should translate and publish them for the good of the United

States."[29] The translator's attempt at establishing Mehemet's credibility, however, shifts focus from what is in fact at stake.[30] Mehemet's creditworthiness ultimately cannot be established because the translation itself cannot be verified; in translating from the Arabic, the translator has all but effaced the Arabic text, affecting the conversion from one idiom to another as a means of exposing it to the circulatory structure of the market. Only by abrogating the cultural singularity that establishes their use-value can Mehemet's letters be put to use; and translated from their specific cultural idiom, it becomes impossible to establish their value as truth.

Paired with the hasty conversion scene that occurs at the novel's end, this opening gesture encloses the text within a formal meditation on the "double appearance" of the commodity as both value and use-value. Predicated upon the loss of his property and his wife, Mehemet's conversion is again underwritten by the movement of fictitious capital. "The Rabbi, with whom thou had some acquaintance at Lisbon, has effected thy ruin by the blackest calumnies . . . [He] has represented you to the regency as a Christian and a fugitive from thy country."[31] By having his Jewish creditors question his credibility as a Muslim and an Algerian, Mehemet's access to capital is withdrawn, as are the trappings of his station in Algiers. His lands are seized, his property liquidated, and his wife absconds with a freed Christian slave. In this gesture Mehemet's identity as an Algerian and a Muslim is itself revealed to be dependent upon finance in that what wealth or status he enjoyed was conditional upon his credibility as such. Islam here appears as coextensive with the domain of fictitious capital, a point Markoe underscores by casual reference to the Orientalist myth that constructs the Qur'an as the cooperative heresy of a Nestorian Christian monk and a Jewish cleric. "How confirmed in error must that infidel be, who can utter so improbable a fiction?" Mehemet asks at one point; yet his conversion would seem to confirm the truth of that error as well as the possibility of moving from the realm of the fictitious into that of real, concrete values.[32] The opening discourse on his creditworthiness ironizes this gesture, however, inasmuch as it implies a movement of conscience that cannot be empirically verified. Forged within the circulatory matrix of capital, Mehemet's identity can never exceed or transcend its point of origins. Just as the concrete capacities of specific use-values are necessarily overwhelmed by their immaterial status as bearers of value, Markoe's Mehemet is continually fated to be an alien, an "other," a spy.

Conversion and the Instability of Value

In *The Algerine Captive*, Islam appears as a figure of financially driven social and cultural mutability; yet, where Markoe's use of that trope cross circuits his polemical agenda, that figure supports the political intervention of Tyler's novel, particularly insofar as it encounters Islam through the trope of conversion. This trope is, of course, familiar to any reader of proto-Orientalist anglophone literature, where the conversion of fictional Muslims offered confirmation of Christianity's moral authority, even in the face of Islam's clear political and economic superiority, while the threat of "turning Turk" evoked the empty heart of the European political order.[33] As a sociohistorical phenomenon, conversions in fact went both ways, with perhaps the greatest portion embracing Islam, if only as a matter of economic expediency.[34] Until the rise of Britain at the end of the eighteenth century, the Ottoman Sultan led what was, quite clearly, the most powerful empire in the world, one in which Muslims had distinct social and political advantages. "Despite what is often cited as 'Ottoman tolerance' of non-Muslim creeds," Selim Deringil writes, "there is no doubt that Muslims in the Ottoman Empire were the ruling class . . . A change of creed or ritual, grave as it was, was not necessarily a terribly intellectual or cerebral choice."[35] Under Islamic law and custom, Christians and Jews living within Dar al-Islam—the world united under Muslim hegemony—were to be respected and protected, yet they were never to be fully integrated. By contrast, Christians from Dar al-Harb—the "world of war" or those lands outside Muslim dominion—could be taken as captives and enslaved. Within a society at least nominally governed by Islamic law, conversion to Islam would have provided even the lowliest European with access to privileges routinely afforded Muslims, the most significant of which was their own freedom.[36]

Conversion figures prominently in *The Algerine Captive*. Where *The Algerine Spy* uses conversion to evoke the possibility of a system of value based upon concrete social relations and spiritual principles (what would later become the animating principle of Jeffersonian Republicanism), for Royall Tyler's Updike Underhill, the question of conversion suggests the irremediable loss of such concrete values and the necessity of making an arbitrary choice by which one might reestablish their hierarchy. *The Algerine Captive* thus elaborates the historical process by which a general equivalent emerges as the material embodiment of value, and it presents that historical process as the result of a willful political decision.[37]

First published in 1797, Tyler's *The Algerine Captive, or, The Life and Adventures of Doctor Updike Underhill* has enjoyed far greater critical attention than *The Algerine Spy*. This is in large part due to Tyler's relationship with the John Adams family. Because of his courtship of Adams's daughter, Nabby, several references to Tyler are made in the Adams's family correspondence. Tyler, of course, was also extraordinarily important to the development of the New York theater scene, writing the first American comedy to be staged in the city. After failing to win over Nabby Adams's mercurial father, Tyler served briefly in the Massachusetts militia that put down the Shays' Rebellion before being dispatched to New York City—then the capital of the nation—as a diplomat. "Tyler had never been to Manhattan," Caleb Crain notes in his introduction to *The Algerine Captive*. "Within three weeks, he had written a play. Within five . . . he had seen it performed."[38]

Staged on April 16, 1787, *The Contrast* was a sentimental comedy of manners in which two contrasting suitors—one a "Chesterfieldian" rake, one an "altruistic, and impoverished" Revolutionary War veteran—vie for the attention of genteel young ladies who, despite their best intentions, yearn for the pleasures of a fashionable court life. In many respects the contrast of the title suggests the parameters of Tyler's emergent Federalism while evoking the dynamics of the arbitrary yet necessary choice that he would restage—figuratively—in *The Algerine Captive*. Standing, respectively, for the opposition of European courtly values to American social mores, the characters of Dimple and Manley present contrasting versions of materially ungrounded aristocratic pretension. Neither character has money; both would seek to achieve financial security through marriage. The contrast, then, is between Dimple, who makes his intentions plain, and Manley, whose discretion and valor will eventually win the day. Tyler's Federalism, from this perspective, is less a deeply felt commitment to a particular form of social organization than a political expedient, a check upon liberty's descent into license.[39]

The necessity of making an arbitrary choice as a hedge against disorder is much more clearly evoked in *The Algerine Captive*, where it is figurative linked to the question of conversion. After having been abducted by Algerian pirates and sold into slavery in Algiers, Tyler's protagonist, Updike Underhill, encounters an Englishman from Birmingham who has secured his liberty by converting to Islam. "Embraced and protected by the rich and powerful, I have now a house in the city, a country residence on the Saffran, two beautiful wives, a train of domestics; and a respectable place in the Dey's customs defrays the expense."[40] The young man appeals to Underhill to meet with the mullah. "He will remove your scruples, and, in a few days, you will be as free and happy as I am." Underhill refuses. "Your body is at liberty, but your soul is in the most abject slavery," he tells the Englishman. "You have sold your God for filthy lucre; and 'what it shall profit you, if you gain the whole word and lose your own soul, or what shall a man give in exchange for his soul.'"[41] The Englishman, however, does not relent. "I have conversed with the Mollah, and I am convinced of the errours of my education. Converse with him likewise. If he does not convince you, you may glory in the christian faith; as that faith will be founded on rational preference, and not merely on your ignorance of any other religious system."[42] After some consideration, Underhill relents. "The prospect of some alleviation from labour, and perhaps a curiosity to hear what could be said in favour of so detestably ridiculous a system, as the Mahometan imposture, induced me . . . to signify my consent to converse with the Mollah."[43]

The change in Underhill's condition is immediate. "The next day, an order came from the Mufti to my master, who received the order . . . and directed me to be instantly delivered to the Mollah. I was carried to the college, a large gloomy building on the outside; but within the walls, it was an earthly paradise." Under the protection of the mullah, Underhill is presented with any number of sensual delights. "The stately rooms, refreshing baths, cooling fountains, luxuriant gardens, ample larders, rich carpets, downy sofas, and silken mattresses, offered with profusion all those soft excitements to indolent pleasure which even the most refined voluptuary could desire." Upon arrival, Underhill is taken to the hammam and bathed by a team of attendants. "[They] rubbed me so hard with their hands and flesh brushes, that I verily thought they would have flayed me." After bathing, he is anointed with balm of Mecca. "This application excited a very uneasy sensation, similar to the stroke of the water pepper, to which 'the liberal shepherds give a grosser name.'" Within a day, his "sun browned" skin peels away, to reveal the white man underneath, "as fair as a child . . . of six months old."[44]

In these passages Tyler stages what amounts to a baptism, rendering literal the course of metamorphoses that have brought Underhill to this point. Throughout the first half of the novel Underhill has served as a model for a new, postrevolutionary type of person, one who is in-becoming rather than being, whose identity is not given in relation to an inherited social structure but is, rather, speculative. Like Markoe's

Mehemet, he shifts his identity over the course of the first half of the novel as he blunders blindly from position to position, place to place. Sent to school as a boy, Underhill soon acquires "a taste for Greek," which kills his "love for labor."[45] Home on his father's farm, Underhill is worse than lost, giving Greek names to his farming implements and enacting scenes from Homer and Virgil during his working hours. "My father's hired men, after a tedious day's labour in the woods . . . for refreshment . . . found Homer's Iliad, Virgil's Delphini and Shrevelius's Lexicon, in the basket."[46] Unable to support his son's education but no longer willing to have him work on the farm, Underhill's father gives into his son's fantasies about embracing a profession and sells off part of his farm to continue funding his studies. The effort is for naught, ultimately, as Underhill fritters away what wages he makes in idle living, and the father continues to carve up his farm to support the son.

Throughout the first half of the novel Tyler treats education as little less than a Ponzi scheme, an inconclusive yet always seductive confidence game that continually reproduces its conditions of possibility. Whether as a student, a scholar, a poet, a schoolmaster, a doctor, or a slave trader, Underhill is useless to anyone, and it is his quest to valorize the fact of his education that eventually leads him to working on a slave ship— against his better principles—and finally into slavery itself. The elusive and unending quest to realize value through speculative deferral is here rendered as its own sort of slavery, perhaps playing upon contemporaneous discourses about the emergent financial culture of the trans-Atlantic slave trade.[47] From this perspective the bathing scene emerges as the latest in a series of metaleptic movements, one position or status substituted for another, with the sloughing off of dead skin materializing the fact of Underhill's arbitrary course of transformative movements. Significantly, this final metamorphosis is feminizing in that the balm of Mecca is indirectly likened to sexual penetration. At first roughed up and "flayed" by his attendants, Underhill describes the sensation of the balm as similar to the stroke of the water pepper, to which "the liberal shepherds give a grosser name."

Quoting Gertrude's description, from act 4 of *Hamlet*, of the "dead men's fingers" that surround the site of Ophelia's death, Tyler invites the reader to consider the implications of the "grosser name" that Shakespeare alluded to, whether it be cuckoo cock, dogstones, or priest's pintel.[48] Here Tyler again enacts another metaleptic conversion, one that harkens, like the end of *The Algerine Spy*, to the double appearance of the commodity in Marx's analysis of capital. As an orchid, the *Orchis mascula* to which Tyler refers evokes the simultaneity of the yonic and the phallic. By its uncanny alliteration, Underhill's name effects a similar doubling. Even as the repetition of the letter "U" evokes identity, the couplet up/under suggests difference as well as the possibility of conversion or exchange. The name itself transfers this trope from the diegetic and registers at the level of the formal. Evoking both the inverse movement of a Greek chorus, and the back and forth of a contrary call and response, "Updike Underhill" might be read as an instance of antistrophe, the rhetorical figure for conversion.

After his ritual ablutions, Underhill is left to wait for the next eleven days, after which he is joined by the mullah. "He was a man of about thirty years of age, of the most pleasing countenance and engaging deportment. He was born at Antioch, and educated a christian of the Greek church. He was designed by his parents for a preferment in that church, when he was captured by the Algerines, and almost immediately, conformed to the mussulman faith; and was in high esteem in the sacred colleges of the priests."[49] The mullah proceeds to indicate to Underhill his great aptitude for inspiring converts and his preference to win adherents through reason. "He said, the holy faith, he offered to my embraces, disdained the use of other powers that rational argument; that he left to the church of Rome, and its merciless inquisitors, all the honour and profit of conversion by faggots, dungeons, and racks."[50] While Islam, as a rule, does not seek converts through force or intimidation, the mullah's appeal to reason, in this instance, seems less a matter of Islamic principle than an attempt at evoking a specific postrevolutionary American anxiety concerning the fetish of reason and its centrality to U.S. political culture. Although the Enlightenment had enshrined reason as the substance of truth, with American political institutions founded on the principle that reasoned debate between representative citizens would inevitably elucidate the common good, the entrenchment of political parties and the failure of the federal government to resolve a range of political crises had polluted this primitive faith. Reason, after all, could be marshaled to the defense of error, as the mullah's discourse would go on to demonstrate.

Over the next chapter, Underhill and the mullah engage in a spirited though largely one-sided debate over the merits of their respective religious traditions. From the start, the mullah gets the upper hand, pointing out, correctly, that Underhill's Christianity is an accident of birth. "Born in New England . . . you are a christian purified by Calvin. Born in the Campania of Rome, you had been a papist. Nursed by the Hindoos, you would have entered the pagoda with reverence, and worshipped the soul of your ancestor in a duck."[51] Over the next five days the mullah goes on to demolish every defensive argument that Underhill puts forth, leaving him apoplectic and, briefly, speechless, with no recourse but to adamantly refuse to engage. "After five days conversation, disgusted with his fables, abashed by his assurance, and almost confounded by his sophistry, I resumed my slave's attire, and sought safety in my former servitude."[52]

As contemporary critics were quick to note, Tyler's handling of this scene is remarkably ambiguous. Through their dialogue, Tyler evokes the effective equality of Christianity and Islam, if not the actual superiority of the Islamic revelation. While Underhill insists upon the moral superiority of Christianity from the standpoint of Enlightenment principles of reason, the mullah presents a superior argument, one grounded in the history of Islam itself. His discourse forces Underhill to resign, defeated but unmoved, to retain his Christianity with his slave status. While Underhill's faith has never been anything more than an ambient presence in the novel until this point, the mullah's discourse reveals his passionate, fundamentally irrational attachment to Christianity as a marker of identity, one that is nonetheless absent any deeply felt sense of positive conviction. Underhill's defense of Christianity reveals no particular insight into the faith as a living spiritual tradition; rather, it is an entirely academic defense predicated upon what he imagines to be the failings of Islam. His Christianity is entirely unconscious and accidental, an embodied remnant of a cultural tradition unbound by any particular catechism. In choosing to retain his Christianity, Underhill thus chooses to make an entirely irrational decision with respect to both the theological and historical discussion at hand as well as the matter of conviction itself.

Absurd though it may be, Underhill's choice suggests the dynamics of faith at work in the Enlightenment discourse of reason. As A. Kiarina Kordela has pointed out with respect to the poststructuralist evacuation of the transcendental, if there are no first principles, if every regime of knowledge is equally ungrounded, and if the distinction between regimes of truth is altogether arbitrary, then all truths are derived from an act of decision that is, in effect, not a decision but a leap of faith.[53] Enlightenment reason is, in effect, founded upon faith; Tyler's handling of the conversion scene thus evokes the unconsciousness of faith as that which supports reason and the values it entails in order to insist upon the necessity of treating this leap as a willful act of political choice. Even though it is based upon a spurious line of reasoning, Underhill's decision to retain his Christianity and his slave status represents the first positive decisions that he makes concerning his status and his identity. Prior to this moment, he has been content to drift, perpetually deferring the question of who he is and what he is becoming, all too content to move with the speculative course of fictitious value that has underwritten his ambitions. In choosing to remain a Christian and a slave, Underhill effectively decides for the first time to become something, eschewing the course of perpetual becoming. Like Mehemet's conversion to Christianity, Underhill's attachment to his faith signifies the possibility of embracing a hierarchy of values that are stable, concrete; but where Markoe posed Mehemet's conversion as the movement between a set of values that were fictitious (Islam) and those that were concrete (Christianity), Tyler allows that both are equally arbitrary and ungrounded. The only ground for value is faith, and faith, for Tyler, is ultimately to be regarded as the concern of politics.

The necessity of making a choice between regimes of value in order to adjudicate a hierarchy of values is later underscored in Underhill's dealings with the Jewish merchants of Algiers. As in Markoe, it is through the Jewish characters that questions about value and political order emerge, again, as questions about financial value and the fictitious. Much more clearly than in *The Algerine Spy*, the Jewish characters that Underhill encounters are hucksters, Shylocks, all too willing to sell out their convictions and obligations to make a quick profit. "This cunning race . . . have contrived to compensate themselves for the loss of Palestine, 'by engrossing the wealth, and often the luxuries of every other land; and, wearied with the expectation of their heavenly king,' who shall repossess them of the holy city, and put their enemies beneath their feet, now solace themselves with a Messiah, whose glory is enshrined in their coffers."[54] Despite his misgivings about their intentions, Underhill contracts with Adonah Ben Benjamin, an Algerian Jewish merchant, to help secure his release. Over several weeks, he turns over to Ben Benjamin what money he can on the promise that Ben Benjamin will act as his agent in negotiations with the Dey. After protracted debates over the price of an

American hostage, the parties settle upon a ransom of $2,000, which Underhill eventually succeeds in raising. Suddenly assured of his freedom, Underhill is jubilant until his hopes are crushed by Ben Benjamin's death. "[Upon] applying to his son for his assistance in perfecting my freedom, which his good father had so happily begun, he professed the utmost ignorance of the whole transaction; declared that he did not know the name of the agent . . . and gave no credit to my account of the monies I had lodged with his father."[55] What could easily be dismissed as an unfortunate coincidence is quickly revealed to be the product of artifice. "The artful Jew, who had contracted for my ransom, fearing he should have to advance the money himself, spread a report that I was immensely rich in my own country. This coming to the ears of my master, he raised my ransom to six thousand dollars, which the wily Israelite declining to pay, the contract was dissolved."[56]

Although Ben Benjamin's son later recants, eventually effecting Underhill's release, the double-dealing and dissimulation of the Jewish characters in these scenes suggests the arbitrary and ungrounded character of finance itself, as well as the political necessity of removing financial considerations from the machinations and cupidity of "the Jews." At once stealing Underhill's money while inflating his value, the Jewish merchants trap Underhill in a form of slavery more thoroughgoing than anything he has experienced before, a form of debt peonage from which he has little hope of emerging. Bound by no obligation except to their own interests, "the Jews" are free to pursue any course they choose, even those that offend all ethical considerations of commerce and sociality. Formally, the identification of these "Jews" with finance is again rendered through the repetitiveness of their name. Where Underhill's name evoked the double appearance of the commodity as use-value and value, in "Ben Benjamin" the repetition of the syllable "ben," the Algerian rendering of the Arabic prefix "ibn" or "son of," suggests the unbound potentiality of self-generation through finance, a train of metaleptic substitutions, of sons repeating fathers, stretching on to fiscal infinity. By embedding the Jewish merchants within a historical discourse that underscores their connection to the land of Palestine and the "holy city" of Jerusalem, however, Tyler poses the identification of "the Jews" in his text with the merchant elite of the United States, most of whom narrated their origins in relation to a settler population that was motivated by the search for their own redemption in the New Jerusalem.

Diabolical Enterprises: Islam, Alchemy, and Financial Speculation

First published in 1832, much of Washington Irving's *Tales of the Alhambra* was composed during a brief stay at the Alhambra in 1828, while Irving was living in Spain researching his biography of Christopher Columbus and his later *Chronicle of the Conquest of Granada*. Despite a lukewarm critical response and his own misgivings about the literary merits of the text, *Tales of the Alhambra* proved enormously successful, inspiring a vogue for all things Andalusian in the United States. Indeed, *Tales of the Alhambra* was the first book Irving published in the United States after his return from a nearly fifteen-year sojourn abroad, living in London, Paris, and Madrid. Some aspect of the book's popularity was no doubt owed to the fact that he returned to the United States an international literary celebrity.

Unlike Markoe's and Tyler's, Irving's work was far more explicitly attuned to questions of finance, speculation, and fictitious value. While *Tales of the Alhambra* does not devote itself to such an investigation, considerations of financial and fictive values appear throughout the body of Irving's published work. Of these, perhaps the most direct and striking reference to financial speculation emerges in his 1840 essay, "An Unexampled Time of Prosperity: The Great Mississippi Bubble," where he explicitly addresses in the most unflattering light the practices that occasioned speculation in real estate and the creation of fortunes out of paper promises. Far more oblique but just as telling is his reference to the great buttonwood tree that dwarfs the manor house of his Dutch protagonist in "Wolfert Webber; or, Golden Dreams." In context, the buttonwood comments upon the vegetable proclivities of the Webber family while symbolically manifesting the genealogy of the dynasty that Irving has traced. The family lives under the shadow of the tree, Irving writes, "which little by little grew so great as to entirely overshadow their palace."[57] This image summons a financial excess. As contemporary readers would no doubt have known, the buttonwood had been associated with the New York Stock Exchange since its founding on May 17, 1792, when the first collection of traders met under a buttonwood tree near 68 Wall Street.[58] In "Wolfert Webber," the expansive growth of the tree prefigures the expansive growth of New York City, which becomes a source of great anxiety of Wolfert Webber and the reason why he begins to dig up his cabbages in search of Stuyvesant gold. Trying to become rich, Wolfert loses all, the opposition between gold and cabbage effectively underscoring Irving's impatience with those who would pursue illusory forms of value for those forms of value that are more substantive or real. "Let but a doubt enter, and the 'season of unexampled prosperity' is at an end. The coinage of words is suddenly curtailed; the promissory capital begins to vanish into smoke; a panic succeeds, and the whole superstructure, built upon credit and reared by speculation, crumbles to the ground, leaving scarce a wreck behind."[59]

Stories of hidden treasure recur throughout *Tales of the Alhambra*, and they project Irving's underlying concern with fictitious value. Beginning from the first chapter, where Irving's squire, Sancho, is taken in by reports of secret Moorish gold, Irving relates these tales as fables, with clear moral imperatives.

> There was once a fountain ... [and] the water gushed from the mouth of a bull's head, carved of stone. Underneath the head was inscribed: EL FRENTE DEL TORO SE HALLEN TESORO. (In front of the bull there is treasure.)
>
> Many digged in the fountain but lost their labor, and found no money. At last, one knowing fellow construed the motto a different way. It is in the forehead ... of the bull that the treasure is to be found, said he to himself, and I am the man to find it. Accordingly, he came late at night, with a mallet, and knocked the head to pieces; and what do you think he found?
>
> "Plenty of gold and diamonds!" cried Sancho eagerly.
>
> "He found nothing," rejoined mine host ... "and he ruined the fountain."[60]

In this tale, the logic of speculation in pursuit of fictitious value is rendered quite literally. Like the "lying reports" that form the basis of speculative frenzies, there is nothing secret about the secret treasure; the mere possibility of the secret treasure is enough to overrule reasonable concerns about either evidence or waste. One after another, men dig into the fountain looking for gold. They lose their labor, Irving tells us, and find no money. This waste of time and energy is occasioned by the flimsiest of promises augmented by increasingly arcane interpretations of the statue's motto. In the end desperate men destroy the statue, seeking to discover the wealth within. What they find, of course, is the very emptiness of the original promise, the motto and the statue now destroyed in the process of their unveiling. There is no gold, there are no diamonds, and the ruined statue stands as a lesson to those who would act on the advice of such meaningless gossip. At the same time, the destruction of the fountain renders it useless as a means of sustaining life: it can no longer deliver water. As if to drive home the connection with financial speculation, Irving casts his fountainhead in the form of a bull, the totemic representation of rising prices and financial expansion.

The parable of the fountain serves to connect Irving's tales of secret Andalusian gold back to the figure of Islam. Although Islam maintains a largely spectral presence in Irving's *Tales*, suffused as they are with haunted ruins and Moorish ghosts, the fountain is one of his more unobtrusive spirits, symbolically invoking the Qur'an's insistence on the holiness of water and a general Islamic commitment to a communitarian ethics of water use.[61] From this perspective, the destruction of the fountain would seem to suggest the literal effacement of Spain's Islamic heritage, here constructed as a concrete use-value akin to the water it delivers.[62] "I have remarked that the stories of treasure buried by the Moors, so popular throughout Spain, are most current among the poorest people. . . . The thirsty man dreams of fountains and running streams, the hungry man of banquets, and the poor man of heaps of hidden gold."[63] Likening the appetite for myth to the physical attributes of thirst, Irving constructs history as itself a source of nourishment, one that stands in a position of some ambivalence with respect to the currency of mythological motifs. For Irving, myth and history are opposed to one another as gold is to cabbages, abstract to real. Spain's Islamic heritage may exist in the real, but insofar as its remains act as a supplement to the most ludicrous flights of fancy, it serves as a figure for the spectrality of financial speculation.

Irving highlights this point by repeated references throughout the whole of his works on Al-Andalus to the mythological origins of Alhambra in alchemy. "The Moorish king who built [the Alhambra] was a great magician," Irving writes, "or, as some believed, he had sold himself to the devil, and had laid the whole fortress under a magic spell."[64] Throughout, alchemy becomes the motif by which he draws the mythological legacies of Spanish Islam into conversation with the anti-Semitic discourse of finance. Irving presents many literal Islamic specters, many of whom use promises of secret Moorish gold to lure hapless Christians to their doom. In one such tale Irving evokes the relationship between alchemy and financial speculation through descriptions of the Signet of Solomon, an occult device that grants access to a secret cache of Moorish treasure. "Everybody has heard of the Cave of St. Cyprian at Salamanca, where in old times judicial astronomy, necromancy, chiromancy, and other dark and damnable arts were secretly taught by an ancient sacristan; or, as some will have it, by the devil himself, in that disguise."[65] It is in the Cave of St. Cyprian that one Don Vicente discovers the Signet of Solomon. The signet, he learns, is the key that unlocks an ancient enchantment that will allow the bearer to discover a long forgotten stash of Moorish gold. It is also, Irving avows, a powerful source of wealth in its own right. "On picking [the Signet] up, it proved to be a seal ring of mixed metal, in which gold and silver appeared to be blended. It bore as a device two triangles crossing each other, so as to form a star. This device is said to be a cabbalistic sign, invented by King Solomon the wise, and of mighty power in all cases of enchantment."[66] Irving continues in this vein in his "historical" notes on this myth, where he affirms the origins of the tale within Islamic culture: "According to Arab tradition, when the Most High gave Solomon the choice of blessings, and he chose wisdom, there came from heaven a ring, on which this sign was engraven. This mystic talisman was the arcanum of his wisdom, felicity, and grandeur; by this he governed and prospered."[67] Through the Signet of Solomon, Irving gives literal shape to the occult and abstractive power of financial speculation while constructing a genealogy of fictitious value that anchors it in a civilizational narrative of Jewish origins. As in the works of Markoe and Tyler, Islam here is rendered a proxy for Judaism, its amplification and augmentation.

Nonetheless, Irving's collection begins to suggest a mode of engagement with Islam that was far less abstracted than those of Markoe, Tyler, or their contemporaries. Having lived in Andalusia for an extended period, Irving was attentive to the myriad ways in which the culture of southern Spain was inflected by Islam, both as a historical trace and a contemporary formation. Indeed, Irving's sojourn at the Alhambra began only after he was prohibited from entering Tangier, then under bombardment by the French as part of the first phase of their North African colonization scheme. Irving's tales were literary creations, but they drew upon an experience of encounter with a place and a people that was previously unavailable, an experience that would blossom into a more concerted engagement with Islamic world cultures as a contemporary social formations. After *Tales of the Alhambra*, Irving would go on to write a history of the Reconquista as well as a two-volume history of Islam that spanned the period between the birth of the Prophet Mohammed and the passage to Al-Andalus. Over the course of his life, Irving's literary invocations of Islam moved from the imaginative to the imperious, from Islam as a set piece or Islam as a sign of Oriental voluptuousness to Islam as an object of knowledge that might be used to some social or political purchase. Irving's work, in this sense, marks the passage of U.S. literary culture into a more recognizably Orientalist engagement with Islam and the greater Arab world, an engagement conditioned by Orientalism as a knowledge project bent to imperial practice.

Notes

1. Edward Said, *Covering Islam: How the Media and the Experts Determine How We See the Rest of the World* (New York: Vintage, 1997).

2. Ibid., 14–15.

3. Timothy Marr, *The Cultural Roots of American Islamicism* (Cambridge: Cambridge University Press, 2006).

4. Timothy Marr, "Strangers in the Spider's House: Transcultural Intelligence in American-(Middle)-Eastern Encounters," *American Literary History* 23, no. 1 (2011): 189–204, at 190.

5. Wai Chee Dimock, "Hemispheric Islam: Continents and Centuries for American Literature," *American Literary History* 21, no. 1 (2009): 28–52; and Wai-Chee Dimock, *Through Other Continents: American Literature across Deep Time* (Princeton, N.J.: Princeton University Press, 2006).

6. Jacob Rama Berman, *American Arabesque: Arabs and Islam in the Nineteenth Century Imaginary* (New York: New York University Press, 2012).

7. Said, *Covering Islam*, 13.

8. Dimock, "Hemispheric Islam," 30.

9. Ibid., 28–52.

10. Saree Makdisi, "Occidentalism" (Presentation delivered at the American University of Beirut in Beirut, Lebanon, on April 30, 2012).

11. David Anthony, *Paper Money Men: Commerce, Manhood, and the Sensational Public Sphere in Antebellum America* (Columbus: Ohio State University Press, 2009).

12. Jennifer J. Baker, *Securing the Commonwealth: Debt, Speculation, and Writing in the Making of Early America* (Baltimore: Johns Hopkins University Press, 2005); and Bruce H. Mann, *Republic of Debtors: Bankruptcy in the Age of American Independence* (Cambridge, Mass.: Harvard University Press, 2009).

13. Georg Lukács, "Reification and the Consciousness of the Proletariat," in *History and Class Consciousness: Studies in Marxist Dialectics* (Cambridge, Mass.: MIT Press, 1972), 93.

14. Karl Marx and Friedrich Engels, *The Communist Manifesto* (New York: Penguin, 2002), 6.

15. Lukács, "Reification and the Consciousness of the Proletariat," 93.

16. Moishe Postone, "Anti-Semitism and National Socialism: Notes on the German Reaction to 'Holocaust,'" *New German Critique* 19, no. 1 (Winter 1980): 107.

17. Moishe Postone, "Anti-Semitism and National Socialism: Notes on the German Reaction to 'Holocaust,'" *New German Critique* 19, no. 1 (Winter 1980): 97–115.

18. On anticolonial epistemologies and the coracialization of Jews and Muslims, see Santiago E. Slobadsky, "Talmudic Terrorism in Bethlehem," in *Biblical Texts: Ur-Contexts and Contemporary Realities* (Bethlehem: Dyer Publishers, forthcoming).

19. Postone, "Anti-Semitism and National Socialism,'" 106.

20. Anna Kornbluh, *Realizing Capital: Financial and Psychic Economies in Victorian Form* (Oxford: Oxford University Press, 2013); and Anna Kornbluh, "The Economic Problem of Sympathy: Parabasis, Interest, and Realist Form in *Middlemarch*," *ELH* 77, no. 4 (2010): 941–67, at 953.

21. On Markoe and the question of "the first American novel," see Cathy Davidson, *Revolution and the Word: The Rise of the Novel in America* (Oxford: Oxford University Press, 2004), 155.

22. Robert Battistini, "Glimpses of the Other before Orientalism: The Muslim World in Early American Periodicals, 1785–1800," *Early American Studies* 8, no. 2 (Spring 2010): 446–74. On the general history of Barbary corsairs and Barbary captivity narratives, see Paul Baepler, ed., *White Slaves, African Masters: An Anthology of American Barbary Captivity Narratives* (Chicago: University of Chicago Press, 1999); and Peter Lamborn Wilson, *Pirate Utopias: Moorish Corsairs and European Renegadoes*, 2nd ed. (New York: Autonomedia, 2003).

23. Timothy Marr, Introduction to *The Algerine Spy in Pennsylvania*, by Peter Markoe (Yardley, Pa.: Westholme, 2008).

24. Peter Markoe, *The Algerine Spy in Pennsylvania* (Yardley, Pa.: Westholme, 2008), 34.

25. Anthony, *Paper Money Men*, 76–77.

26. Postone, "Anti-Semitism and National Socialism."

27. Markoe, *Algerine Spy in Pennsylvania*, 7.

28. Ibid., 5.

29. Ibid.

30. Ibid.

31. Ibid., 112.

32. Ibid., 34.

33. For a fuller discussion of conversion narratives in proto- and pre-Orientalist English literature, see Daniel Vitkus, *Turning Turk: Theater and the Multicultural Mediterranean* (New York: Palgrave Macmillan, 2003).

34. On the sociohistorical phenomenon of Christian conversion, see Nabil Matar, *Islam in Britain, 1558–1685* (Edinburgh: Cambridge University Press, 1998).

35. Selim Deringil, "'There Is No Compulsion in Religion': On Conversion and Apostasy in the Late Ottoman Empire: 1839–1856," *Comparative Studies in Society and History* 42, no. 3 (July 2000): 547–75, at 548–49.

36. For yet another take on the question of English conversion narratives and the "compensatory strategies" deployed by British writers in the early modern period, see Jonathan Burton, "English Anxiety and the Muslim Power of Conversion:

Five Perspectives on 'Turning Turk' in Early Modern Texts," *Journal for Early Modern Cultural Studies* 2, no. 1 (2002): 35–67.

37. On general equivalency, race, and the mediation of difference, see Michael LeBlanc, "The Color of Confidence: Racial Con Games and the Logic of Gold," *Cultural Critique* 73 (Fall 2009): 1–46.

38. Caleb Crain, Introduction to *The Algerine Captive, or, The Life and Adventures of Doctor Updike Underhill*, by Royall Tyler (New York: Modern Library Classics, 2002), xxiii.

39. This reading has been informed by Ed White's recent analysis of *The Algerine Captive*, in which White points to the theoretical incoherence of early American conservatism as embodied in the Federalist Party. Reading the novel within the ideological field generated through captivity and slave narratives, White suggests that the text does not mount a critique of slavery as such but rather a critique of the critique of slavery as that critique circulated within the Federalist movement. In his words, "a key test for conservative sensibility was to know how to resist slavery correctly." Slavery was to be resisted not because of any sentimental moral obligation to democratize liberty, but because it was degrading to the civic culture of the republic—in large part because it formed the basis of Republican political power. Slavery, in other words, was perfectly commensurate with a Federalist worldview; except insofar as African slavery underwrote the power of the Jeffersonian political bloc. In its particulars, White's reading of early American conservatism seems to agree with Corey Robin's treatment of the same. See Ed White, "Divided We Stand: Emergent Conservatism in Royall Tyler's *The Algerine Captive*," *Studies in American Fiction* 37, no. 1 (Spring 2010): 5–27; see also Corey Robin, *The Reactionary Mind: Conservatism from Edmund Burke to Sarah Palin* (Oxford: Oxford University Press, 2011).

40. Royall Tyler, *The Algerine Captive, or, The Life and Adventures of Doctor Updike Underhill* (New York: Modern Library Classics, 2002), 126.

41. Ibid.

42. Ibid., 127.

43. Ibid.

44. Ibid., 128–29.

45. Ibid., 29.

46. Ibid.

47. On the relationship between the trans-Atlantic economy of slavery and the culture of finance, see Ian Baucom, *Specters of the Atlantic: Finance Capital, Slavery, and the Philosophy of History* (Durham, N.C.: Duke University Press, 2005).

48. Marjorie Garber, *Coming of Age in Shakespeare* (New York: Routledge, 1997), 171–72.

49. Tyler, *Algerine Captive*, 129.

50. Ibid., 130.

51. Ibid., 131.

52. Ibid., 136.

53. A. Kiarina Kordela, "Marx, Condensed and Displaced," in *The Dreams of Interpretation: A Century Down the Royal Road*, ed. Catherine Liu, John Mowitt,

Thomas Pepper, and Jakki Spicer (Minneapolis: University of Minnesota Press, 2007), 303–20.

54. Tyler, *The Algerine Captive*, 194–95.

55. Ibid., 204.

56. Ibid., 204–5.

57. Washington Irving, "Wolfert Webber; or, Golden Dreams," in *The Complete Tales of Washington Irving*, ed. Charles Neider (Boston: DaCapo Press, 1998), 489.

58. Doug Henwood, *Wall Street: How It Works and For Whom* (London: Verso, 1998).

59. Washington Irving, "A Time of Unexampled Prosperity: The Mississippi Bubble," in *Complete Tales of Washington Irving*, 305.

60. Washington Irving, *Tales of the Alhambra* (New York: AMS Press, 1973).

61. Francesca De Chatel, *Water Sheiks and Dam Builders: Stories of People and Water in the Middle East* (New Brunswick, N.J.: Transaction Publishers, 2007).

62. On the effacement and negotiation of Spain's Islamic heritage, see Patricia E. Grieve, *The Eve of Spain: Myths of Origins in the History of Christian, Muslim, and Jewish Conflict* (Baltimore: Johns Hopkins University Press, 2009).

63. Irving, *Tales of the Alhambra*, 41.

64. Ibid., 61–62.

65. Ibid., 62.

66. Ibid., 489.

67. Ibid., 505.

Salim the Algerine

The Muslim Who Strayed into Colonial Virginia

JUDITH E. TUCKER

I first encountered the story of Salim the Algerine in the form of an Appalachian tale recorded by Felix G. Robinson, a minister and local historian from West Virginia.[1] It was one of a series of local stories and legends he had collected in western Maryland and West Virginia in the 1950s and 1960s, but it stood out as the most exotic: this so-called Appalachian tale told of Salim, son of an Ottoman official from Algiers, who was abducted by Spanish pirates in the western Mediterranean in the mid-eighteenth century on his homeward journey from studies in Istanbul, transported to Louisiana on a French cargo vessel, and sold into slavery on a local plantation. Within less than a year, he had escaped plantation life and fled northward, only to be captured by the Shawnee. He managed to escape once more and came close to perishing in the woods before he was rescued by an English settler out on a late fall hunting excursion, who then lodged him with another backwoodsman in Augusta County, Virginia, until he recovered his strength and learned enough English to tell his story and express his desire to return to his home in Algiers. His hosts sent him along to Williamsburg, Virginia, where he received the patronage of local gentry who helped sponsor his repatriation to Algiers, sending him on to London with a request that his journey home be facilitated. He disappeared from view for a few years, then surfaced again in their midst in Williamsburg sometime in the 1770s, ostensibly having left Algiers once more, a changed man who had clearly suffered some great disappointment. He settled down locally and was taken under the wing of Virginia gentry, particularly the Page family of Rosewell Plantation. He eventually acquired the reputation of a harmless eccentric who hovered on the edge of sanity and then drifted into obscurity.

As he crisscrossed the Atlantic, Salim was the hapless protagonist in a drama of displacements and connections among far-flung regions globalized eighteenth-century style. Over the past few years I have looked for Salim in eighteenth-century materials, including biographical dictionaries and chronicles from Algiers, Istanbul archives, western Mediterranean travel accounts, narratives of captivity among Ohio Valley American Indians, and the papers and letters of Virginia gentry with Williamsburg connections. I have come up largely empty-handed: the story of Salim has been told and retold in various versions as an Appalachian legend or as the tale of a local character in Augusta and Bath Counties (Virginia)—I have found eleven extant versions—but the search for historical materials to document this story has been rather disappointing.[2] The fact that we do not know his lineage works against finding him in Arab-Ottoman sources. But I have found evidence, as we shall see, that he was a historical person who lived most of his adult life in the Williamsburg area.

There are, needless to say, many dimensions to the Salim story as it touches on eighteenth-century Ottoman social practices, patterns of piracy and diplomacy in the Mediterranean, experiences of slavery in Louisiana, interactions on the American frontier, and the intricacies of Tidewater Virginia society. It is the last of these that I consider here: as Salim crossed cultural borders, what contributed to his success or failure at making it in a new context? What did Salim represent for those who interacted with him? How did he reshape his identity in an environment of extreme dislocation? Salim's adaptation to life in colonial Virginia can be deemed only a partial success. He acquired powerful patrons in the form of members of the Tidewater gentry and achieved recognition as a learned "gentleman," yet he remained a man apart, known for his eccentricities and even his questionable sanity. I explore the limits of his integration, the facilitators and obstacles to his sea change in light of the differences in play, including those of race, religion, culture, and rank—all markers of identity that proved to be more or less negotiable after he arrived in colonial Virginia.

Racial Boundaries

Race was a major issue in the Tidewater slave-owning society in which Salim found himself. Surely he was different from the predominantly English settlers in appearance, but how different is difficult to tell. We learn from the sources that Salim was reportedly of mixed parentage: his father was an Ottoman official stationed in Algiers while his mother was a local Arab woman. The Ottoman father might have had any manner of racial background, given the multiracial character of the Ottoman elite.

As a result of this mixed parentage, Salim would have been known in Algiers society as a *kuloghlu*, the offspring of a member of the Ottoman elite and a local. The ranks of Ottoman officialdom were closed, in principle, to *kuloghlus*: even *kuloghli* sons of the Dey of Algiers could be denied access to state office. We have ample evidence, however, that *kuloghlus* obtained official posts despite strong ideological currents downplaying their Turkishness and excluding them from playing such roles.[3] Salim's mixed background did not prevent him in any case from receiving an elite education in Istanbul, a privilege usually reserved for those destined for the Ottoman elite. But given his liminal position in Algerian society, Salim would have been someone well acquainted with boundaries established by birth, although these were not racial boundaries, strictly speaking.

Would Salim have arrived in the Americas with some home-grown notions about racial barriers based on skin color as well? Although there are virtually no racial distinctions to be found in the Qur'an or hadith, Arab writers no doubt familiar to an educated man like Salim, such as al-Dimashqi (d. 1327) and Ibn Khaldun (d. 1406), subscribed to an environmental theory of skin color, namely that different zones of habitation produced different shades of color, from Black people in equatorial zones of Africa to White people in the cold northern climes. There is no indication in their writings, however, that skin color per se produced inferiority. Both Ibn Khaldun and the traveler Ibn Battuta held that sub-Saharan Blacks and the Whites of the far north were indeed inferior, but this was a function of civilizational difference resulting from the harshness of their environments. Skin color was just one of many attributes resulting from climate, including in the case of northerners large bodies, slow minds, and irascible tempers that impeded the development of higher civilization. Barbarity abounded in the hot and cold extremes inhabited by Blacks and Whites, but it was a barbarity signaled not by skin color but by the presence of grotesque customs and the absence of developed states and laws.[4]

Salim's racial consciousness may well have been shaped by a peculiar chapter in the history of North Africa. In the late seventeenth century, the ruler of Morocco, Mawlay Isma'il, created an army of Black soldiers by drafting Black men, both slave and free, including the *haratin*, a population of agriculturalists from the south of the country. Members of the *'ulama'* were enlisted to opine that Blacks were by definition former slaves and could therefore be re-enslaved as soldiers, thereby eliding color with slave status in a novel fashion. This Black slave army was to endure in neighboring Morocco up to 1757, into the time of Salim's teen years.[5] We have no evidence for any parallel institution in Algiers, however, so such racial distinctions might have been something Salim heard about but did not experience firsthand.

On the other side of the Atlantic, how was Salim perceived in the racially charged atmosphere of Tidewater Virginia? A lack of crisp racial classification appears in an American portrait. Charles Willson Peale painted a portrait of Salim, identified as "a young Algerine of good family," in Philadelphia in 1789, the subject having accompanied his patron, John Page, to his post in Congress.[6] The portrait was lost during the Civil War, but a surviving woodcut depicts a dark-haired, dark-browed, seemingly swarthy individual with a largish mouth and generous pointed nose, who "was painted Indian fashion, with a blanket round his shoulders, a straw hat on his head, tied on with a check handkerchief."[7] There is no clear commitment to a racial category here but rather a visual allusion to native American dress, suggesting, perhaps, that while this "Algerine of good family" was not exactly White, neither was he to be considered Black, an identity that would certainly have barred him from the social acceptance he received.

The attitudes toward race, and Blacks in particular, in the Williamsburg circles in which Salim found himself are captured in the writings of St. George Tucker, a lawyer, professor of law, and eventual judge who was a very close friend of Salim's benefactor, John Page.[8] Tucker went on to write, in the 1790s, a dissertation on slavery in which he advocated for the abolition of the institution in Virginia on the grounds that it was ultimately incompatible with the values of a democratic society, although his plan was a very gradual one with ample compensation to owners and methods to secure Black labor by other means. In the course of exploring the history of slavery in America, Tucker notes that, in the seventeenth century, all non-Christians brought into White settlements in servitude, including "Negroes, Moors, mulattoes or Indians," were by definition slaves, "except Turks and Moors in amity with Great Britain"—in other words, those subjects of the Ottoman Empire or the North Africa regencies whose states had treaty relations with Great Britain at the time.[9] In Tucker's own time, however, it is race that is paramount, and Black Africans have been enslaved because of their racial—not religious or political—identity. Racial identity serves as the justification for slavery and the source of Black inferiority:

In general their existence appears to participate more of sensation than of reflection. Comparing them by their faculties of memory, reason and imagination, it appears that in memory they are equal to the whites; in reason much inferior; that in imagination they are dull, tasteless and anomalous. Etc. The improvement of the blacks in body and mind, in the first instance of their mixture with whites, has been observed by everyone, and proves that their inferiority is not the effect merely of their condition of life.[10]

Although Tucker goes on to say that he lacks, perhaps, the empirical evidence required to draw definitive conclusions, he still suspects that "the blacks, whether originally a distinct race, or made distinct by time and circumstances, are inferior to the Whites both in the endowments of body and mind."[11] The inference is clear: Blacks have been enslaved as a result of this racial inferiority and may be freed from slavery but not from the inferior status conferred by being Black. The Black/White dichotomy that preoccupies Tucker would have worked to Salim's advantage. By not being "Black," with all that meant in the Tidewater circles he frequented, Salim was able to make his way as an acceptable "other" in White society.

Salim's position of racial indeterminacy may well have been aided by the fact that his initial point of entry to colonial society was from the west, through the frontier. Out on this frontier, settlers encountered "a host of strangers of different races, cultures, and social origins," as has been remarked in the context of Kentucky in the 1770s, and is equally applicable to western Virginia in the 1750s when the frontier settler Samuel Givens came across a near-naked and starving Salim in the woods.[12] In the absence of a common language, Givens could not, by all accounts, make out who this person might be, but frontier inclusiveness worked in Salim's favor. Givens revived him and handed him off to one Captain Dickerson, another settler in Augusta country, thereby initiating a string of contacts that passed Salim along eastward, from the frontier to the county seat and then on to Williamsburg. The inclusiveness of these frontiersmen and the absence of any indication that the question of race gave them pause may well have set the tone for Salim's acceptance in Williamsburg, a place where racial distinctions mattered deeply.

Along the way Salim acquired enough English to tell his own story, to establish his identity as an Ottoman subject from Algiers. North Africans, or "Moors," as they were usually designated, were not being subjected to rigid systems of racial categorization in America: eighteenth-century writers tended to describe Moors as "sun-burnt," and noted how the absence of time in the sun preserved the White complexions of Moorish women.[13] "Moors" were not Black, and as skin color became ever more closely linked to the legality of slavery, we find instances in which slaves laid claim to North African origins in order to petition the courts for release from slavery on the grounds of illegal servitude. In 1753, for example, two slaves requested their freedom before a South Carolina royal council on the grounds that they were originally military captives from the Moroccan port of Salé. In a similar petition in 1790 submitted to the South Carolina General Assembly, four men and their wives claimed the legal rights of Whites, saying they were "free Moors."[14] As racial classifications gained more complexity around the turn of the century and the question of the enslavement of Americans by North African corsairs heightened indignation, the discourse on race was to shift somewhat, and North Africans came to be firmly ensconced in a non-White, although not Black, category.[15] Salim arrived on the scene well before these developments, however, and race did not as a result present a significant barrier to his social mobility. By laying claim to "Moorish" identity, he positioned himself as a candidate for admission to White, not Black slave, society.

So a combination of factors—the focus on blackness and the ambiguity of other racial categories at the time at least as far as North Africans were concerned, Salim's introduction to colonial society through one of its less particular portals, and, no doubt, his own prior experience with inhabiting and negotiating a liminal social position—all worked to minimize the impact of race on his social integration.

Religious Connections

Religion might well be expected to pose a greater obstacle. Salim would have arrived with his own store of knowledge of the religiously framed confrontations of the eighteenth-century Mediterranean. Al-Tilimsānī, the chronicler of Algiers who began his narrative with the year 1516 and ended in 1779, captured the spirit of his age in his opening lines: "The pages of this book are written to instill this spirit of defense of the faith into the heart of the timid, and to rouse the brave to an even greater ardor."[16] The following account often pits the Muslims of Algiers against the Christian infidels, and it is God who grants victory to the defenders of the true faith, just as he occasions the infidels to be killed or taken prisoner. In Islamic legal literature as well, Muslim–Christian lines were drawn. The jurist Wansharisi's collection of North African and Andalusian legal opinions (fatwas), although assembled at the turn of the sixteenth century, was widely circulated and referenced throughout the early modern period. These legal opinions assume that pirates or "thieves of the sea" (*lusus al-bahr*) that prey on Muslim ships are *rum* (Roman), a fluid term used for Christians, or simply *nasrani* (Christian). The pirate encounter is invariably one between Christian "thieves" and Muslim victims.[17] There is also due attention paid to the presence of Christian captives in Muslim lands, at least some of whom were presumably taken by corsairs. The status of these captives has everything to do with their religious identity. There is mention of only Christian captives, and those who convert to Islam render their status as slaves problematic.[18] In all the legal opinions, it is Muslimness and Christianness that defines the legitimacy of capture, enslavement, and ransom, in keeping with the fact that North African corsairs were celebrated at home as warriors for the faith, *al-ghuzat*, engaged in sea-borne jihad.

Despite the power and pervasiveness of this rhetoric, it would be a mistake to conclude that Muslim–Christian confrontation would have played an exclusive role in shaping the young Salim's views of Christians and Christianity. In the Algiers of his boyhood, he would have crossed paths with significant numbers of Christians of different backgrounds. For one thing, there were many European captives in Algiers. When, in the spring of 1816, almost all captured Christian slaves being held in the North African regencies were freed, their numbers amounted to 1,660 in Algiers.[19] As a native son of Algiers, Salim would have been accustomed to interacting with Europeans, both these Christian captives who pursued various trades and provided services in the city and the converts to Islam who were active or retired *renegados*, who are discussed in greater detail below. In addition, European consuls, the crews from the ships of European powers at peace with Algiers, and a number of European merchants based in the city bred some familiarity with Christian beliefs and practices. And Istanbul, where he studied, was arguably one of the most cosmopolitan cities of the era. Although population statistics for the eighteenth century are far from precise, estimates place the population of the city in the range of 400,000 to 500,000 residents, of whom well over 40 percent were non-Muslims, primarily Christians.[20] Salim would not have arrived in Virginia completely ignorant of Christianity and of the nuances of difference between, for example, the Ottoman Eastern Orthodox, Catholic French, and Protestant English.

Salim himself was of Muslim background, and this identity might be expected to have posed challenges for him in colonial Virginia. As Thomas Kidd has shown, the available literature on Islam was not, however, all of a piece. The educated elite of the Tidewater could be expected to be familiar with Humphrey Prideaux's *The True Nature of Imposture Fully Displayed in the Life of Mahomet*, first published in 1697 and subsequently reprinted a number of times. As the title suggests, Prideaux focused on the fakery of Muhammad's claim to prophesy and further depicted Islam as a religion of superstition and irrationality, a religion that promoted the "base instincts" of its adherents.[21] But there were also more positive accounts of Islam in circulation, including Henri de Boulainvillier's *The Life of Mahomet*, published in 1731, which questioned the view of Muhammad as imposter and attributed the development of Islam, in part, to the Reformation theme of the corruption of Christian clergy.[22]

The local gentry of the Williamsburg area, who were to play such a significant role in Salim's integration, demonstrated an interest in learning about Islam as part of their broader universalism. We now know the story of Thomas Jefferson's engagement with Islam. Like others of his circle, he had read Freiherr von Pufendorf's *Of the Law of Nature and Nations*, which posited that the teachings of the Qur'an were "consistent with Greco-Roman beliefs and natural law."[23] He also purchased a copy of the Qur'an in 1765 in the form of George Sale's English-language translation; Sale asserted in the introduction that "to be acquainted with the various law and constitutions of civilized nations, especially those of who flourish in our own time, is, perhaps, the most useful part of knowledge."[24] Jefferson appeared to put this commitment to universalism into practice in his proposed Bill for Establishing Religious Freedom in 1777 in Virginia, under which he clearly intended to extend freedom of religion to Muslims.[25] But, according to Denise Spellberg, who has scrutinized Jefferson's writings, including his copious reading notes in the period between 1765 and 1776, there is no evidence that he engaged with Sale's positive discussion of Islamic practices and beliefs in any depth. Indeed, Jefferson's views of Islam appear to have been shaped more by Voltaire's depiction of Islam in his *Essai sur les moeurs et l'esprit des nations* as a militant faith and an enemy of science.[26] Although sources assume that Jefferson knew Salim and spent time discussing religious issues with him, I have not found any direct mention of Salim in

Jefferson's papers. And Spellberg asserts that, prior to his 1786 negotiations with the ambassador from Tripoli, "Jefferson had never met a Muslim."[27]

Closer to home, John Page, on whose plantation Salim found refuge as an informal tutor, ruminated that Islam as a religion, while flawed, was worthy of some serious consideration:

> Is not the Religion of Mahomet which was borrowed in a great Measure from Judaism and from Christianity and which was more agreeable to the People of Asia and Africa than the latter as it indulged their favorite Passion, I say is not this Religion the prevailing Religion in those countries—and do they not teach two great important doctrines of the Gospel the being of God, his Justice and Power and a future state of Rewards and Punishments?[28]

Page makes here a fairly standard reference to the hypersexuality of Asians and Africans, which was nicely accommodated in Islam by the institution of polygyny. Despite this moral laxity, he is quite willing to locate Islam within the Judeo-Christian tradition and even give doctrinal credit for adherence to positions that track Christian views on the nature of the Divine and the afterlife. Unfortunately, Muslims' embrace of polygyny, in keeping with the satisfaction of their "favorite Passion," stood in the way of their readiness to receive the Christian gospel.[29] Page was not as certain as Jefferson about extending equal political rights to Muslims, although he did not dismiss the idea outright.[30]

What seems incontrovertible is that Salim stepped into a milieu in which educated men were engaged in serious discussion of Islam as a religion that shared some fundamental beliefs with Christianity, and of Muslims as fellow human beings who might even lay some claim to civic brotherhood. But there were precious few Muslims available to join the conversation. There were significant numbers of Muslims—whose religious affiliation was often unknown to their owners—among the enslaved portions of the population in the Carolinas and Georgia. Most runaways with Muslim names came from South Carolina, Georgia, and colonial Louisiana, where planters paid attention to ethnicity and preferred slaves from the Islamized areas of Senegambia and Sierra Leone because they were practiced in the cultivation of rice and indigo.[31] Virginians seemed less attentive to the ethnic origins of their slaves and, in any event, did not privilege slaves from these regions, so there were far fewer Muslims to be found among Tidewater slaves; in any case, we can assume that theological debates were not going to take place between master and slave.[32]

The presence of Salim therefore offered a rare opportunity to talk with an educated Muslim who presumably brought a schooled knowledge of Islam to the discussion as well as prior knowledge of Christianity from at least two separate angles. As a resident of Algiers, he would have been aware of the churches housed in various *baños*, the detention facilities for Europeans who had been captured by corsairs. Captive priests were permitted to say Mass and celebrate other rituals and holy days, and friars ventured out onto the streets of Algiers on a weekly basis to ask for alms to support the hospitals for captives.[33] This early exposure to Catholicism and Protestantism in the captive population was followed by encounters with Orthodox Christianity as a result of his residence in eighteenth-century Istanbul where Christians made up a significant part of the population. Salim would have arrived in Virginia, then, with far more knowledge of Christianity than his interlocutors would have had of Islam. I can only imagine that he was more than ready to engage in sophisticated discussions of religion.

As the story of Salim came to be told and retold in local Virginia legend, a new religious element eventually appeared, namely a conversion narrative. Guided by dreams and clerical instruction, Salim comes to embrace Christianity.[34] There are no early sources for this conversion story, so it may well be that this later addition served to bring him into line with a global imaginary of the spread of Christianity, a kind of ex post facto adjustment of the Salim story that signals the transition in the nineteenth century to a less eclectic and more parochial engagement with the world.[35] In any event, Salim's conversion comes to form a major chapter of his story and is made to serve as a vindication of the superiority of Christianity, particularly of Protestantism. According to the mid-nineteenth-century author Bishop William Meade, Salim refused French attempts to convert him because of their idolatrous practices; only when he encountered Presbyterian practices in the English settlements did Christianity begin to appeal to him and he embraced the new faith.[36] Whether Salim converted at all is an open question, although one can imagine that this might have been a good move as far as making his way in local society.

Religion was, in any case, a significant marker of identity for Salim in his new world but not an impediment to his integration. Whether he remained a Muslim who could attract the interest and respect of educated men or a convert who could testify to the virtues of Christianity, religion was not likely at any rate to have blocked his path. In a curious twist, it may well be that Salim's Muslim background lent him considerable social capital among the Virginia gentry, especially in the Williamsburg circles where philosophical and theological issues could take a universalist turn.

Cultural Encounters

What I can surmise about Salim's wider cultural background largely rests on his skeletal biography. His birthplace, Algiers, was a major port with a long history of connections to other shores of the Mediterranean. There was the phenomenon of *renegados*, for example, those Europeans who had thrown in their lot with North African corsairs and sailed as crew or even captains of North African corsairing vessels. Their numbers were significant: in 1582, of the thirty-five captains of corsairing ships sailing out of Algiers, twenty-two can be identified as *renegados*.[37] In 1675, the English consul in Algiers estimated that three thousand *renegados* resided in that city.[38] This phenomenon endured well into the eighteenth century so that as a boy Salim would have been aware of the cosmopolitan nature of the Algiers' elite. Then he spent his formative years in schooling in Istanbul, a large imperial city with a mixed population of Muslims, Christians, and Jews, both Ottoman subjects and members of foreign communities. He had been exposed to different religions and ethnicities. He knew languages: Arabic, Ottoman Turkish, Greek, and probably Persian. Salim was heir to the rich Ottoman-Arab-Islamic heritage that was still on offer in the mid-eighteenth century. In his manner of dress, foodways, and lifestyle, we can assume that he was sophisticated and urbane and might well have been recognized as such. Again, the timing of his arrival on America's shore was critical: the Ottomans could still be regarded in the mid-eighteenth century as powerful and civilized opponents, and the vilification of the "Barbary States" as true barbarians was not to reach a crescendo until later in the century, in the 1780s and 1790s, when corsairs from Algiers targeted the ships of the newly independent American nation.[39]

To our and his bad fortune, however, no outward manifestations of this rich culture accompanied Salim to colonial America. He arrived destitute, a victim of piracy and captivity who had lost everything along the way. As one later account of his rescue in the woods has it, "he was stark naked except for some rags wrapped around his feet. His body was emaciated, and his skin was thickly marked by scars and scabs."[40] He began his life in the English settlements as if newborn: he had to be clothed, fed, and taught comprehensible speech. Insofar as Salim entered his new society as a tabula rasa, as someone who could be inscribed with a new culture of dress, food, language, and deportment, he could be easily assimilated. Indeed, that is what appears to have happened, at least according to one descendant of the Page family who recounted how Salim, after he returned from his journey to Algiers, met Virginia governor John Page "who took him to his home, 'Rosewell,' in Gloucester County, Virginia. Here, Selim became domesticated, and he was a general favorite with all who knew him."[41] And his portrait hung for many years in the family portrait gallery at Rosewell, "side by side with the stately dames, warriors and courtiers."[42]

The Virginia gentry may have brought some cross-cultural knowledge of a particular sort to this encounter. "Eastern tales" and accounts of travel to the East were popular genres in the mid-eighteenth century, and it is likely that Page and his cohort were familiar with some of them. Antione Galland's French edition of the *1001 Arabian Nights* was translated into English and circulated in America. Other fanciful travel accounts cum tales, such as *The Adventures of Abdullah, Son of Hanif*, published in French in 1712 and in English in 1729, were available. Two East India Company employees, James Ridley and Alexander Dow, had also published popular Eastern tales: Ridley's *Tales of the Genii* appeared in 1764 and Dow's *Tales of Inatulla* in 1797.[43] These publications no doubt served as an inspiration for an "Eastern tale" composed by St. George Tucker, a piece that he tantalizingly titled "The Vision of Selim."

The protagonist of Tucker's tale is one "Selim," the son of the "Sultan Haroon Alraschid." While Sultan Harun al-Rashid was indeed an 'Abbasid ruler in the late eighth and early ninth century Baghdad, there is no evidence that he had a son by the name of Salim, so Tucker may well have found the name closer to home. The tale recounts the vision that appeared to Selim during the three days and nights he spent in a deep trance. His vision is one of travel: Selim sets off on a journey to the East fraught with various perils. He experiences extreme privation in the desert, relieved only by the hospitality of Arab tribesmen. He is captured by Malaccan pirates. When his ship is subsequently becalmed and the passengers threatened with starvation, a European merchant on board proposes that they murder one of the company and eat him. Despite

Selim's protestations, this lot falls to Hali, Selim's faithful companion, and he witnesses Hali's murder before a storm arises and drowns all on-board except for Selim. Upon awaking from his trance before the eyes of his concerned family and the real-life Hali who are gathered around his bedside, Selim has a revelation: "O holy Alla! Now I perceive the blessings, which Hali taught me to expect, in this *new Life*; of which, 'till now, I could form no conception! Blessed, be the name of Alla, forever, and ever."[44]

Tucker's tale paints an engaging portrait of the East. Selim is a thoughtful young prince, surrounded by loving family members and retainers. His imagined journey highlights the nobility of the Bedouin and the faithfulness and wisdom of his companion, Hali. Indeed, the critical moment of savagery in the form of murder and cannibalism comes at the behest of a European, and Selim himself is appalled and repelled by both acts. Tucker not only sketches an Eastern culture of generosity and refinement, he also chooses to make this an allegorical tale that crosses religious boundaries with ease. In Tucker's words: "How far this little Tale may convey to the rational mind some faint Idea of the extatic [*sic*] emotions of a Soul which has just quitted its mortal mansion, and entered the portals of Immortality, is submitted to your better Judgement, and that of your Readers."[45] So an Eastern Muslim's vision could help Christian readers in America explore the mysteries of death and immortality. Tucker's tale reflects a romance with Eastern culture, at least in a distilled literary form, and a willingness to consider affinities in the moral and spiritual realms. The Salim from Algiers no doubt benefited from these interests of the Virginia gentry, which could encourage interest in, and respect for, his cultural background.

Regardless of the interest taken in Salim's cultural heritage, there were costs for his social acceptance. Accounts of Salim's life allude repeatedly to eccentricities, instability, or even outright insanity. He was known to abhor the indoors, choosing to sleep rough rather than in the comfort of a host's guestroom. He was said to wear outlandish costumes, such as the "Indian" garb in which Peale painted him. He wandered town and country trying to find "a friend." Rumor had it that he spent time in the Williamsburg "Hospital for Lunatiks," although this has proved difficult to confirm.[46] Overall, he gives the impression of a man who has lost his cultural moorings. Given that he did not have the ability and resources to reproduce his cultural practices in the new environment, the rich culture to which he was heir could not have been all that relevant to his reception in colonial America. The Arab-Ottoman culture seems to survive in his person mainly as nostalgic remnants that create imbalance without challenging local cultural assumptions.

Privileges of Rank

In the absence of the lifestyle that would establish him as a person of consequence, how then did Salim command respect at all? Here the final marker of identity, that of social rank, comes into play. In a letter dated July 12, 1768, from John Blair, clerk of the Royal Governor's Council in Williamsburg, to Lord Hilsborough, secretary of state for the colonies, Blair reports:

> I beg leave to inform your Lordship that the Council have by me paid the Passage to London of a most unfortunate Algereen young man named Salim, who appears to be a Gentlemans Son there. At 17 years of age in a voyage to Phez in Morrocco, where was to stay some time with a Relation there, he was unfortunately taken by a French ship, and by their traders carried among the Mingo Indians and left there a Captive. He spent three years among them before he made his Escape by the advice of an English man what course to take. He travelled 45 days he says in the woods alone, with herbs, Roots and wild fruit for food, till he was fortunately met with by a kind man of Augusta, a frontier family of ours, almost ready to perish his cloths almost torn off. This kind man brought him to his house, cloathed him, fed and Physicked him till quite well. Then a gentleman there took him to his house. Thus he spent two years in Augusta before he found means to get to this Town where his good behavior gain'd him a kind reception with some. It appeared on Examination he has been learning some Greek and Hebrew which speaks him a Gentlemans Son. He hopes to meet an Algereen Ambassador at London. Perhaps your Lordship may think fit to take some advice of him and oblige the Dey of Algiers by kindly contriving him home to his Father and Mother, who no doubt will be greatly pleased to receive their long lost Son, by favour from the English Nation.[47]

The brief story he relates has some features that depart from the legends and tales: Salim was kidnapped in the western Mediterranean, but on a voyage to Fez rather than on the way home to Algiers, he was taken by

French traders directly into Indian captivity among the Mingo, not the Shawnee, and there is no mention of being a slave on a plantation, perhaps the conscious omission of an episode that would undermine the claim of rank and even raise doubts about his race. Blair's account of Salim's subsequent escape from captivity, adoption by English frontier settlers, and eventual arrival in Williamsburg tracks the other stories. And we finally divine the secret behind Salim's social success among the Virginia gentry: it is Salim's social capital in the form of his knowledge of languages, and specifically those languages that served as a marker of male gentility. So Salim, despite the fact that he was a swarthy Muslim with connections to "Turks" and "Barbary States," could be recognized as a fellow gentleman by virtue of his education. It was this education, and specifically his knowledge of Greek, that opened doors for him in Tidewater Virginia, where he socialized with professors from the College of William and Mary and read Greek with the Page sons.

His Virginia patrons were certainly predisposed to be taken by his knowledge of Greek. Thomas Jefferson, for example, had been a close friend of John Page since their days as fellow students at the College of William and Mary, as reflected in a voluminous and intimate correspondence between the two, including during the 1780s, when Salim was frequenting Rosewell. In a letter to Page written in August of 1785, Jefferson contemplated European designs on Ottoman territory, ready to approve only if the object were to establish "the native Greeks in the sovereignty of their own country," an outcome much to be desired because "the modern Greek is not yet so far departed from its ancient model but that we might still hope to see the language of Homer and Demosthenes flow with purity from the lips of a free and ingenious people."[48] Salim's knowledge of Greek was not only the carrying card of a gentleman, it was a key to a rich intellectual tradition much prized by this group of Tidewater gentry.

Respect for learning and the learned in general permeated the Jefferson–Page correspondence. They shared information and opinions in the fields of astronomy, meteorology, medicine, and philosophy. As men pressed into public service, they commiserated on their mutual inability to engage their intellectual interests. Jefferson mused in 1803 from Monticello on years past:

> We have both been drawn from our natural passion for study and tranquility by times which took from us the freedom of choice.

Times however which planting a new world with the seeds of just government have produced a remarkable era in the history of mankind. It was incumbent on those therefore who fell into them to give up every favorite pursuit, and lay their shoulder to the work of the day.[49]

But while they might have been forced to surrender such pursuits, they remained active patrons of others. Page waxed enthusiastic to Jefferson about his discovery of David Rittenhouse, a Pennsylvania man of rather humble origins who had attended Rutgers on scholarship, and a man who according to Page was "a great and ingenious Mechanic and profound Astronomer and Philosopher making excellent Telescopes, Time Pieces, and Sextons . . . this Genius had penetrated deep into the Secrets of the moral and political World, as into those of the natural."[50] Page swung into action, wanting to promote this man he thought neglected by the "learned World," so he invited Rittenhouse to join their learned society and also sponsored him for a position at William and Mary. While Page does not mention Salim in his letters to Jefferson, his interactions with Rittenhouse suggest that perceived talent and education could indeed secure an individual enthusiastic support in the social world of the Tidewater. Rank was about birth, no doubt, but also about educational and intellectual achievements. Learned men from outside local society could attain rank and lay claim to the respect and fellowship of the gentry. And this rank, however acquired, could trump all other facets of identity.

Many of the later accounts of Salim's life gravitate toward the theme of learning. The story of his initial acceptance and even his conversion came to hinge on his educational accomplishments: "He found a New Testament in the original Greek in which it was written, and hugged it to his breast, and began to read it quickly, for he knew Greek far better than he knew English. In two weeks he had studied the whole question of the truth of Christianity, and said he was convinced that there was no other true religion."[51] And the local gentry's penchant for seeking out the learned was thought to work strongly in his favor after his return from Algiers: "the professors of William and Mary became aware of the fact that Selim was a learned man in the classics, and he became a favorite companion in the exclusive circle of learning, and John Page, afterwards Governor Page, seeing Selim and becoming attracted to him took him home and kept him all the rest of his long and useful life."[52]

But Salim's brand of learning did not always secure a place. We have the slightly later example of a man called "S'Quash," who had been imported into Charleston in 1807, just before the ban on the slave trade took effect. He was said to have looked "like a Moor," and a descendant of his original owner wrote that he was "an Arab of a family long educated of his day and class in that he had been to Cairo and could read Greek as well as Arabic. Greek was probably his first means of communication, as that language was then part of a gentleman's classical education."[53] But unlike Salim, S'Quash seems to have spent his life in slavery, rising to the privileged position of overseer but remaining a slave, never attaining the freedom and respect that Salim enjoyed. The difference may have been as simple as one of timing—S'Quash missed the window of opportunity that intellectual and political currents had afforded Salim.

Conclusion

By way of conclusion, I return to the theme of crossing borders, of dislocated lives, to the question of how someone like Salim could make it, or not, in the context of a radical sea change. His race and religion were less problematic than one might expect: there was enough fluidity in racial categories and sufficient interest in Islam for these differences to be either elided or engaged in a positive spirit. His cultural identity as a North African Ottoman subject did not trigger the negative reactions it would just a few years later, when open hostilities would lead to vicious denigration of the Barbary States. Race, religion, and culture were not huge barriers although, at the same time, they did not ensure a welcome for this unique individual. At the end of the day, it was his rank as a gentleman, or at least the ability of the Virginia gentry to accept him as one across racial, religious, and cultural boundaries, that paved his way in the new world. It was all too clear, however, that the experience was painful and ultimately destabilizing for him. If success is measured in the ability to assimilate and leave the past behind, Salim was a failure, doomed to live as a deeply troubled man who never felt comfortable in his new society despite the fact that he had been welcomed. How much we ascribe this failure to his personality as opposed to his context is a question to ponder. And we have the sense, in any case, that Salim's story is part of a closing act. By the turn of the century, more rigid racial, religious, and cultural lines will be drawn, consigning North African Muslims to an unbridgeable divide. It seems unlikely that Salim's experience could have been replicated in those years to come.

There is a final question that hovers in the margins of Salim's story. Despite many attempts to find corroborating material about Salim in chronicles and biographical dictionaries from Algiers, records of pirate activity held in Istanbul, and diplomatic correspondence between London and Algiers, Salim's trail grows cold beyond the confines of Virginia. Might this suggest a well-crafted and largely fictional story, one that was told perhaps by a young man of humble or irregular origins but with some education who was trying to make his way? Certainly his narrative had the great virtue of recounting experiences that spoke to not just one but a number of the traumatic (and exciting) events that occupied the popular imagination: attack by pirates, enslavement, Indian captivity, escape. The way it spoke to many of the anxieties and preoccupations of the time not only helped win Salim a welcome in the Tidewater but also ensured that his story found a place in folk culture and lived on into recent times. Was he an extraordinarily clever imposter? We will probably never know for certain, but the story of his life holds up a mirror in which we glimpse the society that accepted and domesticated him.

Notes

1. "The Allegheny Story: Selim the Algerine," Felix G. Robinson Papers, Box 3, Folder 37, Georgetown University Library, Special Collections Division, Washington, D.C

2. The story of Salim appears in various versions in the following, listed in chronological order by date of composition: William Meade, *Old Churches, Ministers and Families of Virginia*, vol. 2. (1857; repr. J. B. Lippincott, 1900); John Esten Cooke, *Stories of the Old Dominion: From the Settlement to the End of the Revolution* (Harper and Cruthers, 1879), 278–88; J. Lewis Peyton, *History of Augusta County, Virginia* (Frank Prufer & Son, 1882); John P. Hale, *Trans-Allegheny Pioneers: Historical Sketches of the First White Settlements West of the Allegenies* (1886), 256–57; Hezekiah Butterworth, *In the Days of Jefferson or, The Six Golden Horseshoes: A Tale of Republican Simplicity* (New York: D. Appleton, 1901); Andrew Price, *Selim the Algerine: Adventures of a Prisoner of Spain, France, and Shawnees, Rescued in Pocahantas County in 1759* (Times Book Co., 1924); Roberta Page Saunders, "A Lost Picture," *William and Mary Quarterly* 14, no. 1 (1934): 57–59; Mary Wiatt Gray, *Gloucester County (Virginia)* (Richmond, Va.: Cottrell & Cooke, 1936), 77–80; Felix G. Robinson Papers, Box 3, Folder 37, Georgetown University Library, Special Collections Division, Washington, D.C; Hugh S. Gwin, *Historically Speaking: True Tales of Bath County, Virginia* (Warm Springs, Va.: Bath County Historical Society,

2001); and Gene Crotty, *Jefferson's Western Travels: Over Virginia's Blue Ridge Mountains* (Charlottesville, Va.: Gene Crotty, 2002).

3. For a discussion of the *kuloghlu* in Algiers in the period, see Tal Shuval, "The Ottoman Algerian Elite and Its Ideology," *International Journal of Middle East Studies* 32, no 3 (August 2000): 332–33.

4. Chouki El Hamel, "Blacks and Slavery in Morocco: The Question of the Haratin at the End of the Seventeenth Century," in *Diasporic Africa: A Reader*, ed. Michael Gomez, 177–99 (New York: New York University, 2006); and Aziz Al-Azmeh, "Barbarians in Arab Eyes," *Past and Present*, no. 134 (February 1992): 3–18.

5. El Hamel, "Blacks and Slavery in Morocco," 190–95.

6. Why Salim is identified as "young" in 1789, when he should have been in his late forties according to other evidence, remains one of the many puzzles in this life narrative.

7. Meade, *Old Churches, Ministers and Families of Virginia*, 348.

8. The closeness and intimacy of the friendship is on display in letters written by Tucker to Page in which Tucker discusses, among other things, their sharing of sorrow occasioned by the death of their first wives as well as the joy that was theirs in the making of second marriages. See Tucker's letters to Page, "Letters to John Page," *St. George Tucker Collection*, 1771–1821. John D. Rockefeller, Jr. Library, Special Collections, Williamsburg, Virginia, Acc.42.4, Folder 1.

9. St. George Tucker, *A Dissertation on Slavery: With a Proposal for the Gradual Abolition of It, in the State of Virginia. By St. George Tucker, Professor of Law in the University of William and Mary, and One of the Judges of the General Court, in Virginia. [Four Lines from Montesquieu]* (Philadelphia: Printed for Mathew Carey, No. 118, Market-Street, 1796), 36–37.

10. Ibid., 87.

11. Ibid.

12. Elizabeth A. Perkins, "Distinctions and Partitions Among Us," in *Contact Points: American Frontiers from the Mohawk Valley to the Mississippi, 1750–1830*, ed. Andrew R. L. Cayton and Fredericka J. Teute (Chapel Hill, N.C.: University of North Carolina Press, 1998), 206.

13. Ann Thomson, *Barbary and Enlightenment: European Attitudes towards the Maghreb in the 18th Century*, vol. 2 (Leiden: Brill Academic Publishers, 1987), 68.

14. Michael A. Gomez, *Black Crescent: The Experience and Legacy of African Muslims in the Americas* (Cambridge: Cambridge University Press, 2005), 149.

15. Thomson, *Barbary and Enlightenment*, 68–69.

16. Al-Tilimsānī, Muhammad bin Muhammad, *El-Zohrat El-Nayerat*, tr. Alphonse Rousseau (Algiers: n.p., 1841), 1.

17. al-Wansharisi, Ahmad ibn Yahya. *al-Mi'yār al-mu'rib wa-al-jāmi' al-mughrib 'an fatāwá ahl Ifrīqīyah wa-al-Andalus wa-al-Maghrib* (Rabat: Wizarat al-awqaf, 1981–83), vol. 2, 18; vol. 8, 300–302.

18. Ibid., vol. 2, 158–59, 165, 179.

19. Daniel Panzac, *The Barbary Corsairs: The End of a Legend, 1800–1820*, vol. 29 (Leiden: Brill, 2005), 114–15.

20. Betul Besaran, "The 1829 Census and Istanbul's Population," in *Studies on Istanbul and Beyond: The Freely Papers,* vol. 1, ed. Robert G. Ousterhout, 58–60 (Philadelphia: University of Pennsylvania Press, 2007).

21. Thomas S. Kidd, *American Christians and Islam: Evangelical Culture and Muslims from the Colonial Period to the Age of Terrorism* (Princeton, N.J.: Princeton University Press, 2009), 9.

22. Ibid., 10.

23. Sean Foley, "Muslims and Social Change in the Atlantic Basin." *Journal of World History* 20, no. 3 (2009): 377–98, at 394.

24. Ibid., 394.

25. For a discussion of the evidence that Jefferson's vision of national religious equality implicitly included Muslims, see Spellberg, Denise A. *Thomas Jefferson's Qur'an: Islam and the Founders* (New York: Vintage, 2013), 117–20.

26. Ibid., 97–99.

27. Ibid., 123. Jefferson may well have unknowingly come into contact with Muslims among the slaves held on his estate or those of his friends.

28. John Page, "Memorandum Book," Special Collections Research Center, Earl Greg Swem Library, College of William and Mary, Williamsburg, Virginia, MsV, Mc 4, 138–39.

29. T. B. McCord, *John Page of Rosewell: Reason, Religion, and Republican Government from the Perspective of a Virginia Planter, 1743–1808* (Ann Arbor, Mich.: University Microfilms, 1991), 402.

30. Ibid., 148.

31. Gomez, *Black Crescent,* 150.

32. Kidd, *American Christians and Islam,* 1.

33. Ellen G. Friedman, *Spanish Captives in North Africa in the Early Modern Age* (Madison: University of Wisconsin Press, 1983), 80–83, 98.

34. The story of Salim's conversion first appears, as far as I can tell, in Meade, *Old Churches, Ministers and Families of Virginia,* initially published in 1857.

35. For a discussion of this expanding global imaginary, see Walter Mignolo, *Local Histories/Global Designs: Coloniality, Subaltern Knowledges, and Border Thinking* (Princeton, N.J.: Princeton University Press, 2000), 280–81.

36. Meade, *Old Churches, Ministers and Families of Virginia,* 344–45.

37. Michel Fontenay and Alberto Tenenti. "Course et piraterie méditerranéennes de la fin du Moyen-Age au début du XIXème siècle," *Course et piraterie* 1 (1975): 78–126, at 114.

38. Samuel Martin, "Report on State of Algiers," Public Record Office, The National Archives, United Kingdom. SP 71/2/71.

39. Timothy Marr, *The Cultural Roots of American Islamicism* (Cambridge: Cambridge University Press, 2006), 27–29.

40. Oren Frederic Morton, *Annals of Bath County* (Staunton, Va.: McClure, 1917), 101.

41. Saunders, "A Lost Picture," 58.

42. Ibid., 59.

43. For a discussion of the Eastern tales available to Virginia gentry, see Angela H. Patmore, "St. George Tucker's 'Vision of Selim': An Edited Text with Introduction and Critique" (1975), 62–63. Thesis (M.A.) in typescript, College of William and Mary, Earl Greg Swem Library, Williamsburg, Virginia.

44. Ibid., 39.

45. Ibid., 39–40.

46. There is no record of Salim in the extant intake records of the Williamsburg Hospital for Lunatiks, held in the John D. Rockefeller Library in Williamsburg, Virginia.

47. "Letter from John Blair to Lord Hilsborough." July 12, 1768, Public Record Office, The National Archives, United Kingdom, CO 5/1346/167.

48. Thomas Jefferson to John Page, August 20, 1785, Thomas Jefferson Papers at the Library of Congress, Series 1: General Correspondence, 1651–1827, Microfilm Reel 004, http://hdl.loc.gov/loc.mss/mtj.mtjbib001236.

49. Thomas Jefferson to John Page, March 18, 1803, in ibid., http://hdl.loc.gov/loc.mss/mtj.mtjbib012255.

50. John Page to Thomas Jefferson, April 28, 1785, in ibid., http://hdl.loc.gov/loc.mss/mtj.mtjbib001052.

51. Cooke, *Stories of the Old Dominion*, 285.

52. Price, *Selim the Algerine*, n.p.

53. Gomez, *Black Crescent*, 148, citing Paul B. Barringer, *The Natural Bent: The Memoirs of Dr. Paul B. Barringer* (Chapel Hill: University of North Carolina Press, 1949), 3–13.

"Race" and "Blackness" in Moroccan Rap
Voicing Local Experiences of Marginality

CRISTINA MORENO ALMEIDA

Dominant narratives of hip-hop's genesis has its beginning during the 1970s in Afro-Caribbean, African American, and Latino neighborhoods in New York.[1] Urban policies marginalizing Black and Latino neighborhoods as well as social changes occurring in the United States during what Tricia Rose calls "postindustrial New York" helped forge this youth culture.[2] Rappers appeared in street parties and gained importance over a short period of time.[3] Hip-hop's transatlantic voyage was to a large extent driven by Afrika Bambaataa, a member of a New York street gang, who transformed himself into a hip-hop activist and organized the Zulu Nation that traveled to France in the early 1980s.[4] In the beginning of the 1990s, rap music became rooted in Algeria, where groups gathered privately, as is the case of the rap crew Intik (Cool) and MBS (Le Micro Brise le Silence, or "The microphone breaks the silence").[5] Throughout this time, rap music and hip-hop culture also began to germinate in Morocco with break-dancers, rappers, and graffiti artists getting together in the country's urban spaces during the mid-1990s. In Morocco, as in many other local scenes, the blooming of hip-hop among the urban youth has created an open conversation between local experiences of exclusion. Despite the fact that this conversation has frequently been framed simplistically as cultural imperialism, this theory remains reductionist when dealing with global flows and has been contested by a great number of scholars.[6]

This chapter seeks to unravel the specificities of the transatlantic connection between the U.S. rap scene and Morocco. In particular, it looks at how issues of racism, marginality, and the struggle for civil rights have been capitalized by some rappers to explore their own local urban youth marginality. The chapter starts by presenting the socioeconomic context of contemporary urban Moroccan youth. Then it proceeds to examine the construction of "race" and "blackness" in the context of Morocco and the ways Moroccan music has conveyed the idea of a multiracial Morocco that opposes dominant narratives of Moroccan identity as

"Arab Muslim." The following sections examine the music production of two Moroccan rappers, Dizzy DROS and Mobydick, to provide evidence of different artistic strategies through which rappers in Morocco seek to empower local marginalized. In order to relate to social inequalities, Dizzy DROS's songs reshape a derogative word, "darija," which refers to Black people in Morocco, into a "trendy" word to name himself, his friends, his audience, and urban underclass youth in general. Mobydick, on the other hand, reshapes narratives of marginality by including cartoons, video clip characters, singers, or sportsmen inspired from U.S. popular culture. Both Dizzy DROS and Mobydick aim in their music narrative to transform derogative words that directly signal youth marginality into signifiers of empowered youth. This chapter suggests that hip-hop has opened up a dialogue between the United States and Moroccan urban excluded youth through which rappers in Morocco have creatively articulated and reshaped local discourses on race and marginality.

Hip-Hop in Morocco and Urban Youth Marginality

The 1980s and 1990s economic reforms transformed postcolonial Morocco into a neoliberal state. This shift stimulated an intense human rural–urban migration that, together with rapid population growth (from 12 million to 31 million people between 1961 and 2003) and a governmental program of privatization, foregrounded what became Morocco's contemporary economic problems.[7] At the beginning of the 1990s, the European Union promoted the same sort of privatization policy in the region, as George Joffé explains, via neoliberal economic reforms in the Middle East–North Africa (MENA) region as part of a strategy to counter economic migration into Europe by stimulating domestic employment.[8] Concealed by the language of free markets, these neoliberal reforms conveyed new forms of patronage and exploitation "in which the state apparatus changed its modes of intervention but sill played a crucial role."[9] The cosmetic character of years of social, economic, and political reforms had—perhaps predictably—not had any effect, as the country continues to suffer from high rates of poverty, unemployment, and illiteracy.[10] In particular, removing the state from the economic process proved to be inefficient in reducing unemployment or poverty rates.[11] The bulk of Morocco's population (30 percent aged from fifteen to twenty-nine[12]) still feels marginalized from the rest of society. Poverty and unemployment affects a large percentage of urban youth, with 30 percent of those educated past the primary level unemployed.[13] A 2012 report from the World Bank argues that youths have been largely marginalized from the country's economic growth in the last decade.[14] As the report claims, the high level of unemployment only partially explains the exclusion of Moroccan youth from economic life. In this sense, gender disparities, lack of education, and a failure of governmental programs aiding job searches and placement have increased this exclusion. Feelings of failure and distress are increased by the fact that young men in particular are expected to become breadwinners and take care of their future families. According to a Human Development Report commissioned by the United Nations Development Programme, despite the fact that young people in Morocco constitute the largest segment of population, politicians have failed to integrate youth within society. The report emphasizes the number of disenchanted responses among the youth over their future in Morocco.[15]

By the time the neoliberal reforms started, the urban music scene had already began a radical change with the emergence of popular music groups such as Nass El Ghiwane or Jil Jilala during the 1970s. These groups reinvented the Moroccan music scene by introducing socially and politically engaged lyrics that, since independence in 1956, had previously been dominated by oriental Arabic music and patriotic music.[16] In the mid-1990s Moroccan rap albums were informally released as audiocassettes even if rap was still not played on public media. During these first years, rap was seen as a foreign, "Western" genre and an attack on Moroccan identity.[17] By the end of the 1990s Hicham Abkari, president of the Underground Foundation, director of the Mohammed VI Theatre in Casablanca, and former programmer of the *Festival de Casablanca*, organized and recorded videos of rap crews and break-dancing battles in the neighborhod of Hay Mohammadi in Casablanca, proving the rapid popularity that hip-hop had gained in Moroccan urban centers. At the beginning of the following decade, groups that have since become extremely popular began to form, such as H-Kayne in Meknes, Fnaïre in Marrakech, and Thug Gang and rapper Don Bigg in Casablanca. Although the state headed by the Makhzen, that is, the royal court and the ruling elites, has efficiently co-opted some rappers, the Moroccan rap scene has proved to be an extremely heterogeneous and creative scene, keen on finding creative ways in which to transmit feelings of exclusion and empowering local youth.[18] One way in which Moroccan rappers have voiced the social situation of Moroccan youth is by drawing on "race" and "blackness" as a signifier of marginality.

"Race" and "Blackness" in Morocco

In her "Postmodern Blackness," bell hooks establishes a link between the experience of marginality between Black people in the United States and other experiences of exclusion.[19] She argues that "blackness" has become a signifier of marginality that relates with, for example, Moroccan urban underclass youth in their mutual feeling of disconnection with their local context. This consideration of blackness allows us to argue that there is a common experience between groups such as the young underprivileged in Morocco and the inner-city Black youth of the United States. Thus, as hooks's suggestion reveals, the feelings of alienation and despair shared by people across boundaries of class, gender, and "race" can be a base to construct solidarities. These solidarities are transmitted by rap music from performers to listeners around the globe and embodied in the relationship between different hip-hop scenes around the world, as Halifu Osumare points out with the notion of "connective marginalities."[20] In her book, Osumare suggests the notion of connective marginalities as a theoretical frame to understand youth's associations when it comes to global hip-hop. These connective marginalities are inspired by the urban Black and Latino youth experience of marginality, which formed the origin of hip-hop culture. Osumare advocates for any investigation of hip-hop to include the consideration of the issue of race, its place in the United States, and the different ways blackness has been appropriated and exported.[21] Therefore, Osumare argues, alongside hooks, that the concept of blackness embodied in hip-hop culture and rap music is "a methodology for voicing marginality by other historical oppressed peoples."[22]

The connection of global marginalities to the U.S. experience of blackness can be seen in figures such as Malcolm X who have become symbols of resistance and fight against oppression for Moroccan rappers. In *Rebel Music*, Hisham Aidi claims that the figures of Malcolm X and the Black Panthers contemporarily feature abundantly in Europe's Muslim youth discourse, even more than they do in America.[23] Although issues of race or racism have not been focal points of Moroccan rap, many rappers draw on prominent African American activists such as Martin Luther King Jr. or Malcolm X in relation to their own local context of oppression and despair. Rapper Philosof from Thug Gang has claimed that Malcolm X is one of his main inspirations because of his fight for the rights of the marginalized Black community in the United States.[24] Rapper Mobydick associates his artistic person with Malcolm X as a source of empowerment as argued in this chapter. In Don Bigg's song "Casanegra" (2009) the rapper was inspired by the well-known "I Have a Dream" speech, delivered by King on August 28, 1963, in which King called for racial equality and for an end to discrimination.[25] The song "Casanegra"—just as many others in Moroccan rap—deals mainly with the local situation of social inequalities between the rich and poor, the decay of society, corruption, poverty, terrorism, and migration, among other topics. Toward the end of the song, Don Bigg addresses the audience in Darija, or Moroccan Arabic, recreating the popular speech, saying "Yesterday I had a dream."[26] As Don Bigg says, he dreams of

> A Morocco with human rights for you and me. . . . A Morocco with an infrastructure and not many complaints / A Morocco with roads without holes / A Morocco with lot of generosity. . . . A Morocco with government full of good ministers and without thieves / A literate Morocco not an angry Morocco.[27]

Don Bigg's enumeration of the country's problems is followed in this song by a line where the rapper draws on a key slogan in President Barack Obama's first presidential campaign. The line states that he dreams of "a Morocco of 'Yes we can' not a Morocco of yes if only."[28] The resonance to the racial struggle allows the Moroccan rapper to connect with marginality here represented by blackness and the struggle against racism. Although Don Bigg uses Dr. King's speech and Obama's campaign to relate social and economic problems in Morocco, race and racism are absent in the rapper's narrative because these are not significantly perceived as a problem in Morocco.

Until recently in Morocco, issues of race, racism, or slavery have been absent from the public sphere. The official discourse is denial and silence on racial attitudes and racism on the basis of skin color.[29] This dominant narrative is the result of the construction of the dominant Morocco as an Arab Muslim nation during the struggle for independence.[30] Since independence in 1956, Morocco has been constructed as a country racially and ethnically homogenous, blind to the existent racial and ethnic differences. At the turn of century, the establishment of the Royal Institute of Amazigh Cultures in 2002 and the incorporation of Amazigh as an official language together with Arabic in the 2011 constitution both contributed to the official recognition of the country as ethnically heterogeneous.[31] However, between 2012 and 2014, the media, King Mohammed VI, and the government have paid increasing attention to racial issues in the country. Several articles appeared in *Slate Afrique*, *Jadaliyya*, and *Jeune Afrique*, among others, voicing the racism that Black foreign migrants waiting to cross to Europe as well as students suffer in Morocco.[32] In September 2013 King Mohammed VI presided over a working session in Casablanca to review various aspects related to the issue of African immigration in Morocco.[33] Then, in the monthly magazine *Zamane* (Time, in Arabic) included in the November 2013 issue a dossier of various articles discussing the origins of racism in Morocco. This dossier was the basis for Chouki El Hamel's argument that Moroccan society was divided by skin color in the late seventeenth century and that "racist ideologies sprung in order to establish and preserve the social boundaries that demarcate the identities and privileges of the Arabs and the Berbers."[34] Yet, behind this current recast in the official discourse stands the increase in sub-Saharan migrants to Morocco, migrants that no longer use Morocco as mere door to Europe.[35] This new social context has awakened society's concern with racism that is targeted against the sub-Saharan migrants.

Despite the lack of attention to racial issues in Morocco, music and the music cultural scene—music festivals and associations—have acted as catalysts to insert narratives on race and an African consciousness within the discourse of the predominantly Arab Muslim Moroccan identity. The Gnawa tradition and music with origins in West Africa have preserved the few narratives on slavery and race that exist in Moroccan culture.[36] El Hamel's research provides evidence that the term "Gnawa" was used to designate Blacks from that African region.[37] In contemporary Morocco, Gnawa are considered as a distinct ethnic group with a marginal collective status.[38] In the 1970s the mythical group Nass El Ghiwane highlighted Gnawa's position within Moroccan musical tradition by employing instruments like the *gembri* in their songs.[39] Even if blackness in Morocco is not uniquely related to Gnawa traditions and music, the construction of Gnawa as Black African turns blackness into a form of otherness and displays it as an exclusive characteristic of Gnawa.[40] While Gnawa is considered a Moroccan genre, it is constructed in contemporary terms as the music of the racial 'other,' and its foreign origin is often highlighted as an important component of this music.[41] Gnawa's connection to Moroccan identity inspired Fnaïre, and the group capitalized on Gnawa sounds to construct their *taqlidi* rap narrative. However, in their discourse, Fnaïre declares that Morocco is a country free of racism, as they claim in the documentary *I Love Hip Hop in Morocco* (2007). In this documentary the rap crew alleges that, while racism is a problem for the United States, it is absent in Morocco, where the real problem is poverty. In this sense, as Chouki El Hamel's *Black Morocco* argues, there is the belief that Morocco is free from racism and slavery and that these problems are often connected with the United States.[42] The reluctance to discuss slavery and race in Morocco is to a large extent caused by the pride that Islam is devoid of prejudice and oppression.[43] Therefore, blackness in the Moroccan rap context as well as in Gnawa music does not necessarily convey a political move against acts of racism but conveys the establishment of a cultural link to marginality. Reenacting speeches and slogans emanating from the U.S. context helps to transform blackness as a global signifier of marginality and difference "marked already in other countries."[44]

Race persists as an identity signifier of the non-Moroccan—even if there are many Black Moroccans—and is associated with migrants from sub-Saharan Africa so that blackness in Morocco is associated with slavery and inferiority.[45] The dominant culture has marginalized Blacks in Morocco, referring to them as *'abid* (slaves, in Arabic), *haratin* (free Black people), Sudan (Black Africans), Gnawa (Black West Africans), and Sahrawa (Blacks from the Sahara region).[46] Although El Hamel does not include this term, in Morocco there is also a common and derogative word meaning "Black person": *'azzy* (Standard Arabic transliteration) or *3azzy* (Darija). In Standard Arabic, the term is one of respect meaning "my protector that who is the source of my prestige and my glory," however, it is used in Morocco to refer to "Black man" in a derogative manner and is commonly perceived as racist.[47] Although race is not the focus of many of Moroccan rappers, the work of rapper Dizzy DROS has aimed at reshaping this derogative word, bestowing it positive meanings.

Blackness in the Spotlight in Rapper Dizzy DROS's Narrative

The term *3azzy* has taken a new meaning in Dizzy DROS's music. In his work, the word embodies the idea of U.S. inner-city underprivileged Black and Latino youth; however, the use of the word in Darija addresses his local audience. In Dizzy DROS's narrative, the word *3azzy* is framed in a similar manner to the word "nigga" largely used in Black American English. The word "nigga" in the U.S. context became a dominant term with the emergence of hard-core gangster rap by the end of the 1980s. Although it is increasingly accepted in hip-hop culture, the word remains controversial.[48] In hip-hop, the word refers to a Black man; however, as Imani Perry points out, this does not mean it is a simple synonym for Black.[49] The use of the word in the United States has gone beyond denoting "race," including a reference to conditions of marginality as opposed to the Black middle class.[50] As Ronald Judy states: "Nigga is that which emerges from the demise of human capital, what gets articulated when the field nigger loses value as labour. The nigga is unemployed, null and void."[51] In this sense, "nigga" is connected to the idea of blackness suggested by bell hooks, which involves a sense of marginality and disempowerment within society.[52] Nevertheless, the word also constructs the idea of friendship and intimacy.[53] The focus of the polemic is not the word per se but its use in the public sphere.[54] As H. Samy Alim states, the word has positive in-group meanings and pejorative out-group meanings.[55] Yet this division is complicated when it comes to biracial interaction.[56] As Alim suggests, the transformation in spelling—from "nigger" to "nigga"—emphasizes such a distinction. Although the word refers to a Black male, recently the term can be used to refer to any male—"the white nigga"—or to a female.[57] Moreover, other groups in the United States such as the Latino rap group Cypress Hill use the word in construction of a multiracial identity.[58] The word "nigga" or "negro" is also used in other hip-hop scenes such as Brazil.[59] Within the MENA region, rappers from the Egyptian underground scene use the word in English to identify themselves with perceived concepts of blackness.[60] While there is little research on the use of the word in hip-hop scenes outside the United States, it is possible to find terms in different languages that embody the use and meaning of the word "nigga."[61]

In Morocco, the use of word "*3azzy*" in hip-hop is limited to the work of Dizzy DROS, who employs the word in Darija to transmit to his audience a sense of social marginality but also a sense of empowerment. The rapper capitalizes on the word and its local and global signifiers to create a social group that embodies the connection or friendship of Moroccan urban underclass youth. In this endeavor, DROS employs this word as a moniker, as a common noun in his songs to refer to himself, his friends, or the rest of the Moroccan youth, in his first album titled *3azzy 3ando Stylo* (Nigga got style, 2013), and as part of his artistic motto. Dizzy DROS often shouts *"3fat a 3azzy"* (Step *nigga!*) a motto—or shout-out—through which the rapper encourages the *3azzy* to take a step, or rather to leave their mark. The word is, moreover, from the rapper's daily life. As DROS states, he and his DJ and his hype man all started to use the term in reference to one another. DROS says that the term reminds the group of their identity and the lifestyle that is reproduced in his music.

In the song "Cazafonia" (2011), Dizzy DROS employs the term not only in reference to his friends and himself but also to further connote loyalty to the group: *"3wazza* (niggaz) are watching my back," or "You never see me around Cazafonia without spotting my *3azzy* by my side."[62] In this way, *3wazza*, plural for *3azzy*, are not only friends but are those that protect you. Dizzy DROS also uses other words like *achiri* (homie) or *khouti* (brothers), commonly used by other rappers to create the notion of brotherhood among Moroccan youth. In concerts, the audience refers to Dizzy DROS as *3azzy*, for example, in the first song performed at the release of the rapper's first album in 2013.[63] The continuous performance of the word *"3azzy"* allows the rapper to connect with Moroccan youth, despite their social backgrounds, through the idea of marginality expressed in *3azzy*. However, by embodying the word in his own artistic persona and claiming the *3wazza* as part of his group, the rapper reshapes the feeling of despair into a powerful cry for group strength in the same manner as Mobydick does, as discussed in the following section.

This idea of group solidarity is also performed in the video clip of "Cazafonia" in the use of a dog that stands with Dizzy DROS and his crew. The use of a dog is significant due to its negative connotations in the popular Muslim imaginary, inherited from pre-Islamic Semitic traditions.[64] Although traditionally dogs are not popular animals in Moroccan urban centers, they have become very popular as pets in cities like Casablanca and Rabat. The idea of friendship transmitted in the term *"3azzy"* is reenacted through the dog in what Dizzy DROS calls "the dog mentality":

It's a part of showing people the street ... there is something that we represent too. It's like ... I don't like to call it like this, but is like a dog mentality, a part of our mentalities that refers to dogs. Dogs are the most faithful in the relationship to men; a dog would never leave you alone. But if you start to disrespect a dog, he will bite you. And I think this is the mentality and this is the significance of showing a dog in the video clip.[65]

Even if dogs are popular with some members of the Moroccan hip-hop community, by showing a dog in the video clip and using "*kelb*" (dog) as a synonym of "*ʒazzy*," DROS emphasizes the idea of marginality but also protection and solidarity.

The use of dogs, however, may also be seen as the imitation of the U.S. system, just as the same video uses as symbols the Range Rover car or bandanas. At the same time that the rapper benefits from the ways in which hip-hop has channeled the struggle for social justice such as civil rights and Black Power movements globally, Dizzy DROS also draws on hip-hop images that emphasize a cool lifestyle.[66] In this sense, as Moroccan rappers capitalize on the power of rap to articulate Black marginality in contemporary American culture, they are also influenced by hip-hop's commodification.[67] In the video clip of "Cazafonia," Dizzy DROS appears dressed in khaki trousers, red Converse shoes, golden chains, a baseball cap, and a bandana, which he wears as he drives around Casablanca in a Range Rover car. The image reenacts the song with reference to hip-hop garments like New Era caps and bandanas: "New Era on the head to one side and the bandana."[68] The artist also performs the signature walk of the West Coast gang the Crips, to which he also refers in the lyrics: "If we had guns the jails would be full of red and green people like the Crips and Blood."[69] In this sense, Dizzy DROS searches for links and differences between the West Coast and Casablanca, insisting on local specificities by naming West Coast gangs but also the colors red and green to identify Moroccan football teams. These colors not only reference the Moroccan national flag but also the respective colors of the two most famous football teams in Casablanca: Wydad and Raja. The references to California might also be associated with the homonymous rich neighborhood of Casablanca. California or Californie, in its French denomination, is situated in the south of the city and is mainly composed of big, luxurious villas surrounded by palm trees. Through the title of the song the rapper creatively establishes a connection between the high classes of both California localities in Casablanca and the United States.

The lyrics of "Cazafonia" also dwell on social inequities in different aspects of the city: "In this huge city / everyone gets his daily payment stealing or begging."[70] The fact that Dizzy DROS reflects on social inequities while traveling in a Range Rover in the video clip of the song is problematic. He claims to belong to the popular neighborhood of Bine Lamedoun; however, a Range Rover suggests an association between Dizzy DROS and the upper classes and the new rich.[71] At the same time, this is part of the rapper's strategy to show the two poles of Moroccan urban society while narrating the youth's ambitions to climb up the social ladder. The song "Cazafonia" succeeds in transmitting the feeling of empowerment by claiming ownership of the city by youths disowned by society. When Dizzy DROS and his audience sing *Cazafonia dylna dyalna*," meaning Cazafonia or Casablanca is ours, they are claiming agency and the right to own their own city. This chorus prompts the youths to occupy and conquer public space—that is, youths' everyday space—despite the fact that youth in the MENA region are only allowed to use the streets passively.[72] In this sense DROS argues that rappers do not receive help in claiming a presence in media, including radio or TV: "We're struggling to make everything by ourselves, no one, no one came to us and said 'look, we're gonna pass your songs on the radio, we're gonna pass you on TV.' So we did impose ourselves. And this is a particularity that I really appreciate in Moroccan rap."[73] Claiming ownership of public spaces such as the street resembles the genesis of hip-hop culture, as DROS noted in our interview: "When you start to search about hip-hop, the thing that gets stuck in your mind is that it's music created by people who had nothing. So they really struggled for it to face racism, to face the social problems that they had in the U.S. in the middle of the '70s and beginning of the '80s."[74] The transmission of hip-hop culture is not limited to commodification but to historical narratives that relate hip-hop culture to social struggle within the Black communities in the United States. In "Cazafonia," Dizzy DROS engages locally with the alienation of Moroccan youth, emphasizing their lack of control over the cities. DROS further emphasizes the lack of mobility of the urban underclass in the chorus of "Cazafonia:" "We live in Cazafonia / we die in Cazafonia / we go around and we don't get far from Cazafonia."[75] In these lines the city becomes a claustrophobic space without hope for change. DROS attempts to own the city because it is the only chance for change. In other words, as the city of Casablanca becomes the only space for the underclass youth to live, DROS claims that this youth must gain control over it and reshape it. In the song, ownership is enacted by writing the city's name with a "z" instead of an "s"; this is a normal practice in the writing of the plural "niggaz" (or in other words such as the U.S. rapper Eazy E's own name and his solo *Eazy Duz It* [1988]) and can be interpreted in a similar way here. This is how DROS makes use of his aesthetics skills—flow, voice, rhymes, and creative language—to establish a link with urban youth. This minor change in Casablanca's name as well as the use of other languages (*3azzy* and *kelb*) gives Dizzy DROS a distinctive creative identity.

Like other Moroccan rappers, Dizzy DROS's cultural production includes references to Malcolm X, which are particularly interesting because of their direct focus on race and racial issues. DROS includes in the introduction to the song "3alam" (Crazy/World, 2013) a fragment of a speech delivered by Malcolm X in which he asks his African American audience about its self-hatred.[76] Part of the speech is quoted in the song:

> Who taught you to hate the color of your skin? Who taught you to hate the texture of your hair? Who taught you to hate the shape of your nose and the shape of your lips? Who taught you to hate yourself from the top of your head to the soles of your feet? Who taught you to hate your own kind? Who taught you to hate the race that you belong to so much so that you don't want to be around each other?

Using a speech that deals with issues that affect both Moroccan society and global problems allows Dizzy DROS to use blackness as a symbol of otherness and marginality. In combining the song with the Malcolm X speech, the rapper initiates a dialogue between the Moroccan context and the U.S. civil rights movement. Dizzy DROS, as well as Don Bigg before him, does not require a deep knowledge of the civil rights movements to make the connection because the mere hint toward such events provides the rappers with a link to what they represent: agency, resistance, the fight for civil rights, and marginality. Moreover, the use of this speech is an act of empowerment where DROS demands his audience to reflect on self-hatred. This speech allows DROS not only to create awareness of racism in Morocco but also to reflect on the role of the country's elites in creating this continuous aversion against the lower class.

The work of Dizzy DROS has been praised by the weekly magazine *TelQuel*, which considered the rapper's album *3azzy 3ando Stylo* (2013) as one of the best hip-hop works of the past decade in Morocco, and his skills as a rapper were acknowledged in an earlier article by the same magazine in which the journalist wrote highly of DROS' style, his voice, his punchlines, and his slang.[77] *TelQuel*'s assessments are backed up by DROS' gain in audience. The skills of a rapper, including good rhymes, lyrics, flow, punchlines, creative language, and the creativity of cultural production, can thus be seen as attracting rap listeners and establishing a relationship between the rapper and the marginalized urban youth. The creative use of blackness and race in Dizzy DROS's work as well as his acknowledgment of Malcolm X may be directly linked to the hip-hop community as rap conveys a sense of group in which youth can share experiences and enter into a translocal dialogue. The fact that Dizzy DROS's narrative employs race as a conveyor of marginality in order to connect with urban youth is not random. The idea of race and racism is a public issue in contemporary Morocco. Despite the fact that the media and antiracist campaigns relate racism to sub-Saharan migrants, a rapper like DROS incorporates race in the everyday life of its hip-hop audience. The rapper refers to class inequities and social exclusion through language that relates the ideas to the suffering of Black Moroccans. The next section presents the case of Mobydick to further argue for the role of creativity and popular culture in connecting with marginal youth. As in the case of Dizzy DROS, Mobydick displays an ability to connect with local youth by creating a dialogue between global popular culture and local slang. However, Mobidick's artistic creativity stages a wide variety of characters from U.S. popular culture, Japanese manga comics, or popular singers as well as a unique style that highlights humor as a tool for social critique.

Strategies of Rapper Mobydick to Empower Local Marginalities

The case of Mobydick provides evidence of the important role of creatively using popular culture, both local and global, to build a space of shared ideas and feelings where, even if the national borders are blurred, local specificities remain in the spotlight. Although Mobydick's work also connects rap with blackness, this has been one way to embody youth's global marginality. The use of fictional characters or Moroccan TV shows in lyrics become powerful referents for Moroccan youth because they can relate to them as part of their everyday lives. The work of Mobydick provides evidence of the wide range of creativity in the Moroccan rap scene.

In his music production, Mobydick embodies the marginal local figure of Lmoutchou; a name that Mobydick explained in our interview comes from Darija and Spanish: "Lmoutchou, comes from the real Moroccan dialect, from Darija. . . . It is a name given to young people brought from the countryside to do household chores, *lmoutchou*. Yeah! It's the young people that push the gas bottles and stuff, the young people that have the dirty jobs, *lmoutchou*."[78] In Spanish this word is "muchacho," defined by the Royal Spanish Academy as a young person who works as a servant.[79] Mobydick explained that the reason behind this name was to give value these people who are often teased and marginalized:

> I told myself that I need to give value to this word because there are many that are called in this way, you see, we call them like this, I told myself why not to get in the shoes of this young people that are stuck with the hard jobs to value. At least if as a consequence of giving this name it becomes a bit famous, then these young people, when they are called as *lmoutchou* they won't feel humiliated.[80]

In a song called "Checkmate,"[81] included in the mixtape *Dars Khass Ba3da L'Album* (Particular Lesson After the Album, 2011), the rapper dwells on the idea of marginality through popular culture using representative figures of African American culture, including singers like Marvin Gaye and Michael Jackson, sportsmen like Cassius Clay (Muhammad Ali) and Penny Hardaway, and popular rappers like Notorious B.I.G. and Ice-T. Through this list of names, Mobydick establishes a link with a wider range of Black U.S. culture, claiming the popularity of these figures within their own domains in spite of the U.S. history of racial segregation. Mobydick embodies the notion of Black Power by establishing a link between Malcolm X and himself as Lmoutchou and thus connects two local experiences of marginality. This idea is expressed in "Checkmate" when Mobydick dedicates this song to "all those who struggled and sacrificed."[82] In our interview Mobydick highlighted the relationship between the Black urban marginalized youth in the United States with rappers in Morocco:

> Here in Morocco it is not the young people from ghettos that make rap. Here in Morocco it's young people that go to school that make rap. The poor people from ghettos here are not even able to write their name, we have to leave them aside. It's another level, you know what I mean. Let's say we [Moroccan rappers] are the equivalent to U.S. ghettos.[83]

Mobydick reflects on the fact that even if most of Moroccan rappers come from poor or modest backgrounds, they are literate. Mobydick capitalizes on a well-known African American rapper, Notorious B.I.G., to whom he also refers to in the song as "Big Poppa," to credit the local idea of marginality embodied in Lmoutchou: "A lot of MC's have empty words, they see life only in pink, playing on the beat of Notorious B.I.G. . . . Homie, I don't want to make money by flattering someone, even though I have the opportunity, *lmoutchou* is authentic like Big Poppa."[84] He goes further in the song and refers to other hard-core hip-hop crews such as Onyx or Fu-Schnickens.

In aiming to accentuate the value of marginal Moroccan youth, Mobydick also appropriates comic characters, especially fictional heroes such as Batman, Superman, and the Incredible Hulk, that he used to watch on television as a child.[85] The influence of superheroes in his narrative is present not only in his lyrics but also on the clothes he wears and the walls of his studio, Adghal Records in Salé. Moreover, the rapper has appropriated the Superman symbol to create his logo in which he substitutes the "S" for an "M." Mobydick employs his own version of this symbol in many of his cultural productions, including pictures and garments, and he used it for the cover of his mixtape *Dars Khass Ba3da L'Album* (Particular Lesson After the Album, 2011) and on caps and T-shirts that he often wears in concerts.[86] In this manner Mobydick also wears garments with other American superheroes like the Incredible Hulk and Batman, as on the cap he wore during our interview.[87]

These comic characters, normally referred to as superheroes, carry controversial cultural baggage, partially because they were all created in the United States. Superheroes became popular in the United States during the economic depression of the 1930s.[88] Superhero comic books have also been related to warfare and are part of an ideological narrative structured around fighting in the name of good and honest citizens.[89] Moreover, superheroes are frequently victorious in the struggle against evil.[90] This narrative is associated with a white nationalist fantasy, as the case of Captain America suggests.[91] Although these characters have evolved and are today more ethnically and racially diverse, gender remains problematic in the superhero narrative.[92] Superhero narratives are also dominated by childhood nostalgia and fail to reflect the "ethical complexities of adulthood."[93]

Despite the numerous, diverse, and complex issues around superhero comics, Mobydick employs the characters in their capacity to empower

Lmoutchou. A superhero is also a person with extraordinary human powers and capabilities or is fundamentally different.[94] By associating Lmoutchou with superpowers and victory, the rapper constructs an empowered character that fights in the face of the country's evil: the state headed by the Makhzen. The Lmoutchou represent the good and honest, and they demonize the state headed by the Makhzen in favor of the unprivileged classes. This relationship between the rapper, cartoons, and superheroes can be seen in the acknowledgments from his album *Lmoutchou Family* (2011):

> This album has been achieved thanks to the comics that I watched during my childhood, the movies I absorbed, to my fear of police and authorities, to Spiderman, Ironman, Hulk, Thor, Superman, Green Lantern, Batman, Green Arrow, to the Avengers and the Justice League, Darth Vader, Steve Austin, Captain Majid, and especially Grendizer.[95]

Many of the characters on this list, along Willy Wonka, Einstein, and Beethoven, appear in the song "Checkmate." Mobydick continues in the album's credits by thanking "the Moroccan justice system" before thanking his parents, family, and friends for allowing him to satirize the fear of the Makhzen and security apparatus in Morocco. In this creative way Mobydick depicts fictional characters as the only ones capable of saving Moroccan society from injustice. These fictional heroes help the artist combat the numerous obstacles to producing an album, including the Makhzen's persecution, in addition to obstacles of belonging to the margins of society. The fact that none of these fictional character are Moroccan, however, may be problematic in that it may indicate the lack of powerful local characters capable of the fighting the power. Yet Mobydick's character Lmoutchou comes to fill in this gap by creating a new local superhero.

Mobydick also resorts to satire in the song "Checkmate," where he alludes to the uprisings of MENA. In the midst of these uprisings, on February 22, 2011, Muammar Gaddafi, the former Libyan leader, delivered a televised speech denouncing the violence inflicted against his government. In this speech Gaddafi claimed that he would hunt protesters "chiber chiber, bit bit, dar dar, zenga zenga"—that is "inch by inch, room by room, house by house, street by street." Mobydick appropriates the last words of this sentence in "Checkmate" to state: "My audience wears large clothes and have earrings / everyone has *Lmoutchou Family* from house to house, street to street . . . towards the front."[96] In this sense Mobydick describes his audience as part of the hip-hop culture through their clothes aesthetics while creating political satire to criticize an authoritarian leader in the Arabic-speaking region. The reference to such a political character is especially significant since the speech went viral on YouTube as a remixed song called "Zenga Zenga" (Street, Street) that mocks Gaddafi.[97] During my fieldwork in Morocco (2011–13) the song was used as a mobile phone ringtone, and the phrase was used frequently to make fun of Gaddafi. The effect of using sarcasm in his criticism of Moroccan institutions or authoritarian leaders results in a subtle but strong act of engagement with local and translocal contexts.

When asked about using humor in his criticism, Mobydick considers that it is easier to communicate when people are having fun.[98] Even though the rapper believes that a sense of humor is present in U.S. rap, he states that rappers in Morocco often present themselves as extremely serious people.[99] As Mobydick explained in an interview "I don't understand why do our rappers take things so serious. . . . In order to talk about important things, it's not required to have a dramatic tone."[100] In "Checkmate," Mobydick criticizes rappers, linking them to a Moroccan TV program called *Lalla L3arousa* (Married Woman): "Rap in this country is controlled by *Lalla Le3rosa*."[101] This light entertainment program invites several couples to compete to win a free wedding party, highlighting the hardships of young couples to get married due to the high expenses involved in weddings. By comparing Moroccan rappers to this program, Mobydick seeks to ridicule the rap scene, reducing it to an unsophisticated mass media program. Mobydick targets rappers whose narrative does not fully engage with society's margins but remains mainstream. By comparing some Moroccan rappers to the program, Mobydick ridicules the rap scene by reducing it to a machine in search of profit. This criticism of rappers who only engage superficially with hip-hop culture and local issues is also expressed by Mobydick using jargon. In "Checkmate," Mobydick refers to these sorts of rappers as *frex poperop*, which, as he explained to me, describes someone that dresses in a hip-hop style but does not know anything about the culture behind it. As the rapper expresses in "Checkmate": "Fuck *frex poperop* is not about large clothes and caps."[102] Later in the song, Mobydick refers to these people as *bouzebbal* (from Arabic *zbala*, meaning rubbish or garbage), a word commonly used by youth in Morocco to insult another person as a fool or as empty-headed: "Homie be tough, I spray *bouzebbal* with

Baygon."[103] In this line he compares *bouzebbal* with Baygon, a common insecticide. Those who are just into hip-hop as a trendy and "cool" style but who do not engage with it fully are thus equivalent to insects. Although this association may be perceived as harsh, this line is part of to Mobydick's ego trip where the rapper attempts to prove his creativity through humorous metaphors. In this endeavor, Mobydick defines what he perceives "authentic" rappers as those artists with creativity who do not fall for the local market's predicaments.

"Checkmate" draws on sarcasm in different ways to engage locally, translocally, nationally, and globally with the world that surrounds not only Mobydick but to a large extent Moroccan youth. However, the creation of a character like Lmoutchou suggests the rapper's aim to specially connect with and empower Morocco's marginalized urban youth. Mobydick's creativity enables him to capitalize on extremely varied fictional and popular characters to construct an empowered marginal artistic self. The kind of engagement that Mobydick suggests requires rappers to move out of their comfort zone and to experiment with creative artistic narratives that surpass national borders, but mainly engaging with youth's day-to-day life within them. Through humor, African American activists, fictional characters, or local slang, Mobydick develops a strategy that allows him to reflect on local social and political issues, whether these are the Moroccan Makhzen or local rappers who limit their discourse to empty words and neglect to engage with their social and political context.

Conclusion

This chapter provides evidence of the U.S.–Morocco encounter within the experience of urban youth exclusion conveyed by hip-hop culture. This connection is embodied in the notion of blackness that not only denotes race in the Moroccan context but also links Moroccan and U.S. youths' feelings of despair, social marginality, and poverty. The chapter provides evidence of different Moroccan rappers' work encountering paths with eminent African American activists such as Martin Luther King Jr. and Malcolm X. These encounters situate both local scenes within notions of social struggle and racism but most importantly the possibility of youth's empowerment. Mobydick creatively combines renowned characters with fictional heroes such as Superman or Batman to empower his fictional character Lmoutchou, who bestows dignity to Moroccan urban excluded youth. Rapper Dizzy DROS draws on the term "3azzy" to join and reshape the conversation on race that has been excluded from the public arena in Morocco. These examples manifest the limitedness of the cultural imperialism theory that essentializes both U.S. and Moroccan urban youth cultures. The idea of cultural imperialism ignores the complexity of rap scenes in both countries and the many ways in which a fruitful dialogue can take place. In particular, the U.S.–Morocco encounter examined here results in the incorporation of discussions on race in the Moroccan public arena, which unveils the presence of anti-Black racism in the Moroccan society. This case suggests that, beyond the U.S. borders, public discussion on racism may be difficult because of the Islamic pride that considers Islam absent of prejudice and oppression, hence making racism a taboo subject. Inspired by the U.S. experiences of urban youth marginality and struggle for civil rights, Moroccan rappers creatively strive for an open discussion on issues that relate to social exclusion of urban youth, whether this is connected to race or not. Although the encounter with U.S. rap may inspire Moroccan rappers to engage with Moroccan urban unprivileged youth, capitalizing on translocal conversations framed by hip-hop culture is not a product of cultural imperialism. In this vein, this chapter provides evidence that suggests that the U.S.–Morocco encounter motivates Moroccan rappers to artistically imagine creative ways in which to talk about issues otherwise concealed in the Moroccan public arena.

Notes

1. Joseph G. Schloss, *Foundation: B-Boys, B-Girls, and Hip-Hop Culture in New York* (Oxford: Oxford University Press, 2009), 4.

2. Tricia Rose, *Black Noise: Rap Music and Black Culture in Contemporary America* (Middletown, Conn.: Wesleyan University Press, 1994).

3. Ibid., 34–36.

4. The Zulu Nation started as a hip-hop organization in South Bronx focused on channeling young people's anger into music, dance, and graffiti in order to keep them away from gangs. George Lipsitz, *Dangerous Crossroads: Popular Music, Postmodernism and the Poetics of Place* (London: Verso Books, 1994), 26. See also Veronique Helenon, "Africa on Their Mind: Rap, Blackness, and Citizenship in France," in *The Vinyl Ain't Final: Hip Hop and the Globalization of Black Popular Culture*, ed. Dipa Basu and S. Lemelle, 151–66 (London: Pluto Press, 2006), 151.

5. Hadj Miliani, "Culture planétaire et indentités frontalieres: A propos du rap en algérie," *Cahiers d'Études Africaines* 42, no. 168 (2002): 763–78, at 765.

6. Simon Frith, "A Critical Response." In *Music at the Margins: Popular Music and Global Cultural Diversity*, ed. Deanna Campbell Robinson, Elizabeth Buck, and Marlene Cuthbert, 280–87 (Santa Monica, Calif.: Sage, 1991); Reebee Garofalo, "Whose World, What Beat: The Transnational Music Industry, Identity, and Cultural Imperialism," *World of Music* 32, no. 2 (1993): 16–32; Roy Shuker, *Understanding Popular Music* (London: Routledge, 1994); Jocelyne Guibault, "Interpreting World Music: A Challenge in Theory and Practice," *Popular Music* 16, no. 1 (1997): 31–44; Georgina Born and David Hesmondhalgh. "Introduction: On Difference, Representation, and Appropriation in Music," in *Western Music and Its Others: Difference, Representation and Appropriation in Music*, ed. Georgina Born and David Hesmondhalgh (Berkeley: University of California Press, 2000); Tony Mitchell, ed. *Global Noise: Rap and Hip Hop Outside the USA* (Middletown, Conn.: Wesleyan, 2001); Martin Stokes, "Music and the Global Order," *Annual Review of Anthropology* 33 (October 2004): 47–72; Ian Biddle and Vanessa Knights, *Music, National Identity and the Politics of Location: Between the Global and the Local* (Hampshire: Ashgate, 2007); and Tope Omoniyi, " 'So I Choose to Do Am Naija Style': Hip Hop, Language, and Postcolonial Identities," in *Global Linguistic Flows: Hip Hop Cultures, Youth Identities and the Politics of Language*, ed. H. Samy Alim, Awad Ibrahim, and Alastair Pennycook, 113–35 (London: Routledge, 2009).

7. George Joffé, "Morocco's Reform Process: Wider Implications," *Mediterranean Politics* 14, no. 2 (July 2009): 151–64, at 158.

8. Ibid., 159–60.

9. Koenraad Bogaert, "Contextualizing the Arab Revolts: The Politics behind Three Decades of Neoliberalism in the Arab World," *Middle East Critique* 22, no. 3 (September 2, 2013): 213–34, at 223, doi:10.1080/19436149.2013.814945.

10. Shana Cohen and Larabi Jaidi, *Morocco: Globalization and Its Consequences* (New York: Routledge, 2006).

11. Ibid., 38; Joffé, "Morocco's Reform Process," 160; and Jamal Bahmad, "From Casablanca to Casanegra: Neoliberal Globalization and Disaffected Youth in Moroccan Urban Cinema," *Middle East Journal of Culture and Communication* 6 (2013): 15–35, at 17.

12. "Kingdom of Morocco: Promoting Youth Opportunities and Participation," World Bank, Middle East and North Africa Region, Sustainable Development Department, Report No. 68731-MOR, June 2012, http://www-wds.worldbank.org /external/default/WDSContentServer/WDSP/IB/2012/08/13/000333037_20120 813235720/Rendered/PDF/687310REVISED00029020120Box369250B.pdf (August 5, 2014).

13. Cohen and Jaidi, *Morocco*, 39.

14. Ibid.

15. *50 Years of Human Development & Perspectives to 2025: The Future Is Being Built and the Best Is Possible*, HDR50-Summary, United Nations Development Programme, January 2006, http://hdr.undp.org/sites/default/files/nhdr_2005_morocco -en.pdf, p. 11.

16. Antonio Baldassarre, "Moroccan World Beat through the Media." In *Mediterranean Mosaïc: Popular Music and Global Sounds*, ed. Goffredo Plastino, 79–100

(London: Routledge, 2003), 83; Jeffrey Callen, "French Fries in the Tagine: Re-Imagining Moroccan Popular Music" (Ph.D. diss., Department of Ethnomusicology, University of California, 2006), 6; and Mubarak cited in Gonzalo Fernández Parrilla and Helio Islán Fernández, "La Leyenda Nass El Ghiwane," *Al-Andalus Magreb* 16 (2009): 149–61, at 153.

17. Élisabeth Cestor, "L'irruption du rap au Maroc entretien d'Élisabeth Cestor avec Hicham Abkari, Casablanca, May 2008," *Africultures*, October 21, 2008, http://www.africultures.com/php/index.php?nav=article&no=8120.

18. The term "Makhzen" is used in Morocco to refer to the political and economic ruling elite that provide the administrative structure, legal framework, and military manpower to increase the Moroccan Monarchy's authority. Abdeslam Maghraoui, "Political Authority in Crisis: Mohammed VI's Morocco," *Middle East Report* 218 (Spring 2001): 12–17, at 12; and Mohamed Daadaoui, *Moroccan Monarchy and the Islamist Challenge: Maintaining Makhzen Power* (Basingstoke, U.K.: Palgrave Macmillan, 2011), 46.

19. bell hooks, "Postmodern Blackness," *Postmodern Culture* 1, no. 1 (1990): 1–10.

20. Halifu Osumare, *The Africanist Aesthetic in Global Hip-Hop: Power Moves* (New York: Palgrave Macmillan, 2007), 15.

21. Ibid., 8.

22. Ibid., 71.

23. Hisham Aidi, *Rebel Music: Race, Empire, and the New Muslim Youth Culture* (New York: Pantheon Books, 2014), xxx.

24. Philosof, Interviewed by author, Casablanca, May 8, 2013.

25. Don Bigg, "Casanegra," March 26, 2012, http://www.youtube.com/watch?v=67-EvFBDYOo (April 15, 2014).

26. "lbareh hlamt helma."

27. "Mghrib fih 70909 l insan lik o lia . . . Mghrib fih l'infrastructure o 9allat chkwa/Mghrib fih tor9an o 7fari msdouda/Mghrib l karam oljoud walaboudd . . . Mghrib fih wizara mhayba bl wozara o 9éllat chffara/Mghrib 9ari mghrib wa3i machi Mghrib ka3i."

28. "Mghrib dyal 'Yes We Can' machi Mghrib dyal 'Yes law kan.'"

29. Chouki El Hamel, *Black Morocco: A History of Slavery, Race, and Islam* (New York: Cambridge University Press, 2012), 2.

30. Benjamin. Stora, "Algeria/Morocco: The Passions of the Past. Representations of the Nation That Unite and Divide," *Journal of North African Studies* 8, no. 1 (2003): 14–34, at 22.

31. The Royal Institute of the Amazigh Culturehttp://www.ircam.ma/doc/divers/presentation_of_ircam.pdf (November 8, 2013); and the Moroccan Constitution http://www.maroc.ma/en/system/files/documents_page/bo_5964bis_fr_3.pdf (May 2, 2014).

32. "Les étudiants africains, victimes du racisme ordinaire au Maroc," Slate Afrique, November 28, 2012, http://www.slateafrique.com/99053/etudiants-afrique-maroc-rabat-racisme-violences-casa (May 2, 2014); "Complicity and Indifference: Racism in Morocco," Jadaliyya, August 1, 2013, http://www.jadaliyya.com/pages/index/13324/complicity-and-indifference_racism-in-morocco (May 2,

2014); and "Racisme: au Maghreb, les Noirs sont-ils des citoyens comme les autres?," Jeune Afrique, April 29, 2014,http://www.jeuneafrique.com/Article /JA2779p020.xml0/racisme-maghreb-noirs-negre-maghreb-racisme-au -maghreb-les-noirs-sont-ils-des-citoyens-comme-les-autres.html (May 2, 2014).

33. Communiqués du Cabinet Royal, http://www.diplomatie.ma/Portals/0 /Communiqu%C3%A9%202013/Communiqu%C3%A9snew.pdf (May 2, 2014).

34. El Hamel, Black Morocco, 2.

35. Özge Bilgili and Silja Weyel. "Migration in Morocco: History, Current Trends and Future Prospects," Maastricht Graduate School of Governance (2009): 1–56, at 18; and Hein de Hass, "Country Profile: Morocco," Focus Migration no. 16 (2009): 1–11, at 1.

36. El Hamel, Black Morocco, 2.

37. Chouki El Hamel, "Constructing a Diasporic Identity: Tracing the Origins of the Gnawa Spiritual Group in Morocco," Journal of African History 49, no. 02 (September 24, 2008): 241–60, at 247.

38. Ibid.

39. The gembri, also called sintir or hejhouj, is a squared stringed instrument with a bass sound. Callen, "French Fries in the Tagine," 5.

40. Moulay Driss El Maarouf, "Nomadictates: Staging Roots and Routes in the Essaouira Gnawa Festival," Globalizations (2013): 1–17, at 6.

41. See, for example, Tony Langlois, "Music and Politics in North Africa." In Music and the Play of Power in the Middle East, North Africa and Central Asia, edited by Laudan Nooshin, (Hampshire: Ashgate, 2009), 226–47, at 218; and Ziad Bentahar, "The Visibility of African Identity in Moroccan Music," Wasafiri 25, no. 1 (March 2010): 41–48, at 41.

42. El Hamel, Black Morocco, 2.

43. El Hamel, "Constructing a Diasporic Identity," 242.

44. Osumare, Africanist Aesthetic in Global Hip-Hop, 62.

45. John Philip Rode Schaefer, "Moroccan Modern: Race, Aesthetics, and Identity in a Global Culture Market," (Ph.D. diss., Department of Anthropology University of Texas, 2009), 56–57.

46. El Hamel, Black Morocco, 2.

47. A. L. de Prémare, Dictionnaraire arabe-français (Établi sur la base de fichiers, ouvrages, enquêtes, manuscrits, études et documents divers par A. L. de Prémare et collaborateurs), Tome 9 (Paris: L'Harmattan, 1996), 98. Moreover, the collective demonym is used popularly to refer to the inhabitants of Marrakech—ʿazzaoui (plural, ʿazzawa)—and is rooted in the word ʿazzy but is not considered a derogative word.

48. H. Samy Alim, Roc the Mic Right: The Language of Hip Hop Culture (New York: Routledge, 2006), 77.

49. Imani Perry, Prophets of the Hood: Politics and Poetics in Hip Hop (Durham, N.C.: Duke University Press, 2004), 142.

50. Dipa Basu, "What Is Real about "Keeping It Real"?" Postcolonial Studies 1, no. 3 (November 1998): 371–87, at 374; and Ronald A. T. Judy, "On the Question

of Nigga Authenticity," in *That's the Joint! The Hip-Hop Studies Reader*, ed. Murray Forman and Mark Anthony Neal, 105–18 (London: Routledge, 2004), 106.

51. Judy, "On the Question," 106.

52. hooks, "Postmodern Blackness."

53. Perry, *Prophets of the Hood*, 142.

54. Ibid., 143.

55. Alim, *Roc the Mic Right*, 77.

56. Cecilia Cutler. "'You Shouldn't Be Rappin', You Should Be Skateboardin' the X-Games': The Constructions of Whiteness in an MC Battle," in *Global Linguistic Flows: Hip Hop Cultures, Youth Identities and the Politics of Language*, ed. H. Samy Alim, Awad Ibrahim, and Alastair Pennycook, 79–94 (New York: Routledge, 2009), 89.

57. Alim, *Roc the Mic Right*, 78.

58. Pancho McFarland, *Chicano Rap: Gender and Violence in the Postindustrial Barrio* (Austin: University of Texas Press, 2008), 41.

59. Derek Pardue, *Ideologies of Marginality in Brazilian Hip Hop* (New York: Palgrave Macmillan, 2008), 83.

60. Angela Williams, "'We Ain't Terrorists but We Droppin' Bombs': Language Use and Localization of Egyptian Hip Hop," in *The Languages of Global Hip Hop*, ed. Marina Terkourafi (London: Continuum, 2010), 67–95, at 84.

61. For the use of *"noir"* in French rap, see Steve Gadet, *La fusion de la culture hip-hop et du mouvement Rastafari* (Paris: L'Harmattan, 2010); and for the use of *"Kanak"* in Germany, see Timothy S. Brown, "Keeping It Real' in a Different 'Hood: (African-)Americanization and Hip Hop in Germany," in *The Vinyl Ain't Final: Hip Hop and the Globalization of Black Popular Culture*, ed. Dipa Basu and Sidney J. Lemelle (London: Pluto Press, 2006), 137–50.

62. Dizzy DROS, "Cazafonia," November 11, 2011, https://www.youtube.com /watch?v=YCYj4vbCr4o (August 23, 2014). "3wazza koulchi mora dahri mkali"; and "3amrek ghatchoufni ghadi; Wast Cazafonia bla matchouf l3azzy 7daya b7alla haz m3aya hadi."

63. Dizzy DROS, "Ta7ad Ma3arf (Live)," December 4, 2013, https://www .youtube.com/watch?v=UJyocRirU7A (May 2, 2014).

64. Richard C. Foltz, *Animals in Islamic Tradition and Muslim Cultures* (Oxford: Oneworld, 2006), 129.

65. Dizzy DROS, Interviewed by author, Casablanca, February 15, 2012.

66. Marcyliena Morgan and Dionneb Ennett. "Hip-Hop & the Global Imprint of a Black Cultural Form," *Daedalus: The Journal of the American Academy of Arts & Sciences* 140, no. 2 (2011): 176–96, at 189; and Osumare, *Africanist Aesthetic in Global Hip-Hop*, 150.

67. Rose, *Black Noise*, 3.

68. "New Era foug rass tay7a jenb wl bandana."

69. "Koun kanou 3andna frada kourra l7abss ghada tnod Bin l7mar m3a lkhdar b7al l'Crips wl Bloods."

70. "F'had lmdina dyal sakht/Koulchi baghi yjib nharo Ya b'chafra ya b'llaht."

71. Dizzy DROS includes references to Bine Lamedoun, a popular neighborhood of Casablanca, in many of his songs such as "Cazafonia" (2011) or "Men Hna" (2012).

72. Asef Bayat, *Life as Politics: How Ordinary People Change the Middle East*, (Amsterdam: Amsterdam University Press, 2010), 11.

73. Dizzy DROS, Interviewed by author, Casablanca, February 15, 2012.

74. Ibid.

75. "Kan3icho Cazafonia / Kanmoutou Cazafonia / Kandoro ga3 l9nat w ga3ma nfoutou Cazafonia."

76. The title of the song plays with the expression "3alam," which Moroccans employ to react to something that is unbelievable or astonishing. In this case, the expression translates as "it's crazy." Dizzy DROS employs the word that also means "world" in Arabic to discuss worldwide illnesses. Dizzy DROS, "3alam," November 21, 2013, https://www.youtube.com/watch?v=Y-rdesHDCsE (May 23, 2014); see also "Malcom X: Who Taught Your to Hate Yourself," June 6, 2007 http://www.youtube.com/watch?v=gRSgUTWffMQ (May 23, 2014).

77. "Dizzy Dros, le rappeur qui monte," Telquel, December 8, 2013, http://telquel.ma/2013/12/08/dizzy-dros-le-rappeur-qui-monte_9949 (April 29, 2014); and "Festival. Tremplin, le bain urbain," Telquel, October 3, 2013, http://telquel-online.com/content/festival-tremplin-le-bain-urbain (April 29, 2014).

78. "Lmoutchou, ça sort de la vrai dialecte Marocaine, ça sort de la darija . . . C'est un pseudonyme qu'on donne aux jeunes qu'on ramène du bled pour qu'ils fassent les tasses ménagères, lmoutchou. Wé! C'est les petits qui poussent les bonbonnes du gaz et ça, c'est les petit qui font le sale boulot, lmoutchou." Mobydick, Interviewed by author, Salé, July 5, 2013.

79. "mozo que sirve de criado." Diccionario de la lengua española http://lema.rae.es/drae/?val=muchacho (October 10, 2013).

80. "Je me suis dit qu'il faut que je valorise ce mot parce qu'ils sont pleins qui portent ce pseudonyme, tu vois, on les appelle comme ça, je me suis dit pourquoi ne se mettre dans la peaux de ce petit gars là qui se tape les taches dures pour valoriser au moins si par la suivre je rendre ce nom et il devient un peu famous, les jeunes quand ils se vont rappeler par lmoutchou ils vont pas se sentir humilié." Mobydick, Interviewed by author, Salé, July 5, 2013.

81. Mobydick, "Freestyle Checkmate," November 12, 2011, http://www.youtube.com/watch?v=VxagfDYjHS4 [Accessed August 23, 2014].

82. "li 9assa w'de77a."

83. "Ici au Maroc c'est pas le pauvres du ghetto qui font le rap. Ici au Maroc c'est les jeunes scolarisés qui font du rap. Les pauvres du ghetto chez nous ils peuvent pas même écrire leur nom donc le ghetto au Maroc laisse tomber, c'est un autre échèle. Tu vois c'est-ce que je veut dire? On va dire on est l'équivalent des ghettos Américains" (Mobydick, Interviewed by author, Salé, July 5, 2013).

84. "9ouwwt les MC's fihoum lfara, chayef deniya ghi b'le7mouriya, la3eb foug l'beat d'Notorious Big . . . 3chiri ma bghitch ndir l'flous b'l7iss l'cappa, wakha lforsa kayna, lmoutchou authentique ki Big Poppa."

85. Mobydick, Interviewed by author, Salé, July 5, 2013.

86. In his Facebook profile he has posted caricatures where he is also wearing a Superman cap and holds the symbol of this superhero modified by him or dressed with Superman's garment. Mobydick Facebook Account, December 27, 2012, https://www.facebook.com/media/set/?set=a.10151311520599594.492262.7234204593&type=3; and Mobydick Facebook Account, December 31, 2012, https://www.facebook.com/photo.php?fbid=10151318794374594&set=a.433057804593.232721.7234204593&type=3&theater (May 2, 2013).

87. Mobydick Facebook Account, https://www.facebook.com/media/set/?set=a.433057804593.232721.7234204593&type=3 (May 2, 2013).

88. Jiří G. Růžička, "American Superheroes and the Politics of Good and Evil," *American Phenomena* (Summer 2010): 46–49, at 46.

89. M. J. Costello, *Secret Identity Crisis: Comic Books and the Unmasking of Cold War America. Vasa* (New York: Continuum, 2009), 5.

90. Růžička, "American Superheroes," 46; and Lawrence Rubin, "Superheroes on the Couch: Exploring Our Limits," *Journal of Popular Culture* 45, no. 2 (2012): 410–31, at 411.

91. Dittmer, Jason. "Captain America's Empire: Reflections on Identity, Popular Culture, and Post-9/11 Geopolitics," *Annals of the Association of American Geographers* 95, no. 3 (2005): 626–43, at 627; and Costello, *Secret Identity Crisis*, 5–6.

92. Carol Stabile, "'Sweetheart, This Ain't Gender Studies': Sexism and Superheroes," *Communication and Critical/Cultural Studies* 6, no. 1 (March 2009): 86–92, at 87. doi:10.1080/14791420802663686.

93. Isaac Cates, "On the Literary Use of Superheroes; Or, Batman and Superman Fistfight in Heaven," *American Literature* 83, no. 4 (January 19, 2011): 831–57, at 853.

94. Roz Kaveney, *Superheroes! Capes and Crusaders in Comics and Films* (London: I. B. Tauris, 2008), 4.

95. Captain Majid is the Arabic name for the Japanese manga Captain Tsubasa known as Flash Kicker in the United States. "Cet album est réalisé grâce . . . Aux dessins animés que j'ai dû voir dans ma vie de gosse, aux films que j'absorbe, à ma peur des flics et des autorités, à Spiderman, Ironman, Hulk, Thor, Superman, Green Lanthern, Batman, Green Arrow, aux Avengers et à la Justice League, Darth Vader, Steve Austin, Captain Majid, et surtout Grendizer . . ."

96. "joumhouri dareb large we dayer tangua/koulchi 3endo lmoutchou family men "dar l'dar, zanga zanga . . . ila amame."

97. Noy Alooshe Remix, "Zenga Zenga Song," February 22, 2011, http://www.youtube.com/watch?v=cBY-on4esNY (April 15, 2014); and "Qaddafi YouTube Spoof by Israeli Gets Arab Fans," New York Times, February 27, 2011, http://www.nytimes.com/2011/02/28/world/middleeast/28youtube.html (May 23, 2014).

98. Mobydick, Interviewed by author, Salé, July 5, 2013.

99. Ibid.

100. Ibid.

101. "Rap fle'blad, chaddah lalla le3rosa."

102. "Fuck frex popérop ma b9atch fel large wl'casquette."

103. "3chiri koun khsime, rach bouzebbal b'Baygon."

Call and Response, Radical Belonging, and Arabic Hip-Hop in "the West"

RAYYA EL ZEIN

Enthusiasm about the paradigm-shifting events of the Arab uprisings of 2010–13 has been marked by notable attention to creative cultural production by Arab youth. Journalists have diversified their coverage of the "Arab street" in recent years to marvel at the creative politics in graffiti, street art, underground music, and theater. In the academe, musicologists and performance studies scholars have addressed how music and dance in city streets and during the occupations of town squares have the capacity to enact resistance while scholars of literature have turned to rich traditions of Arabic poetry to explain the contemporary political expression in protest chants.[1] Perhaps no single genre of cultural production has received more of this attention in recent years than Arabic rap and hip-hop. In 2011 *Time* magazine named Hamada Ben Amor, the Tunisian rapper known as El Général, one of the top one hundred most influential people of the year. Since then, almost every major anglophone news network from *Time* to the *New York Times* and the *BBC* to *NPR* has aired or published multiple features about emcees and hip-hop heads in Arab cities since the Tunisian Revolution. What are we to make of this "Western" fascination with a Bronx-born form transplanted to the streets of Beirut and Benghazi?

Much of the literature on creative cultural production around the Arab uprisings has expanded the range within which political messages in the Arab world can be read. Authors taken by the refreshing, youthful energy of this revolutionary period suggest that politics may also be understood as creatively enacted by a variety of cultural activities and imaginations. However, despite the political attentiveness scholars and journalists in these fields have displayed, this literature has not yet addressed how the particularities of the processes of cultural production create experiences that help define specific political bearing. In other words, analysis of cultural production around the so-called Arab Spring has yet to push the discussion past the location or celebration of politics in certain youth cultures. I want to further the conversation of cultural production and politics in the Arab world by asking: how can some rap and hip-hop in Arabic be understood as specific political practice? What do specific pieces and their live performances generate that allow the genre to be read as politically or culturally significant? If Arabic rap and hip-hop is exciting in the wake of the Arab uprisings, why is it so? What can analyzing this cultural production reveal about the emergent forms of political belonging enacted and developed in these practices?

In the pages that follow, I pursue these questions via an analysis of live performances of different tracks. The multiple arrangements of "Long Live Palestine, Part Two" (Lowkey et al.), "*Kollon 3endon Dababaat*" (Shadia Mansour), and "Destiny" (Omar Offendum) in live performances present a concise but deep archive across which to track variations on themes of the development of community, the performance of Arab identity, and the collective articulation of specific political messages. In these performances, I pay special attention to interactions between audience and performer as well as other factors that structure audience behavior and reception. I argue that considering the performance structures and performative gestures of these three tracks helps understand the co-construction of community and identity—what I call "radical belonging"—in some contemporary Arabic rap. I suggest that radical belonging is a way of understanding horizontal networking, multitudinous *communitas*, and the articulation of hybrid identities that this cultural production generates. These social features and ways of interacting are not unlike those that undergirded political action in the occupations of city squares from Tunis to Cairo to New York City. Finally, exploring the radical potential of some rap and hip-hop in Arabic benefits from considering how state institutions and the neoliberal media are also attempting to co-opt and manipulate this cultural production into a specific political narrative. In the third and final section, I consider the political performance of the emcee himself or herself in different contexts.

To be sure, Arabic rap was not born with the Arab Spring. The first widely recognized raps in Arabic were produced in the mid to late 1980s in Algeria and Morocco, notably with the formation of two influential rap crews, Le Micro Brise le Silence ("the microphone breaks the Silence," or MBS) and Intik. By the late 1990s the Arab-Israeli group DAM had formed and by the early 2000s were also beginning to rap in Arabic. The number of groups and quality of their work has multiplied exponentially across the Levant, North Africa, and the diaspora throughout the 2000s. Rappers and emcees in Morocco, Tunisia, Algeria, Libya, Egypt, Sudan, Syria, Lebanon, Jordan, the Palestinian territories, Bahrain, and even Saudi Arabia generate and share material online and through formal production houses in this period. In Algeria in the mid-1990s rap groups responded to the Algerian civil war; by the late 1990s members of the group DAM were growing out of an initial collaboration with the Israeli rapper Subliminal and reformulating their work to approach the experiences of Palestinians in the West Bank in the lead up to the second intifada; in Lebanon, Palestinians in refugee camps in the outskirts of Beirut have been discussing the webs of corruption and negligence imposed upon them by the Lebanese and the market of nongovernmental organizations. In North Africa, state censorship made it extremely difficult for artists to disseminate their work via official channels, whereas in Lebanon and the West Bank, official festivals have showcased local rap talent, some of it quite critical of the establishment. Funk, experimental music, acoustic, and hardcore elements have all appeared in different parts of different musicians' work. All of which is to say that the aesthetic and political strategies in contemporary rap and hip-hop in the Arab world have precursors and catalysts beyond the immediate events of 2010–13. It is important to point to the panoply of aesthetic, political, and economic influences that have developed the gestures that perform politics in this genre through transnational and intergenerational exchange over several decades.

In the following pages I focus my attention on what Diana Taylor would call performatic strategies in rap concerts.[2] I concentrate on different uses of call and response, costuming, and "warm up" and "cool down" techniques to theorize how rap performances might work to build political community, what I call here radical belonging.[3] In the first section I connect the use of antiphony (call and response) and polyphony (multiple, simultaneous lyrical threads) in various performances of Lowkey's track "Long Live Palestine, Part Two" to contemporary political theorists' formulations of lateral sociality known as the "multitude." In the second section I apply literature on the generation of community in contemporary interactive art and performance practice to an analysis of Shadia Mansour's pedagogical strategies and costuming during live performances of the track *"Kollon 3endon Dababaat"* ["They have tanks"].[4] In the final section I explore the relatively different contexts in which Omar Offendum has performed his track "Destiny." I consider how his carefully cultivated Arab American persona, central to this track, initiates a sort of phatic intercultural communication where the process of presenting the emcee *himself* off the stage can be understood as a "call and response" in the shifting borders between the Arab world and the United States and Europe. In this section I also consider how the State Department and partnering art institutions, via the "Rhythm Road" initiative and other cultural engagements, transposes an interpretation of African American culture and experience into a constructed Arab/Muslim American identity, crafting a specific model of political engagement. My analyses of these performances leads me to a conclusion that suggests paying attention to the institutional representation of Arab rappers and their work can further shift borders in the forging of transnational alliances in years to come.

Polyphony and Multitude: "Long Live Palestine, Part Two"

H. Samy Alim has suggested that call and response in contemporary U.S. hip-hop and rap music developed from similar interactions in funk music performances, like this basic one: "[Rapper] Say 'Hoooo!' [Audience] 'Hoooooooo!' [Rapper] Say 'Ho! Ho!' [Audience] 'Ho! Ho!'" etc.[5] As this generic textualization of the practice shows, call and response is, at its essence, the invited involvement of the audience (responder) by the performer (caller). Literature on call and response, sometimes called antiphonal exchange or communication, in hip-hop studies, anthropological accounts of African musical forms, studies of preaching styles in African American churches, and assessments of protest strategies in Occupy Wall Street all suggest that these responsive utterances are additionally significant in that they are able to create community during the performance event.[6] Robert Farris Thompson calls call and response "perfected social interaction" in that it brings individuals together to act as one body.[7] Jack L. Daniel and Geneva Smitherman concur adding, "call and response seeks to synthesize 'speakers' and 'listeners' in a unified movement."[8] Arab rappers and emcees, like their counterparts who perform rap in other languages around the world, also use antiphonal strategies to connect with and activate their audiences. In this section, I consider how the use of simple call and response (between a single performer and a relatively congealed audience), as well as multiple or polyvocal calling and responding (what I call here polyphony) between multiple performers and ostensibly heterogeneous audiences, succeeds in building particular community.

Kareem Dennis, alias Lowkey, received critical acclaim from U.K. hip-hop circles upon the independent release of three volumes of his own mix tapes. London-based, born of an Iraqi mother and an English father, he started rapping at the age of twelve, first imitating an American accent before resorting to his specific London cadence of speech.[9] To date, one of his biggest successes is a collaboration he directed with nine other artists, released in December of 2009.[10] "Long Live Palestine, Part Two," followed on the significant success of Lowkey's initial solo track with a similar message and the same beat and refrain in March of 2009. "Part Two" also featured verses from nine different artists: Tamer Nafar and Suhell Nafar of DAM (Palestinians from Lyd, Israel), The Narcicyst (Iraqi Canadian), Eslam Jawaad (Anglo-Syria), Shadia Mansour (Anglo-Palestinian), Hichkas (from Tehran, Iran), Reveal (Anglo-Iranian), and Hasan Salaam (African American). It topped the Amazon hip-hop charts shortly after its release, which was timed to commemorate the one-year anniversary of the invasion of Gaza by the Israeli Defense Forces (sometimes known as Operation Cast Lead).[11] Four of the verses are in English; four of the verses are in Arabic; one verse (that of Hichkas) is in Farsi. Lowkey connects the verses with a chorus in English. It consists of a call and response wherein Lowkey prompts, "Free, free!" and the other rappers respond "Palestine!" The caller (Lowkey's) voice is singular. The response (his collaborators together) is a chorus of voices. This creates a specific effect wherein "Palestine" is vocalized or, indeed, claimed in the plural. This recurring plurality presents a way of understanding how identity, political action, and community or solidarity is articulated and understood in some Arabic rap.

Michael Hardt and Antonio Negri have theorized a contemporary form of community they call a "multitude." A distinguishing feature of this social formation is the replacement of vertical hierarchy with horizontal networking. Moreover, individual identities within the "multitude" do not melt together in the kind of sociality encouraged by the image of the "melting pot"; nor do they disappear in the quest for power as in the figure of "the people" or "the proletariat." The multitude, rather, suggests clusters of activity, laterally connected together in a network, where difference proliferates. Hardt and Negri suggest: "The multitude is a multiplicity of . . . singular differences."[12] The multitude offers a way of understanding difference as belonging.

The mix of languages Lowkey coordinates in this piece makes it almost certain that the vast majority of listeners will not understand at least part of the track. However, the fact that Arab listeners may not understand Hichkas's verse or that Iranian listeners might not understand DAM's (or that anglophone listeners may not understand either) does not weaken the piece but, contrary to traditional understandings of lyrical comprehension, strengthens it. By collaborating in this way, the prominent line of the refrain, "It's about time we globalize the *Intifada*" takes on a second meaning. It may mean, "It's time we all fight to liberate Palestine"; but it may simultaneously suggest that, like the social media campaigns that connected youth around the world in 2011–12, "We are all Palestine." The plural responses of "Palestine" initiate a polyvocal claim to its political struggle while the multilingual verses are polyphonic, lyrical exchanges between collaborating rappers. Thus the formal structuring elements of this track function as an expansive container which holds a multiplication of voices. This is even more obvious when the track is performed live.

The Gazan rap group DARG Team performed their own iteration of "Long Live Palestine" at Geneva's annual Fête de la Musique in 2010. None of the members of the group performing were originally featured on the track. DARG (Da Arabian Revolution of Gaza) Team are three emcees and a beatmaker, Sami Srour, Bassam El Massri, Mohammed El Massri, and Ahmed Badran. In their iteration of "Long Live Palestine," the call and response of the chorus and the original beat and melodic refrain are used to bookend the original verses of the Gazan artists. All of DARG Team's verses are in Arabic. Further, the group also translated the chorus "Free, free Palestine!" into Arabic, chanting instead "Falasteen 7urra!"[13] Interestingly, in the international contexts in which the piece is performed, these changes do not undo the polyphonic elements built into Lowkey's 2009 collaboration. On the contrary, interactions between the audience and performers in international contexts demonstrate a further multitudinous dimension than the international collaboration Lowkey originally orchestrated.

An amateur video posted on YouTube records the audience's warm welcome of the group when they take the stage in Geneva. The emcee introducing the visiting artists incites the audience in French, "S'il vous plait! Faites une bruit pour cette groupe de quatre artistes qui vont chanter en langue arabique!" [Please make some noise for this group of four artists who will sing in Arabic!][14] As the rappers perform, the audience picks up the Arabic refrain "Falasteen 7urra," which does not appear in either of the first two iterations of the track produced by Lowkey—with no prompting in French or English. The call and response plays like so: "[DARG Team] Falasteen! [Audience] 7urra!" Moreover, around the half-way point of the performance, the four members of DARG transition from the Arabic antiphonal "Falasteen 7urra!" to the English "Free, free Palestine!" pointing their mics toward the crowd for the plural response "Palestine," as in the Lowkey collaboration. The audience boldly returns "Palest*ine*," with anglophone (not francophone, i.e., Palest*een*) intonation from the first prompt, without a hint from the performers. We might reasonably assume the audience is predominantly French-speaking from the linguistic choices of the emcee who introduced the Gazan group. Nevertheless, it picks up and performs linguistic cues in both Arabic and English. This is significant *even if* we concede that a portion of audience is likely diasporic and bi- or trilingual. Indeed, paying attention to the build in participation over the course of each chorus suggests that the performers effectively relied on a certain co-facilitation of the call and response by some audience members, who recognized and helped pronounce appropriate words and syllables, effectively leading others in the antiphonal exchange the performers initiated. This points to a polyphonal layering of audience participation, suggesting that performers acknowledge that the makeup of an audience need not be homogeneous.

It is more accurate to say, perhaps, that the framework of this piece does not merely *suggest* that an audience need not be homogenous, it assumes that it *already is not*. Most importantly, the performers do not perceive this as an obstacle; rather they seem to rely on it as a strength that further facilitates the active articulation of the piece's political project. Thus, one of the liberating aspects of Lowkey and his collaborators' work here lies in the fact that it recognizes and embraces the radical strength of a culturally, linguistically, and ethnically multitudinous community.

Moreover, this use of audience co-facilitation importantly displaces the exclusive ownership of the artistic production from a single artist and spreads it among the network of individuals—performers and spectators. An important aspect of antiphonal exchanges in live performances is that they activate the audience. Maggie Sale suggests that call and response "depends and thrives upon audience performance and improvisation."[15] In other words, the performer's performance is only one node in a network of performance activity that gives the piece potency. The political quality of the work exists in its ability to activate its audiences. The liberating, radical action may be a simple declaration, like this track's "Free, free Palestine!" In spaces where it is actively discouraged, the unapologetic articulation of a politically unpopular project becomes political action.

In April of 2010, a tour brought Lowkey, The Narcicyst, DAM, and Shadia Mansour to Southpaw, a five-thousand-square-foot venue in Park Slope, Brooklyn, where they performed most of "Long Live Palestine, Part Two."[16] A remarkable and immediately recognizable interaction between performers and their audience in that venue is the explosion of the crowd into cheers after Lowkey's line "Nothing is more anti-Semitic than Zionism." The accusation of anti-Semitism associated with support for Palestine is resoundingly rejected in the heart of a neighborhood known for its politely liberal but staunchly pro-Israel politics.[17] Moreover, the release catalyzed by Lowkey's line allows for and encourages a stronger response in the antiphonal exchange that follows. As in Geneva at the DARG show, enthusiastic chants of "Palestine!" in response to "Free, free!" function as the main political act.

Furthermore, the footage of the performance in Park Slope especially suggests that the call and response has an embodied aspect in addition to its linguistic or oral one. Georg Fuchs notes that "rhythmic movements of the human body in space" are able to "infec[t] other people with the same or similar rhythmic vibrations, putting them in a state of ecstasy."[18] Artists are obviously aware of this relationship as the encouragement of physical and vocal participation is constant and varied. In Park Slope, artists are especially keen to promote a specific choreography in rhythm with the music. Audiences are asked to put two fingers in the air and wave them side to side. The linguistic and embodied elements of the call and response, this suggests, are not separate but intricately wrapped up in each other. The movement of the body to a rhythm, even singing along with the verses, encourages that the political punch of participation in the "Free, free Palestine!" refrain resounds.

The polyphony recorded in this track and embraced in performance recalls Paolo Virno's stipulation that the "multitude is the form of social and political existence *for the many, seen as being many*."[19] The activation of plural and recognizably different voices in the polyphonal exchanges in the piece's structure creates a space that encourages instead of limits the multiplication of difference within a network. At the same time, this difference is channeled into a constant energy and the articulation of a political statement. I suggested that the polyvocal chants of "Palestine" suggest multiple meanings for the phrase, but performers unquestionably seek to have the call and response performed, regardless of how individuals interpret it. This suggests that while the heterogeneous nature of the participation and of the crowd is acknowledged and encouraged, a single community or resonance is formed nevertheless. That is to say, the piece holds the potential for myriad variations on a theme; this ensures that it not only speaks to a multitude but *performs one*. The performances themselves enact the multitude, calling a network of different voices standing together into being. Thus, the radical potency lies not just in the lyrics "It's about time we globalize the intifada" but in the realization that the intifada is already globalized and furthermore is already active; chants of "7urra!" and "Palestine!" suggest that the global intifada may be there, around you, in the concert space.

Performative Pedagogy: "Kollon 3endon Dababaat"

In her book *The Transformative Power of Performance*, renowned theater historian and theoretician Erika Fischer-Lichte develops the concept of the "autopoetic feedback loop" to describe exchanges between performers and spectators in avant-garde performance practices since the 1970s.[20] This concept applies to various performatic arrangements wherein the roles between spectators and performers are reversed (spectators act, performers watch or listen), community is generated, and intimacy and distance in the performance space is actively negotiated. Importantly, as Fischer-Lichte tracks this aesthetic shift in performance art since the 1970s, she emphasizes the changes in its social nature. Performances she looks at do not *represent* community generation or intimacy, rather, "they actually create instances of these processes. The spectators do not merely witness these situations . . . they are made to physically experience them."[21] Her analysis presents a history of how contemporary performance practices largely in the United States and Europe (also Japan) came to integrate and rely on these strategies—from directors' emphasis on the physical spaces used as theatres, to dramatic shifts in dramaturgy and staging. This attention begins to parse out the different kinds of community live performance may potentially generate.

In my analysis of Shadia Mansour's performances in this section, I am particularly interested in the analysis Fischer-Lichte makes of intimacy and distance in the performance space and in the duration of community generated by performance. Fischer-Lichte suggests that, in the performance practices she considers, the community generated is "fleeting."

She suggests that a "community of co-subjects . . . became possible only for very short periods of time. It was not sustained for the entire duration of a performance but merely over fluctuating and limited spans."[22] If the claims I made in the previous section about the generation of multitudinous community via live performances are convincing, it is appropriate to inquire further about the nature of this engaged collectivity. Does "radical belonging" last? Or is it, as in the context of avant-garde performance, merely a "temporary social reality?"[23]

Shadia Mansour's performance style is particularly noteworthy in the way she activates her audiences' awareness of Arab identity through vocal and embodied exchanges. Mansour herself is British, of Palestinian descent. In late November 2011 she took the stage at the Shrine, a "World Music venue" in Harlem, dressed in a traditional Palestinian robe or *thob*.[24] In many of her performances she dons this long-sleeved, floor-length, colorful costuming choice. When she does, she points to the persona of a "traditional" Arab woman, and specifically to Palestinian heritage, not far perhaps from what Cheryl L. Keyes has categorized as the persona of "Queen Mother" cultivated by some Black female rappers.[25]

The use of an easily identifiable marker of "Palestinian-ness" functions like Keyes suggests the use of Kente cloth or ankh-stylized jewelry has for African American women rappers such as Queen Latifah or Queen Kenya of the group Zulu Nation, attributing certain dignity to the performing Arab female body. While the *thob* outwardly identifies pride of her Palestinian heritage, it also marks her as distinctly "Other" on the stage and in the performance venue. The long gown separates her from her male collaborators, who are always dressed in simple T-shirts and jeans. It creates a specific performance aura around her petite frame quite different from the one male rappers and audience members of both genders sometimes invoke by draping the kuffiyeh, the black-and-white- or red-and-white-checked scarf that has come to symbolize Palestinian resistance worldwide, about their neck or around their shoulders.[26] Moreover, Mansour's use of call and response allows her to navigate the distance she creates with this performance persona.

In her book *Strange Encounters*, Sara Ahmed theorizes how the processes of encountering different bodies may be understood as forming collectivity. She suggests, "Collectivities are formed through the *very work that has to be done* in order to get closer to other others."[27] Mansour's gestures and strategies in performance suggest that the generation of community in some Arab rap performances depends on understanding the potential for belonging in the ways Ahmed suggests. Mansour plays with intimacy, physical space, and pedagogy in call and response to generate a sort of belonging that is intricately rapped up with recognizing and claiming Arab identity. This collectivity and this understanding of identity is formed by Mansour's prompts to "get closer"—physically and metaphorically—to other Arabs.

"This is hip hop, it's not some industry party," Mansour said when she took the microphone at the Shrine. "I need your energy," she continued, "Come close." The group consented, bringing an audience of fifty to sixty closer to the tiny stage. With audience members shoulder to shoulder, almost touching, she continued to warm up the crowd, now seeking to build intimacy of a different sort. "Who here speaks Arabic?" she asked. A spattering of hands and cheers emerged from the crowd. "No," Mansour began again, "Who here *really* speaks Arabic, not . . . 'Ana be7eb el la7meh ktir!'"

Mansour was referring to a parody rap video that went viral in 2006. In it two young Arabs rap about their love of "*la7me*" ("meat," in Arabic, as translated by the video's publishers).[28] It was perhaps the first example of what has become a series of rap spoofs that celebrate or satirize outward trappings of Arab identity. The most popular of such productions to date, "Saudis in Audis" by the West Virginia–based comedian Remy Munasifi, is a parody of young Gulf Arabs, and at the time of writing had over 7.5 million hits on YouTube.[29] The videos are made by Arab American men with the ostensible intent of reclaiming negative stereotypes about Arabs by making the self-recognition of particular traits humorous. They identify particular habits or behaviors (eating meat, mustaches, pronunciation of some words, especially the difficulty of the aspirated "p" for Arabic speakers) as "alien" and poke fun at them using a mixture of Arabic and English, or "Arablish."[30] In referring to the "La7me" video (a track with at least three times as many hits as the most popular of her own tracks), Mansour tapped into the imagined community it had generated.[31] This points to a variation in the development of community in live rap performances discussed in the previous section. Instead of embracing all sorts of linguistic difference—as the collaboration with Lowkey does—Mansour effectively shuts down the possibility of other communication by deliberately opening with what was essentially an inside joke. This has a dual function: it surely connects the insiders who understand the joke, but it also clearly demarcates and excludes those who do not.

In doing so, Mansour figuratively drew a circle around her audience, further distinguishing them from casual listeners or non-interested customers at the bar. Speaking specifically *to Arabs* and getting them to speak is a notable feature of the way Mansour structures her performances. This has to do with the specific political environment in which young Arabs find themselves in the world today, where they are frequently identified as dangerous, backward, extremist, or any number of negative qualifiers in a "post-9/11" landscape. Moustafa Bayoumi suggests that since the beginning of the wars in Afghanistan and Iraq, "Arabs and Muslims, two groups virtually unknown to most Americans prior to 2001, now hold the dubious distinction of being the first new communities of suspicion [in the United States] after the hard-won victories of the civil-rights era."[32] In New York and other cities, the infiltration of Muslim and Arab communities by police and undercover investigators has had devastating impacts on these communities' abilities to relate to each other and to the rest of society. The American Civil Liberties' Union describes these practices as having "deeply negative effects" on Muslim and Arab communities' constitutional rights "by chilling speech and religious practice" and further "fraying the social fabric" of these communities "by breeding anxiety, distrust, and fear."[33] These negative impacts are not limited to Arab and Muslim communities in the United States. Mansour has performed this same track with almost the exact gesture and strategies I describe below in the West Bank and Gaza. This suggests that the way this piece attempts to generate community is focused around how it challenges or overcomes the anxiety and fear that comes with identifying as, being seen as, or simply "being with" other Arabs. While the particularities of this fear and anxiety in New York and Gaza are different, Mansour's performances suggest that the need to confront these shared feelings is similar.

So her question of *who speaks Arabic* is not a simple linguistic temperature check. Rather, her act of demarcating her audience as Arabic-speaking, and urging that audience to articulate choruses and refrains in Arabic together, works to identify and empower a denigrated and hesitant demographic. Mansour specifically asks who *speaks* Arabic and not, as any number of performers or speakers, aware that their language of choice is not the dominant one, who *understands* Arabic. This is because, as we saw in the last section, the *audience speaking* is a crucial part of the politics of the performance. Shadia Mansour activates these audience responses in several tracks that use pedagogical techniques wherein she teaches her audience a line or two of Arabic, which they then sing back to her in the chorus. Particularly good examples of this are her performances of the piece "Kollon 3endon Dababaat" ["They have tanks"].[34]

The track's title and refrain "Kollon 3endon debabaat wa i7na 3endna 7jar" [They all have tanks and we have stones] is a riff off the popular children's song "Kullon 3endon Siyarat," ["They have cars"] written by Jad Rahbani.[35] In the original, the refrain runs, "They have cars and my grandfather has a donkey." The song's message for young audiences is a celebration of lack through laughter. The lyrics detail how the town makes fun of the speaker's grandfather, who cannot afford a car, but the tone and melody of the piece make light of this ostracism and reclaim it, importantly figuring the speaker as a collective "we."

Mansour's appropriation of this piece speaks directly to a pedagogical strain in her work. The recycling of the children's refrain has a certain political affect (overtly identifying herself with Palestinian children), but it also allows listeners with a slighter grasp on the language into the meaning of her original piece. Diasporic listeners will recognize the music and the dichotomy set up in the refrain even if they miss the in-tricacies of the (much more complicated) original verse. Similarly, like the reference to the parody rap videos, Mansour again taps into an ex-isting imagined community and appropriates it into contemporary po-litical action. This is embodied in the audience speaking in the following call and response: "[Mansour] Kollon 3endon dababaat wa i7na 3endna? [They have tanks and we have?]; [Audience]: 7jar! [stones!]. If an audi-ence responds timidly at first, she pretends not to have heard properly and asks, confused, "5yar?" [cucumbers?] or "jazar?" [carrots?].[36] Both Arabic words rhyme with the correct answer, "7jar" [stones], thus creat-ing an antiphonal exchange that very much mirrors a teacher or parent's playful attempts to goad children into more emphatic pronouncements. Mansour uses this strategy in performances in and outside the United States and Europe. When she performs for Palestinian audiences, the em-phasis is decidedly not on whether or not audiences speak Arabic but on their willingness to gather and claim political strategies (like rocks, to fight tanks) together.[37]

Significantly, the use of language articulation as an embodiment and activation of identity presents a community that is aware of difference even within its continuity. In the footage of the performance at the Shrine, the varying levels of familiarity with Arabic are made painfully clear in the multiple attempts Mansour makes to produce a refrain of the chorus that is understandable (she says exasperatingly at one point, "I've sang it *a million* times, so everyone should know the words!"). It is not enough to suggest that a series of insider references enacted live create a single and cohesive, collective body. Rather, Mansour's different performance strategies highlight the need to understand, as Sara Ahmed suggests, how "to complicate what it means to be 'with,' such that 'with-ness' is a site, not of shared co-habitance, but of differentiation."[38] If we understand Mansour's navigation of what is clearly *not* a homogenous audience or performance space in this way, we can see how her attention to physical closeness in performance spaces, articulation in Arabic of specific political strategies, and self-identifying as "Other" contributes to an understanding of differentiated community. Mansour's deliberate provocation of difference and strangeness visually and orally/aurally draws attention to the heterogeneous nature of the Arab community she speaks to while co-constructing the space that allows audiences to embody and feel the strength of that cultural and political belonging. Ultimately, this suggests that the performances build awareness that lingers outside the performance spaces, generating community that lasts after the "fleeting" moments in the venue. Recordings of all of the performances I have discussed so far register at several points that some individual audience members are familiar with a given track and are coming back for more. This repeat attendance suggests a community that returns to form again, not in exactly the same form, but that returns nevertheless. Mansour' performance strategies—her use of call and response and her navigations of distance and difference—point to the particular co-construction of identity and community—a radical, returning belonging in the context of Arabic rap.

Staging Politics

In 2005 the U.S. State Department, along with Jazz at Lincoln Center, and the Brooklyn Academy of Music (BAM), launched an international music tour dubbed "Rhythm Road." The project, which continues today, is modeled off of the so-called Jazz Ambassador tours of the Cold War, wherein predominantly African American jazz musicians toured countries in Africa, Eastern Europe, the Middle East, and South Asia as a part of President Dwight Eisenhower's cultural diplomacy to defeat communism. Proposed by Rep. Adam Clayton Powell Jr., the Jazz Ambassador tours, dubbed the United States' "Secret Sonic Weapon" by the *New York*

Times, featured Dizzy Gillespie, Louis Armstrong, Duke Ellington, and Benny Goodman, among others.[39] The idea was to counter the restrictive cultural environment of Soviet communism with the free improvisation of American jazz. The original tours also had a second political function in the late 1950s and 1960s. Musicians playing overseas in mixed-race bands powerfully corrected the negative images of segregation and racism that the civil rights' fight against Jim Crow laws brought to international attention.[40]

The "Rhythm Road" tours were launched in the wake of the Abu Ghraib prison scandal. They originally featured hip-hop and rap acts and, Hisham Aidi has argued, deliberately exploited a perceived connection between the Muslim, African American roots of hip-hop and dissent and critique in the legacy of Malcolm X.[41] Former secretary of state Hillary Clinton has publicly referred to the "hip-hop envoys" and the Rhythm Road tours as an important "chess piece" in U.S. foreign policy. While the Rhythm Road tours now include a range of music including folk, country, and gospel, they began featuring American hip-hop acts, particularly those made up of young Black and Muslim musicians.

Aidi has suggested that the significance of the tours lies in the efforts of the State Department to use cultural production toward political ends in the war on terror. More specifically, he argues that the tours engaged in "blackwashing" the unfavorable image of the United States in the Arab and Muslim world by attempting to relate to young generations susceptible to "Islamic fundamentalism" with cultural production understood as "hip," "Black," and "Muslim." The tours' purported aim of "promot[ing] democracy and foster[ing] dissent" is moreover underscored by the seeming integration of Muslims within the fabric American life of via their performing bodies producing an ostensibly "American" music form.[42] Central in this representation of hip-hop in the Arab world for undeniably political ends is the staging of identity and race. Aidi's attention to the political ideology underpinning the cultural programming of the U.S. State Department makes for fascinating reading. Flipping Aidi's project around slightly, I here want to explore the political ideology that can be discerned in how hip-hop acts are hosted by art institutions "at home" in the United States.

The consideration that cultural production is also underscored by political ideology "at home," not only when taken abroad, is relevant even if the institutional players were unconnected.[43] In 2013 BAM, one of the collaborators on the Rhythm Road tours, and host of the annual Next

Wave Festival, hosted an evening "celebrating the spitfire rhymes and rhythms of the Middle East." "Mic Check: Hip Hop from the Middle East and North Africa" featured El Deeb, from Egypt; Shadia Mansour; El Général; the much touted Tunisian crew; and Amkoullel, from Mali. In this section, I explore how representations of race and identity under an umbrella of "politics" can communicate quite different politics than those I ventured in the analyses above. I consider these dynamics in order to divest my analysis from a celebration of the genre of rap and hip-hop in Arabic as *essentially* liberatory. This is a version of the problematic assumption that the authors of the Brookings report quoted by Aidi have articulated. Moreover, a careful look at the staging of "politics" in cultural production reveals that the ever-growing enthusiasm for political expression in cultural production from the Arab world can mask quite different politics. In this section, I want to explore how the representation and staging of an abstract but alluring "politics" are employed to *depoliticize* emcees and their work.

During the continuation of the Arab uprisings, the global mass media struggled to find interlocutors to explain what was happening on Arab streets. As attention to and production of Arabic rap and hip-hop grew, North American– and European-based Arabs in the diaspora were frequently called upon to interpret the significance of these events and the cultural production surrounding them. The attention Syrian American rapper and architect Omar Offendum received around the Egyptian revolution and the release of his collaboration track "#Jan25," named for the hashtag activists and journalists were using to connect on Twitter, is exemplary of this phenomena. In live interviews and at live events, the rapper was staged to appear as an accessible representative of the "Arab street" despite his physical distance from it. The remarkable enthusiasm for the presence and perspectives of some young Arab journalists in the diaspora in this period—such as Ayman Mohyeldin, then a correspondent for Al Jazeera English, and Sharif Kouddous of Democracy Now!—further illustrates this phenomenon. On Twitter, what is best described as a steadily growing fan base eagerly followed Mohyeldin's urgent reports from Tahrir. Hosts at the studio in Doha could barely contain their curiosity about the experiences of their leather jacket–clad Egyptian American colleague. On international platforms in a changing global context, the demand for perspectives about the upheavals in Arab streets resulted in the restaging of the identity and experiences of some Arab Americans.

When pushed to deliver what they thought the events on the Arab street meant or felt like, however, rapper Omar Offendum and journalist Ayman Mohyeldin both immediately backed away from suggestions that their experiences may "represent" those of Cairenes or other Arabs. An Al Jazeera English interview with Offendum on February 8, 2011, is one good example of just how awkward these presentations of a politicized Arab identity can be.[44] Invited to discuss his track "#Jan25," clips from the official video for Offendum's track "Destiny" were instead aired underneath the interview. Generally, the Los Angeles–based rapper is asked to explain what Arab youth think or feel about the 2011 Egyptian revolution, generalizations he tries to eschew. Offendum makes a point to invoke only "solidarity with" their struggle. The host stumbles over his questions, answering them himself occasionally. About the medium Offendum and his colleagues used to express this solidarity, the host offers, "And . . . I was going to say, 'why rap music?' You're a rapper, that's why." On the same channel on February 11, 2011, the day then–Egyptian president Hosni Mubarak stepped down, Mohyeldin encountered similarly stammering questions. Hosts in the studio asked how he felt *as an Egyptian* while on air, reporting from Tahrir Square, interactions he has talked about publicly as curious if not problematic.[45] Offendum, Mohyeldin, and others likely eschew these sorts of questions because they are conscious of the differentiation within a larger Arab community that their role as professionals and members of the diaspora presents.[46] This reflection is perhaps more obvious than a consideration of how narratives and stagings of hybridity and intercultural subjectivity fit into neoliberal frameworks of power.

Antonio Gramsci saw liberation for certain classes through the development and integration of so-called organic intellectuals into mainstream or traditional political processes. Underrepresented classes, he argued, needed to think and theorize from their own subject positions. Only through intellectual activity that was "organic" to each class could a more just government and more equitable distribution of power be executed.[47] This construct relies on the ability of an individual or individuals to effectively represent their communities to a larger whole and more specifically to power. It also requires that individuals are able to identify with the larger group for whom they are meant to speak. This has been notoriously complicated for diasporic artists and thinkers in general. Stuart Hall, for example, in engaging with this question offered, "We were organic intellectuals without any organic point of reference."[48]

Many diasporic Arab rappers are especially cognizant that their potential roles as organic intellectuals are more complicated than Gramsci's theorizations can initially accommodate. For example, The Narcisyst, who raps mostly in English, asks earnestly, "And if I go back to Basra, will it ever receive me?"[49] A life in the United States, or Canada, or the United Kingdom makes it quite difficult to, with any healthy sense of compassion, speak earnestly "for" or "as" the myriad ethnic and cultural classes from which one may hail but in which one may no longer be immersed. Instead, Offendum's "Destiny" identifies pride of the experience of Hall's "without an organic point of reference" as he explores the implications of living between "East" and "West." With verses in Arabic and English on either side, the chorus repeats:

> It's hard living in the West when I know the East's got the best of me
> Could be looking in my eyes but you never really see the rest of me
> Can you hear me *masiree* [my destiny]
> Bilingual's what I'm blessed to be.
> Hamamet salameh fte7i ajnihateki wa tiree [dove of peace, open
>   your wings and fly][50]

Given this conscientious navigation of how they are seen by others, it is no accident that articulations of identity form an overwhelmingly central focus of many rap and hip-hop artists living and producing in the diaspora. As I argued in the previous section, it is something that Shadia Mansour's performances actively navigate. The exploration of identity, however, can take on different meanings when it is deliberately staged as attractive "hybridity."

Promoted as a way to categorize "uncharacterizable" musics, the genre of "World Music" came to indicate a specific way that musicians and producers broached different markets and sold the sonic interactions between "West" and "non-West" heard in a given work. The search for more authentic "sounds" prompted U.K.- and U.S.-based record producers to record material with musicians from Africa, South East Asia, and the Middle East. Popular music–scholar Simon Frith suggests that in World Music "the 'authentic' worked in retail terms as a redescription of the 'exotic.'"[51] As World Music has continued to grow and develop with subgenres such as the South Asian bhangra, *raï* music, and hip-hop in numerous languages, Timothy Taylor suggests that the Western consumer's desire for and exoticization of authenticity in World Music has been replaced. Instead, Taylor suggests, "*hybrid* has become the new authentic."[52]

In a media age that has consistently and deliberately presented largely negative images of Arab men and meek or oppressed Arab women, clean-cut, hip, articulate, young Arabs who move from Arabic to English articulate liberal political arguments and speak "as" both "Arab" and "Western" present a new radical hybridity that can emerge to remake the image of a changing Arab world. Iraqi Canadian rapper The Narcicyst has talked at length about the experience of being simultaneously courted and surveilled by the FBI and the role that he perceives outward trappings of self-presentation—like facial hair and fashion choices—have played in these interactions.[53] In the celebration of some diasporic Arab artists and musicians as intercultural communicators, more than a simple celebration of diasporic culture is taking place. The staging of these identities in the framing of cultural events like rap concerts also functions politically but quite differently from the radical modes of belonging I pointed to in the previous sections. Asked to stand in for or represent Arab experiences and identity, Arab Americans in media spotlights confront the prospect of performing a recognizable and approachable authenticity. This hybridity represented in sartorial choices, accents, and linguistic fluency has a counterpart in hip-hop and rap in Arabic, which seemingly brings "East" and "West" together in an alluring way.

For example, the Mic Check event at BAM brought together four rap acts. El Deeb, from Egypt opened the concert; Shadia Mansour took the stage next; Tunisia's El Général followed; and the Malian rapper Amkoullel closed out the set. Beats were provided onstage by DJ Johnny Juice of Public Enemy and traditional musical interludes interspersed between sets by Moroccan musician Brahim Fribgane on the oud and Yacouba Sissoko, a griot and musician from Mali, on drums. The event not only brought together these four rap acts but also effectively melded "tradition"—embodied in the oud and drums as well as in Amkoullel and Mansour's costuming choices—with "modernity"—manifest in Deeb and El Général's T-shirt/sweatshirt and jean combinations and Johnny Juice's digitized beats. This was a selling point of the evening, advertised as an event that "brings together a host of intrepid anthem writers alongside more traditional musicians."[54] Deeb, bald, clean shaven, with Black frame glasses wearing a Brooklyn t-shirt brought a hipster counterpart to Amkoullel's Malian garb of a wide brimmed straw hat, and loose, embroidered pants and slippers. The four rappers alternated between French and English and different dialects of Arabic. All together, the concert staged an alluring—and authentic, because hybrid—urban performance experience, very much in the vein of BAM's tag line "home for adventurous artists, audiences, and ideas."[55]

My point is that these stagings of allure, excitement, and hybridity are not only curious; they are pointedly political. That is, they perform a political ideology, one that is not necessarily radical but specifically neoliberal. The Mic Check event, curated by Zeyba Rahman, was described in BAM literature thus:

> From the recent revolutions in North Africa and the Middle East, rappers have emerged as torchbearers of the movement's progressive energy and restless, defiant spirit. For *Mic Check*, BAM brings together a host of these intrepid anthem writers alongside more traditional musicians for an evening of contemporary music born from radical social and political change.[56]

In a talkback with the artists the night before the concert, DJ/rupture (the artist and writer Jace Clayton) led a discussion about politics and revolution and the ability of hip-hop to conduct this energy in their respective languages. Without exception, all the artists confirmed that they, too, see politics in their work. The corroboration by artists that their work is political is important in elaborating how the representative framework of the event worked. But this fact of their agreement about the *presence* of politics in their work need not intimate they share a united particular political project. The celebration of this music as being "born from radical social and political change" nevertheless implies a framework of understanding the inherently liberatory nature of this creative expression of dissent. My interest is not in claiming that the work of these rappers is "actually" conservative or reactionary. Rather, my concern is the ease with which words like "defiant," "change," "radical," and "political" are used as referent-less place holders, which an audience nevertheless seems to understand. What does "change" imply about the people "changing"? Why is it alluring? Why is music borne from it compelling? What "politics" are appearing—or are being staged—in this event? In a concert in which most of the lyrics were not in English and left untranslated save for program notes audience members held in the darkened opera house, what political communication was transferring between the musicians and their Brooklyn audience?

Earlier I claimed that the call and response interactions between artists and their audiences are particularly important vehicles for interpreting political meaning. In my analyses in the previous sections, I suggested that the use of language in the call and response invoked or formed community in specific ways. The same holds true at the BAM event. For example, Deeb, who opened the concert, attempted a call and response to close his song "Beeladee." The call and response, after the Arabic rap, was in English. He interrupted the Arabic lyrics to say, "When I say 'Egypt'; you say 'Free! Egypt'—" and then he pointed his mic to the house. This was followed by "Syria!" "Free!"; "Tunis!" "Free!"; "Palestine!" "Free" and then: "The World!" "Free." Deeb's final refrain of "The World/Free" after the series of specific Arab countries was nothing short of awkward, as if a concession to the overtly politicized chants that preceded it. "Free Egypt, Tunis, and Syria" have distinct connotations, specifically tied to the Arab uprisings and their demands. "Free Palestine" likewise has a specific political project attached to it. The specifics of a free world, on the other hand, are much harder to pin down, perhaps fitting instead into the narrative of a globalized utopia. While the disappearance of national borders certainly has its place in a utopian political imaginary, this positive approach to globalization is not typically associated with the revolutionary ethos of the Arab uprisings or of any number of contemporary political youth movements. The refrain fell flat.

Amkoullel, whose set closed the concert before a collaborative finale, performed a very different sort of interaction with the audience. He opened his set with the song, "SOS" in which the chorus sings, "SOS, SOS, we're in a state of emergency / this must change." And he closed the set by asking the audience to dance with him in his last piece, "Come Dance." Removing his hat and shirt, he suggested that even though artists deal with politics in their work, sometimes they also just need to have fun. He urged the audience to stand up and move their hips with his, and to join him in the refrain "We are all Africa." There are several remarkable features of Amkoullel's set, especially when considered in the company of the other artists with whom he shared the stage and under the framework of BAM's description of the event and its insinuations to both the Arab uprisings and Occupy Wall Street.[57]

We should recall that in the spring of 2013, the French were escalating military exercises against armed Islamic rebels in northern Mali in a new frontier of the war on terror. Amkoullel's "SOS" is not a call for solidarity *against* this kind of imperial intervention. Rather the arrival of the French seems to be in line with the kind of SOS the song calls for. Wherever one falls on the question, surely it is clear that asking for imperial intervention is a different politics than insisting that colonial interference desist. Further, Amkoullel's closing pieces at the end of the show, the refrain "we are all Africa" and an invitation to "shake your body," are a startling curatorial interpretation of the emerging politics of the region over the past few years. The fact that the concert of "intrepid anthem writers . . . born from radical social and political change" ended with the literal performance of a half naked, dancing Black body on stage, entreating the audience to a dance party despite their differences, demands a more careful consideration of how art institutions like BAM use the exotic allure associated with diasporic or foreign performers, "hybrid" aesthetics, and the "politics" they attribute to their work. The curatorial framework of the event used the strange familiarity of Black musical culture in order to render alluring the distinctly different tongues and strange politics of the Arab world and North Africa through the voices of hip, young Arabs and Africans. Leaning on Aidi's work on the Rhythm Road tours, this curatorial framing of Amkoullel, El Général, Deeb, and Mansour's work seems to try to "blackwash" the radical political energy of some contemporary rap music into a multicultural call to heal the world through dance.

The curatorial drive appears to be to exhibit radical, Black, Arab, and Muslim politics in a hip cultural environment, but the effect is to reproduce neoliberal narratives of multicultural appreciation and celebration, akin to what Wendy Brown has discussed in her work on "tolerance." What is particularly relevant about Brown's discussion to my own here is how this neoliberal mode of governmentality depoliticizes even while invoking the name of political activity as its allure. Brown writes: "Depoliticization involves removing a political phenomenon from comprehension of its *historical* emergence and from a recognition of the *powers* that produce and contour it. No matter its particular form and mechanics, depoliticization always eschews power and history in the representation of its subject."[58]

By lumping the four artists together—whose personal histories, contexts, and politics are quite different—the event's framework obscures the sharp political messages in each. Consider first the three Arab artists. One could say that El Général raps about government corruption and censorship; Deeb about Egyptian belonging and nationality; Mansour about the Israeli occupation. Even this very simplistic mapping of their work reveals that each is concerned with very different political problems, born of specific contexts. The inclusion of Amkoullel's work—with which the other three Arab artists admitted in the artist talkback preceding the event that they had not heard of before being approached by BAM's curating team—within the frame of musicians from the Middle East and North Africa further distances each of the performers from their material and historical contexts. Indeed, it is curious at least to consider the Malien musician "North African," as the latter category typically refers to the Arab-speaking countries, the bulk of whose geographical domain is north of the Sahara. Mali, which shares neither the cultural influence of Islam nor the common linguistic denominator of Arabic, is not typically included in this categorization.

This somewhat arbitrary geographical (and some would say race-based) consideration aside, the political concerns and means employed Amkoullel's tracks are also markedly different from his colleagues.[59] For example, in the track "SOS," despite the line "Nous avons trop entendu / j'en ai marre d'avoir la main tendue" (We've heard too much / I'm sick of holding out my hand), the footage under the refrain that sings "SOS, SOS, on est on état d'urgence" (SOS, SOS, we are in a state of emergency) is of donations being gathered and unloaded. Indeed, the track advertises that proceeds from its purchase will be donated to victims of the violence in northern Mali.

At some point in all their work, all four artists address directly or indirectly the presence of Islamic fundamentalism or religious conservatism in their societies. However, removing a consideration of the specific historical, colonial, and economic contexts in which that fundamentalism as political power has grown and making it difficult to understand the lyrical content of the raps as they are being voiced, as the BAM curation did, has the effect of framing the artists as all together rapping for a vague notion of "freedom" that they do not have but that the New York / Brooklyn-based audience does, or that it at least possesses to a greater extent. Understanding the political "change" of which this music is borne is thus framed as understanding "how we can help them," a very particular neoliberal ideology, manifest worldwide in a reciprocal relationship of forced governmental debt and an economy of foreign nongovernmental organizations.[60] The fact that this ethos of a neoliberal imperialism, recognized in the staging of cultural activity exported abroad, can also be found in a cultural event in New York City should not be surprising, although its critique has been less pronounced. The curation of the "Mic Check" event is pointedly political because, instead of encouraging a discussion of the similarities and differences between the contexts of these four artists under the umbrella of "politics," it obscured those material contexts. In this way it masked how specific political players, among them the United States and its allies, create the difference, poverty, oppression, and so on, to which these rappers respond. This effectively depoliticizes their work. Moreover, these four musicians have such different styles and politics that it seems unlikely a collaboration between them would be organic; the framework imposed upon them suggests instead that other aesthetic and political considerations were at play. Indeed a balance of modernity, tradition, gender, and tone in a multicultural, hybrid celebration of creative dissent can be seen in much of BAM's programming. The stagings of Arab rappers thus can also produce politics—albeit markedly different from the "radical belonging" that I suggested may be generated in other performances.

Conclusion: Analyzing Cultural Production to Shift Borders

> "Our music foretells our future. Let us lend it an ear."
>
> —JACQUES ATTALI, *Noise: The Political Economy of Music*

In this chapter, I have suggested paying closer attention to what politics are produced in rap and hip-hop concerts in Arabic. On the one hand, I have proposed "radical belonging" as a way to understand the political potential in some live performances of some Arabic rap. On the other, I have suggested that curatorial frameworks can also depoliticize pointed political critiques by masking or obscuring the material contexts from which the lyrics speak. My attention to particular strategies of incorporating call and response in rap performances attempts to understand how exchanges between performers and audiences and among audiences help communicate political meaning in these performances. I have done so in order to further a conversation about what political creative production by young Arabs does. Specifically, I have used these examples to suggest how Arabic rap and hip-hop concerts can be seen as a site of struggle over the meaning of quickly developing politics in the Arab world. This has stemmed from a conviction that it is not enough to locate politics in cultural production in the wake of the Arab uprisings. For cultural production to deepen understanding of our contemporary moment, careful attention to specific cultural practices is needed. Moreover, as the context between the United States and the Arab world in the wake of the Arab Spring continues to evolve, this kind of analysis of cultural production may be poised to make significant contributions to comprehension of these changes. Like Attali suggests, critical attention may "lend an ear" to forthcoming changes. Attention to how individuals and communities interact may help deepen understanding of how borders are shifting, disintegrating, or reforming transnationally in years to come.

Notes

I would like to thank Julia Goldstein, Jean Graham-Jones, Eero Laine, Elizabeth Adams, Maurya Wickstrom, and participants in the 2012 CASAR conference at the American University of Beirut for their comments on early iterations of this essay. Any shortcomings are exclusively my own.

1. See for example Elliott Colla, "In Praise of Insult: Slogan Genres, Slogan Repertoires and Innovation," *Review of Middle East Studies* 47 (2013): 37–48; Brinda Mehta, "Staging Tahrir: Laila Solimon's Revolutionary Theatre," *Review of Middle East Studies* 47 (2013): 49–55; and Shayna Silverstein, "Syria's Radical Dabke," *Middle East Report* 263 (2012): 33–37. See also Walid El Hamamsy and Mounira Solimon, eds., *Popular Culture in the Middle East and North Africa: A Postcolonial Outlook* (New York: Routledge, 2013); and Thomas Burkhalter, Kay Dickinson, and Benjamin J. Harbert, eds., *The Arab Avant-Garde: Music, Politics, Modernity* (Middletown, Conn.: Wesleyan University Press, 2013).

2. This means that the lyrical strategies of these artists are largely not my focus here. Much literature in hip-hop studies globally concentrates on rap lyrics. I attempt to push this study in a different direction. By using "performatic" in this essay, I adopt Diana Taylor's term meaning of or related to performance, as distinguished from J. L. Austin's discursive notion of the "performative." Diana Taylor, *The Archive and the Repertoire* (Durham, N.C.: Duke University Press, 2003), 6.

3. I am leaning on Victor Turner and Richard Schechner's work on the "whole performance sequence." See Victor Turner, *From Ritual to Theatre: The Human Seriousness of Play* (New York: PAJ Books, 2001); and Richard Schechner, *Between Theater and Anthropology* (Philadelphia: University of Pennsylvania Press, 1985).

4. In this essay I adopt the transcription practice common in much popular and web-based discourse around this musical subculture and other youth practices in the Arab world wherein a numeral stands in place of an Arabic phoneme or letter that does not have a simple equivalent in the romance alphabet. In this codification, the number "3" stands in for the Arabic letter "ع" (pronounced as a guttural "*ah*").

5. H. Samy Alim, *Roc the Mic Right: The Language of Hip Hop Culture* (New York: Routledge, 2006), 79–80.

6. See, for example, Jack L. Daniel and Geneva Smitherman, "How I Got Over: Communication Dynamics in the Black Community," *Quarterly Journal of Speech* 62 (1976): 26–39; Maggie Sale, "Call and Response as Critical Method: African American Oral Traditions in *Beloved*," *African American Review* 26 (1992): 41–50; Oliver Jackson, Preface to *Kuntu Drama*, ed. Paul Harrison, ix–xiii (New York: Grove, 1974); Geneva Smitherman, *Talkin' and Testifyin': The Language of Black*

America (Detroit: Wayne State University Press, 1977); Robert Farris Thompson, *African Art in Motion: Icon and Act* (Los Angeles: University of California Press, 1974); Edward D. Miller, "Authoring the Occupation: The Mic Check, the Human Microphone, and the Loudness of Listening," in *Media Authorship*, ed. Cynthia Chris and David A. Gerstner, 180–93 (New York: Routledge, 2013); and H. Samy Alim, *Roc the Mic Right*, 54–56.

7. Thompson, *African Art in Motion*, 28.

8. Daniel and Smitherman, "How I Got Over," 33.

9. Nikesh Shukla, "Lowkey Interview," *Original UK Hip Hop*, December 29, 2005, accessed November 21, 2013, http://www.ukhh.com/features/oldinterviews /lowkey/index1.html.

10. "Lowkey-Long Live Palestine Part 2 (Lyrics)," YouTube video clip, 4:59, posted by "baddaman234," January 1, 2010, accessed November 21, 2013, http://www .youtube.com/watch?v=4PgxMjmKEoc.

11. "Lowkey Marks Gaza's One Year War with Top Spot in Charts," *British Hip Hop*, January 5, 2010, accessed November 21, 2013, http://www.britishhiphop.co .uk/news/latest/lowkey_marks_gaza_s_one_year_war_with_top_spot_in_charts .html.

12. Michael Hardt and Antonio Negri, *Multitude: War and Democracy in the Age of Empire* (New York: Penguin Books, 2004), xiv.

13. The number "7" stands in for the Arabic letter "ح" (pronounced as a hard "*h*"). See note 4.

14. "Long Live Palestine—DARG TEAM—fete de la musique Live, Geneva Switzerland," 5:39, YouTube video clip, posted by "DARG TEAM," July 1, 2010, accessed November 21, 2013, http://www.youtube.com/watch?v=9LSgRscUwnQ &feature=player_embedded.

15. Sale, "Call and Response as Critical Method," 41.

16. "Lowkey-Long Live Palestine (Live in Brooklyn, NY)," YouTube video, 4:12, posted by "FacelesswithEyesOpen," March 26, 2011, accessed December 18, 2015, https://www.youtube.com/watch?v=aFGQ7Roodao&ab_channel=Faceless withEyesOpen.

17. Discussions about Palestine and Israel in New York City are markedly more conservative than they are in other Western cities, especially those in Western Europe. And while the political climate in the United States may be changing, recent events indicate that despite their liberal reputations compared with the rest of the United States, New Yorkers remain conflicted in terms of their position on the policies of the state of Israel toward Palestinians. In November of 2011 controversy was sparked among participants in "Occupy Wall Street" when some members spoke in the name of the group and expressed solidarity with the Turkish flotilla's efforts to break the blockade on Gaza on Twitter. Other members strongly disagreed with the sentiment, revealing that even New York's political activists on the Left remain "divided" on Palestine. See Ben Lorber, "Flotilla Controversy within Occupy Wall Street Shows Palestine Continues to Be a Fault Line," *Mondoweiss*, November 4, 2011, accessed November 21, 2013, http:// mondoweiss.net/2011/11/flotilla-controversy-within-occupy-wall-street-shows

-palestine-continues-to-be-a-fault-line.html. And in March 2012 the Park Slope Food Coop (a sixteen-thousand-plus member cooperative market located in same neighborhood in which Lowkey and his colleagues played in 2010) held a vote about whether or not *to hold a vote* to join the Boycott, Divest, and Sanction movement. Members overwhelmingly voted not to vote.

18. Georg Fuchs, *Der Tanz* (Stuttgart: Verlang von Strecker and Schroeder, 1906), 13, qtd. in Erika Fischer-Lichte, *The Transformative Power of Performance: A New Aesthetics*, trans. Saskya Iris Jain (New York: Routledge, 2008), 58. The enthomusicological literature on music and trance is extensive. In the larger dissertation project of which this research is a part, I explore affective exchanges and *tarab* in particular as a way of looking at the political experiences of participating in rap and hip hop concerts. *Tarab*, traditionally confined to the sphere of classical Arabic music, refers to a state of emotional transformation catalyzed by powerful performances. See, among others, A. J. Racy, *Making Music in the Arab World: The Culture and Artistry of Tarab* (Cambridge: Cambridge University Press, 2004).

19. Paolo Virno, *A Grammar of the Multitude*, trans. Isabella Bertoletti, James Cascaito, and Andrea Casson (New York: Semiotexte, 2004), 21; emphasis added.

20. Fischer-Lichte, *The Transformative Power of Performance*.

21. Ibid., 40.

22. Ibid., 53.

23. Ibid., 55.

24. "Shadia Mansour [kollon 3endon dababaat], live at the shrine, harlem nyc," Vimeo video clip, 4:21, posted by "spinderella," accessed December 18, 2015, https://vimeo.com/32243309.

25. Mansour is sometimes referred to as the "Queen of Palestinian Hip Hop." Cheryl L. Keyes, "Empowering Self, Making Choices, Creating Spaces: Black Female Identity via Rap Music Performance," in *Ethnomusicology: A Contemporary Reader*, ed. Jennifer C. Post, 97–108 (New York: Routledge, 2006).

26. At other times, when she is not wearing a *thob,* Mansour can be seen performing in jeans, a T-shirt, and kuffiyeh. Her track with M1 of Dead Prez, "Koffeyye Arabeyye" addresses the cultural appropriation of the kuffiyeh by Israelis, like the ones for sale at https://thesemitic.com/item-category/keffiyehs/ (accessed November 22, 2015).

27. Sara Ahmed, *Strange Encounters* (London: Routledge, 2000), 17, original emphasis.

28. "Arab Meat (Lahme) Song," January 19, 2006, video clip, accessed November 21, 2013, YouTube, http://www.youtube.com/watch?v=ali1PgunFWtc&feature =related. At time of writing the video has over 1.8 million hits on YouTube. According to the posting, the two men in the video are lip-synching to lyrics and beat originally recorded by Florida-based brothers Firas and Tarek Shrourou and the production company Top Notch.

29. "Saudis in Audis," October 21, 2010, video clip, accessed November 21, 2013, YouTube, http://www.youtube.com/watch?v=lqJDuZIcQ34.

30. Slang for the "interlanguage" between Arabic and English, Arablish "refers to the phenomenon of code-switching between the two languages. It is alterna-

tively named Arablizi," which combines Arabic and "Inglizi," the word for "English" in Arabic. "Arablish," *Wikipedia: The Free Encyclopedia*, accessed November 21, 2013, http://en.wikipedia.org/wiki/Arablish. Importantly, despite a clear recognition of Arab stereotyping, these parodies are not overtly political in nature, in the sense that they do not articulate, claim, or even approach a particular project. On the contrary, some of this energy can easily be seen as a further "Othering" of "unassimilated" Middle Eastern Arabs by second generation Americans. The "Saudis in Audis" track in particular distances the U.S.-based comedian from his "foreign" Saudi counterparts. In short, the affective content of the rap spoofs is wholly distinct from that in the "serious" rap production offered by the other artists I consider here. I use "serious" only to distinguish it from the "spoof" videos and raps, not to suggest a hierarchy of value. Indeed the popularity of the latter as measured in hits on YouTube suggests these parodies merit at least as much critical attention.

31. Here not by print but electronic media. Benedict Anderson, *Imagined Communities* (New York: Verso, 1983).

32. Moustafa Bayoumi, *How Does It Feel to Be a Problem? Being Young and Arab in America* (New York: Penguin Books, 2008), 3.

33. Noa Yachot, "125 Groups ask DOJ to Probe Un-American NYPD Surveillance," *American Civil Liberties Union*, October 24, 2013, accessed November 21, 2013, https://www.aclu.org/blog/national-security-religion-belief-technology-and-liberty/125-groups-ask-doj-probe-un-american. See also Faiza Patel and Amos Toh, "NYPD Muslim Spying Operation Takes 'Security' to an Unjustified Extreme," *Guardian,* February 6, 2013, accessed November 21, 2013, http://www.theguardian.com/commentisfree/2013/feb/06/nypd-muslim-spying-handschu-guidelines.

34. "Shadia Mansour '*Kollon 3endon Dababaat*'" YouTube video clip, 3:54, posted by "titoaauj," January 30, 2009, accessed November 21, 2013, http://www.youtube.com/watch?v=XI7qa1z63mE; for footage of this track at the Shrine in November 2011 see note 24.

35. "Kullon 3ndon siyarat w jidi 3ndo 7mar" [in Arabic], YouTube video clip, 2:29, posted by "qana beit el 3rab" [in Arabic], June 15, 2011, accessed December 18, 2015, https://www.youtube.com/watch?v=RecJjzgCLUk&ab_channel=BiTAlarab.

36. 5 stands in for the Arabic letter "خ," pronounced "*kh*" (see note 4).

37. See "Shadia Mansour—Kolon 3indon Dababat Live 7efa [They all have tanks live in Haifa]," YouTube video clip, 3:53, posted by "Shady Khafaga," July 30, 2011, accessed November 21, 2013, http://www.youtube.com/watch?v=daYyrAfiito.

38. Ahmed, *Strange Encounters*, 48.

39. Fred Kaplan, "When Ambassadors Had Rhythm," *New York Times*, June 29, 2008, accessed August 15, 2014, http://www.nytimes.com/2008/06/29/arts/music/29kapl.html?pagewanted=all&_r=0.

40. See Penny von Eschen, *Satchmo Blows up the World: Jazz Ambassadors Play the Cold War* (Cambridge, Mass.: Harvard University Press, 2004); and Lisa Davenport, *Jazz Diplomacy: Promoting America in the Cold War Era* (Jackson, Miss.: University Press of Mississippi, 2009).

41. Aidi quotes a 2008 Brookings report that noted sensitive connective tissue between the United States and the Muslim world in the bodies and work of inner-city Muslim rappers who "carry on an African American Muslim tradition of protest against authority, most powerfully represented by Malcolm X." Aidi notes that the study calls for "greater exploitation of this natural connector to the Muslim world." Cynthia Schneider and Kristina Nelson, *Mightier than the Sword: Arts and Culture in the US–Muslim World Relationship* (Brookings Institute), qtd. in Hisham Aidi, "America's Hip-Hop Foreign Policy: How Rap Became a Battleground in the War on Terror," *Atlantic,* March 20, 2014, accessed August 15, 2014, http://www.theatlantic.com/international/archive/2014/03/americas-hip-hop-foreign-policy/284522/?single_page=true.

42. Hisham Aidi, *Rebel Music: Race, Empire, and the New Muslim Youth Culture* (New York: Pantheon, 2014), 221–57.

43. See Dipesh Chakrabarty, *Provincializing Europe: Postcolonial Thought and Historical Difference* (Princeton, N.J.: Princeton University Press, 2000).

44. "Omar Offendum on Al Jazeera—#Jan25 Egypt," YouTube video clip, 4:13, posted by "Al Jazeera English," February 8, 2011, accessed November 21, 2013, http://www.youtube.com/watch?v=tSLWbIMxd88.

45. "Media Coverage of the Arab Revolutions: A Discussion with Al Jazeera Correspondent Ayman Mohyeldin," moderated by Helga Tawil-Souri, Institute for Public Knowledge, New York University, March 22, 2011.

46. Yassin Alsalman writes, "We as Arabs are not and probably never have been one." Yassin Alsalman, *The Diatribes of a Dying Tribe* (Toronto: Write or Wrong Publishing, 2011).

47. Antonio Gramsci, *Selections from the Prison Notebooks*, trans. and ed. Quintin Hoare and Geoffrey Nowell Smith (New York: International Publishers, 1971).

48. Stuart Hall, "Cultural Studies and Its Theoretical Legacies," in *Stuart Hall: Critical Dialogues in Cultural Studies,* ed. David Morley and Kuan-Hsing Chen, (London: Routledge, 1996), 261–74, at 267.

49. "The Narcicyst featuring Shadia Mansour 'Hamdulilah' Official Music Video," YouTube video clip, 4:19, posted by "Channel Narcy," September 14, 2010, accessed November 21, 2013, http://www.youtube.com/watch?v=oISHZQJdeSw.

50. "Omar Offendum—Destiny (Official Video HD)," YouTube video clip, 3:49, posted by "londonsfynest," July 4, 2010, accessed November 21, 2013, http://www.youtube.com/watch?v=WGl7BFDCVGA.

51. Simon Frith, "The Discourse of World Music," in *Western Music and Its Others*, ed. Georgina Born and David Hesmondhalgh, (Berkeley: University of California Press, 2000), 305–22, at 308.

52. Timothy Taylor, *Beyond Exoticism: Western Music and the World* (Durham, N.C.: Duke University Press, 2007).

53. Yassin Alsalman (the emcee known as The Narcicyst) gives his assessment of his and his colleagues' reception by the FBI at the 2007 convention of the American-Arab Anti-Discrimination Committee. See Alsalman, *Diatribes of a Dying Tribe.*

54. "Mic Check" *BAM*, accessed August 15, 2014, http://www.bam.org/music/2013/mic-check.

55. "About" *BAM*, accessed December 18, 2015, http://www.bam.org/about.

56. Ibid.

57. A "mic check" was a strategy used by Occupy Wall Street protesters to communicate protest logistics and chants in the fall and winter of 2011–12.

58. Wendy Brown, *Regulating Aversion: Tolerance in the Age of Identity and Empire* (Princeton, N.J.: Princeton University Press, 2006), 15, original emphasis.

59. North Africa—today largely populated by Arabs—is often used in contradistinction to Sub-Saharan Africa, which has been decried as lumping all of "Black" Africa into one amorphous category.

60. David Harvey discusses the so-called Washington Consensus of economic policy behind the lending practices of the International Monetary Fund and the World Bank as a central feature of neoliberalism. At the same time that governments of the Global South are forced to accept predatory conditions on loans that privatize their economies and shrink the role of the state in providing social services, a growing market of international organizations dubbed nongovernmental organizations is increasingly in place to "help" a population where the state once would. This economy of nongovernmental organizations has been criticized as perpetuating a demographic of "helpless" citizens, as opposed to empowering communities to problem solve themselves. David Harvey, *A Brief History of Neoliberalism* (Oxford: Oxford University Press, 2007).

The Reception of U.S. Discourse on the Egyptian Revolution

Between the Popular and the Official

MOUNIRA SOLIMAN

> The first line that ought to be written in the Book of Our
> Revolution, and read a thousand times each day, is that we
> must decide for ourselves to believe in mankind's power and
> omnipotence, and erase from our minds the unceasing and
> overpowering delusion that man is a weak and insignificant
> creature.
>
> —ZAKI NAJIB MAHMUD, "My Days in America"

During the eighteen days of the first wave of the January 25, 2011, Egyptian revolution, America certainly had a presence in Tahrir Square. On one side of the square stood the American University in Cairo, empty buildings with broken window panes and vandalized offices behind closed gates, some of the rooftops of its buildings hiding snipers ready to shoot at the protesters filling up Tahrir Square. On the other side of the square, darkened and dismantled, stood the renowned Nile Hilton hotel, the first of its chain in Egypt, a remnant of a bygone era, awaiting renovation as the new Ritz Carlton. To the side, on Mohamed Mahmoud Street, opposite the campus of the American University in Cairo, in one straight line side by side, McDonalds, Pizza Hut, and Hardees poured into Tahrir Square to join forces with the infamous Kentucky Fried Chicken.[1] The American fast-food chains, a beehive in busy and crowded downtown Cairo, closed their doors in the face of millions of Egyptians who poured into the square, nursing smashed window panes, their doors now covered with cardboard signs that read "No to Mubarak, the U.S. agent!" The broken image of America was hard to miss; the closed American chains were a visual representation of how Egyptians felt toward the position of the United States on the Egyptian revolution.

In answer to skeptical queries on the role of the United States of America in the Arab Spring and its possible motives, Secretary of State Hillary Clinton, in her keynote address at the National Democratic Institute in 2011, responded: "Along with our economic and technical help, America will also use [its] presence, influence and global leadership to support change."[2] The response was typically noncommittal, shying away from a direct answer that would force the United States to adopt a clear position on relevant issues, act upon it, and be held accountable. As is customary, the United States sent mixed messages that could be read in numerous ways, allowing it to maintain multiple and contradictory relationships with the regime, the different political powers, and the people. In short, the United States attempted to appeal to all three parties and to ensure at the same time that neither its interests nor its global image were jeopardized. These mixed messages were not lost on Arab populations; in fact, they were picked up and reciprocated through popular reactions.

Egyptian protesters' reactions to U.S. power have been described as a "campaign of hatred"—by the people and not the governments—against the United States. This is a term that was first used by President Dwight Eisenhower in 1958 when he expressed his concern over the general sentiments of the Arab people toward the United States. In response, the National Security Council then issued a report explaining that the reason for this hatred against the United States was its support of authoritarian regimes in the Middle East, the repression of democracy, and forestalling development, all for the purpose of controlling the energy resources in the region.[3] Commenting on the Arab Spring, Noam Chomsky explains that the scene has not changed much since 1958—in fact, it has grown worse:

> Take a look at what's happening in the Middle East today. There's a campaign of hatred against the United States, in Tunisia against France, against Britain, for supporting brutal, harsh dictators, repressive, vicious, imposing poverty and suffering in the midst of great wealth, blocking democracy and development, and doing so because of the primary goal, which remains to maintain control over the energy resources of the region. What the National Security Council wrote in 1958 could be restated today in almost the same words.[4]

But the history of the relationship between the United States and the Middle East / Arab world has not always been antagonistic, especially when it comes to Egypt. There have been periods when the United States has been seen in a much better light than it is today. Indeed, in the first half of the twentieth century Egyptians viewed America as a symbol of independence, freedom, and equal opportunities; America was a dream desired by many people. Even with the disillusionment of that dream, Egyptians maintained their respect for Americans, consciously aware that the double-standard foreign policy of the United States does not represent its people.[5] The duality of this love/hate relationship is ironic: Why do Egyptians continue to enthusiastically consume American culture while harboring an increasing sense of animosity toward the U.S. government that facilitates the production of this culture and, more importantly, exports it to the world? Despite the vilification of Arabs and Muslims in U.S. media, which have created an atmosphere of fear and have forever changed the image of the Arab to a terrorist, especially after the events of 9/11, Egyptian media has represented America differently. Egyptian media has had its share of stereotypical images of promiscuous American ladies and the famous Uncle Sam with his dollar sack, but these stereotypes are representations of cultural differences rather than attempts to "other" the American people. In the end these images of America remain benign expressions and if anything have made American culture even more appealing to Egyptian audiences.

Scholarly discussions about the decline of United States hegemony and the end of the American century remains a sophisticated debate within academic circles that have not been translated into an Egyptian popular perception. In other words, Egyptians and Arabs in general still perceive the United States as the world's superpower, which is manifested in United States military force and aid programs. The current economic crisis in the United States, which is connected to U.S. influence in the Arab region, does not have a direct impact on the way people in Egypt, and generally in the Middle East, continue to look upon the United States as an invincible power. What does have an impact on popular perception, however, is the unconditional support that the United States provides Israel and its double-standard policies toward Palestinians. But even with the case of the United States–Israel special relationship, people are discerning enough to distinguish between those who sit at negotiation tables and the rest of the population. Moreover, despite the uneven role that the United States plays in the Israeli–Palestinian conflict, its efforts to bring about a negotiated peace between the Israelis and the Palestinians intermediary efforts nevertheless remain uncontested. In other words, such efforts are perceived as part of the global role that the United States has assumed since World War II, that of the benevolent protector of human rights. It is the image that the United States persistently exports to the world partly through its popular culture. In an article titled "The Reception of American Culture in the Middle East after 'The Arab Spring,'" Nazmi Al-Shalabi, Marwan Obeidat, and Shadi Neimneh argue against the double-standard policies of the United States when it comes to the Israeli–Palestinian conflict, policies that have been the cause of much anger, frustration, and disappointment among Arab populations. It is interesting, however, that, although critical of U.S. practices in the region, the authors unwittingly endorse the same image that the United States has propagated for almost a century, taking it for granted that America is exceptionally in a position that allows it to assume such a global role. Taking sides with Israel, the United States has been isolating itself, sacrificing its interests, undermining the peace process, losing its credibility, and damaging its reputation as a leading power. To regain this status, the United States should set a good example for others. It should play its cards well, and argue in support of people's—including Palestinians—demanding freedom and human rights.[6]

Such statements clearly indicate the ambivalent nature of the relationship between the Arab world and the United States. Amy Goodman, in an interview with Noam Chomsky on the Arab Spring, hinted at such ambivalence when she pointedly asked him what he thought of the banner that people were holding in Tahrir Square that said, "Yes, we can too."[7] The reference is to Barack Obama's famous slogan during his first presidential campaign. In fact, this is not the first time that the slogan has been used in Egypt. Ever since Obama won the presidency of the United States in 2008, the slogan has appeared on many different occasions in the Egyptian context. While some argue that this is a sign of Egyptians' warming up to America, others, including Chomsky, hint at the subversive use of the slogan, claiming that unlike Obama and his administration, the Egyptians actually mean it.[8] In either case, it is an example of the intersection of politics and popular culture in Egypt, which characterizes people's reactions toward their government as well as toward various forms of foreign intervention. This intersection crystalized during the January 25 revolution and the position of the United States toward it, highlighting a tripartite relationship, one that involved the political rhetoric of the United States on the revolution, the official Egyptian response, and the reaction of the Egyptian public toward both. The position of the Obama administration received popular reaction because of its fluctuating responses, wavering between support for the regime and consequently its own political interests on the one hand and, on the other hand, trying to gain the trust and faith of the Egyptian youth, thereby feeding into the idealistic image of America as the epitome of freedom and democracy. Naturally, the youth who instigated the revolution expected the Obama administration to legitimize its position on the side of the people and act as an outside pressure that would help them fight their battle and realize their dreams. However, the response of the Obama administration was both insipid and frustrating to the Tahrir youth, who in turn heavily criticized the United States for its position on the revolution. Ironically, the position of the United States was so ambiguous that it did not please the Egyptian regime either, which was perceived as having forfeited the support it has unconditionally provided the Egyptian government throughout the past thirty years of Mubarak's reign.

In this chapter I offer a reading of people's criticism of the ambiguous position of the United States as manifested in jokes, songs, slogans, and graffiti that directly targeted America and exposed its shortcomings. The analysis of such popular reactions sheds light on the Egyptian public's perceptions of United States foreign policies in the Middle East with particular focus on Egypt. It also highlights how popular responses to the Mubarak regime or the United States administration were often related in ways that emphasized the tripartite relationship referred to before as well as the convergence of politics and popular culture. The chapter follows a timeline of simultaneous official positions and popular reactions and responses involving the Egyptian government, the U.S. government, and the Egyptian people. The timeline will cover the critical period leading up to January 25, 2011, since roughly 2009, the eighteen days of the revolution, and concluding with the first anniversary in 2012. The analysis will highlight the power of peaceful resistance, which is one of the important tenets upon which the revolution was based, and the role of popular culture toward realizing that end.

The Intersection of Politics and Popular Culture

In analyzing the Egyptian response to the United States position on the revolution, I rely on the Birmingham school's understanding of popular culture as a key site of political contestation and negotiation. There are a number of determining factors that characterized the January 25 revolution and that led to the success of its first wave, which ended with the ousting of Hosni Mubarak and his government. First, Egyptian youth mobilized unprecedented numbers of Egyptians who took to Tahrir Square and other squares in other cities in Egypt, calling for freedom, dignity, and social justice, and demanding the removal of the regime. Second, "the people" from different social, economic, and ideological backgrounds were awakened and united, ultimately creating Stuart Hall's concept of the "popular democratic cultural force." And finally, "the people" took to the streets to demonstrate their anger and frustration against the "power bloc" in a peaceful as well as an artistic manner through various manifestations of popular culture that included songs, slogans, street performances, graffiti, jokes, and so on. This cultural apparatus was, and continues to be, the people's way of resisting the domination of the power bloc through reconstructing a "hidden transcript" of popular cultural and artistic production.

Significantly, this was not the first time that the people's democratic voice was manifested through mass culture. In *Ordinary Egyptians*, Ziad Fahmy maps out a similar scenario during the 1919 national revolution against British occupation of Egypt, when demonstrators chanted songs in colloquial Arabic, publicly insulting Britain and demanding an end to its imperialist project in Egypt. Fahmy explains that

> the efficacy of the new mass media and their potential for mass mobilization were best demonstrated during times of national crisis. The 1906 Dinshaway incident and the 1919 Revolution in particular reveal how all forms of mass media functioned together to effectively document, memorialize, celebrate, and mobilize on a national scale. The growth of popular Egyptian mass culture was the pivotal factor in the popularization and dissemination of an Egyptian national identity.[9]

The January 25 revolution witnessed a similar redefinition of Egyptian identity based on the ability of the people to organize themselves in their struggle against a power bloc represented through an authoritarian regime that had been supported by the United States during the entire thirty years of its governance. The ability to overcome this power bloc, forcing it to recognize the power of the people, has indeed led to a redefinition of Egyptian identity perhaps best exemplified through the slogan "Raise your head up high / you're Egyptian," which was heard on the streets of Egypt for the first time on February 11, 2011, the night Mubarak stepped down.

From Cairo Speech to Pseudo-Democracy

In June 2009, a few months after his election, President Barack Obama gave his promised speech to the Muslim world from Cairo University in Egypt. The visit, which was an attempt to mend the relationship between America and the Muslim world, was heralded as a new beginning and was generally well received, although with "guarded optimism."[10] The young Egyptian students listening to Obama's words that day, glorifying America as a nation "born out of revolution against an empire [... and] founded upon the ideal that all are created equal, and [...] have shed blood and struggled for centuries to give meaning to those words— within [its] borders, and around the world," identified with his ideas of freedom and liberty.[11] Obama's words certainly resonated with that which young Arabs all over the region yearned for: "But I do have an unyielding belief that all people yearn for certain things: the ability to speak your mind and have a say in how you are governed; confidence in the rule of law and the equal administration of justice; government that is transparent and doesn't steal from the people; the freedom to live as you choose. Those are not just American ideas, they are human rights, and that is why we will support them everywhere."[12] Most Arab intellectuals and journalists, both supporters and detractors of Obama, described his speech as "honeyed" or "sugary," explaining that "the principles outlined in Obama's speech have to be backed up by action. In other words, Obama will be judged on what he achieves on the ground rather than his skilled oratory."[13] This was also reflected in the Egyptian popular reaction, which regarded Obama with an undeniable measure of hope but remained skeptical as to what he could achieve in reality. The popular Egyptian singer Shaaban Abdel Rahim translated these sentiments in his famous song about Obama in which he compared him to his predecessor, George Bush:

> I can see the smile
> And the happiness on the faces
> I just wish Obama is not the same as Bush
> Bush, damn him, messed us up for days and years
> Obama, people think, will turn out to be Saladin

What can Obama do about the catastrophes which Bush and his
    father left behind
They haven't left a place undestroyed[14]

Abdel Rahim goes on to warn people that they need to be careful where
they place their hopes so that their dreams do not turn into nightmares.

Of course, two years after the Cairo speech, not much had changed
where U.S. foreign policy was concerned, and what was once received
with a guarded measure of optimism was later rejected in full disappointment. Between 2009 and 2011 the United States proved over and again
that while it preaches one thing, it often does the opposite. On most of
the issues raised during Obama's infamous Cairo speech, the Obama administration adopted a double-standard position similar to previous administrations when it came to protecting its interests at the expense of
professed principles and ideals. Its failure in the Israeli–Palestinian conflict and similar failure in Iraq and Afghanistan; its position on Iran, and
particularly the Iranian presidential elections in 2009; and its tepid reactions to the atrocities of Arab authoritarian regimes were all indications
of the failure of the U.S. government once more to meet the expectations of the Arab people, and the disappointment of the latter particularly in the Obama administration for betraying the global role America
always professes to have. In a series of cartoons published in *Al-Ahram
Weekly* newspaper in December 2010, a month before the January 25 revolution, Egyptian cartoonists Gomaa and Ossama, projected the popular image of America at the end of 2010. The cartoons reflect the failure
of the United States to fulfill its promises on all fronts. Gomaa, for example, shows Obama sticking out of the Israeli prime minister's pocket
and raising a warning hand at the latter. An amused, full of himself Netanyahu, looks down upon the admonishing Obama, reflecting an Israel
confident in its power over the United States despite Obama's actions.[15]
Ossama, on the other hand, shows an Uncle Sam preparing to leave
behind a bloodied Iraq divided among Sunnis, Shias, and Kurds, having
obviously failed in implementing the United States' pseudo-mission of
democracy in Iraq.[16] Similarly, Gomaa portrays a diabolic Uncle Sam before and after the release of the WikiLeaks documents that incriminated the United States for violating the very human rights it promised
to uphold in Iraq and Afghanistan.[17] It is worth mentioning that these
cartoons and many others, in fact, were published in a state-owned newspaper that allowed the publication of such critical material as long as it

avoided criticizing the Egyptian government and its supportive role toward American practices in the Middle East.

Mohamed ElBaradei, former director of the International Atomic Energy Agency, explains America's loss of credibility in the Middle East and attributes it to the refusal of the United States to take a clear stance on unequivocal issues:

> If you would like to know why the United States does not have credibility in the Middle East, that is precisely the answer. People were absolutely disappointed in the way you reacted to Egypt's last election. You reaffirmed their belief that you are applying a double standard for your friends, and siding with an authoritarian regime just because you think it represents your interests. We are staring at social disintegration, economic stagnation, political repression, and we do not hear anything from you, the Americans, or, for that matter, from the Europeans.[18]

In referring to the November 2010 parliamentary elections in Egypt where the ruling National Democratic Party then left the opposition with only 3 percent of the seats, ElBaradei condemned the U.S. government whose position on the clearly fraudulent results was "dismay."[19] The United States concluded its statement on the elections by attempting, as usual, to appease both the government and the people: "The United States has a longstanding partnership with the government and the people of Egypt, rooted in common interests and shared aspirations for the future. We look forward to continuing to work with the Egyptian government and with Egypt's vibrant civil society to help them achieve their political, social, and economic aspirations."[20]

Such lukewarm, equivocal reactions have been typical of the U.S. government; however, this time it was quite audacious and very ironic after almost a decade of nonstop talk about implementing democracy in the Middle East. As Robert Fisk put it in his commentary on the events of January 25 in Egypt and the position of the United States toward it, it was a "failure of moral leadership . . . resulting in a [blight] of history [that] will now involve a U.S. president who held out his hand to the Islamic world and then clenched his fist when it fought a dictatorship and demanded democracy."[21] It certainly went against all previous talk on the rule of the law, justice, and freedom that Obama extensively detailed in his Cairo speech. As ElBaradei put it, "well, frankly, I was dismayed that all [the American administration] could say is that it was dismayed. The word was hardly adequate to express the way the Egyptian people felt."[22]

The Revolution: January 2011

As the Tunisians poured into the streets of the country in unprecedented numbers, calling out "The people demand the removal of the regime," and while the government was violently cracking down on the protesters, the U.S. government urged all parties to remain calm, calling upon the Tunisian government to "hold free and fair elections in the near future that reflect the true will and aspirations of the Tunisian people."[23] The United States—and, for that matter, the West—refrained from making its position clear until the ousting of Zine El Abidine Ben Ali, when it became obvious that the will of the people had prevailed. Only then did Obama declare: "And tonight, let us be clear: The United States of America stands with the people of Tunisia, and supports the democratic aspirations of all people."[24]

On the same day, January 25, 2011, in Cairo and other major cities in Egypt, protesters went out in great numbers, heading toward Tahrir Square in a peaceful march calling for "bread, freedom, and social justice." What started as peaceful, though, soon turned into violent demonstrations as the police resorted to violence to disperse the people, and the Egyptian government responded by banning gatherings and cutting off communication channels. For the first few days, when it was still unclear whether the Egyptian government would be able to crush the demonstrations, the U.S. government continued its support of the Mubarak regime despite statements on universal human rights, peaceful assembly, and opportunities for reform intended to appease the Egyptian people. In answer to a question on whether Washington was concerned about the stability of the Egyptian government and the demonstrations in Egypt, Secretary of State Hillary Clinton, after calling on all parties to exercise restraint, responded, "our assessment is that the Egyptian Government is stable and is looking for ways to respond to the legitimate needs and interests of the Egyptian people."[25] Her answer echoed the same statement made less than a month earlier regarding Tunisia, and it certainly enraged the people.

ElBaradei criticized the use of the word "stability," bluntly accusing the United States of supporting the corrupt Egyptian regime and of exercising double standards when it comes to protecting its interests: "What did she mean by stable, and at what price? Is it the stability of 29 years of 'emergency' laws, a president with imperial power for 30 years, a Parliament that is almost a mockery, a judiciary that is not independent? Is that what you call stability? I am sure it is not. And I am positive that it is not the standard you apply to other countries."[26]

Chomsky satirically comments on the litheness of the word "stability," comparing it to the way the United States uses the word "democracy": "Stability is—it's kind of like democracy. Stability means conformity to our interests."[27] Hinting again at the double-standard policies of the United States, he explains: "When Iran tries to expand its influence in Afghanistan and Iraq, neighboring countries, that's called 'destabilizing.' It's part of the threat of Iran. It's destabilizing the region. On the other hand, when the U.S. invades those countries, occupies them, half destroys them, that's to achieve stability."[28] Similar statements on stability in Egypt were repeated by Robert Gibbs, who, when asked whether the White House believed the Egyptian government was stable, answered affirmatively; he added, in answer to whether the United States still backs Mubarak, "Egypt is a strong ally."[29] The same statement was emphasized by Obama, "Egypt's been an ally of ours on a lot of critical issues: They made peace with Israel; President Mubarak has been very helpful on a range of tough issues in the Middle East."[30] Vice President Joe Biden reiterated the same statement, declaring, "I would not refer to [Mubarak] as a dictator."[31]

Back in Tahrir Square, demonstrators responded by condemning the Mubarak regime and denouncing the intervention of the United States, especially after hearing Obama's warning to protesters against resorting to violence at a time when they were defending themselves against the brutality of the Egyptian security forces. Slogans and banners rejecting the interference of the United States in Egyptian affairs filled the square as protesters' chanted "No to America / Egypt for Egyptians," "No Mubarak, No Suleiman / No more agents for the Americans," and held signs in written in English that accused America of betraying the protesters: "USA, Why you support Dectatour."[32] And, whereas the message of the United States to the Egyptians was vague and failed to meet their expectations, the popular response of the protesters was very clear, leaving no doubt as to people's real sentiments toward U.S. foreign policy and its close ties to Mubarak's repressive regime. Significantly, people perceived Mubarak as merely a puppet of the United States. Indeed, one of the pictures which appeared in Tahrir Square was a poster of Mubarak, showing a likeness to the Obama campaign posters but with a caption that read "No you can't."[33] This sentiment was further emphasized by the infamous slogan "Oh Mubarak you coward, you agent of the Americans," which directly accused him of being a traitor who betrayed his own people. The use of both picture and slogan are quite interesting. The picture is a reference to Obama's broken promises and people's disillusionment, whereas the slogan is a reference to the late president Anwar Sadat, who was also popularly perceived as an American accomplice especially after the Camp David Accords, which estranged Egypt from the rest of the Arab world. Both picture and slogan indicate a public perception that can be traced back to the increased presence of America in Egypt and the Middle East, particularly toward the second half of the twentieth century. More importantly, they point to one of the major grievances in the relationship between Egypt—and, for that matter, the Arab world—and the United States, and that is the Israeli–Palestinian conflict. In an interesting cartoon by Jihad Waleed (solicited through a competition held by *Al Jazeera* in January–February 2011), Mubarak, in one of his last speeches during the eighteen days of the revolution, is seen running out of battery, significantly made in Israel, while he himself is perceived as an American stooge.[34] The reference is of course to a regime that is running out of steam and practically seeing its last days. Ironically, though, when asked whether it was time for Mubarak to step down, Vice President Biden answered: "No, I think the time has come for President Mubarak to begin to move in the direction [...]—to be more responsive to some of the needs of the people out there."[35]

Tahrir City: The Orderly Transition

When Frank Wisner, the U.S. envoy, arrived in Cairo on February 1, Tahrir was in full swing as the protesters took over the square and set up an alternative micro city. In the absence of appropriate artistic tools that would express people's frustration against the regime and the supporting world powers, it was natural for protesters to resort to a repertoire of national songs that dated back to the 1950–70s era. Many of the popular songs that were heard in the square were produced in another context yet were very relevant to the moment. Indeed, Wisner's proclamations that "President Mubarak's continued leadership is critical: it's his opportunity to write his own legacy" was met with sarcasm and ridicule, especially after the Obama administration tried to distance it-self from Wisner's remarks, claiming that they were made in a personal capacity.[36] The famous song of the duo Ahmed Fouad Negm and Sheikh Imam, "Sharaft ya Nixon Baba" (Welcome Father Nixon), was heard in the square as protesters gathered at night and wiled away the long, cold hours by singing popular national songs:

> You've honored us Father Nixon
> O you of Watergate They gave you so many honors
> These exploiters of the people.
> They festooned the widest path
> From Ras-El-Tine to Mecca
> So that from there you could go to Accra
> And that it could be said he made the pilgrimage.
> It was a real traveling circus,
> Your benediction Parents of the Prophet.[37]

The famous song, dating back to Richard Nixon's visit to Egypt in 1974, was arguably used to parody Wisner's visit. The reference is of course to the corruption of the U.S. government embodied through the figures of Nixon and Wisner, especially after Robert Fisk revealed that Wisner is employed by a law firm that works for Mubarak's government.[38] Despite distancing itself from Wisner's remarks, the harm to Obama's adminis-tration was beyond repair because people realized that he was simply out-lining an established policy, that of stability over democracy, despite proclamations otherwise. This was clearly the message that was passed on to the youth in Tahrir Square, who in turn responded by further sati-rizing the United States. "Cowboy Dynamo," the famous song by the late Egyptian poet Fouad Haddad, written in the 1960s during his im-prisonment, was heard in Tahrir city as the protesters made fun of the United States and its intentions:

> Cowboy dynamo
> Herding his sheep
> Hung a banner across the countryside:
> Let America
> Colonize you—
> Honorable woman with an honorable cause.[39]

Indeed the sentiments of the people seemed to echo what ElBaradei put in a nutshell:

The United States and its allies have spent the better part of the last decade, at a cost of hundreds of billions of dollars and countless lives, fighting wars to establish democracy in Iraq and Afghanistan. Now that the youth of Cairo, armed with nothing but Facebook and the power of their convictions, have drawn millions into the street to demand a true Egyptian democracy, it would be absurd to continue to tacitly endorse the rule of a regime that has lost its own people's trust.[40]

The undertone of sarcasm detected in ElBaradei's comment echoed a public reaction not just in Cairo but worldwide, where the United States became the butt of jokes. The Brazilian cartoonist Carlos Latuff made fun of both Mubarak and Obama, showing an archaic-looking Mubarak glued to the presidential seat, resisting any attempts of removal, and behind him, standing in support, is Obama with a pot of glue at his feet.[41] Likewise, Stephen Hoban, on *Political Comedy*, made fun of Obama's reactions to the revolution. Joking about how hard it is to write comedy on events happening around the world, he explains: "If the President, whose job it is to have opinions about these events, can't come up with a coherent response to developments in Egypt for a week, think about how hard it must be for comedians to react immediately, to predict what the unformed public opinion will be, and to do it funny."[42] Similarly, Imran Garda sarcastically provides a template for U.S. foreign policy based on its similar reactions to the different revolutions and uprisings in the Arab region. Assuming a mocking tone, he impersonates a spokesman for the United States government: "We continue to monitor the situation and are very concerned about recent events in _____. We call for restraint on both sides. We urge President/Prime Minister/King _____ to facilitate dialogue and provide concrete steps towards a peaceful resolution."[43]

However, in spite of the general perception, both nationally and internationally, that the United States was obviously siding with the Mubarak regime at the expense of the protesters, the Egyptian government was not happy with the reaction of the Obama administration, which in itself was a further indication of the ambiguity of that position. Despite statements from the Obama administration that it was not siding with either party—"this isn't a choice between the government and the people of Egypt," as Robert Gibbs put it[44]—the Egyptian government understood that times were changing. With increasing remarks about "an orderly transition," the Egyptian government felt that the United States was forfeiting the unconditional support it had provided Mubarak for the last thirty years. When Christiane Amanpour asked Mubarak, in an exclusive interview on February 3, 2011, whether he felt betrayed by the United States' calls for him to step down sooner rather than later, he said he had told Obama: "You don't understand the Egyptian culture and what would happen if I step down now."[45] In his last couple of speeches, Mubarak would even go a step further, hinting at a foreign conspiracy involving the Tahrir protesters. His newly appointed vice president, Omar Suleiman, former chief of intelligence, would in fact state it bluntly to Amanpour, claiming, "for sure, these people have been supported by foreigners," adding, "what I hear from President Obama is that he is supporting the people."[46] On February 10, 2011, the day before he stepped down, Mubarak declared that he "will not accept ever [...] to listen to the talks coming from abroad, [whomever] it's coming from or for whatever reason or pretexts or excuses."[47] Feeding into people's anger, the Egyptian state media propagated more lies about foreign conspiracies and the manipulation of protesters by giving them one hundred dollars each and a meal from Kentucky Fried Chicken if they would agree to go to Tahrir Square. The "Kentucky Dudes," as the protesters referred to themselves, nonchalantly responded to the lies by singing "We Are the Kentucky Dudes":

> They called us the Kentucky dudes
> They said we will remove the eagle in the flag
> and put a chicken in its place
> ... We want Kentucky in all the squares
> we want Kentucky to be the official sponsor of the revolution
> they called us the Kentucky dudes
> and we were only sacrificing our lives for you Egypt[48]

The popular response of the people in Tahrir Square showed an instinctive awareness of the political game being played at their expense, and they were determined to beat it. Their message was clear: the times have changed. Indeed, as Obama put it, "through thousands of years, Egypt has known many moments of transformation. The voices of the Egyptian people tell us that this is one of those moments; this is one of those times."[49] But the people also knew that these were hollow words; and that in reality the protesters were on their own. As Shadi Hamid put it, "people want moral support; they want to hear words of encouragement. Right now, they don't have that. They feel the world doesn't care and the world is working against them."[50] Indeed, people realized that change needed to come from within them, and to many this was a moment of illumination as it forced people from across different social, economic, ideological strata to face up to themselves and to realize that if they wanted the removal of the regime, they had to come together as one voice and one collective action.

In "Once Upon a Time," the popular poet Amin Haddad addresses this change in people's attitude. The poem, which was written in 2004 to condemn the United States' invasion of Iraq and the passivity of the Arab nations in the face of such aggression, was rewritten during the January 25, 2011, revolution.[51] The new version starts off on the same note as the earlier one, criticizing the United States and Israel:

Story has it that . . . that what?
they stole our country, the bad guys
Story has it that once upon a time
they stole our country . . . the Americans
Story has it that generation after another
they stole Palestine . . . the Israelis
Story has it grandchildren . . . that America has invaded Baghdad
Story has it . . . believe it or not that America is striking mercilessly
They'll storm Baghdad by the afternoon
And by sunset they would be in Egypt.[52]

In the original version, however, Haddad makes fun of the passivity of the Arabs and their inability to stand up to the United States and Israel. It is the same note of defeat we hear in Shaaban Abdel Rahim's song on Obama referred to earlier, when he claims that the Arabs are waiting for Obama to rectify the policies of former administrations: "Arabs are waiting for Obama to take their hand, to protect them / But mind you Arabs, neither Bush nor Obama will ever think of you / Only your hands will protect you."[53] In a way, Abdel Rahim's song foretells the advent of the Arab Spring and the eminent change that will happen to people in different parts of the Arab world. Indeed, the second version of Amin Haddad's poem "Once Upon a Time" takes a different turn when it comes to people's reaction against authoritarian regimes and Western hegemony. Haddad salutes the rebirth of the Egyptians and the Arab nation:

The Story goes that the people finally held the light with their
    own hands
that once upon a time whatever the people wanted they got
The story goes that generation after another Egypt was born in
    Tahrir Square
It is said children the sun of the revolution emanated from the
    martyrs
oh freedom, ours is an Arab revolution
Dawn, noon, sunset, afternoon across Tunisia, Libya, Syria, Egypt.[54]

Conclusion: A Year Later, January 25, 2012

In her memoir, *Cairo: My City, Our Revolution*, Ahdaf Soueif meditates
on how easy it was for the revolution to turn into a violent spectacle had
not Egyptians from across the spectrum insisted on keeping it peaceful.
She explains, rightfully so, that it was a struggle between "a tenacious,
brutal and corrupt government, using all the apparatus of the state, and
a great and varied body of citizens, armed with nothing but words and
music and legitimacy and hope."[55] Indeed, with the coming together of
the people, a "nobrow" sociocultural space was created through which
Egyptians were able not only to conquer an autocratic regime and force
it to step down but, more importantly, to conquer the divide created by
that regime to weaken this body of citizenship and keep it apart for thirty
years. I would argue that it is this particular aspect of the revolution—
the realization of the power *of* the people—that has instigated a very personal and unprecedented response from people worldwide, in a way
forcing their governments to acknowledge this newly awakened empathy and solidarity on behalf of their citizens toward the protesters in
Tahrir Square. It is this moment of affinity that would later on lead to
similar movements and uprisings from neighboring Syria, to Spain, and
across the Atlantic, giving, in Soueif's words, "voice and power to civilian citizens everywhere."[56]

Obama's words to the American people, therefore, on February 11,
2011, the day Mubarak stepped down, in which he professed that "the
United States will continue to be a friend and partner to Egypt. . . . We
stand ready to provide whatever assistance is necessary—and asked for—
to pursue a credible transition to a democracy," raise some important
questions.[57] Foremost of which is, who is Obama representing when he

talks about the "United States" and uses the pronoun "we"? The American workers protesting in Madison, Wisconsin, and drawing the support of the protesters in Tahrir Square?[58] Or the people occupying Zuccotti Park, marching in New York City and calling out to "Turn Wall Street into Tahrir Square"?[59] Or is he simply reiterating the same stale position of his and previous administrations, once more offering empty promises to "the people"? In fact, who is Obama addressing when he claims that the United States will continue being a friend and partner to Egypt? The Egyptian people? Or the present Egyptian administration represented through the Supreme Council of Armed Forces (SCAF)? What kind of partnership is he referring to, and partners in what? Most importantly, what kind of assistance, and at the expense of what? People's lives? The tear gas canisters and cartridges fired against the protesters in Tahrir Square in January 2011 and at every renewed clash between the protesters and the SCAF throughout the past year since the fall of Mubarak's regime have been made in the United States and authorized to be sold to Egypt at a time when the abuse of the Egyptian security forces against protesters was, and remains, common knowledge worldwide. In a cartoon commenting on the events of November 2011, popularly referred to as the Mohamed Mahmoud events or the second wave of the revolution, Carlos Latuff shows an Egyptian security officer carrying Uncle Sam's hat full of deadly CR gas canisters, "proudly made in United States," and hurling them at protesters.[60] Later in the same month, November 2011, a group of workers from the port of Suez would refuse to allow a U.S. shipment of lethal tear gas into Egypt. The Egyptian government, however, would intercede and order the shipment to be released. Resonating responses of anger would appear in different forms all over Egypt. Graffiti stencils showing the price of one imported tear gas canister as equal to twenty-five dollars would appear on the streets of Cairo alongside calls for the downfall of America's agents.[61]

In a comparison between Eastern Europe in 1989 and Egypt in 2011 and the role of America in both movements, Pierre Tristam argues that this time around the United States is certainly on the wrong side of history, having lost the respect of the people and with it any possible influence over the development of events: "You don't see on Tahrir Square, as you did in Tiananmen Square 22 years ago, anyone brandishing replicas of the Statue of Liberty. You won't even see Barack Obama's face on placards and mugs, as you did in Cairo two years ago, when he delivered another one of what, in retrospect, was an empty-hope speech about the West's relations with the Muslim world."[62]

Instead, what we see today in Tahrir Square and other public spaces in Egypt are warning messages from the people to the U.S. government to stop interfering in Egyptian affairs.[63] However, such calls as "We will not be ruled by America" are not only meant for the U.S. government, but, more importantly, such messages target the current Egyptian administration, which is perceived now as Mubarak's alter ego and another American stooge. The tripartite relationship between the current Egyptian ruling authority, the U.S. government, and the Egyptian people continues. No more was this complex relationship clearly manifested as when the SCAF decided to crack down on foreign-based nongovernmental organizations in Egypt including United States election-monitoring and democracy-promoting groups, raiding their offices, confiscating computers and documents, and arresting forty-three civil society workers, including nineteen Americans. The U.S. government responded by threatening to cut off military and economic aid to Egypt, which in turn forced the Egyptian authorities to allow the American civil workers on trial to depart the country. This latest episode of the "Tom and Jerry"–like relationship is not lost on the Egyptian people, who have been conscious for some time of the strained relationship between the Egyptian and the U.S. administrations, even prior to the January 25 revolution, especially with the increased criticism of the United States on the violation of human rights in Egypt and the absence of democracy. It is another indication of the kind of game played by both administrations at the expense of the people who understand that proclamations such as the Egyptian prime minister's—"Egypt will not kneel down to anybody"—and threats from the U.S. government to cut off aid are merely hollow words.[64] At the end of the day, neither will risk severing that relationship. However, as the game continues and with the change of the political scene in Egypt, the people are becoming key players. They are determined to protect what they fought for and achieved in the eighteen days of the first wave of the January 25 revolution. A year later, on the same day, while calling out "down with military rule in Egypt," the Kentucky dudes were simultaneously sending out messages that the fried chicken meals are ready to be picked up in Tahrir Square! Interestingly, the shift that people have undergone, becoming a "popular democratic cultural force," cannot be disregarded and will not be easily thwarted either, a fact that both the Egyptian and the U.S. government are starting to realize, and it goes toward determining their actions now as well as redefining their future relations with this newly awakened force.

Notes

1. Fast-food franchise chains like McDonalds, Pizza Hut, and Hardees are very popular in Egypt. Kentucky Fried Chicken is even more famous because of its logo. Colonel Harland Sanders' visage is recognized all over Egypt and is often parodied in advertisements.

2. Hillary Clinton, Keynote Address at the National Democratic Institute's 2011 Democracy Awards Dinner, November 7, 2011, http://www.state.gov/secretary /20092013clinton/rm/2011/11/176750.htm (May 10, 2012).

3. Noam Chomsky, Interview on *Democracy Now*, February 2, 2011, http://www .democracynow.org/blog/2011/2/2/part_2_noam_chomsky_this_is_the_most_re markable_regional_uprising_that_i_can_remember (May 11, 2012).

4. Ibid.

5. For further discussion on this point, see Mounira Soliman, "The Image of America in Egyptian Cinema: A Socio-political Reading," in *Liberty and Justice: America and the Middle East Conference Proceedings*, ed. Patrick McGreevy (Beirut: American University of Beirut, 2008), 369–79.

6. Nazmi Al-Shalabi, Marwan Obeidat, and Shadi Neimneh, "The Reception of American Culture in the Middle East after "The Arab Spring," *Canadian Social Science* 7, no. 5 (2011): 156–61.

7. Noam Chomsky, Interview on *Democracy Now*, February 2, 2011.

8. Ibid.

9. Ziad Fahmy, *Ordinary Egyptians: Creating the Modern Nation through Popular Culture* (Palo Alto, Calif.: Stanford University Press, 2011). 172.

10. Layla Al-Zubaidi and Doreen Khoury, "Guarded Optimism in the Arab World," *Heinrick Boll Stuftung: Middle East*, June 15, 2009, http://lb.boell.org/sites /default/files/downloads/Al-Zubaidi_Khoury-Guarded_Optimism_in_the _Arab_World.pdf (November 23, 2015).

11. Barack Obama, Cairo speech, June 4, 2009, http://www.guardian.co.uk /world/2009/jun/04/barack-obama-keynote-speech-egypt (May 3, 2012).

12. Ibid.

13. Al-Zubaidi and Khoury, "Guarded Optimism in the Arab World."

14. My translation. Shaaban Abdel Rehim, Obama Song, http://youtu.be/jT5-D1OPABo (May 3, 2012).

15. Gomaa, *Al-Ahram Weekly Online*, December 16–22, 2010, http://gomaatoon .com/toon_archive.aspx (May 3, 2012).

16. Ossama, *Al-Ahram Weekly Online*, December 16–22, 2010, http://gomaatoon .com/toon_archive.aspx (May 3, 2012).

17. Gomaa, *Al-Ahram Weekly Online*, December 9–15, 2010, http://gomaatoon .com/toon_archive.aspx (May 3, 2012).

18. Mohamed ElBaradei, "The Return of the Challenger," *Newsweek*, January 26, 2011, http://www.newsweek.com/mohamed-elbaradei-return-challenger-66789 (May 3, 2012).

19. Ibid.

20. "Egypt's Parliamentary Elections," U.S. Department of State website, November 29, 2010, http://www.state.gov/r/pa/prs/ps/2010/11/152097.htm (May 11, 2012).

21. Robert Fisk, "Secular and Devout. Rich and Poor. They Marched Together with One Goal," *Independent,* February 2, 2011, http://www.independent.co.uk /opinion/commentators/fisk/robert-fisk-secular-and-devout-rich-and-poor -they-marched-together-with-one-goal-2201504.html (May 3, 2012).

22. ElBaradei, "The Return of the Challenger."

23. "Obama Calls for Free and Fair Tunisia Elections," Ahram Online, January 14, 2011, http://english.ahram.org.eg/NewsContent/2/8/3900/World/Region/ Obama-calls-for-free-and-fair-Tunisia-elections.aspx (November 22, 2015).

24. Barack Obama, "State of the Union 2011: President Obama's Full Speech," *ABC News,* January 25, 2011, http://abcnews.go.com/Politics/State_of_the_Union /state-of-the-union-2011-full-transcript/story?id=12759395#.T6KwE8Xjr7c (May 3, 2012).

25. "United States Urges Restraint in Egypt, Says Government Stable," *Reuters,* January 25, 2011, http://af.reuters.com/article/topNews/idAFJOE70O0KF20110125 (May 3, 2012).

26. ElBaradei, "The Return of the Challenger."

27. Noam Chomsky, Interview on *Democracy Now,* May 11, 2011, http://www .democracynow.org/seo/2011/5/11/noam_chomsky_the_us_and_its (May 3, 2012).

28. Ibid.

29. "Press Gaggle by Robert Gibbs en route Green Bay, Wisconsin," January 26, 2011, http://www.whitehouse.gov/the-press-office/2011/01/26/press-gaggle- robert-gibbs-en-route-green-bay-wisconsin (May 3, 2012).

30. "Your Interview with the President 2011," January 27, 2011), http://www .youtube.com/watch?v=nqoeuIlaxRc#t=16m45s (May 3, 2012).

31. Hao Li, "Joe Biden: Mubarak is no dictator and should not step down," ibtimes, January 28, 2011, http://www.ibtimes.com/joe-biden-mubarak-no-dictator -should-not-step-down-video-full-text-260929 (Dec 23, 2015).

32. Glenn Greenwald, "Obama's Man in Cairo," *Salon,* February 8, 2011, http:// www.salon.com/2011/02/08/suleiman/ (May 3, 2012).

33. "The Egyptians Understand Obama," *Rush Limbaugh Show* [transcript], February 15, 2011, http://www.rushlimbaugh.com/daily/2011/02/15/the_egyptians _understand_obama_just_ask_cnn_s_nic_robertson (May 3, 2012).

34. Jihad Waleed, "Egyptian Dictatorship, Made in USA," *MRZine,* February 9, 2011, http://mrzine.monthlyreview.org/2011/waleed090211.html (May 3, 2012).

35. Hao Li, "Joe Biden: Mubarak is no dictator and should not step down," ibtimes, January 28, 2011, (Dec 23, 2015).

36. Julian Borger, "The Egyptian Crisis: Another Day, Another Two United States Policies," *Guardian,* February 6, 2011, http://www.guardian.co.uk/world /julian-borger-global-security-blog/2011/feb/06/egypt-obama-administration (May 3, 2012).

37. My translation. Ahmed Fouad Negm, *Al A'mal Al She'raiyah Al Kamilah* [The complete poetic works] (Cairo: Merit Publishing House, 2005), 474–76.

38. Robert Fisk, "United States Envoy's Business Link to Egypt," *Independent*, February 7, 2011, http://www.independent.co.uk/news/world/americas/us -envoys-business-link-to-egypt-2206329.html (May 3, 2012).

39. My translation. Fouad Haddad, *Dīwān al-arājūz yaḍribu ʿalá al-wajīʿah wa-yulāqī ʿalá al-ṭibṭāb* [The trickster] (Cairo: Sina Publishing House, 1987).

40. Mohamed ElBaradei, "The Next Step for Egypt's Opposition," *New York Times*, February 10, 2011, http://www.nytimes.com/2011/02/11/opinion/11elbaradei .html (May 10, 2012).

41. Carlos Latuff, "Obama Policy on Egypt: Back the Dictator," February 9, 2011, http://twitpic.com/3xydm8 (May 10, 2012).

42. Stephen Hoban, "Making Jokes about Egypt," *Splitsider*, February 4, 2011, http://splitsider.com/2011/02/making-jokes-about-egypt/ (May 10, 2012).

43. Imran Garda, "Templates for responding to excesses of an ally," *Al Jazeera*, January 31, 2011, http://blogs.aljazeera.net/americas/2011/01/31/templates-responding-excesses-ally (May 10, 2012).

44. "Press Gaggle by Robert Gibbs."

45. Christiane Amanpour, "Mubarak: If I Resign Today There Will Be Chaos," *ABC News*, February 3, 2011, http://abcnews.go.com/International/egypt-abc -news-christiane-amanpour-exclusive-interview-president/story?id=12833673# .T6vTLsXjr7d> (May 10, 2012).

46. Ibid.

47. "TRANSCRIPT: Hosni Mubarak TV address to Egypt," *CBC News*, February 10, 2011, http://www.cbc.ca/news/world/story/2011/02/10/f-egypt-mubarak -transcript.html (May 10, 2012).

48. Lefty-M, *Kentucky New Song*, http://www.youtube.com/watch?v=42h3m _GlubI (May 3, 2012).

49. "Remarks by the President on the Situation in Egypt," White House Office of the Press Secretary, February 1, 2011, http://www.whitehouse.gov/the-press -office/2011/02/01/remarks-president-situation-egypt (May 10, 2012).

50. Quoted in Heather Hurlburt, "Five Things to Understand about the Egyptian Riots," *New Republic* January 28, 2011, http://www.tnr.com/blog/jonathan -cohn/82416/five-things-you-should-know-about-the-riots-in-egypt (May 10, 2012).

51. Amin Haddad, *Fī al-mawt ḥanʿīsh* [In death we live] (Cairo: Merit Publishing House, 2004).

52. My translation. Amin Haddad, "Yohka Anna," [Once upon a time] http:// www.youtube.com/watch?v=eubYlovN3ko (May 10, 2012).

53. Rehim, Obama Song.

54. My translation. Haddad, "Yohka Anna."

55. Ahdaf Soueif, *Cairo: My City, Our Revolution* (London: Bloomsbury Publishing, 2012), 179.

56. Ibid.

57. "Remarks by the President on the Situation in Egypt."

58. "Egypt Supports Wisconsin Workers," http://twitpic.com/419nfm (May 11, 2012).

59. Andre Spatz, "Occupy Wall Street Protest Joined by Unions-Manhattan," October 5, 2011, http://www.demotix.com/photo/858694/occupy-wall-street-protest-joined-unions-manhattan (May 11, 2012); and "Occupy Wall Street—Beware GOP the American Autumn Is Rising," *Politicalmonkey2010,* October 8, 2011, http://politicalmonkey2010.wordpress.com/2011/10/08/occupy-wall-street-beware-gop-the-american-autumn-is-rising/ (May 11, 2012).

60. Carlos Latuff, "CR Gas, Proudly made in the USA," http://haimbresheeth .com/gaza/2011/11/24/ (May 11, 2012).

61. Hossam el-Hamalawy, "We're Not Leaving Until Mubarak Leaves," https://libcom.org/library/"we're-not-leaving-until-mubarak-leaves" (Dec 23, 2015); and Hossam el-Hamalawy, "Down with America's Agents," November 21, 2011, http://www.flickr.com/photos/elhamalawy/6380119383/in/photostream/ (May 11, 2012).

62. Pierre Tristam, "The Egyptian Revolution in the Context of U.S. Policy in the Middle East," *About News,* http://middleeast.about.com/od/egypt/a/us -egyptian-revolution.htm (May 11, 2012).

63. Hossam el-Hamalawy, "We Will Not Be Ruled by America," November 25, 2011, http://www.flickr.com/photos/elhamalawy/6400958721/ (May 11, 2012).

64. Shaimaa Behery, "News Analysis: NGOs Case Brings Tension to Egyptian-U.S. Relations," *English.news.cn,* February 11, 2012), http://news.xinhuanet.com /english/world/2012-02/11/c_131403865.htm (May 11, 2012).

Arab Spring, American Autumn

BRIAN T. EDWARDS

Within the interdisciplinary field of American studies, critical self-examination has long been central and crucial to the vitality of its academic project. Middle East studies, another interdisciplinary field, has had a different trajectory within the U.S. academy but has been no less fraught.[1] In the first decade and a half of the twenty-first century, the establishment of new American studies programs in the Middle East and North Africa has been one of the more interesting places where the two interdisciplinary projects merge—sometimes uncomfortably but always instructively.

Since December 2005, when the newly established Center for American Studies and Research (CASAR) at the American University of Beirut (AUB) hosted its first international conference, Middle East and U.S.-based scholars of American studies have come together for biennial meetings. Over this time, the collective conversation has grown increasingly to become a comparative Middle East studies–American studies meeting, with scholars from the two fields converging in the same halls. In the United States, the annual meetings of the American Studies Association (ASA) and the Middle East Studies Association tend not to overlap in terms of attendance, so this merging of scholars at the CASAR events is notable.

Having participated in all five of the conferences between 2005 and 2014 as both an observer of discussions of American studies in the Middle East and a participant in them, I was struck by the tenor of the 2014 event. By 2014 the Middle East had changed dramatically. Geopolitical events in the intervening eight years was a major part of this shift, particularly the so-called Arab Spring, but it was not the only factor.[2] In U.S.-based discussions as well, the persistent debate about the field of American studies and its indebtedness to the long legacy of the ideology of American exceptionalism had moved into a new stage, in fits and starts. A field now in its eighth decade was again experiencing a paradigm shift.

American studies as an interdisciplinary formation has long offered something new to the more stable and stubborn disciplines in the U.S.

academy, but by now a sense of belatedness is prevalent. The important intervention by Amy Kaplan, in her now classic essay of 1993 "Left Alone with America," that American studies needed to pay attention to cultures of U.S. imperialism, the title of her landmark collection edited with Donald Pease, opened up a profound reassessment of the ways in which the field itself was stuck within a methodology too indebted to some of the very myths that scholars in the field had been interested in disassembling since at least the early 1970s.[3] In the two decades since Kaplan's essay, a variety of methods and approaches to freeing the field from this intellectual legacy have been put forward, from post-nationalist and comparative American studies, and from hemispheric to transatlantic to transpacific approaches. With my colleague Dilip Gaonkar, my own intervention in this discussion has been to argue for "globalizing American studies"—by which we did not mean to volley the common meaning of "globalization," which one might reasonably recast as a neoliberal project to reduce non-American difference to a playing field for American capital.[4] Rather, we argued that scholars should attend to the ways in which American culture and cultural forms circulate transnationally as fragments, entering into new contexts often disassociated from their rich meanings in the United States, and are remade, recoded, and reused in new local contexts. By so doing, we may learn much about American culture from outside of the United States, an area that the field of American studies had been professionally suspect about.[5] This has been true about the latest generation of American studies programs outside the United States, most notably in the Middle East, where scholars—including many who attended the CASAR meetings—have offered strikingly original perspectives on canonical American authors, texts, and social formations, often rejecting the presuppositions of U.S.-based accounts of these same figures.[6] But the movement of America as a fragment is also to be found far from academia, in the realms of popular culture, literature, and cinema and in the social movements that have riveted our attention yet again, during and in the wake of the Arab uprisings of 2010–11.

Three years after the Arab Spring, the January 2014 meeting in Beirut offered an interesting moment of disjuncture, what I have elsewhere called a "preposterous encounter."[7] Such moments are always instructive and crucial, so it is worth pausing briefly on this one. In Beirut two crises converged: first, the crisis faced by the U.S.-based ASA since its November 2013 resolution to boycott Israeli universities and academic institutions—ratified by the ASA membership in a vote in December—which lead to a massive amount of external backlash against the ASA, an internal debate within its membership, and a great deal of press coverage. Second, the political situation in Lebanon had arrived at a different crisis, where the ongoing cataclysm in neighboring Syria continued to manifest itself in a spate of political violence locally. In Beirut, two car bombs in quick succession—December 27, 2013, eight dead; and January 2, 2014, five dead, sixty wounded—just prior to the CASAR conference, which was held January 6–9, had nerves frazzled. As Americans and Americanists gathered in a Beirut hotel on the Corniche, the U.S. State Department issued a travel warning, widely circulated in the English language press:

> Following recent bombings in Beirut and other instances of violence that have occurred in Lebanon in recent months, the U.S. government strongly urges U.S. citizens in Lebanon to exercise extreme caution and to avoid hotels, western-style shopping centers, including western-style grocery chain stores, and any public or social events where U.S. citizens normally congregate, as these sites are likely targets for terrorist attacks for at least the near term.[8]

The irony was not lost on some participants: a gathering of U.S. citizens discussing American studies in a hotel, all sponsored by the AUB, what could be a more likely target? Perhaps predictably, many U.S.-based scholars canceled their trips at the eleventh hour. Others, including those based in Beirut and elsewhere in the Middle East, and U.S.-based scholars who had made the trip, did not keep silent about their disappointment in their colleagues, though mostly in hushed tones.[9] Near the registration desk, the list of cancellations among participants was significantly longer than in previous conferences. Surely not everyone who canceled did so out of fear of personal safety, but the numbers were startling.

Both the ASA boycott resolution and the ongoing violence in Syria and Lebanon haunted the conference. They haunted the event in the sense that French philosopher Jacques Derrida has taught us to think of haunting as constitutive of being itself (*hauntologie* and *ontologie* are near homonyms in French, and Derrida plays on the ways the invented word "hauntology" sounds like "ontology" in French). The haunting could be quite spooky as well: conservative journalists and neo-Zionist bloggers took advantage of the extensive conference website to mock the event in U.S. media outlets, frequently with ad hominem attacks, even while not venturing far from their computer screens in the United States. And in Beirut, the pervading sense among many local residents that another spectacular act of political violence was imminent was frequently expressed (indeed, a car bomb went off in the Bekaa Valley on January 16 shortly after the conference, and then another in Beirut on January 21, both with multiple casualties). Thus, Middle East politics and U.S. politics regarding the Middle East were ever present during the conference, though differently for the participants. The benefits of gathering—for those who made the trip—was the potential to put them in dialogue, as happened frequently both in the sessions and in the coffee breaks and meals.

And yet there were moments of disjuncture: the absence of so many U.S.-based scholars on the printed schedule; the different critical modes that American studies and Middle East studies value; the ways in which travel itself is a privilege differently experienced by participants coming from underfunded state institutions in the Middle East and relatively wealthy ones in the United States, and in turn the ways Beirut itself, ever present danger aside, could offer a relief for those who had traveled from yet more fraught Cairo, to say nothing of the absent Iranians and Syrians. These were moments of "disjuncture" in the sense that Arjun Appadurai opened up in his classic essay on the cultural aspects of globalization: moments revealed by the overlap of different experiences as gaps are exposed.[10]

How does circulation help us explain this disjuncture? And how does a rigorous examination of the ways in which American cultural production (including American studies itself) circulates in the Middle East and North Africa open up our understanding of the limits of American self-understanding, even that emanating from its most radical critics?

The premise of my current work is that if one looks at the global circulation of American ideas, modes, and representations as they make their way in the world, the way they are fragmented and move as jump cuts has the potential to unseat the logics of American exceptionalism, including the critique of that exceptionalism.[11] Ironically, it was the profound lesson of American studies that texts, particularly cultural texts, could best be interpreted if their rich historical and social contexts were taken into account. So it would seem perverse to suggest that as American cultural products and forms circulate outside the contexts in which they were created, they might accrue some new or richer meaning that could reflect back on the field itself.

The Arab Spring offered such a provocation to American studies and allowed us a way to reimagine "America" as in its own late stage, a period I have been calling "After the American Century" and will also call here the American Autumn. These are not temporal demarcations so much as theoretical ones or even methodological ones. My primary interest is not merely to critique U.S. neo-imperialism on the political front, not to show how the foreign policies of the United States during the twentieth and twenty-first centuries have been opposed to its discourse about freedom and democracy. These are important arguments to make, to be sure, but I will leave it to the historians and political scientists to expose the gap between policy and pronouncement.

Rather, I am interested in the ways in which the so-called Arab Spring was productive in changing many mainstream American attitudes toward the Arab world, forcing many to revise the previous sense of the Arab world as stuck in centuries of history (Orientalism) and offered an opening to a sense of the Arab world as young, vibrant, and multivalent. Still, many of those who championed the Tahrir uprisings, and those in Tunisia and elsewhere, gave too much centrality to the role of American forms (especially social networking media) in their accounts of the Arab Spring.

Against these accounts, I argue that as American cultural products and cultural forms are taken up by disparate publics, the new meanings that accrue to them are not to be understood as evidence of U.S. cultural hegemony, nor do they prove the persistence of the American Century. Rather, the innovative ways in which Egyptians and others use U.S. cultural forms for local projects demonstrates what the end of the American Century looks like and offers an energized means by which to interpret North African and Middle Eastern literature and cultural production in the digital age.

Putting these two strands together—the revision of the American narrative of the Arab world effected by the Arab Spring and the necessary engagement of the fields of Middle East studies and American studies in its autumn—we craft the relationship between Arab Spring and American Autumn.

Autumn of America

The "Autumn" of America designates a way to understand the period which follows the so-called American Century, namely that which comes after the particular form of U.S. hegemony that was operative between World War II and the late Cold War within which the economic and geopolitical predominance of the United States was confused with the global popularity of its cultural products. The logics of the American Century were powerful; indeed, they circumscribed the ways in which American studies understood the relationship of American culture to geopolitics and material history.

In their contribution to the 2011 collection *Business as Usual: The Roots of the Global Financial Meltdown*, Beverly Silver and the late Giovanni Arrighi propose that the 2008 financial meltdown is "one of the latest indicators" that we are in the midst of the "'autumn' of U.S. world hegemony."[12] Rehearsing and extending the argument of Arrighi's now classic *The Long Twentieth Century*, and expanding on the thesis of French historian Fernand Braudel, Silver and Arrighi argue that four major periods of "systemwide financial expansion" have taken place within the history of capitalism, each of them repeating a common pattern while innovating on its predecessor.

For Silver and Arrighi, Braudel's identification of the massive financial expansions that took place in the Italian city-states and the Republic of Genoa from the fifteenth century to the early-seventeenth century, in Holland from the late-sixteenth through the eighteenth centuries, and in the United Kingdom from the late-eighteenth to early twentieth centuries should be complemented by an analysis of the fourth expansion of global capitalism beginning in the late-nineteenth century, with the United States as the new center. In the third period of expansion, the United Kingdom was both a "fully developed national state" and one with a "world-encompassing commercial and territorial empire that gave its ruling groups and its capitalist class an unprecedented command over the world's human and natural resources."[13] With a global empire, the British did not need to rely on foreign powers for protection, as the Italian states had in their period of ascendancy during the Renaissance, so the British internalized their own protection costs. As an industrial center, the British also produced their own manufactured goods, which Silver and Arrighi argue was central to the "profitability of [their] commercial activities," and thus internalized their production costs. During the British period, the expansion of the financial system therefore went yet further than it had under their Dutch and Italian forebears.

As British industrial capitalism waned, the United States emerged with a different set of arrangements. Instead of a colonial empire on the

British model, the United States was, in Silver and Arrighi's words, a "continental military-industrial complex with the power to provide effective protection for itself and its allies and to make credible threats of economic strangulation or military annihilation toward its enemies." Thus, the power, size, insularity and "natural wealth" of the United States could internalize both protection and production costs, as had the British. The innovation, however, was the formation of "vertically integrated multinational corporations," which allowed the American capitalist class to internalize what the authors call the "transaction costs" of capital expansion: "to *internalize the markets* on which the self-expansion of its capital depended."[14]

The American Century, from the perspective of worlds-systems analysis, is therefore a cycle of accumulation in which the multinational corporation takes the place of Britain's global, colonial empire, but not in the same way. It innovates on the British model and has more in common with the Dutch Republic of the seventeenth and eighteenth centuries. Silver and Arrighi point out that as each of these cycles of accumulation ran its course, as expansion of the financial system reached its limit, a period of financialization set in: the autumn of each cycle. They point to Marx's *Capital*, volume 1, wherein Marx himself noted a pattern "whereby expansions of the financial system . . . played a key role in the transfer of surplus capital from declining to rising geographical centers of capitalist trade and production":[15] Venice "in her decadence" (quoting Marx) lent massive sums to Holland; Holland, in its late period, lent huge sums to England; and England had already been giving large amounts of credit to the United States as Marx was writing *Capital*. The autumn of each financial expansion is the spring for another system.

Worlds-systems analysis is not without its problems or its critics, of course, particularly from the field of history. For students of literary and cultural studies, the putative theoretical shortcomings are less important than the apparent disconnect to our work: reading the analyses of great systemic shifts, the escalation of one cycle of accumulation and diminution of another, one hardly feels that the analysis of individual texts or authors matter to the grand pattern. Perhaps we might understand social movements and protest—decolonization and the civil rights movement, or globalization and the antiglobalization protests, and the literary and film texts that document them—in a different light if we see them in terms of the waxing and waning of massive cycles and systems, but it is not immediately apparent how. Still, we need a foothold, some sort of stable ground from which to reexamine the "state" of American studies, and this may provide a surprisingly useful one. For in the long and animated discussion of the limits and persistence of American exceptionalism—and the resurgence of claims for American exceptionality in public discourse, particularly on the American right and center-right—it is clear that there is an anxiety about the financial meltdown and a process of coming to terms with the exuberance of the 1990s and the various economic bubbles that closed the last century.

Arrighi, in a long essay called "Hegemony Unravelling," published in two parts in the *New Left Review* in 2005, noted the contradictory aspects of the apparent revival of the U.S. economy in the 1990s: the escalation of U.S. foreign debt "without precedent in world history" and the "emergence of a new U.S. imperial project," namely the Project for a New American Century. He asks "whether and how the New American Century project and its adoption by the Bush Administration relate to the turbulence of the global political economy since 1970."[16] Arrighi thus connects the Project for a New American Century and its "adoption as official U.S. policy" not only with a domestic response by conservatives to the perceived moral profligacy of the 1990s under the Clinton Administration, but, following David Harvey, with "an attempt to maintain the hegemonic position of the U.S. under the conditions of unprecedented global economic integration created by endless capital accumulation at the end of the twentieth century."[17]

Arrighi makes a compelling case that we understand the Project for a New American Century in terms of the unraveling of U.S. global hegemony, an anxious awareness that the conditions of the so-called American Century are now in their autumn. (In this he differs from Harvey, who points to the project as a key example of "the New Imperialism."[18]) Still, we may adapt these lessons and bring them into the realm of American studies and its own unraveling academic hegemony by shifting the focus to the patterns of knowing—the changing context for literary and cultural production—that were also emerging in the 1990s and have now emerged as our current episteme.

In other words, when the anxious discourse in the 1990s about the "end of history" and loss of moral center was disrupted by the cataclysmic events of September 11, 2001, and the announcement of a war on terror that lasted through the two terms of the George W. Bush administration, the neo-imperialism of the Project for the New American Century and the critique it occasioned from American studies also served as a distraction from a changed episteme. What was occluded was the way in which the new ways of knowing that the digital revolution had opened up (global village, global cultural economy, collapsing of borders, states of diaspora, etc.) were marking the transition from one way of inhabiting the world within the long American Century into yet another. This awareness ran ahead of the patterns those of us in American studies had developed for understanding the interplay of text and politics, of representation and history, a methodology that had of course emerged during the height of American ascendancy even as it was refined and debated through the long Cold War.

One might say that in the early period of American studies (the 1940s and 1950s), American studies mirrored the American cycle of accumulation itself. The multinational corporations so key to the American Century were similar to American studies, and vice versa, in that they were blind to the ways in which the markets they were exploiting—and in the case of American studies, the texts and contexts they were grappling with—had their own particularities and did not buy American goods silently. They "internalized the markets on which the[ir] self-expansion . . . depended," to borrow Arrighi's phrase about multinational corporations. It was not always easy to read or to even perceive the discrepancies. American studies was by and large monolingual, and as it waned, it exposed the problems and logics of exceptionalism, without shifting the frame or externalizing the object of study or moving outside its borders, language, and archives, except in spatialized ways. Thus the hemispheric approaches, an obsession with borders, and so on, that have offered us important lessons and opened up key new archives but also are stubbornly spatial and centrifugal in their attempt to reconfigure the field.

The title of my new book—*After the American Century*—is a provocation both for American studies as a discipline and more generally.[19] As I use the term, "the American Century" is more than a temporal demarcation for the twentieth century. It is an *episteme*, a way of understanding the present during a period of massive expansion, one we can now see beyond. Thus, I am trying to open up a methodology by which to read the text that is able to account for its placement—and its movement—in an expanding or contracting system. In so doing, I borrow the phrase "American Century" from its key proponent, Henry Luce, to suggest that "the American Century" names not simply a unit of time or a geospatial term for marking the political and economic dominance of the United States but a way of understanding the role of American culture in the world during a period when new technologies and media played a major role in circulating American cultural products as commodities. That those circulating objects of American culture were, of course, more than commodities, and that they moved off their prescribed or anticipated pathways will offer the occasion to wonder whether we are indeed in the autumn of the American Century and what such an awareness may mean to literary and cultural analysis. Attention to the circulation of American cultural objects in the "autumn" of the American Century also permits, I argue, an opportunity to move beyond the logic that has animated American studies as a disciplinary formation—and as a method—including in the late period of critique with its attention to the limits of the exceptionalist thesis.

The Arab Spring

How does the Arab Spring intersect with this reading methodology, this disruption to the modes and methods of American studies?

During the years leading up to the Arab Spring, I was following the work of an exceptionally interesting group of young writers based in Cairo—novelists, essayists, dialect poets, and comic artists, all of whom publish in Arabic. The Egyptian revolution—or what might more accurately be called the January 25 movement—highlighted the complicated ways in which American patronage and American innovation have affected the Egyptian cultural landscape, and the diverse ways in which young Egyptians reflect back on U.S. political hegemony in its autumn and on American cultural production. In the case of American cultural products, we must include not only the usual suspects—novels, films, music, and so on—but also cultural forms, the most prominent of which from this decade emerge from the realm of the digital: social networking media and the various logics and cultural products it has inspired.

In the first decade of the twenty-first century, Egyptian literary and cultural production developed innovative ways to incorporate American cultural forms, whether it was the cyberpunk novels of Ahmed Alaidy or the graphic novels and comics of Magdy El Shafee, to pick two examples from recent Egyptian literature that made their way back into U.S. discussions.[20]

Formally, much new Egyptian literature seems to refract circulation-based capitalism in startlingly original ways: it borrows from global forms and language (the graphic novel, serious comic, the vocabulary and spelling of TXT messaging, as recalibrated in Arabic). At the same time, the strongest texts expressed a young Egyptian consciousness, one that is mediated by the technologies of globalization and global culture but is simultaneously local—which means "national" or Egyptian—and as a result remains difficult to translate into an American idiom. The reach of American forms into Egyptian literature (prominent examples are the language of text messaging and the form and layout of comic books) might seem to signal the elasticity of American culture, but I think such would be a mistake. Egyptian literature would thereby be understood as derivative, secondary, and not worthy of more than secondary attention. In other words, as global forms make their way into Egyptian fiction, it is not a question of influence, that pernicious old pattern for reading the movement of one literature into another, or a simple lesson about the enlarged meanings of the original text derived from the surprising readings of a new public (an erroneous idea that Azar Nafisi's *Reading Lolita in Tehran* popularized).

Rather, if we attend to the ways in which the movement of an American form—abstracted, condensed, stripped of its former contextualized meaning—opens up a new set of meanings, how it jumps publics in a way that does not reflect on the original public from which it has traveled, we may move beyond the anachronism of the American studies vernacular tradition as we inhabit and attempt to understand the twenty-first century. We might derive what Dilip Gaonkar and I call a cosmopolitan approach to American studies wherein "America" is understood as a node, as an agent of capitalist modernity, and as I suggested at the beginning of this essay, wherein American hegemony is in its autumn, ceding to a new set of arrangements.[21]

Consider, then, how the Egyptian revolution was understood in the mainstream American media, the ways in which the otherwise clear refusal of American hegemony, both political and cultural, was negotiated. The role of the Internet and of social networking media in the January 25 movement was referred to frequently in American accounts. Yet putting the Internet in such a privileged or authorial position became a way to give credit to the West for creating and developing a technology that lead to a new cultural form: social networking and a new genre of productive texts that might flow from it. This is a way for left-center Americans to manage the guilt for the excesses of the Bush administration, counter-ing responsibility for the unwelcome gift of "democracy" via invasion and occupation by recourse to a different American gift, that of technol-ogy. In other words, the United States may have sent military invasion your way, which was bad, but we also sent Facebook and Twitter, which is good. This, I think, is what lay beneath the media emphasis on the digital aspects of the Arab Spring.

Of course, the technologies of the digital revolution did play a role in the series of uprisings that spread from Tunisia, to Egypt, and then quickly around the Arab world. The digital circulation of images, rhe-toric, and advice across the region was a significant factor and apparently a novel one in linking movements in diverse locations with a rapidity and intimacy that had not been present—or had not been as available to so many—in previous global contexts.

By telling the story this way, American commentators had found a way to negotiate the more uncomfortable message coming from Tahrir Square: that the massive support the U.S. government had given the Hosni Mubarak regime, and, indeed, the Tunisian president Zine El Abidine Ben Ali's regime, put the United States on the side of the opponents of change. Thus, when Hillary Clinton visited Cairo in March 2011, the month following Mubarak's fall, the January 25 youth refused to meet with her, a story that barely registered in American media. The carry-over of Cold War political calculus in supporting the Mubarak and Ben Ali regimes—that they were steadfast partners in the so-called war on terror—was more than obvious to young Egyptians as precisely that: the anachronism of extending a twentieth-century geopolitical logic into the twenty-first century, the erroneous assumption that it was not the au-tumn of American hegemony. Thus, by telling the story of the January 25 movement as one created by a Google chief, or as only possible because of Facebook and Twitter, the American media and its hungry public could manage the contradictions that were perhaps too painful to ac-knowledge.

By taking recourse to a reading practice that emphasizes circulation—one that sees America as a key node, but not the only one, in a global network of nodes—the hope is that we can escape the persistent logics of the twentieth century, the logics of the American Century wherein circulation only went in one direction. That this logic was so influential in circumscribing American studies itself—American studies in its ver-nacular tradition, not the emergent cosmopolitan tradition that was there but overlooked—is a reason to reject it, and embrace that which comes after.

This discussion of events in Egypt is "outside" of American studies, particularly if we heed the reasonable critique of the transnational turn in American studies: that it mirrors the very expansionist impulse of the American Imperium it would seek to resist. Yet the American Autumn overlaps with the digital age within which the circulation of abstracted American forms is a major part of the cultural landscape of places like Egypt. In both Egypt and the United States, the ways of knowing "after the American Century" are not merely ones in which the United States as political entity and American culture are understood in the context of the waning of global hegemony but also are known as fragments via a variety of digital technologies. Thus, by bringing an account of recent Egyptian politics and cultural production into a discussion about American studies, rather than suggest that American studies is the appropriate framework for understanding contemporary Egypt, I mean to suggest the reverse: that a nuanced account of contemporary Egyptian recalibrations of American cultural production productively disrupts American studies in its own autumn.

An earlier version of the second and third parts of this essay appeared as "After the American Century," *REAL: Yearbook of Research in English and American Literature*, Vol. 27, Special issue: "States of Emergency - States of Crisis" ed. by Winfried Fluck, et al. (Tuebingen, Germany: Gunter Narr Verlag, 2011): 57–72.

Notes

1. See Zachary Lochman, *Contending Visions of the Middle East: The History and Politics of Orientalism* (New York: Cambridge University Press, 2004). See also my introduction to *On the Ground: New Directions in Middle East and North African Studies*, ed. Brian T. Edwards (Doha: Northwestern University in Qatar, 2013; electronic edition, 2014).

2. The term "Arab Spring" was popularized in global media, and is of course both a misnomer (since many of the uprisings took place in the winter) and a way of framing political protests in terms of rebirth and youth. The more generally accepted terms now in use are Arab uprisings or Middle East uprisings, both of which I prefer for analytical purposes. When I use "Arab Spring" here, then, it is to emphasize the ways in which the series of events from December 2010 through February 2011, especially in Tunisia and Egypt, were represented in U.S. and other global media.

3. Amy Kaplan, "Left Alone with America," *Cultures of United States Imperialism*, ed. Amy Kaplan and Donald E. Pease (Durham, N.C.: Duke University Press, 1993), 3–21.

4. Brian T. Edwards and Dilip Parameshwar Gaonkar, "Introduction: Globalizing American Studies," *Globalizing American Studies*, ed. Brian T. Edwards and Dilip P. Gaonkar (Chicago: University of Chicago Press, 2010), 1–44.

5. See Brian T. Edwards, "Fragments of America: Response to Marius Jucan," *America, British and Canadian Studies* 14 (June 2010): 96–103.

6. I advance this argument in my essay "American Studies in Motion: Tehran, Hyderabad, Cairo," in *Globalizing American Studies*, 300–21.

7. By "preposterous encounter," I mean to acknowledge the ways in which American studies must account for both the postcolonial and the imperial aspects of American culture and history. This is developed in my essay "Preposterous Encounters: Interrupting American Studies with the (Post)colonial, or *Casablanca* in the American Century," *Comparative Studies of South Asia, Africa and the Middle East* 23, no. 1–2 (2003): 70–86, Special issue: "Comparative (Post)colonialisms."

8. Embassy of the United States, Beirut, Lebanon, "Security Message for U.S. Citizens: Personnel Travel Restrictions, January 5, 2014. http://lebanon.usembassy .gov/sm_010514.html.

9. CASAR director Alex Lubin addressed the absence of U.S.-based colleagues in his opening remarks to the conference.

10. Arjun Appadurai, "Disjuncture and Difference in the Global Cultural Economy," in *Modernity at Large: Cultural Dimensions of Globalization* (Minneapolis: University of Minnesota Press, 1993), 27–47.

11. For a comprehensive history and critique of the term, see Donald E. Pease, "American Studies after American Exceptionalism? Toward a Comparative Analysis of Imperial State Exceptionalisms," in *Globalizing American Studies* (Chicago: University of Chicago Press, 2010), 47–83.

12. Beverly J. Silver and Giovanni Arrighi, "The End of the Long Twentieth Century," in *Business as Usual: The Roots of the Global Financial Meltdown*, ed. Craig Calhoun and Georgi Derluguian (New York: New York University Press, 2011), 55.

13. Ibid., 61.

14. Ibid., 62. Emphasis added.

15. Ibid., 59.

16. Giovanni Arrighi, "Hegemony Unraveling—I," *New Left Review* 32 (2005): 26.

17. Ibid., 26, 30.

18. See David Harvey, *The New Imperialism* (New York: Oxford University Press, 2003).

19. Brian T. Edwards, *After the American Century: The Ends of U.S. Culture in the Middle East* (New York: Columbia University Press, 2016).

20. See my "Jumping Publics: Magdy El Shafee's Cairo Comics," *NOVEL: A Forum on Fiction* 47, no. 1 (Spring 2014): 67–89, Special issue: "Is the Novel Democratic?"

21. Brian T. Edwards and Dilip P. Gaonkar, Introduction to *Globalizing American Studies*.

PART II | Infrastructures of Control

*From Mythmaking
to Drone Warfare*

The Uses of Modernization Theory

American Foreign Policy and
Mythmaking in the Arab World

WALEED HAZBUN

In the run-up to the 2003 American invasion of Iraq, Fouad Ajami was one of many analysts who argued that "the driving motivation of a new American endeavor in Iraq and in neighboring Arab lands should be modernizing the Arab World."[1] While the George W. Bush administration used images of "weapons of mass destruction" and post-9/11 fears of terrorist threats to generate support for the war, a central component of the administration's Middle East strategy depicted the region as in need of American-led political and socioeconomic transformation. The notion of an American mission to modernize the Arab world has, in fact, long played a role in shaping U.S. policy toward the region.

This chapter traces the post–World War II arc of a particular set of ideas about the ability of the United States to transform the Arab world in ways that serve both the Arab world's people and American interests. These ideas reached their greatest prominence in the 1950s and 1960s with the popularization of ideas associated with the social scientific notion of "modernization theory."[2] This approach understands the American model of mass consumer society in the 1950s as representing the universal template for modernity and suggests the United States can promote socioeconomic transformations in the Arab world resulting in governments and societies that would evolve to have interests more aligned with the United States and ready to embrace an American role in the region. At the same time, this view identifies threats to U.S. interests as the product of limited or failed socioeconomic and political change. I refer to such arguments that use modernization theory to guide U.S. policy making as positing the strategic logic of modernization. While often contested by rival political and intellectual views, these ideas have animated much academic scholarship, policy making, and media commentary about the region since the 1950s suggesting how the United States and the Arab world can forge closer ties based on common interests.

The strategic logic of modernization has long appealed to many to U.S. policymakers and scholars of the region as its seems to suggest how the United States can offer economic aid and deploy "soft power"—by means such as technical assistance and building American-style education institutions abroad—rather than rely primarily on military power to pursue its strategic interests.[3] Such a dualist approach, however, masks more than it reveals. I argue that the strategic logic of modernization effectively *facilitated*—rather than offered an alternative to—the development of a regional posture based on the deployment of military force and the backing of repressive regimes. I show how the strategic logic of modernization suggests a long-term project that could potentially transform the region and generate for the United States a set of more stable, modern states to serve as regional allies. But the notion of a "long run" in which the socioeconomic change in the Arab world reduces the contradiction between some strategic U.S. interests and the interests of peoples and states in the Arab world is only a fiction enabled by how modernization theory misreads patterns of political change. The long run always remains a distant, unrealized but potential future. This map of the future is fictitious as it is predicated on a refusal to recognize the autonomous agency of modernizing Arab subjects. It is also blind to other political forces and authorities in society and thus ignores them or assumes they will succumb to the forces of modernization. This framework has the effect of justifying increased repression to counter existing forms of authority and political mobilization as well as the growing challenge of modernizing political forces seeking greater agency. As a result, the strategic logic of modernization ends up suggesting the need for the backing of forces that can secure order. By the early 1960s, American advocates of modernization theory would embrace the military as agents of modernization and recast the conservative regimes the United States increasingly relies on as "reformers" on the evolutionary path to modernization while discounting the ability of the nationalists to realize modernization in the American image. By the 1970s the strategic logic of modernization would be replaced in policy circles and some scholarship on the region by a more explicit embrace of the need for order and the suppression of radical nationalist and Islamist forces understood as opposing U.S. regional interests. This chapter suggests that the shift in strategy represents a logical evolution in U.S. policy based on its interests and thus the deployment of ideas derived from modernization theory have been sustained more by America's self-image as a beneficent force in the region and as a strategy to navigate America's contradictory interests in the Arab world than by changes in or better understandings of the region or processes of socioeconomic change. In short, the strategic logic of modernization has usefully served as a toolkit for American mythmaking in the Arab world.

The chapter then briefly considers the post-9/11 rise of "neomodernization" approaches that seemed to suggest the revival of an American approach to the region and scope for policy-relevant scholarship about the region that could embrace Arab agency. These approaches arose with a recognition of the contradictions of a U.S. strategy reliant on repressive regimes while projecting the goal of a U.S.-led liberal global order and proclaiming the need for political and economic liberalization in the Arab world. Neomodernization approaches, however, have tended to support the fiction that the Iraq war could be used as a tool to help resolve these contradictions and provided a logic for American liberals to support the war.

I conclude by suggesting how in the wake of the Arab uprising and the (limited) retreat of U.S. power projection in the region, new spaces for alternative modes of U.S.–Arab world engagement and knowledge production might open up. I use the example of American-style educational institutions in the Arab world that U.S. policymakers have often sought to support as tools of American soft power. But I call for abandoning the notion that these institutions can serve as tools of American soft power and suggest, instead, how they might contribute to efforts to imagine new modes of American engagement with the Arab world.

The American Gaze of Modernization

The vision of America as a powerful force for promoting modernizing transformations across the globe was vividly expressed in Henry Luce's 1941 essay "The American Century."[4] Writing before the United States became fully engaged in World War II, Luce envisioned "an America which will send out through the world its technical and artistic skills. Engineers, scientists, doctors, movie men, makers of entertainment, developers of airlines, builders of roads, teachers, educators. Throughout the world, these skills, this training, this leadership is needed and will be eagerly welcomed, if only we have the imagination to see it and the sincerity and good will to create the world of the 20th Century."[5] Luce helped popularize the geopolitical vision that, for America to realize itself, Americans must engage the world beyond its shores and help forge a U.S.-centered global order based on American values and ideals.

In the wake of World War II, American policymakers sought to establish a U.S.-led liberal capitalist world order. The order was centered on North America and Western Europe, where, with the Marshall Plan, the United States promoted postwar economic recovery and, with NATO, established a security community to counter the threat posed by the now hostile USSR. With the rise of the Cold War and the global expansion of commerce, communication, and the means of war, the American geopolitical vision extended to the global scale. The implications of these changes were reflected in NSC-68, an internal policy doctrine written in 1950 that spelled out "in a shrinking world the absence of order among nations is becoming less and less tolerable."[6] David Ekbladh explains, "As the Cold War expanded and deepened, modernization found an important strategic role.... For the United States, its version of modernization offered a means to contain communist development and promote a stable, liberal world order."[7]

One can trace the roots of modernization theory as a social scientific theory to Weberian sociology, the "liberal tradition" of American political thought, and notions of American exceptionalism.[8] Scholars such as Michael Hunt have also noted how in many ways modernization theory replicated some of the hierarchical and racial ideas of pre–world war approaches to the nonwhite world.[9] But the production and popularization of modernization in the 1950s, across both academia and policymaking circles, was largely a product of knowledge production efforts driven by American strategic concerns. In fact, as David Ekbladh explains, "as the United States made more and deeper commitments in the 'Third World,' modernization quickly grew connected to counterinsurgency efforts. Its emphasis on developing better roads, electrification, improved communication, or new agricultural techniques would offer peoples in conflict zones a better standard of living. This would breed modern outlooks, but more importantly turn these individuals toward the regime that the United States was attempting to buttress with such efforts."[10]

Scholars affiliated with the MIT Center for International Studies, founded in 1952 by Max F. Millikan to produce policy-oriented research, produced some of the most influential studies that outlined the tenets modernization theory. The CIA funded much of the initial research conducted by the center, focused on issues of counterinsurgency and anticommunist propaganda.[11] These studies became part of a new wave of scholarship about the Middle East and other developing regions that was defined by a distinctly American gaze of modernization, which imagined a U.S.-led project of regional transformation. One of the best-known studies was Daniel Lerner's *The Passing of Traditional Societies: Modernizing the Middle East*, published in 1958.[12] This research was a product of surveys Lerner conducted, beginning in Turkey, on the impact of modern media communications in developing societies. Funded by the U.S. government, the study's goal was to improve the political impact of American radio broadcasting abroad. In his comparative study, Turkey came to serve as a model for a society that reflected progress in the process of modernization. Embedded in this template was the legacy of Ataturk's modernization and secularization efforts and Turkey's more recent development of security ties to the United States as a member of NATO. As Zachary Lockman explains, according to the theory of modernization that Lerner developed, "The social, economic and cultural changes which Middle Easterners were experiencing—urbanization, greater physical mobility, the spread of mass media, and so on—all helped foster the ability of individuals to shed their traditional styles of life and adopt the mobile and empathetic personality characteristic of people in modern societies like the United States."[13] Lerner summarizes his findings by noting, "Western society still provides the most developed model of societal attributes (power, wealth, skill, rationality) which Middle East spokesmen continue to advocate as their own goal. . . . From the West came the stimuli which undermined traditional society in the Middle East; for reconstruction of a modern society . . . the West is still a useful model. What the West is, in this sense, the Middle East seeks to become."[14] In Lerner's theory the success of the Western model and the erosion of bases of traditional society suggests a linear model of change along a narrow tract.

At the same time that Lerner's theory suggested how modernization could lead to societies more sympathetic to American interests and a U.S.-led order, it spelled out the bases for threats to U.S. interests: "newly-mobile men and women, liberated by their imagination of better things from reverence toward what *is*, become frustrated and depressed, or antagonistic and aggressive, when their social institutions provide inadequate opportunities for mobility. They move toward the extremes of political action, attracted toward the instruments of propaganda, agitation and violence, by which they hope to disrupt the settled order and to speed their way toward a more satisfying way of life."[15]

Meanwhile, Lerner's MIT colleague economic historian Walt W. Rostow had been developing an evolutionary theory of economic development based on a similar notion of convergence. In 1960 he published the highly influential *The Stages of Economic Growth*, which plots the conditions that enable economies to reach what he dubbed the "take-off stage" leading to the development of a high mass consumption economy, as existed in the United States and Western Europe.[16] Subtitling his study "A Non-Communist Manifesto," Rostow viewed his theory as a tool in the Cold War struggle. He had a similar view of the sources of threat to the United States in describing communism as "a kind of disease which can befall a transitional society if it fails ... to get on with the job of modernization."[17]

The Strategic Logic of Modernization Theory in the Arab World

Regarding the Middle East, the rise of modernization theory assisted in a transformation of the forms of scholarship and policy options pursued by Americans. Due to its oil resources and strategic location, the region was a critical concern for early Cold War policy planners. Meanwhile, the beginnings of decolonization and the retreat of the European colonial powers encouraged a greater role for the United States. While committed to close ties to its west European allies, the United States sought to distance itself from their colonial legacies and project itself as the leader of a more liberal global order. The rise of modernization theory was influenced by these geopolitical concerns and, at the same time, helped define new means to pursue U.S. goals.

The development of a modernizing gaze helped foster new forms of knowledge about the region. The discourse of classical Orientalism that emphasizes the persistence of premodern social structure and political cultures defined by Islam and Islamic civilization framed much of the existing U.S.-based scholarship on the Arab world.[18] But in contrast to the discourse of Orientalism, the American gaze of modernization imagined the modernizing transformation of the Middle East while discounting the lingering importance of traditional culture and religion. In this process, the United States had a privileged position as representing the universal model for the region as well as the agent of change.

As Matthew Jacobs notes, in the early postwar Middle East, specialists inside the U.S. government argued that "promoting economic development offered the best chances of bringing controlled change to the Middle East," but policymakers initially opposed a direct role for the U.S. government leaving the task to American transnational firms such as the oil companies.[19] As a step toward greater government involvement, in what is now referred to as the Truman Doctrine, in 1947 the United States pledged economic aid to Cold War allies in Greece and Turkey as the British began their retreat from their past economic and military commitments in the region. Still devoting limited funds, in the late 1940s and 1950s the United States promoted technical economic assistance through the Point Four Program. While these expressed American good will and showcased its technical know-how, the impact of the programs, even if fully implemented, was understood as too limited to produce the sort of structural transformations scholars of the region viewed as necessary.

The influence of modernization theory on U.S. policymakers grew in the context of American efforts to develop strategies to promote its U.S. Cold War interests at a time of growing Third World nationalism. Initially in the early 1950s members of the Eisenhower administration supported Gamal Abdel Nasser's rise to power in Egypt viewing him as a valuable anticommunist nationalist leader, but soon the United States entered an era of shifting relations with the Arab world's largest and most powerful state.[20] The United States was frustrated by Nasser's resistance to viewing the USSR as a regional threat while insisting that the lingering influence of the former colonial powers and the newly formed state of Israel posed the most pressing threats to Egypt's security.[21] In 1955, when the United States would not sell Egypt the weapon systems Nasser felt he needed to face the growing threat of Israel following the Gaza raid, Nasser displayed his mastery of playing the super powers off each other by making an arms deal with the USSR (through Czechoslovakia), which shocked the Americans. Even after this deal, Eisenhower considered backing Nasser's request for a loan from the World Bank to finance Egypt's effort to build the Aswan High Dam to serve Egypt's irrigation and electricity generation needs. But after the United States withdrew support, Nasser took the bold step of nationalizing the British- and French-owned Suez Canal Company and claiming the fees generated by the canal. While the United States had reservations about Nasser's behavior, Eisenhower nevertheless opposed the subsequent British, French, and Israel invasion and effort to topple Nasser. Eisenhower wanted the United States to stand apart from the former colonial powers and feared alienating the Arab masses.

The challenge for U.S. policymakers grew in the wake of the Suez crisis as Nasser seemed victorious and his regional popularity grew. Of concern to the United States was not only Nasser's willingness to deal with the USSR but also his strong opposition to the American vision for a regional security architecture to contain the USSR. Nasser opposed several U.S.- and U.K.-backed regional security schemes, such as the Baghdad Pact, and inspired demonstrations across the region, leading even Jordan—a monarchy highly dependent on Western support for its own security—to refuse to join. In an effort to meet these challenges, in 1957 the Eisenhower administration implemented a new strategy that would later be referred to as the Eisenhower Doctrine, which pledged economic and military support to allies in the region. The shift in American policy represented by the Eisenhower Doctrine, which sought to contain the influence of Egyptian-led Pan-Arabism, was driven by the view that Nasserism was destabilizing friendly, conservative regimes and making the region vulnerable to communist influence.

It was the American struggle to address the growing influence of Arab nationalism that led to the development of the strategic logic of modernization theory and its expanded influence on American Middle East policy making. Eisenhower's January 1957 message to congress introducing the policy was met by mixed reactions, and many American policymakers and congressmen feared getting the United States dragged into a military engagement in the region, but many also felt the policy would not be enough to shore up American allies in the face of rising challenges from Arab nationalist and populist movements.

Following the speech, the MIT economic historian Walt Rostow published a commentary in the *Washington Post* entitled "Mideast Policy Must Look Beyond This Crisis."[22] In it Rostow outlined a new logic for U.S. policy that he would first offer to the Eisenhower administration as it reformulated its Middle East policy in the wake of developments in 1958. The approach would later be adopted by the Kennedy administration, in which Rostow would serve in a high-ranking capacity. In the op-ed Rostow argues that the "major strategic interest" of the United States in the developing world is "modernizing their societies in the widest sense."[23] He calls on the United States to "to hold up a vision of what in the long pull these societies might achieve," noting that "in no region of the world is the individual citizen poorer or harder pressed than in the Middle East."[24] Rostow also argues that "our standards for allocating aid should be economic, not political or military standards."[25] In other words, he argues that the United States should "join them in a carefully calculated but openhearted effort to develop and modernize their societies."[26]

While Rostow's op-ed focused on American challenges in the Middle East, he and his MIT colleagues Max F. Millikan and others had recently published "A Proposal: Key to an Effective Foreign Policy," which offers a more extensive general statement on the strategic logic of modernization.[27] This text directly challenged existing foreign aid and economic diplomacy efforts that focused on short-term military and strategic concerns, such as the Eisenhower Doctrine, and sought to use aid as a barging chip. Millikan and Rostow argued that instead, with large amounts of unconditional aid, the United States could help developing states, regardless of their political orientation, reach the "take-off" stage.

Rostow would play a key role in the shift in U.S. policy. He first worked as a consultant to the Eisenhower administration as it formulated a response to the Iraqi Free Officers coup of 1958 when many U.S. policymakers came to view the wave of Arab nationalists as too powerful to directly oppose. Then in 1960 a group of MIT scholars, including Rostow, submitted a report to the Senate Committee on Foreign Relations. The next year the report was published as *The Emerging Nations: Their Growth and United States Policy* with Max F. Millikan and Donald L. M. Blackmer serving as editors. The report extends the strategic logic of modernization theory beyond the question of aid policy and outlines how U.S. policy could "help these societies move in directions compatible both with their long-run interests and with our own."[28] Such an approach diverged from the existing orientation and approach of U.S. policy. Modernization theory recognized the critical importance of rising social forces and nationalism in shaping the preferences of states and the policy options of their leaders. The MIT scholars noted that "relationships must be grounded in a shared interest in furthering a process of modernization which will enable the transitional societies to develop their own versions of responsible government to play a cooperative role in a new world order."[29] At the same time, this view suggested an imperative for the United States to go beyond its current focus on political regimes and develop ideas and tools for influencing socioeconomic development in the "new" states.

The Lure of Modernization and Arab Nationalism
in Middle East Studies

While the theorists of modernization had developed an argument for how and why the United States should accommodate the rise of Third World nationalism and support its leaders' desires for modernization, many scholars trained in Middle East studies who closely followed the great political upheavals in the Arab world made parallel arguments about how the United States could support the hopes and dreams of the Arabs by supporting their modernization efforts and accommodating the rise of Arab nationalism. Many of these scholars were associated with the newly founded centers for Middle East studies at U.S. universities that gained U.S. government funding in the mid-1950s as part of its early Cold War–era push for the development of area studies scholarship. While these scholars published important academic works, their approach to the region could also be translated into policy-relevant arguments as presented in the many policy journals they also published in.

For example, in the July 1958 issue of *Foreign Affairs* Richard H. Nolte and William R. Polk presented an assessment of U.S. interests and policy entitled "Toward a Policy for the Middle East."[30] Nolte had just returned from an extended residence in Beirut as part of a research fellowship before he would begin teaching at Dartmouth College. Polk was then a professor of Middle East history and politics at Harvard University. Writing before 'Abd al-Karim Qasim's July 1958 nationalist coup in Iraq, their assessment would prove prescient. Writing against the logic of the Eisenhower Doctrine, Nolte and Polk highlight how "the decisive social and political force at work [in the Middle East] is Arab nationalism."[31] They argue that "it is self-defeating to oppose change in an area where reform is a popular idea and rapid fundamental change is inescapable."[32] While these scholars were not theorists of modernization, they viewed the Arab world through a similar lens. At the time, Polk was at work on a monograph about the "impact of the West" on southern Lebanon and would later organize a conference titled "Beginnings of Modernization in the Middle East." Their essay describes how "turmoil [in the Arab world] results from the profound and accelerating social revolution which is taking place as a result of contact with the West" and how a "cultural aspect [of this process] is the gradual replacement of the static, tradition-bound assumptions of the Islamic past by those of the secular, progressive West."[33] Rather than wielding a Cold War lens or focusing on the personality of Nasser, they viewed Arab nationalism as part of a social force driving not only Arab unity but also "a craving for social justice, economic development, industrialization, and internal reforms."[34] It is, they suggest, an expression of a popular desire "to reform and reconstruct their society in the pattern of modern industrialized respectability."[35] Following a logic similar to the one being developed at the time by the modernization theorists at MIT, Nolte and Polk saw modernization not as directly generating pro-American sentiments but rather leading to long-term transformations that would promote state behaviors conducive to American interests. "To be effective," they conclude, "American policy must have nationalist support and this can be won by a clear and steady endorsement of their own constructive purposes."[36] American objectives, they note, "do not inherently conflict with those of the progressive nationalists," and "indeed, with the moral and material backing of the United States, Arab progress towards achieving these things could also become progress toward securing American objectives."[37] They even suggest that "the present nationalist hostility toward the whole range of other American interests in the Middle East would tend to fade away."[38]

In the wake of the 1958 "revolution" in Iraq and under the impression that the wave of Arab nationalism sweeping the region was unstoppable while noting with concern the new Iraqi regime's growing ties to the Iraqi Communist Party, the Eisenhower administration shifted away from a policy of containing Nasserism to one of accommodating Arab nationalism and Egypt's growing power. This new policy was outlined in the November 1958 National Security Council report NSC 5820/1 and stated the United States would "accept and seek to work with radical pan-Arab nationalism."[39] At the same time, the report recognized the reduced influence of Saudi Arabia, the need for Israel to become accepted in the regional system, and the possibility that Jordan might face partition or internal political realignment.[40] While the shift in U.S. policy can be explained in realpolitik terms as a reaction to inability of the United States to contain Nasser at a moment of growing regional influence, the strategic logic of modernization imagined a way to transcend the need for realpolitik balancing by promoting a shift in the interests of regional states to better align them with those of the United States. Writing in the December 1958 issue of the popular American magazine the *Atlantic Monthly*, Polk outlined the logic for such a shift in his essay "The Lesson of Iraq."[41] His analysis explains the coup by the Iraqi Free Officers as a product of the failure of the old regime governing Iraq's British-installed Hashemite monarchy to promote development and modernization. Polk highlights the frustrations of "the emerging middle class . . . who had been most exposed to Western life and thought and upon whose technical abilities, acquired during that exposure, the old regime depended."[42] He continues, "Thus, while the government depended upon the newly educated generation for all of its schemes of economic and social betterment and indeed for all of its technical functions, from the operation of the telephone company to the weaving of cloth, yet the government was immune to the political ideas of this new generation."[43] Polk also notes a similar dynamics in the military, as "many officers had studied abroad. . . . In the process of acquiring Western technical skills, they also acquired Western values and expectations."[44] In later writings Polk would emphasize how the military in places like Iraq serves as a school of nationalism to help produce the "new men" needed to promote modernization: "At the upper echelons, the former army officer is the 'doer' of the new order. . . . As a factory manager or senior bureaucrat he will play a dominant role in modernizing the country."[45] At the same time, echoing warnings in the NSC 5820/1 report, in his *Atlantic Monthly* essay Polk noted the need for the conservative monarchies in Saudi Arabia and Jordan to grow politically and the danger of the United States indentifying so closely with them. Following his modernization-framed analysis, Polk concludes that the region needs development aid more than arms shipments and that in many ways U.S. and Arab interests are aligned. "The new generation of nationalists," he notes, are planning "large-scale development programs"; thus both the United States and the Arabs desire peace and the steady flow of oil (needed by Western economies as an energy source but also a critical revenue source needed to serve Arab development).[46] Polk concludes the essay: "Let us not forget that our essential policy interests are identical with those of the Arabs."[47]

Toward a "New Frontier" in the Middle East

The influence of modernization theory in U.S. foreign policy reached its greatest prominence with the inauguration of John F. Kennedy as president in 1961. As a senator, Kennedy had spoken out in favor of Algerian independence and the need for the United States to recognize the force of nationalism in the developing world.[48] In taking office, Kennedy told Americans that they stood at the edge of a "new frontier" and sought to implement a regional Middle East policy that accommodated Third World nationalism and the strategic logic of modernization. To do this, Polk would be tapped to serve as the Middle East expert on the State Department's Policy Planning Council while Rostow was given the post of deputy national security advisor from where he sought to launch a revolution in American foreign aid and development policies.

In the Middle East, the Kennedy administration sought to reformulate U.S. policy toward Nasser at a time when, as a CIA report explained, "the long-term outlook for conservative and Western-aligned regimes is bleak. . . . Neutralism, social reform, and pan-Arab unity were the wave of the future; the conservative monarchies risked being swept away."[49] Laying the foundations for such a move, Kennedy appointed John S. Badeau as U.S. ambassador in Cairo. Badeau had been a professor of religion and Middle East studies and had served as president of the American University in Cairo. While not a theorist of modernization, he had practical experience in development. He served as director of the Near East Foundation, which ran technical assistance programs across the Middle East. The Near East Foundation's emphasis on "very simple programs operating at the village level" exemplified the new approach to development that Kennedy sought to advance with the founding of the Peace Corps.[50] Writing in 1958, Badeau understood that "social and economic development is clearly a priority in the Middle East" and warned that "it is extremely difficult to implement without a revolution."[51] He likened the "Egyptian revolution" of Nasser to the French Revolution, noting that "it, too, had its self-seeking leaders, its power cliques, its political nationalism; but it let loose forces that finally changed the pattern of social life in most of Europe. That is what the Egyptian revolution has begun to do in the Middle East and that is why it strikes fire in some form in every country."[52] It was through such a modernization theory lens that seemingly "socialist" policies such as land reform and centrally planned state-led industrialization could be viewed favorably by some U.S. policymakers and scholars. Badeau concluded that Egyptians "are looking for independence and integrity. We are concerned about alignment; they are concerned about national development. Until, in our sympathies and our foreign policy, we find some way to take account of their basic priorities I doubt if the situation can be greatly improved."[53]

With Rostow's backing, expanded economic aid and development assistance played an important role in the efforts of American–Egyptian rapprochement in the early 1960s. The first steps in 1961 consisted of pledging large amounts of food aid through the Public Law 480, the "Food for Peace" program that allowed the United States to ship surplus agricultural produce to "friendly" states abroad.[54] The United States was soon considering a number of aid requests from the Egyptian government. Polk, again following a strategy Rostow had advocated, pushed for stronger engagement with Egypt as he "identified Egypt's development as the key to regional security."[55] The American goal was to shift Nasser away from external confrontations and geopolitical maneuvering by giving him tools to address Egypt's internal economic problems. In 1962 the United States launched its effort, sending a Harvard economist to Egypt to assess the country's development plans. Kennedy's liaison for Third World affairs, Chester Bowles, along with Polk, then met Nasser and his economic officials. Following the trip, Bowles reported, "If Nasser can gradually be led to forsake the microphone for the bulldozer . . . he may assume a key role in bringing the Middle East peacefully into our modern world."[56]

This brief era of engagement saw the U.S. funding of several Egyptian development projects including the rescuing of several Nubian monuments from areas that were being flooded by the building of the (Soviet-financed) Aswan High Dam.[57] As a result, in 1965 the government of Egypt offered one of these spectacular monuments, the Temple of Dendur, to the United States, and it eventually was relocated to the Metropolitan Museum of Art in New York City. But overall, the modernizers of the Kennedy administration were unable to realize their goal of an extensive U.S.-backed push for modernization in Egypt (or elsewhere in the Arab world) let alone a shift in the country's interests and goals. Even before Kennedy's assassination in 1963, the American rapprochement with Egypt had collapsed, largely over the civil war in Yemen. Nasser felt compelled to support, with Egyptian troops, the republican forces that had overthrown the Saudi-backed monarchy. Nasser viewed supporting such republican, Arab nationalist forces against the "feudal" and reactionary forces of the monarchies as essential to his modernizing vision for the Arab world. American officials, however, became concerned as Egyptian forces bombed near the Saudi border. The Saudis, highly concerned about Nasser's growing influence that came at their expense, asked the United States for support. While seeking to resolve the conflict, American officials drew closer to the Saudis and soon abandoned the accommodation of Nasser, though in 1963 they had hoped the Baathist Arab nationalists in Iraq and Syria might prove useful anticommunist partners.[58]

The U.S. backing of Saudi Arabia and its alignment with other "conservative" states, combined with the development of a closer strategic relationship with Israel, would come to define the core elements of the U.S. strategy in the Middle East. Both the strategic logic of modernization and the realpolitik approach of accommodating nationalists to contain communists were eclipsed by a new approach, eventually termed the "Nixon Doctrine," that identified militarily powerful Cold War allies that could serve as pro-U.S. proxy states to contain the seemingly Soviet-aligned nationalist republican states and the growing radical Palestinian nationalist movement. In this new regional architecture, the United States no longer had conflicting short-term and long-term interests (or so it seemed at the time). After the 1967 Arab–Israeli war, regional politics became more polarized, pushing the United States further toward supporting Israel's regional military dominance and anchoring the United States to the conservative monarchies aligned against what became increasingly Soviet-backed forces of Arab radicalism and Palestinian nationalism.[59]

Modernization Theory and Mythmaking

What are the lessons of the rise and decline of the strategic logic of modernization? In assessing the failures of American policy efforts, many of the advocates of the strategic logic of modernization would blame the lack of will and proper focus on the part of Third World leaders who the United States had sought to support. For example, Rostow would conclude that Nasser was a "romantic" rather than a pragmatic modernizer who was unable "to focus [his] efforts on economic and social developments."[60] Rostow declares, "The romantic revolutionaries of the developing world are not the wave of the future."[61] Others, such as John Badeau, were better able to see how the American vision of modernization was far more narrow than the objectives of Arab nationalists like Nasser had, who understood modernization as part of a broader regional, geopolitical vision.[62]

A closer look at Badeau's analysis reveals a problematic embedded in the strategic logic of modernization. Writing a few years after he resigned from his position in Cairo, Badeau recognized aspects of this problematic. He begins, "It can be argued . . . that the Western interest in stability and progress should result in a policy of supporting progressive—in some cases radical—movements throughout the Arab world, so that the

West may be identified with the emerging future rather than the decaying past."[63] At the same time, Badeau recognizes that the nature of U.S. interests posed a dilemma:

> Yet in some Arab countries where particular American and Western interests are strong, the passage from traditionalism to modernity may wreck the stability of the existing order in which American interest is set. In these circumstances, particular interests in the specific country tend to take precedence . . . . This is partly a time factor. Particular interests in specific countries are immediate, or at best short term, while many interests general to the area are long-term, connected with movements, conditions and policies which will bear fruit only in a remote future. How to define general American interest in the Arab world, yet allow for the reality of specific short-term interests, is a constant problem.[64]

The problem Badeau recognizes, however, *never* goes away. In fact, it is an essential element of the utility of the strategic logic of modernization. American policymakers in the Middle East have long faced the dilemma of seeking to advance a broad range of interests across the conservative oil rich Gulf states, the nationalist revolutionary republics, and Israel. This definition of interests contains within it several contradictions and the strategic logic of modernization offers a flawed map of an *imagined* future in which some of these contradictions get resolved. If revolutionary nationalists focused on modernization, for example, they would be more eager for economic aid and technology from the United States and investment from the oil rich states rather than military power to confront Israel. Eventually, so the theory goes, among their growing middle classes an interest in consumerism would eventually replace the appeal of radical nationalism.

As Badeau points out, the challenge U.S. policymakers define for themselves is the need to develop tactics to pursue the long-term goal of transformation while not abandoning short-term strategic concerns. Such a map, however, is fictitious. America's existing strategic concerns tend to drive policy in the Middle East, and the commitment of diplomatic and military resources to those interests has expanded vastly over time. But by holding out the notion of transformed landscape in the future, policymakers try to suggest that the opposition current policies face from regional societies or the ways they seem at odds with expressed American values (such as backing repressive regimes) are only temporary or part of a transitional phase until the United States has successfully established a new regional order. Badeau, however, writing in retrospect notes that such as future is "remote" rather than imminent.

While figures like Polk and Badeau supported the push for a shift in policy focused on the goals of modernization, when it came to policy making, existing strategic interests remained primary.[65] We can see these concerns in Rostow's 1957 op-ed, "Mideast Policy Must Look Beyond This Crisis," discussed earlier.[66] A close reading of the qualifications and contextualization of his argument reveals how his promotion of the strategic logic of modernization is a tool to secure U.S. strategic interests as they currently exist. Rostow even argues that the people and government of the Middle East who are to benefit from U.S. support for modernization must accept U.S. interests, including the willingness of the United States to use force in the region to "counterpoise against a soviet invasion" or "to suppress a limited war."[67] He also notes that the Arabs "must be convinced that Israel is there to stay" and that the United States will act to ensure the flow of oil resources. Most notable, he declares that "a military and diplomatic stance designed to make these things crystal clear is a necessary condition for any American policy in the Middle East."[68] In other words, while modernization was expected to enhance the American position in the long run by transforming the interests of Arab rivals and stabilizing the regimes of allies, in the short run the United States must maintain if not expand its military posture. Thus, for Rostow and other top policymakers, modernization is not a substitute for power projection but a supplement to it. As Roby Barrett explains, "This faith in economic reform also carried with it a steadfast belief that when necessary political stability had to be maintained by force in order to create a secure environment for development."[69] In fact, in the 1960s as the interests of modernizing nationalist regimes diverged rather than converged with those of the United States, more power projection was required.

The priority of "political stability" helps explain how supporters of the strategic logic of modernization drifted into increasing reliance and support for the military as agents of modernity and in the process rationalized increasingly repressive regimes. American scholars working in the idiom of modernization theory, as Polk notes, were the first to embrace the military as agents of modernization. In 1963, just as some U.S. policymakers were ready to embrace Baathist coup plotters as such agents, Princeton professor of politics Manfred Halpern published *The Politics of Social Change in the Middle East and North Africa*.[70] Halpern had previously worked for the State Department in a variety of intelligence research capacities. *The Politics of Social Change* was based on Halpern's 1960 Ph.D. thesis submitted to the School of Advanced International Studies at Johns Hopkins University. It was published as a report for the Rand Corporation, a think tank established in California with the help of the Douglas Aircraft Company and which reported to Pentagon officials. Halpern's work became known for his thesis about the role of the new middle class, of which the military, he argues, served as its tool.

In an insightful critique of the influence of modernization theory on U.S. policy toward the Middle East, Richard Bulliet makes the biting observation that "the people we supported as agents of modernity became tyrants, their societies police states."[71] Modernization theory misreads the process of change. It offers a map predicated on the refusal to recognize the autonomous agency of modernizing subjects. It is blind to other political forces, ideologies, and authorities in society and thus ignores them or assumes they will succumb to the forces of modernization.[72] As such, states and social forces have no (legitimate) agency outside the narrow confines of paths that will lead them to embrace U.S. interests and its regional role in the Middle East. Thus, rather than suggesting the United States will likely have to make greater accommodation of regional powers as they modernize, it suggests interests will become more aligned. These conditions have the effect of justifying increased repression to counter existing forms of authority and political mobilization as well as the growing challenge of modernizing political forces seeking greater agency.

Bulliet's critique highlights how modernization theory is a product of social research limited to a thin layer of Western-educated Arab elites, totally ignoring Islam and the social values of the vast majority of Arab societies. Bulliet argues that "western-style modernization is identified without convincing rationale as the conscious goal of Middle Eastern society," and "no alternative way of engaging the modern world received serious consideration."[73] More generally, Bulliet argues that American "policy circles seem incapable of imagining a Muslim model of modernity."[74] Viewing the process of modernization as a scholar of Islamic history, he highlights how modernization theorists were blind to existing Islamic institutions and values as well as the need for modernizing elites to destroy existing rival forms of the authority and centralized power (much as modernizing Arab nationalists did in the 1950s and 1960s creating the foundations for authoritarian regimes). The pattern, in fact, only replicated patters of the change in the Middle East in the nineteenth century under the modernizing efforts of Mohammad Ali in Egypt and the Tanzimat of the Ottoman Empire, where modernization went hand-in-hand with political centralization and new regimes of social control.

In the 1960s U.S. policymakers and scholars did not immediately abandon the narrative of modernization theory but sought to safeguard U.S. ties to "the decaying past" by rebranding these regimes as progressive traditionalists and modernizing monarchists who would take the gradual path to modernization. Rostow would refer to these states as the "evolutionists."[75] In Iran, American-backed reform efforts were branded a "White Revolution," but they produced limited "modernizing" results, except widespread social dislocation, and went hand-in-hand with counterinsurgency programs and the building of a police state. In Saudi Arabia the U.S. embrace of Faisal bin Abdulaziz Al Saud was framed by "celebrations of Faisal as a successful reformer who headed of a revolution."[76] But as Robert Vitalis documents, such a view is largely a myth with almost none of the reforms announced in 1962 ever being fulfilled even though the image of Faisal as modernizing leader has been continually recycled ever since.[77]

Throughout the era of the high phase of modernization theory and U.S. efforts to accommodate Nasser and other Arab nationalists, the United States continued to develop its ability to project military power and became increasingly reliant (like the British before them) on naval and air power using offshore bases like Diego Garcia. By the 1960s American concern for land-based containment capabilities, which the United States had sought in the 1950s with its efforts to develop defense pacts with Arab states, were superseded by a new architecture for global power projection. As William Stivers explains: "Thus [President Kennedy's] conciliatory policy ended as little more than a footnote to history. But his military strategy endured—and constitutes his chief contribution to the development of the future US position in the Middle East. That position would hinge not on America's ability to achieve a modus vivendi with Arab nationalism, or to broker political settlements to regional conflict, but on US military power in the India ocean."[78]

The Eclipse of the Strategic Logic of Modernization

By the late 1960s, modernization theory's map of evolutionary change was being discredited by scholars who noted the failure of convergence between developing and developed societies.[79] As noted earlier, with the development of the Nixon Doctrine, U.S. policy would soon shift to embrace a strategic logic of order that privileged political order and stability and often required the suppression of radical social forces and ideologies. Such a logic was most powerfully expressed by Harvard professor Samuel Huntington, who turned the logic of modernization theory on its head by arguing that socioeconomic change created demands for political participation that often outstrip the capacity of political institutions resulting in instability and what he termed "political decay."[80]

In the 1970s the global economic structure in which the U.S. support national development and import-substitution-industrialization in the Third World was transformed by the decline of the Bretton Woods financial system, the oil price shock, and the failed effort of the developing states to promote a "New International Economic Order."[81] Across the Arab world, in the 1970s and 1980s a wave of social and political mobilization began challenging pro-U.S. regimes in Egypt, Tunisia, Jordan, and Lebanon as well as Iran. These forces included radical nationalist, populist-leftist, youth, and Islamist movements that challenged patterns of state repression, lack of political freedom, socioeconomic inequality, and these regimes' pro-U.S. foreign policies. Regardless of their eroding domestic legitimacy, regimes that served American regional interests were directly supported by American economic and strategic aid. In the 1980s the United States and international financial institutions replaced their goal of promoting economic development with policies focused on neoliberalism and free market reforms. The implantations of these policies led to waves of "bread riots." Meanwhile, most Arab states built ever more repressive forms of authoritarian rule in the face of (real and perceived) threats to regime security from domestic challenges and external rivals. As a result of such a strategy, Ajami notes, "American power" in the region has been "built on relationships with military rulers and monarchs without popular mandate."[82] The legacy of this American approach to the region was starkly expressed in the 1991 congressional testimony of Martin Indyk, who would later serve in the Clinton and Obama administrations. Speaking about the likely consequences of the 1991 war with Iraq war, Indyk explains, "The apathy towards the West that is likely to follow has long been present in the Arab world. It cannot be resolved through accommodation."[83] What matters, he suggests, is not "whether they hate us or love us,"—since he notes, "for the most part, they hate us,"—"but whether they are going to respect our power."[84]

The Rise of Neo-Orientalism and Neomodernization

By the 1980s the blindness to the diverse sources of agency in Arab society endemic in modernization theory became increasingly unsustainable within the scholarship of those who specialize in Middle East studies.[85] New trends in scholarship explored the experience of subaltern communities, such as workers, peasants, women, and informal sector workers, while the continuing relevance of Islam and Islamic social institutions became better understood. Meanwhile, during the 1970s, in terms of the production of policy-relevant knowledge, the strategic logic of modernization was displaced by rival neo-Orientalist understandings that read the political agency of Arab actors—whether Islamists, Palestinian nationalists, or labor activists—as threats to U.S. interests and often understood as driven by traditional, antimodern world views shaped by Islam or Arab culture.[86] This alternative approach to the Middle East, often promoted by scholarship produced in association with think tanks, influenced the shift in policy toward one increasingly reliant on the projection of military power and alliances with authoritarian regimes who suppressed populist social forces (increasingly mobilized by Islamist movements).

The continuing attachment on the part of many U.S. policymakers' notions of American exceptionalism and the self-image of the United States playing a benevolent role in the region only led to increasing the intensity of mythmaking.[87] The threats the United States faced from new social forces and radical states were often exaggerated while America's authoritarian allies were often recast as modernizing or enlighten autocrats who balanced change with stability.

In the wake of 9/11, however, many American policymakers and analysts came to recognize the limits of U.S. regional strategy based on the projection of military power and suppression of social forces. At the same time they highlighted what they saw as the threats posed to U.S. interests by Arab societies, which they viewed as having rejected modernity. As noted earlier, the idea of a U.S. war in Iraq for the purpose of supporting (or imposing) the modernization of the Arab world resonated with the way many Americans wanted to view the U.S. role in the region.[88] But with eclipse of the strategic logic of modernization and its understanding of the short- and long-term tradeoffs, U.S. policymakers and many academics sought to sustain the narrative of modernization, but this time more explicitly backed by the coercive force needed to suppress the now mobilized aspects of societal agency (supposedly) opposed to modernity. Neomodernization approaches were found in both neoconservative and liberal formulations. Rather than being blind to the coercive dynamics of modernization, the Bush administration and its neoconservative backers embraced the so-called Lewis Doctrine with the goal that the Iraq war would lead to the creation of a "a Westernized polity, reconstructed and imposed from above like Kemal's Turkey."[89] At the popular level, influential "liberal hawks" also justified the U.S. invasion along very similar lines. *New York Times* columnist Thomas Friedman, for example, wrote that "if America made clear that it was going into Iraq, not just to disarm Iraq but to empower Iraq's people to implement the *Arab Human Development Report*, well, [Arab terrorists] still wouldn't be with us" but, referring to the broad mass of public opinion, he suggests "the Arab street just might."[90] Such views, however, ignore that American projects of modernization, especially when imposed by force, are even less likely than in the 1960s to lead to state and societal preferences that embrace current American policies and interests in the Middle East. The consequences of the American effort to rebuild Iraq clearly illustrate this point. Ironically, after facing armed resistance to the American occupation, drawing on the same experiences that led officials like Rostow to embrace modernization theory, the U.S. military developed a counterinsurgency strategy based on attempting to provide security as well as economic and social well-being for civilian population.[91]

Engagement without Interests at the End of the American Century?

A little more than three years after the U.S.-led invasion of Iraq—as the country was being torn apart by a violent sectarian civil war—U.S. Secretary of State Condoleezza Rice would again invoke the image of war as a necessary vehicle to promote political transformation in the Middle East. On July 21, 2006, in the midst of a brutal war between Israel and Lebanon's Hezbollah movement, Rice held a press conference. In response to a question about belated U.S. efforts to negotiate a cease-fire, she noted that the United States had "no interest in diplomacy for the sake of returning Lebanon and Israel to the status quo ante."[92] She suggested that if Israel could destroy Hezbollah's military capabilities and decrease its political standing by having it blamed for the wide-scale destruction caused by the war, then Lebanon would finally be able achieve a stable, sovereign, democracy. Rice famously added, "What we're seeing here, in a sense, is the growing birth pangs of a new Middle East. . . . And whatever we do, we have to be certain that we are pushing forward to the new Middle East, not going back to the old one."[93]

Rice's imaginary of a "new" Middle East and the U.S. role in it remained highly contested in the Arab world. It has been challenged not only by political forces opposed to all U.S. presence in the region but also by voices at American-founded institutions—such as at the American University of Beirut (AUB)—operating in the region. Such institutions have often been viewed by many (in the United States and the Arab world) as tools of American soft power. In the remainder of the chapter, however, I want to consider the contribution such voices and centers of knowledge production can make in offering an alternative imaginary for the role the American presences can play in the region. Writing in the aftermath of the 2006 war, Patrick McGreevy, the founding director of the American studies program at AUB, notes "the U.S. role in this war points to a concern that confronts people almost everywhere because the power of the United States is palpable almost everywhere."[94] He refers to "this concern" as "the American question." McGreevy points out that the question arises "in response to a transnational presence that, in the view of many people in many places, poses fundamental cultural, economic, and political challenges." Referring to Rice's comments, McGreevy highlights how "Lebanon's share of these pangs included more than a thousand dead, a million displaced, infrastructure destroyed, beaches and harbors polluted with oil, and millions of cluster bombs scattered over its landscape."[95] He then observes that, "for the students in my class, America was not simply a faraway land; it was a palpable, and sometimes shocking, presence in their lives."[96] McGreevy's "American question" lies at the heart of the motivation for the founding of AUB's American studies program. The program was established in part as a response to the concerns of the Palestinian–American literary scholar Edward Said, who had written in 1991 that such programs are needed because "the United States is by far the largest outside force in the Arab world" and at the time the Arab world had no major center dedicated to its study.[97]

In the years since the 2006 Lebanon war and especially in the wake of the Arab uprisings, McGreevy's American question has taken on a new, more complex resonance as the American military role has been scaled back and its political leverage, as well as its willingness to risk further engagements, has diminished. Meanwhile, new regional and external actors, such as Qatar, Turkey, and Russia, have come to play larger regional roles while the power and influence of nonstate actors, many born as insurgent movement opposed American and Israeli occupation, have expanded. The Arab uprisings begun in Tunisia in late 2010 did not cause these shifts but helped accelerate and consolidate a process we can refer to as the "end of the American Era in the Middle East."[98] While U.S. president Barack Obama has at times tried to suggest that the uprisings could create a new basis for stronger U.S.-Arab ties, these hopes and claims have been neither credible nor sustainable.[99] For example, Obama's repeated references to U.S. support for political and economic reform in the region seem to ignore that many Arab protesters were not interested in economic aid and technical assistance but rather in renegotiating the terms of the Washington Consensus and U.S. backing for neoliberal economic reforms that have been thoroughly exploited by local regimes and economic elites. In the 1950s and early 1960s, many so-called Westernized Arab elites might have shared the vision that American advocates of modernization preached, but few in the Arab world (and beyond) today see the United States as the universal model of modernity. The legacies of recent U.S. policies in Iraq and Palestine also diminish its credibility as an agent for change. Meanwhile, the examples of U.S. policy toward events in Egypt and Syria dramatically highlight how the United States has lost leverage to shape events and seems to have disengaged. The United States seems to be attempting to insulate itself from the likely outcomes of a more repressive regime in Egypt and a violent civil war in Syria that will have a long lasting regional impact.

At the same time, as American relative political influence and leverage declines, we are seeing a more militarized regional posture and a reconfiguration of the means and footprint of American power projection in the Middle East focused on the more limited task of combating terrorist movements through air strikes and assassination missions.[100] Rather than large land-based military forces, the United States is moving toward a networked form of organization based on the use of small units of elite special forces; reliance on high-tech operations using drones, electronic tracking, and cyber war; and closer military-to-military cooperation, often with U.S.-trained forces in the region. Based on long-range mobility and with less need for large bases in the region, this new configuration of power is less visible, and politically it is less transparent, making it harder for political forces and social movements (at home and abroad) to oppose.

While U.S. power and interests are still present, especially in the Gulf, the end of what we might call the projection of the "American Century" in the Middle East has opened the door to a questioning of how U.S. interests are defined and pursued. Between economic constraints at home and the way the uprisings have only expanded the contradictions between U.S. interests and the stated objective of upholding of American values, the notion of an American project to remake the Middle East has become unsustainable if not also no longer credible.

In his contribution to this volume, American studies scholar Brian T. Edwards takes up the question of what forms American presences abroad will take in this new era "after the American Century." In opposition to the image of a universal American model of modernity offered by modernization theory, Edwards suggests that "American culture and cultural forms circulate transnationally as fragments" that get taken up, reinterpreted, appropriated, and transformed by disparate publics. Thus Edwards's approach suggests the possibility for American ideas, commodities, institutions, or other presences to exist in the Arab world but to be detached from a strategic logic and open to appropriation by diverse agents from and in the Arab world.

One such form may be knowledge produced by "American" overseas institutions such as AUB. The location of such institutions and the mix of American and non-American scholars associated with them situates them such that, unlike U.S.-based scholars, they are not expected or rewarded in terms of their ability to produce knowledge, like modernization theory, that seeks to serve the advancement of American interests or influence strategic policy. As a result, this context of knowledge production effectively follows the warning of political scientist Robert Vitalis, who argues that scholars with ties to policymakers seeking to influence policy debates can end up sacrificing "the scholar's primary objective of producing new knowledge."[101] Vitalis does not only suggest that working in collaboration with government-sponsored research consortia might compromise one's objectivity and autonomy, but he is equally wary of scholars whose research programs and theoretical tools are guided by their ideological opposition to American foreign policy. Vitalis has shown in his research on the political economy of Egypt how in the 1970s and 1980s Middle East studies scholars driven by their political opposition to U.S. foreign policy and their solidarity leftist forces in Egypt led them to "metatheorical commitments [in the form of adherence to theories of dependency and neocolonialism] that time and again hobbled analysis."[102]

As we witness the decline of the American era, McGreevy's reflection about the "American question" in the wake of the 2006 war as experienced in Beirut can be transformed to a productive use for knowledge production. Take, for example, the field of security studies. In their programmatic 2006 essay "The Postcolonial Moment in Security Studies," Tarak Barkawi and Mark Laffey not only reconfirm how "security studies [has generally been] by and for western powers" but also suggest a series of moves that might help pluralize the fields of security studies and international relations.[103] As I have suggested elsewhere, perhaps the next turn in security studies and international relations scholarship will lead to the proliferation of scholarship developed by scholars situated in the postcolonial states, especially those exposed to the violence of colonial modernity.[104] I do not think that "the politics of a non-European security studies" need be defined simply, as Barkawi and Laffey suggest, in terms of standing "with the weak against the strong, with the many against the few" and backing their equal right to bear arms. Rather, an alternative way of defining a "Beirut school" approach to scholarship is one outlined by John Waterbury in a *Foreign Affairs* essay he published while president of AUB. Waterbury notes that in "any attempt to deal with the widespread rage against Washington in the Muslim Middle East," institutions such as AUB are "perhaps the strongest weapon in Washington's 'soft power' arsenal."[105]

However, Waterbury does not suggest—as proponents of soft power usually do—that AUB or other such educational institutions can be used as tools to reshape the preferences of other states and societies or increase the attractiveness of American polices.[106] Rather, he suggests that they can provide a basis for the mutual recognition of rival interests. Explaining that "today's crisis is not one of values, let alone civilizations, but one of interests," he argues "the real problem is that the various sides in the crisis do not understand the 'other's' interests or the 'other's' politics. Hence they have not found a way to talk intelligibly and intelligently about the nature of their conflicting interests."[107] To be able to produce knowledge that recognizes these conflicting interests requires scholarship that seeks to understand diverse subjectivities and avoids being hemmed in by frameworks that seek to resolve conflicts and difference. Take, for example, the challenge of the development of scholarship about the Lebanese militant group Hezbollah. Much U.S.-based security scholarship is framed in relationship to the definition of the group as a "terrorist" organization. As a result, this scholarship tends to follow either the neo-Orientalist or neomodernization approaches. This is to say, such scholarship either offers a catalogue of villainous deeds suggesting means for its defeat or, alternatively, attempts to counter such views by portraying the group as having evolved into a political movement with legitimate political goals learning to play by the rules of the Lebanese political system. An example of an alternative approach is the work of two Beirut-based scholars, Mona Harb and Reinoud Leenders, who suggest "that both the labeling of Hizbullah as terrorist and, conversely, its identification as a 'lebanonised' political force that is about to make its conversion into an unarmed political party are misleading and incapable of grasping this organisation's complexities."[108] They note that, "in fact, both 'terrorist' and 'lebanonised' labels produce a quality of knowledge inferior to that produced by Hizbullah's own conceptualisation of its enemies. But most importantly, the debate on Hizbullah's alleged terrorist nature has obscured several of its traits that many should register before passing judgment on it."[109] Harb and Leenders here offer an approach to study Hezbollah that refuses to define its objectives as a priori either opposed to or in support of Hezbollah's political objectives.

While they are not the only places able to produce such an approach, institutions such as AUB are keenly situated to cultivate scholarship and teaching that adopts such an approach to the study of both Hezbollah as well as U.S. policy in the region. At the same time, these institutions foster scholarship formulated in a language and idiom that is widely understood and recognized for scholarly rigor. Waterbury explains the modest role that institutions such as AUB can play in influencing the course of global politics: "Higher education cannot erase clashing interests or inimical policies. But it can have a role in shaping the way conflicts are conducted. . . . It can promote a broader understanding of the route to certain impasses and of alternative roads past them."[110] Waterbury writes in the same issue of *Foreign Affairs*, as Ajami's essay noted earlier, but suggests a radically different scope and method for American efforts to impact the Arab world. He recognizes conflicts of interests between the United States and the Arab world and does not suggest that American influence or institutions can or should produce a convergence of interests by "modernizing" the people of the region. Rather, he makes the limited claim that American institutions of higher learning can promote means for rival parties to understand the other side's interests and alternative means to possibly accommodate those differences.[111] Such a role recognizes a capability that is far more limited than what most American policymakers seeking to expand American soft power are willing to settle for. At the same time, it suggests a mode for American engagement with the Arab world that can be part of an effort to imagine a more pluralist global order.

Notes

1. Fouad Ajami, "Iraq and the Arabs' Future," *Foreign Affairs* 82, no. 1 (January–February 2003): 2.

2. Nils Gilman, *Mandarins of the Future: Modernization Theory in Cold War America* (Baltimore: Johns Hopkins University Press, 2007); and Michael E. Lathman, *The Right Kind of Revolution: Modernization, Development and U.S. Foreign policy from the Cold War to the Present* (Ithaca, N.Y.: Cornell University Press, 2011).

3. On the notion of "soft power," see Joseph Nye, "Soft Power and Higher Education," *Forum Futures* (2005): 11–14. On the AUB as a tool of American soft power, see Rasmus Bertelsen, "Private Foreign-Affiliated Universities, the State, and Soft Power: The American University of Beirut and the American University in Cairo," *Foreign Policy Analysis* 8, no. 3 (July 2012): 1–19.

4. Henry R. Luce, "The American Century," *Life*, February 17, 1941.

5. Henry R. Luce, "The American Century," Reprinted in *Diplomatic History* 23, no. 2 (Spring 1999): 170.

6. Cited in Melani McAlister, *Epic Encounters: Culture, Media, & U.S. Interests in the Middle East since 1945* (Berkeley: University of California Press, 2005), 52.

7. David Ekbladh, "A Pillar's Progress: How Development's History Shapes U.S. Options in the Present," Belfer Center Discussion Paper 2010–03 (Cambridge, Mass.: Harvard Kennedy School, 2010), 6.

8. See Gilman, *Mandarins of the Future*; and Robert A. Packenham, *Liberal America and the Third World* (Princeton, N.J.: Princeton University Press, 1973).

9. See Osamah F. Khalil, "At the Crossroads of Empire: The United States, the Middle East, and the Politics of Knowledge, 1902–2002" (PhD dissertation, Department of History, University of California, Berkeley, 2011), 62.

10. Ekbladh, "A Pillar's Progress," 6.

11. See Gilman, *Mandarins of the Future*, chapter 5.

12. Daniel Lerner, *The Passing of Traditional Societies: Modernizing the Middle East* (New York: Free Press, 1958).

13. Zachary Lockman, *Contending Visions of the Middle East*, 2nd ed. (Cambridge: Cambridge University Press, 2010), 138.

14. Lerner, *Passing of Traditional Societies*, 47.

15. Ibid., 402, as cited in Lockman, *Contending Visions of the Middle East*, 138.

16. Walt W. Rostow, *The Stages of Economic Growth: A Non-Communist Manifesto* (Cambridge: Cambridge University Press, 1960).

17. Ibid., 164.

18. See Lockman, *Contending Visions of the Middle East*, 130–34; See also Matthew Jacobs, *Imagining the Middle East* (Chapel Hill: University of North Carolina Press, 2011), 151–58.

19. Jacobs, *Imagining the Middle East*, 160.

20. See Malik Mufti, "The United States and Nasserist Pan-Arabism," in *The Middle East and the United States: A Historical and Political Reassessment*, ed. David W. Lesch, 141–60 (Boulder, Colo.: Westview, 2007); and Warren Bass, *Support Any Friend: Kennedy's Middle East and the Making of the U.S.–Israel Alliance* (Oxford: Oxford University Press, 2003).

21. On Nasser's Arab nationalist understanding of insecurity, see Steve Niva, "Contested Sovereignties and Postcolonial Insecurities in the Middle East," in *Cultures of Insecurity: States, Communities, and the Production of Danger*, ed. Jutta Weldes, Mark Laffey, Hugh Gusterson, and Raymond Duvall, 147–72 (Minneapolis: University of Minnesota Press, 1999), 160–64.

22. W. W. Rostow, "Mideast Policy Must Look Beyond This Crisis," *Washington Post*, January 13, 1957, E1.

23. Ibid.

24. Ibid.

25. Ibid.

26. Ibid.

27. Max F. Millikan and W. W. Rostow, *A Proposal: Key to an Effective Foreign Policy* (New York: Harper, 1957).

28. Max F. Millikan and Donald L. M. Blackmer, eds., *The Emerging Nations: Their Growth and United States Policy* (Boston: Little, Brown, 1961), x.

29. Ibid., 133.

30. Richard H. Nolte and William E. Polk, "Toward a Policy for the Middle East," *Foreign Affairs* 36, no. 4 (July 1958): 645–58.

31. Ibid., 645.

32. Ibid., 647.

33. Ibid., 649.

34. Ibid., 650.

35. Ibid.

36. Ibid., 653.

37. Ibid.

38. Ibid.

39. Cited in Mufti, "The United States and Nasserist Pan-Arabism," 148.

40. Ibid.

41. Polk, William R. "The Lesson of Iraq," *Atlantic Monthly*, December 1958, http://www.theatlantic.com/magazine/archive/1958/12/the-lesson-of-iraq/306494/.

42. Ibid.

43. Ibid.

44. Ibid.

45. William R. Polk, *The United States and the Arab World* (Cambridge, Mass.: Harvard University Press, 1965), 222, 227.

46. Polk, "The Lesson of Iraq."

47. Ibid.

48. See Ted Widmer, "The Challenge of Imperialism," *Boston Globe*, July 15, 2007; and Waleed Hazbun, "Fragments of a Retrospective History: Senator Kennedy's Geopolitical Vision," in *Connections and Ruptures: America and the Middle East*, ed. Robert Myers, (Beirut: Center for American Studies and Research, American University of Beirut, 2011), 343–55.

49. Bass, Support Any Friend, 77.

50. John S. Badeau, "To Aid Developing Areas," *New York Times*, December 27, 1953.

51. Badeau, John S. "The Middle East: Conflict in Priorities," *Foreign Affairs* 36, no. 2 (January 1958): 240.

52. Ibid.

53. Ibid.

54. Jacobs, *Imagining the Middle East*, 176; and "Public Law 480: 'Better than a Bomber,'" *Middle East Report* (March–April 1987), 25.

55. Nathan J. Citino, "The 'Crush' of Ideologies: The United States, the Arab World, and Cold War Modernisation," *Cold War History* 12, no. 1 (2012): 102.

56. Quoted in Bass, *Support Any Friend*, 89.

57. Jacobs, *Imagining the Middle East*, 176–77.

58. Brandon Wolfe-Hunnicutt, "Embracing Regime Change in Iraq: The American Foreign Policy and the 1963 Coup d'état in Baghdad," *Diplomatic History* 39, no. 1 (December 2014): 98–125.

59. See William Stivers, *America's Confrontation with Revolutionary Change in the Middle East, 1948–83* (New York: St. Martin's Press, 1986).

60. W. W. Rostow, *The Diffusion of Power: An Essay in Recent History* (New York: Macmillan, 1972), 199.

61. W. W. Rostow, *Politics and the Stages of Growth* (Cambridge: Cambridge University Press, 1971), 359.

62. Lathman, *The Right Kind of Revolution*, 83.

63. John S. Badeau, *The American Approach to the Arab World* (New York: Harper & Row for the Council on Foreign Relations, 1968), 16.

64. Ibid.

65. The same can be said about an American long-term interest is resolving the Arab–Israel conflict, which often conflicts with American short-term concerns about Israeli security.

66. Rostow, "Mideast Policy Must Look Beyond This Crisis."

67. Ibid.

68. Ibid.

69. Roby Barrett, *The Greater Middle East and the Cold War: US Foreign Policy under Eisenhower and Kennedy* (London: I. B. Tauris, 2007), 2.

70. Manfred Halpern, *The Politics of Social Change in the Middle East and North Africa* (Princeton, N.J.: Princeton University Press, 1963).

71. Richard W. Bulliet, *The Case for Islamo-Christian Civilization* (New York: Columbia University Press, 2006), 123.

72. On continually saliency of Islamist alternatives, see Citino, "The 'Crush' of Ideologies"; and Bulliet, *The Case for Islamo-Christian Civilization.*

73. Bulliet, *The Case for Islamo-Christian Civilization*, 107.

74. Ibid., 116.

75. Robert Vitalis, *America's Kingdom: Mythmaking on the Saudi Oil Frontier* (London: Verso, 2009), 247–48.

76. Ibid., 244.

77. Ibid. The mythology seems to have spread far and wide. Jonathan Curiel writes "[Grateful] Dead lyricist Robert Hunter, who wrote *Blues for Allah*, once described Faisal as 'a progressive and democratically inclined ruler,' a reference to Faisal's championing of women's rights, his prohibition of slavery, and his other [for Saudi Arabia] liberal measures." See Jonathan Curiel, *Al' America: Travels through America's Arab and Islamic Roots* (New York: New Press, 2008), 125.

78. Stivers, *America's Confrontation*, 43.

79. See Gilman, *Mandarins of the Future*, chapters 6, 7. On the limits of modernization and political development theory, suggesting how they failed to accommodate the demands for populist democracy and mass participation at the heart of Third World nationalisms, see Irene Gendzier, *Managing Political Change: Social Scientists and the Third World* (Boulder, Colo.: Westview, 1985).

80. See Samuel P. Huntington, *Political Order in Changing Societies* (New Haven, Conn.: Yale University Press, 1968).

81. James Gelvin, "American Global Economic Policy and the Civic Order in the Middle East," in *Is There a Middle East? The Evolution of a Geopolitical Concept*, ed. Michael E. Bonine, Michael Gasper, and Abbas Amanat (Stanford, Calif.: Stanford University Press, 2011), 191–206.

82. Ajami, "Iraq and the Arabs' Future," 5.

83. Quoted in Ussama Makdisi, "Anti-Americanism in the Arab World: An Interpretation of a Brief History," *Journal of American History* 89, no. 2 (September 2002): 538.

84. Quoted in ibid.

85. See Lockman, *Contending Visions of the Middle East*, chapters 5, 6.

86. See ibid., 217–37; McAlister, *Epic Encounters*, 216–23; and Fawaz Gerges, *America and Political Islam.* (Cambridge: Cambridge University Press, 1999), 21–28. See also, Ajami, Fouad. *The Arab Predicament: Arab Political Thought and Practice since 1967*, 2nd ed. (Cambridge: Cambridge University Press, 1992).

87. On origins of the notion of "benevolent America" in the Middle East, see Makdisi, "Anti-Americanism in the Arab World."

88. See Waleed Hazbun, "The Middle East through the Lens of Critical Geopolitics: Globalization, Terrorism, and the Iraq War," in *Is There a Middle East? The Evolution of a Geopolitical Concept*, ed. Michael E. Bonine, Michael Gasper, and Abbas Amanat (Stanford, Calif.: Stanford University Press, 2011), 207–30.

89. Michael Hirsch, "Bernard Lewis Revisited," *Washington Monthly*, November 2004, 13. See also Peter Waldman, "A Historian's Take on Islam Steers U.S. in Terrorism Fight," *Wall Street Journal*, February 3, 2004.

90. Thomas L. Friedman, "Under the Arab Street," *New York Times*, October 23, 2002.

91. See Laleh Khalili, *Time in the Shadows: Confinement in Counterinsurgencies* (Stanford, Calif.: Stanford University Press, 2013), 57.

92. CQ Transcripts Wire, "Secretary Rice Holds a News Conference," July 21, 2006, http://www.washingtonpost.com/wp-dyn/content/article/2006/07/21/AR 2006072100889.html.

93. Ibid.

94. McGreevy, Patrick. "The American Question," *Journal of American Studies in Turkey*, 24 (Fall 2007), 15–27.

95. McGreevy, Patrick. "Living against America: Classroom Encounters in Beirut," *Journal of American History* 96, no. 4 (March 2010), 1088.

96. Ibid.

97. Edward W. Said, "Ignorant Armies Clash by Night," *Nation*, February 11, 1991.

98. Stephen Walt, "The End of the American Era," *National Interest,* November–December 2011, 6–16.

99. See Waleed Hazbun, "The Geopolitics of Knowledge and the Challenge of Postcolonial Agency: International Relations, U.S. Policy and the Arab World," in *The Oxford Handbook of Postcolonial Studies*, ed. Graham Huggan (Oxford: Oxford University Press, 2013), 217–34.

100. See Steve Niva, "Disappearing Violence: JSOC and the Pentagon's New Cartography of Networked Warfare," *Security Dialogue* 44, no. 3 (2003): 185–202.

101. Robert Vitalis, "Thinner than Air," *Middle East Report*, no. 242 (Spring 2007): 44.

102. Robert Vitalis, "The End of Third Worldism in Egyptian Studies," *Arab Studies Journal* 4, no. 1 (Spring 1996): 13.

103. Tarak Barkawi and Mark Laffey, "The Postcolonial Moment in Security Studies," *Review of International Studies* 32 (2006): 344.

104. Hazbun, "Geopolitics of Knowledge," 231.

105. John Waterbury, "Hate Your Policies, Love Your Institutions," *Foreign Affairs* 82, no. 1 (January–February 2003): 61.

106. See Nye, "Soft Power and Higher Education"; and Bertelsen, "Private Foreign-Affiliated Universities."

107. Waterbury, "Hate Your Policies," 60.

108. Mona Harb and Reinoud Leenders, "Know Thy Enemy: Hizbullah, 'Terrorism' and the Politics of Perception," *Third World Quarterly* 26, no. 1 (2005): 173.

109. Ibid., 173.

110. Waterbury, "Hate Your Policies," 67.

111. On the politics of teaching American studies abroad, see McGreevy, "The American Question."

Traveling Law

Targeted Killing, Lawfare, and the Deconstruction of the Battlefield

CRAIG JONES

Striking Origins

On the morning of November 9, 2000, Israeli Air Force helicopters were heard above the Palestinian village of Beit Sahour. Then came the explosion. Sitting in his unarmored Jeep, Hussein Abiyat, a senior member of Fatah, went up in flames. The antitank missile killed Abiyat and two innocent elderly women: "collateral damage." Later that day, two months after the outbreak of the second Palestinian intifada, the Israeli military publicly assumed responsibility for the strike: "During an operation initiated by the IDF [Israeli Defense Force], in the area of the village of Beit Sahour, missiles were launched from Air Force helicopters toward the vehicle of a senior activist of the Fatah Tanzim. The pilots reported the target was accurately hit. The activist was killed and his deputy, who was with him, was injured."[1] No mention was made of the murdered elderly women, but aside from this silence, the announcement is vitally important because it marked the beginning of Israel's official assassination policy. The justification and legal contention was that Israel had entered what IDF lawyers called "an armed conflict short of war" and that Israel was entitled to target and kill enemy individuals as permitted by the rules of war outlined in International Humanitarian Law (IHL) (also sometimes known as the Laws of Armed Conflict).[2]

Though it might now seem difficult to believe, the European Union and the United States condemned the attacks and rejected Israel's legal position. British foreign secretary Jack Straw claimed that the assassinations were "unlawful, unjustified and self-defeating."[3] The European Union said the policy amounted to "extrajudicial killings" while U.S. State Department spokesman Richard Boucher said such action was "heavy-handed." The U.S. government made it repeatedly clear that it opposed targeted killings.[4] An international fact-finding mission, established by President Bill Clinton and led by former U.S. senator George

Mitchell refused to accept the Israeli view that the threshold of "armed conflict" had been crossed: the intifada constituted civil unrest, a domestic police issue and not a war. The Mitchell Report dismissed the idea of war as being "overly broad" and noted that the "IDF should adopt crowd-control tactics that minimize the potential for deaths and casualties," urging further that "an effort should be made to differentiate between terrorism and protests."[5] The message was clear: terrorism could not legitimately be dealt with via recourse to war, and Israel should revert back to the more traditional law enforcement approach, a legal regime that places far greater restrictions on the use of lethal force.[6]

The U.S. criticism of Israeli-targeted killing policy was short lived, however. By 2000 the CIA was already flying Predator drones over Afghanistan in search for Osama bin Laden, but the Predators were still unarmed when Israel went public with its targeted killing campaign. In late 2000 the head of the CIA's Counterterrorism Center, Cofer Black, decided to arm the Predator even though the head of the CIA, George Tenet, still had "serious questions about the new killing technology and the ethics and legality behind its use."[7] Shortly after the terror attacks on 9/11 George W. Bush approved a presidential finding that sanctioned CIA strikes on al-Qaeda as a "defensive" measure in the then nascent "global war on terrorism" (GWOT). The first lethal drone missions were conducted in Afghanistan in late 2001 as part of so-called Operation Enduring Freedom. Only a year later armed drones were introduced into Yemen, a fact that demonstrated the malleability of the GWOT concept while also radically expanding its geographies. On November 3, 2002, CIA operatives fired a Hellfire missile from a Predator, killing Qaed Salim Sinan al-Harethi, who was allegedly responsible for organizing the suicide bombing attack on a U.S. Navy missile destroyer, the USS *Cole*, in October 2000. Two days after killing al-Harethi, the then-deputy defense secretary, Paul Wolfowitz, openly confirmed it was a U.S. strike and called it a "very successful tactical operation."[8] The strike, the first by an armed drone outside of Afghanistan—and thus *outside* of any recognized battlefield—resembled and yet also exceeded Israel's attempt to justify assassination by expanding the definition of war. Both the United States and Israel had defied the international consensus on assassination, and in this sense we may read these initial strikes in Palestine and Yemen as the origins of a concerted attempt to legalize and legitimize "targeted killing" (the term itself is a euphemism and conceals the possible imprecision and so-called "secondary" or "incidental" effects of the tactic by promising a violence that is targeted and therefore highly discriminatory[9]). Israel invented the legal model for assassination, and the United States not only adopted but crucially also expanded it, first into Yemen and later into Pakistan and Somalia. These were not mere legal abstractions: the new Israeli and U.S. targeted killing policies challenged the very definition of war. They did so by abandoning the notion that the battlefield should have geographical limitations, whether symbolic or real.[10] These states wanted the legal privilege to kill anywhere, including places that "terrorists *might* go seeking safe haven."[11] Frequently these putative "safe havens" were—and are—not in states or territories bordering actual war zones (such as Iraq and Afghanistan) but are hundreds of miles away, often on a different continent.[12] Paying particular attention to U.S. targeted killing in Yemen and Pakistan, Jeremy Scahill has argued that very early on in the GWOT, at least according to the White House, Pentagon, and the CIA, the whole world became a battlefield.[13] Scahill's account echoes Derek Gregory's argument that the United States and Israel have laid the foundations for what he calls an "everywhere war," though Gregory also insists that the production of a global battlespace is contingent upon a distinct *legal* armature—or armatures—that secure and enable several modalities of military violence, targeted killing and drone strikes among them.[14]

In this chapter I argue that U.S. drone warfare is indebted in several important ways to Israel's targeted killing policy and in particular to Israel's expansionist definition of war. In recent years, U.S. drone warfare has been subject to growing scholarly and popular critique.[15] But far less attention has been paid to Israeli-targeted killing.[16] There may be several explanations for this, but surely among them are the twin facts that targeted killing in Israel has decreased every year since 2006 and that, even at their peak in 2001–4, Israeli-targeted killings were and are dwarfed—in scope and scale—by U.S. targeted killing (Kevin John Heller called the latter "one hell of a killing machine").[17] The casualty statistics are a minefield of their own, but they do communicate some of the scale and breadth of Israeli and U.S. targeted killings in relation to one another. Between September 29, 2000, and July 7, 2014, Israel has killed 543 Palestinians in targeted killing operations; 191 of these were civilians.[18] This is no small number, of course, but in comparison, the United States has killed the following during targeted killing operations: in Pakistan from 2004 to 2014, between 2,347 and 3,792 (of which 416–957 were civilians); in Yemen from 2002 to 2014, between 321 and 512 (of which

24–48 were civilians); and in Somalia from 2007–2014, between 16 and 30 (of which 1 was a civilian).[19] Importantly, these statistics do not include data on what the Bureau of Investigative Journalism terms "possible extra drone strikes" or "other covert operations" (because these operations are difficult to verify) although their estimates suggest that fatalities could be in excess of 1,000 in addition to those numbers given here. The data also does not include targeted killings in Iraq and Afghanistan (data concerning operations in these overt wars is, paradoxically, much more difficult to come by than data for "covert" wars) though targeted killing of known individuals—"priority" or "high-value" persons on a target list—and those persons thought to express a dangerous "pattern of life" have been common throughout the wars in Iraq and Afghanistan and remain an important tactic following the recent resurgence of the Islamic State of Iraq and al-Sham, or ISIS, in Iraq and Syria.

But, lest the dust completely settle on Israeli-targeted killing policy, as Amos Harel argued it already has, my argument is that we might productively approach U.S. drone warfare and targeted killing by examining a key part of its legal origins in and through the Israeli experience.[20] Crucial to my account is the notion that law is a "traveling phenomenon."[21] Israel used the paradigm of war to legally justify its targeted killing policy, and the United States subsequently borrowed and expanded this framework. But, like anything else, law does not travel alone and no legal "transplant" is an exact replica of the "body" from which it came;[22] it requires a carrier as well as a receptive (legal and political) community.

I use the concept of lawfare to explore the circulations of targeted killing law between Israel and the United States. There are several definitions of lawfare (which I will come to), but in conceptualizing targeted killing law as lawfare I mean two things. First, the attempts by Israel and the United States to legalize and normalize targeted killing constitute an abuse and weaponization of law. Second, the debates about lawfare that have emerged over the last decade and a half have become a medium through which targeted killing has been justified and normalized. To ground this argument, I reject conservative definitions of lawfare as something that is conducted only by the "weak" enemy Other.

In the following two sections I review the literature on lawfare, first examining conservative accounts of what I call "diabolical lawfare" before moving to deconstruct the idea that Israel and the United States practice a form of "benign" lawfare. I then outline how Israel sought to legalize targeted killing and how, subsequently, the United States used the war paradigm to radically expand and "deconstruct" the battlefield. These movements between the Israeli legalization of targeted killing and U.S. deconstruction of the battlefield are particularly potent forms of lawfare not only because they seek to legitimize violence that would otherwise be considered illegitimate but also because they expand the scope of said violence such that there may be no escape from the battlefield. By way of conclusion, I argue that targeted killing, lawfare, and the deconstruction of the battlefield help to clarify a shift in the geographical and ontological borders of war at the putative "end of the American Century."[23]

Diabolical Lawfare

Former U.S. Air Force deputy judge advocate general Charles Dunlap popularized the term "lawfare."[24] In his original essay he defined it simply as "the use of law as a weapon of war," but he gave it a pejorative meaning, indicating that lawfare was a new form of warfare that posed a series of potential threats to the United States and its allies.[25] By 2005 the threat was registered in the National Defense Strategy, which stated "our strength as a nation will continue to be challenged by those who employ a strategy of the weak using international fora, judicial processes, and terrorism."[26]

The context for the emergence of the lawfare discourse in the United States was the international outcry over torture, rendition, and indefinite detention in Guantanamo Bay and Abu Ghraib. There are those who view the very existence of these "black sites" as a deliberate attempt to create a space of exception through the law (that is, lawfare par excellence[27]). But others view this as a radical misreading lawfare. Michael J. Lebowitz, for example, argues that the real abuse of law in Guantanamo came not from the torturers or the lawyers who wrote the "torture memos" but from those actually detained in Guantanamo.[28] According to her, "by following what was tantamount to scripted legal advice, detainees and their advocates in the aftermath of the 9/11 attacks launched a massive campaign through various court systems worldwide."[29] In this view, lawfare is synonymous with the tactics of terrorism and, as Eyal Benvenisti explains, humanitarians have albeit unwillingly become "strategic all[ies] of the terrorists because the terrorists benefit indirectly from whatever constraints" humanitarians seek to impose on the state.[30]

Radical views on lawfare are by no means unique to the United States. Israel has also led the charge against the "illegitimate" use of lawfare. Most commentators begin their analysis of lawfare against Israel with the publication of a UN investigation into war crimes committed by Hamas and Israel during Operation Cast Lead, the horrific Israeli assault on Gaza in 2008–9.[31] Dubbed the Goldstone Report after its principal author, Richard Goldstone (a Jewish South African judge who issued several important rulings opposing apartheid and who served as the first chief prosecutor of the UN International Criminal Tribunal for the former Yugoslavia and Rwanda), the report was a damning condemnation of both Israeli and Hamas actions during the three-week war. But most commentators gloss over this fact and fasten on Goldstone as a powerful symbol of the ultimate abuse of law.[32] The lawfare debate in Israel reached a climax in 2010 when Prime Minister Binyamin Netanyahu told the press that Goldstone is a "code word for an attempt to delegitimise Israel's right to self-defense." He listed Goldstone as "one of Israel's most serious security challenges" alongside Iran's nuclear program and Hamas rocket fire.[33] More recently, following Israel's latest large scale military invasion of Gaza—so-called Operation Protective Edge—the IDF has set up a new legal unit and has expanded its Military Advocate General Corps to deal with "legal battles" resulting from the carnage caused by the IDF.[34]

There have been several civil lawsuits concerning U.S. and Israeli courts that have raised the profile of the lawfare debate.[35] These lawsuits raise a number of claims, some of them pertaining to the prohibition against torture and indefinite detention, but more frequently and more recently they concern the fraught legality of targeted killing.[36] These lawsuits have had very limited success in terms of outlawing targeted killing, and courts have helped to normalize and legitimize the tactic both by accepting its legality (as has happened in Israel) and by refusing to hear any cases relating to targeted killing (as has happened in the United States). In a landmark but controversial ruling handed down by the Israeli High Court of Justice (HCJ) in 2006, targeted killing was understood to be within the bounds of the law. The HCJ set four criteria that must be met for targeted killing to be legal. The HCJ held that targeted killing operations must: (1) take precaution to harm only combatants and civilians who are "directly participating in hostilities"; (2) not be used if "less harmful means can be employed" (the principle of necessity); (3) not use excessive harm (the proportionality principle); and (4) be investigated in cases where excessive harm has been caused. I will return to the significance of this ruling below, but here want to underscore the point that although there is no equivalent ruling in the United States, the effect of nonintervention by the U.S. courts has produced much the same permissive effect as the Israeli HCJ ruling. In *Al Aulaki v. Obama et al.*, the DC District Court cited targeted killing as a "nonjusticiable" question and deferred responsibility to an unstated entity in some unknown future: "the serious issues regarding the merits of the alleged authorization of the targeted killing of a U.S. citizen overseas must await another day or another (non-judicial) forum."[37]

The Executive thus determines U.S. targeted killing policy, and the president personally authorizes individual strikes—all without judicial review.[38] Since at least 2012, following the campaigning of Sen. Dianne Feinstein, a special group of staff members from the House and Senate intelligence committees have had some access to intelligence and operational information used by the CIA in their drone strikes.[39] But without disclosure of the full legal standards guiding the policy, critics have complained that such oversight is ultimately ineffective and that the commission of another secret court is anathema to legal and public transparency.[40]

But these measures to bring targeted killing under judicial review constitute a "legal jihad," according to Brooke Goldstein and Aaron Eitan Meyer.[41] Such renderings write the first half of a typology that has always been fundamental to the lawfare debate: lawfare and other illegitimate weapons—from improvised explosive devices to suicide bombings—belong to the enemy Other. To witness the other part we need look no further than to Brook Goldstein's neoconservative Lawfare Project. The project defines lawfare as "the abuse of Western laws and judicial systems to achieve strategic military or political ends." The qualification of lawfare as something that is done *to* Western legal systems is highly significant and as the project's website goes on to note, lawfare "must be defined as a negative phenomenon to have any real meaning. Otherwise, we risk diluting the threat and feeding the inability to distinguish between that which is the correct application of the law, on the one hand, and that which is lawfare, on the other.[42] The typology comes full circle only when we view Western legal and military practice *against* the abusive and diabolical tactics of the Other. In extremis, this means that "we" do not do lawfare (we merely "apply" laws). Thus, what is common to both Israeli and U.S. lawfare discourse is a strain of abusive and diabolical lawfare that commentators suggest belong to and are typical of the enemy Other; ultimately, these traits are unrecognizable in the Western self. Lawfare has therefore become a site through which classic Orientalist tropes have found considerable purchase. What lawfare boils down to, according to Laurie Blank, is the "exploitation of the law of war" by "insurgent groups."[43] The diabolical lawfare of the Other thus involves deliberately placing their own civilians in the line of fire.[44] According to this logic, those civilians become legitimate "collateral damage," and it is the enemy—not the attacking military—who is responsible for their deaths. Thus Dunlap does not merely call the enemy savages but refers rather to the "savagery of the[ir] *illegalities*," suggesting that the other is premodern precisely because he or she has not entered the world of law and civilization.[45] This is a convenient and self-serving argument that displaces the responsibility of modern military forces to protect civilians while also providing a blanket justification for their "accidental" and "incidental" destruction.[46]

The Global War on Terror: Benign Lawfare?

The rise of the lawfare debate is tied intimately to the terrorist attacks of 9/11 and the war on terror that has traveled and expanded in its wake. It was Gregory who showed with unprecedented clarity the way in which imaginative geographies were mobilized in the wake of 9/11 to script the U.S. war in Afghanistan (and later the U.S. and U.K. war in Iraq) and Israel's military campaigns against Palestine as part of the same war.[47] Once terrorism had become the common enemy—and Gregory is careful to show that the conjunction between "Islam" and "terrorism" was established long before 9/11—so too any tactic employed by the enemy was seen as illegitimate and diabolical, including the appeal to international law and human rights, or the use of courts and other legal instruments. This amounted to an abusive and asymmetrical use of law, according to proponents of military lawfare.[48] This explains why Dunlap defined lawfare as a negative phenomenon: he wanted to militate against the use of law by adversaries of the United States and, although he made no mention of Palestine or Israel in his initial foray into the subject, scholars and commentators were quick to adopt his negative definition and to apply it to Palestinian legal claims.[49] The emergence of a lawfare discourse in the United States and Israel over the last decade and a half is not coincidental but has been shaped by the war on terror and by what Gregory memorably called its "architecture of enmity." In fact, the war on terror constitutes a war *on* international law that is by no means universal or widely accepted, and the conceptualization of lawfare as a negative phenomenon should be seen as a sideshow that distracts attention from the fact that the United States and Israel have been trying to change international law through practices that violate it.[50]

Although Dunlap originally cautioned against the use of lawfare, he later reconsidered his position in light of the wars in Iraq and Afghanistan. "The new counterinsurgency doctrine . . . emphasises that lawfare is more than just something adversaries seek to use against law-abiding societies," he wrote in 2009, "it is a resource that democratic militaries can—and should—employ *affirmatively*."[51] Unlike the lawfare deployed by the enemy, Dunlap claims that U.S. lawfare is about abiding by, installing, and promoting the rule of law. The example he gives is the establishment in Baghdad of a rule of law complex, a "self-contained haven" that "permits Iraqis to solve Iraqi problems in relative safety for themselves and their families." The fortified Green Zone provides a secure environment for a "legal infrastructure" we are told, and along with other "law-oriented, effects-based operations," these have become a "critical piece of counterinsurgency strategy."[52] And just like counterinsurgency operations were supposedly about winning "hearts and minds" by minimizing violence and fighting with empathy (the much commented on "armed social work"[53]), Dunlap's new lawfare is invested in limiting violence and exercising law instead. He thus redefined lawfare as the "strategy of using—or misusing—law as a substitute for traditional military means to achieve an operational objective."[54]

There is something disingenuous about the way that the Israeli and U.S. military and their apologists have represented as negative the use of law as a weapon of war, not least because it seems to be a case of the pot calling the kettle black.[55] Dunlap's realization that "democratic militaries" can also use the law as a weapon of war is equally incredulous. It belies the truth that the United States and other imperial powers both today and historically have all too frequently conducted violence in the name of law.[56] There is not the space here to write a critical history of lawfare, but it is worth making the point that colonial powers have for a long time practiced something very similar to what is today called lawfare.[57] Indeed, as legal anthropologists John Comaroff and Jean Comaroff have cogently argued, part of the backlash against colonial power has been directed precisely at the legal institutions of imperialism:

"What imperialism is being indicted for, above all, is its commission of lawfare: its use of its own rules—of its duly enacted penal codes, its administrative law, its states of emergency, its charters and mandates and warrants, its norms of engagement—to impose a sense of order upon its subordinates by means of violence rendered legible, legal, and legitimate by its own sovereign word. And also to commit its own ever-so-civilized, patronizing, high-minded forms of kleptocracy."[58] Again, and as tempting as that last sentence might be, I cannot go there, but I do nonetheless want to keep this colonial history of lawfare in view, not least because it has all kinds of inflections in the way that the United States and Israel conduct warfare and lawfare today. Perhaps most misleading and frustrating about "benign" accounts of lawfare is that they fail to consider the violence inherent in the exercise and foundation of law. We must ask the following: on what authority will Dunlap's "democratic lawfare" be founded if not on a foundational violence and one constantly reinscribed through the very exercise of warfare? I am thinking here, of course, of Walter Benjamin's lesson that all violence is either law making or law preserving.[59] As Jacques Derrida has shown, law is nothing without enforcement, thus raising the question of who will enforce this "democratic" lawfare, and how?[60] These questions, I think, expose the possibility that lawfare is not and has perhaps never been about finding legal alternatives to traditional military means; rather, it is a method that also facilitates and in a very real sense produces violent military means and not just of the "traditional" variety. In the end though, even Dunlap appears unsure as to whether lawfare really is a substitute for warfare. He writes of the legal and the lethal as expressing more of a complementary relationship: the "parallel application of legal weaponry coincident with more traditional arms" he argues, "can have an exceptionally *productive synergistic* effect."[61] Dunlap is closer to the mark with this epiphany, and in what follows I want to show how the lawfare of targeted killing, far from substituting violence with law, seeks to justify the extension of killing *through* the law.

War through Law (or, Lawfare 2.0)

The "legalization" of targeted killing in Israel was contingent on a foundational act of lawfare. Israel constructed a war, in part, *through* law. A similar war, or rather, a similar conceptualization of war was subsequently emulated by the United States and radically expanded to apply—

potentially—everywhere.[62] I do not want to repeat here the broad discursive formations of the GWOT that have already been so well documented but rather want to focus on the way in which these discursive formations have been injected with a mixture of legal argument and lawfare.[63] Moreover, and although we are by no means beyond the GWOT, the language as a legal construct is now dated. Two examples begin to illustrate the point. Although Israel used the post-9/11 language of terrorism and the "axis of evil" to its full advantage, it never legally justified targeted killing in terms of a *global* war on terror as such (thus raising the question of how Israel's war on terror became the US *global* war on terror).[64] Moreover, when Barack Obama assumed office in 2009, then State Department legal adviser Harold Koh advised him to reject the GWOT label, preferring instead to base U.S. military actions on the view that the United States is in an "armed conflict with al-Qaeda, the Taliban and associated forces." And yet, under Obama we have witnessed not the cessation of Bush's GWOT but its rebranding (as "overseas contingency operations"), recalibration, and expansion.[65] But it would also be intellectually lazy to say that nothing has changed except the name; if nothing else, Obama and Koh's legalistic language marks the increasing legalization or "juridification" of later-modern war. This matters to the present analysis because this juridification of war is underwriting simultaneous changes in the spatiality of the battlefield.

In 2000 the International Law Department (ILD) of the IDF published a legal opinion that sought to redefine the second intifada as a war. This was a radically new situation, Israeli military lawyers argued, and there was no basis for comparison between the first intifada (of 1987–92) and the second intifada.[66] There were two essential ingredients to the legal thesis. First, Israel was allegedly no longer in control of the West Bank and Gaza as it had been in 1987 and so could no longer maintain security (of course, this was a fiction—and it remains a fiction). The Oslo Accords did not end the occupation, and although Israel withdrew from some Palestinian population centers in the West Bank (Area A) throughout the 1990s, it remained in partial control of Area B and in full control of Area C. Gaza, too, was still occupied at the start of the second intifada, and it remains de facto occupied today in spite of Israel's putative "withdrawal" in 2005. Second, and related, Palestinians were now armed with serious weapons, forcing Israel's hand. In an Israeli Ministry of Foreign Affairs press briefing, Col. Daniel Reisner summarized the change in legal perspective thus: "The rules of engagement for the

IDF in the West Bank and Gaza Strip have been modified in accordance with the change in the situation. Prior to the violent events, 'police rules of engagement' were applied.... The situation has now changed. The Palestinians are using violence and terrorism on a regular basis. They are using live ammunition at every opportunity. As a result, Israeli soldiers no longer are required to wait until they are actually shot at before they respond."[67] Once this legal architecture was put in place, the IDF were in a position to use the full force of war: the ILD had created a framework whereby the IDF could legally target and kill Palestinians, or so it claimed. Without first defining Israel's relationship with Palestinian groups as one of war (in legal terms, an "armed conflict"), targeted killing would simply be illegal in all but the most exceptional of circumstances.[68] International human rights law and the law enforcement paradigm—the other legal regimes potentially applicable to targeted killing—place far greater restrictions on the use of force, which is why Israel had opted for a war-type model (an "armed conflict short of war"[69]) that is guided by the more permissive and "gray" regime of IHL.[70]

In December 2000 the killing of Dr. Thabet, a political official and member of the Palestinian Authority, prompted the filing of the first petition challenging the legality of Israel's targeted killing policy in the HCJ.[71] A second petition was filed following one of the most controversial air strikes in Israel's repertoire of targeted killings.[72] The Israeli Air Force dropped a one-tonne bomb on the house in which the leader of Hamas' military wing Salah Shehadeh was sleeping. In addition to Shehadeh and his guard, 14 Palestinian civilians, including 8 children were killed, and more than 150 injured. Both petitions, however, were dismissed on January 29, 2002, the court refusing to intervene.[73] A third petition was eventually accepted on January 24, 2002, but by the time the court had reached its judgment on December 15, 2006, 240 Palestinians had already been killed in targeted killing strikes.[74] The verdict has received a significant amount of praise and criticism, but the most relevant to the present analysis is the fact that the court accepted the majority of the IDF's legal opinions, including the designation of the second intifada a war—that is, the ILD's radical legal opinion gained the force and legitimacy of law.[75] Steadily, a "war process" had "replaced the peace process" and politics had become "an extension of war by other means."[76] The significance of the ruling extended beyond Israel though, and, as Anthony Dworkin pointed out at the time, it would likely become "an important precedent for other countries engaging in military action against terrorist groups." Dworkin clearly had the United States in his sights, and so did the judge who gave the opinion, Dworkin argues, "In some ways Justice Barak's opinion appears to be written with the US in mind."[77]

Traveling Law/fare

At first the United States did not accept Israel's interpretation of the second intifada as an armed conflict, and it spoke out against targeted killing.[78] Senior IDF lawyer Daniel Reisner had opined to the Mitchell Committee and had been "aggressively attacked" by the United States and United Kingdom for his legal opinions, but he looks back on the criticism with a measure of irony: "It took four months and four aircraft to change the mind of the US government."[79] The United States quickly saw a need to target suspected terrorists wherever they might be found, even if they were found outside of a conventionally understood battlefield. Early in 2001, the United States had sent delegations to Israel to try to persuade the IDF to stop the targeted killings. After 9/11, however, they returned with a different mission: they wanted to learn from Israel and to study how Israel had developed and justified its targeted killing policy.[80] The exact nature of those meetings is classified, but news sources at the time reported:

> The Bush administration has been seeking Israel's counsel on creating a legal justification for the assassination of terrorism suspects.... Legal experts from the United States and Israel have met in recent months to discuss the issue, and are considering widening the consultation circle to include representatives of America's closest allies in the war against terrorism.... American representatives were anxious to learn details of the legal work that Israeli government jurists have done during the last two years to tackle possible challenges—both domestic and international—to its policy of "targeted killings" of terrorist suspects.[81]

It is impossible to say how formative of U.S. policy these high-level, closed-door political meetings were, and there is no formal and official document that outlines which parts of Israeli policy the United States might have emulated—or at least, if there is one, it remains classified. In any case, whatever might have been directly borrowed then might not be applicable today. But law does not travel in official documents and through secret meetings alone.

In her study of what she calls the "circulations of law" in the colonial context, Iza Hussin writes that law is a "travelling phenomenon, its logic centred upon the balance between the local and the general."[82] This frames quite neatly the issue of targeted killing and the way that it has traveled from Israel to the United States. The "law" of targeted killing was invented and developed by Israel and when it became useful elsewhere—i.e., in the United States—the law traveled. But this is a little too neat. What was it that traveled, and how? Was it formal law or law-*fare*; was it the overall framework or was it specific tactics? The crucial point is not that law(fare) travels but *how* it travels and *why*. Hussin is once again useful because she reminds us that law leads a worldly and social life. Of the British colonial period she notes that "law did not travel alone: it had carriers and agents, who themselves had travelling companions—government officials and diplomats, traders and business-men, missionaries, pilgrims, scholars, privateers. Its departure was often a matter of heated debate; its arrival at each port of call required trans-lation, negotiation and domestication, as well as all-out war."[83] My aim here, then, is not to reconstruct a cause/effect "moment" in which Israeli-targeted killing is merely "transplanted" to the United States. To under-stand how targeted killing law has traveled, it helps to conceive of law as something richer than legal formalism and to consider the way in which—as David Delaney would have it—law is "worlded."[84] Indeed, to push the point even further, and as theorist of comparative law Edward Wise has written, "legal history, to be genuine history, requires, first of all atten-tion to evidence both about law and about the contexts in which it is embedded."[85] Much work has gone into making and shaping targeted killing, and we should remember that an orgy of senior civil and mili-tary lawyers, military commanders, world leaders, legal scholars, and a host of other experts were—and are—involved in packaging, transporting, and unpacking the law(fare) of targeted killing.[86] For sake of space I focus here only on the jurisprudence that has played an especially important role in defining, transporting and transforming the law(fare) of targeted killing.

Several advocates of a more permissive approach to the U.S. targeted killing policy have been inspired by or have drawn heavily upon the Is-raeli experience and the Palestine–Israel conflict more broadly. Former UN special rapporteur on extrajudicial, summary, or arbitrary executions Philip Alston has usefully catalogued some of the most vociferous of these opinions and is worth quoting at length:

[Amos] Guiora ... argues that, "international laws explicitly providing for active self-defense should be formed out of what has been learned from Israel's struggle with terrorism." The tendency to extrapolate from Israel's experience in order to arrive at policy prescriptions for the United States is well illustrated by the title and subtitle of a later article by the same author: "License to Kill: When I advised the Israel Defense Forces, here's how we decided if targeted kills were legal—or not." ... Similarly, [Eyal] Gross criticises the inflexibility of international humanitarian lawyers who are not prepared to "reconsider the merits" of targeted killings, chemical warfare, and attacks on currently protected groups of civilians. ... Almost all of the factual information and case studies are drawn from Israel's policies. ... Other commentators [Gabriella Blum and Phillip Heyman] suggest that there is already an identity of interest and indeed even a degree of symmetry in terms of both law and policy between Israeli and American approaches. Thus they note that both countries have made targeted killings "an essential part of their counterterrorism strategy" and that both have found them to be "an inevitable means of frustrating the activities of terrorists who are directly involved in plotting and instigating attacks from outside their territory."[87]

Alston's review of this literature is tremendously useful in demonstrating the ways in which the debate that legal scholars have become embroiled in is not abstract and academic but is concerned with big political and legal questions, the very stuff of targeted killing. As such, he demonstrates that legal scholars are not neutral arbiters on targeted killing but are rather proactive carriers and shapers of its discourse. The message from this scholarship is that the Israeli-targeted killing experience is one that can and should be emulated. Afsheen Radsan and Richard Murphy push the point even further: if a "small country quite vulnerable to terrorism ... can create and manage a system of accountability for targeted killing, then, on a similar balance, the United States should be able to do so as well."[88] But Alston shows why such arguments are problematic: invariably, they focus on Israel's *stated* policy and on the HCJ's somewhat restrictive approach to targeted killings rather than on the *actual* practice and conduct of targeted killing. His own analysis of Israeli practice reveals severe shortcomings, and ultimately he registers a profound skepticism that Israel serves as a model to be emulated.[89]

A list of differences exists between the U.S. approach and the Israeli approach, and some of the more significant differences have come to the surface very recently. Israel does not, at least as a matter of policy, target and kill its own citizens, whereas the United States has and does. The same Department of Justice white paper that justified the execution of U.S. citizen Anwar al-Awlaki also contained a radically expansive definition of "imminent threat," expanding the scope of who can be targeted and when.[90] Israeli scholars and former IDF military lawyers have spoken out against these and other elements of U.S. targeted killing policy.[91] But the most startling differences are surely over the nature and geography of these wars: the size and geography of the Palestine–Israel conflict is very different from those in Iraq and Afghanistan, to say nothing of the covert wars that the United States is waging in Pakistan, Yemen, and Somalia. The origins of the conflicts are different, and they have been fought differently. Legal scholar Kenneth Anderson is our guide here: "The fact of living cheek by jowl, a conflict going on for generations, a relatively enormous amount of intelligence available for purposes of making meaningful determinations in a limited geographic space on a limited population—it is all fantastically sui generis, and I believe quite inapplicable and irreplicable elsewhere."[92] In a way, of course, both Anderson and Alston are correct: we cannot simply cut and paste from one conflict to another, even less because these conflicts are plural and multifaceted. For example, it is not clear whether Israel is at war only with Palestine (or only Gaza and Hamas?) or whether the armed conflict is also against Lebanon, Syria, and Iran.[93] It is also not clear whether and where cyberwarfare constitutes and triggers armed conflict.[94] Furthermore, the United States is fighting multiple wars, all of which have been of a very different nature and have taken divergent courses: "counterinsurgency" in Iraq and Afghanistan, "counterterror" there and elsewhere, al-Qaeda and the Taliban in Pakistan, al-Shebab in Somalia, and so on. All of these wars are overdetermined, and the idea that one tactic and technology—targeted killing—applies to and should be used in and across these wars in the same way is intellectually (and strategically) lazy. But herein lies the rub with Alston's analysis on the inapplicability of the Israeli-targeted killing model to the United States. He focuses our attention on the practice of targeted killing, and while this is a welcome departure from accounts that merely parrot doctrine and policy, his analysis fails to take into account the broader legal and discursive schema within which targeted killing has been produced and transported. That is, by focusing on the ways in which Israeli and U.S. targeted killings are incongruent, he misses the crucial point that they have been made to coincide through legal recourse to the "paradigm of war." Israel's "armed conflict short of war" has been remade, and it is not so much that targeted killing is taking place "beyond borders" as Alston would have it: targeted killing is taking place through the annihilation and radical redrawing of borders. We must turn to contemporary deconstructions of the battlefield if we are to fully appreciate the lawfare that not only seeks to justify targeted killing but also renders meaningless the borders that might have contained it.

Deconstructing the Battlefield

In this final section I argue that Israel's construction of an expansionist and aggressive paradigm of war proved the most potent form of lawfare that made its way across the Atlantic because it provided the United States with an entire legal framework within which targeted killing could be justified. The war framework has become so expansive that it effectively deconstructs the normative and legal borders of war: once the entire world is constructed as a battlefield, the borders demarcating the inside/outside of war no longer exist: there is no outside. The recent legal battle to redefine and expand the battlefield has not been conceived of as part of the lawfare debate, and yet I believe it is at the cutting edge of politico-scholastic lawfare. Frédéric Mégret has written of a "vanishing battlefield," and while he careful to point out that the "deconstruction of the battlefield" has been under way since the nineteenth century (with the invention of firepower), he also insists that there *is* something new about the deconstructions of the post-9/11 era: "There is no doubt that a deliberate attempt to manipulate what constitutes the battlefield and to transcend it in ways that liberate rather than constrain violence has been at the heart of the response to the terror attacks of 9/11.... The War on Terror essentially combines all the deconstructing effects that have taken their toll on the idea of the battlefield in the 20th Century, to the point of making it barely recognizable."[95] What vanishes for Mégret—the normative legal zones of conflict—appears in Derek Gregory's analysis as an "everywhere war," where he alerts us to new (but always historically contingent) spaces of war, cyberwarfare, drone warfare outside of traditional warzones, and counternarcotics.[96]

These critical—and critically important—analyses respond to recent debates in law about the so-called legal geography of war.[97] Such debates, of course, go back at least to the authorization to use military force passed by Congress on September 14, 2001. The authorization granted the president the authority to use all "necessary and appropriate force" against those whom he determined "planned, authorized, committed or aided" the 9/11 attacks or who harbored those persons or groups.[98] The authority to use military force also came from secret orders, such as the al-Qaeda network execute order signed by Secretary of Defense Donald Rumsfeld in 2004. The order "allowed for JSOC operations "anywhere in the world" where al-Qaeda operatives were known or suspected to be operating or receiving sanctuary."[99] These laws were hardly direct descendants from those passed in Israel, but they bear a striking resemblance in terms of the way that they approached terrorism and, more explicitly, how they conceptualized the fight against terrorism in terms of an expansive armed conflict.

Early in the GWOT, Secretary of State Condoleezza Rice spoke of a "new kind of war" that renders the Geneva Conventions irrelevant and "quaint."[100] Of course, in a way she was right: the original Geneva Conventions are in some ways quaint, and their language can seem antiquated today. But IHL is not a static legal regime, neither in custom nor treaty, and the United States (and Israel) refused to sign the most significant update to IHL—the 1977 Additional Protocols—since the 1949 conventions were founded. So while the conventions may well be out of date, the United States then and now is plainly not prepared to have IHL updated in ways consonant with (most of) the rest of the international community. The updates and "new laws" sought are ones that defy international consensus because they favor a particularly narrow and sui generis way of fighting war: a preemptive, geographically unlimited "counterterror" war. It is no surprise, then, that the United States has attempted to change law not through treaty but through recourse to consensus defying practice.

Today these generalizations that "new wars need new laws" have taken on very specific and almost deregulatory form.[101] The new laws are ones that expand the scope and ontology of war. Laurie Blank, for example, has expressed the need to move away from traditional conceptions of "battlefield" to something called she calls the "zone of combat." But what does it mean, and *where* does it begin and end? Blank defines the zone expansively: "anywhere terrorist attacks are taking place, or perhaps even being planned and financed."[102] Indeed, she goes on to claim, citing Natasha Balendra, that a "war against groups of transnational terrorists, by its very nature, lacks a well-delineated timeline or a traditional battlefield context."[103] The war cannot, in her view, be limited to this static thing called the battlefield but must follow the terrorist wherever he or she may go. In this perspective, the transition from the Israeli battlefield to the vision of the "world as battlefield" is upon us and is allegedly supported by the relevant international law, or at least by lawfare.

But it is Kenneth Anderson who most directly addresses the question of a legal geography of war and its (ir)relevance in the twenty-first century. Anderson does away with the idea that geographical constraints can and should be put on war: "we have swung full circle in the past decade, arriving back at the traditional view there is no legal geography of war."[104] This position, broadly supported by a number of other legal scholars, bears more than a passing resemblance to the current official position of the U.S. government: "The United States is in an armed conflict with al Qaeda, as well as the Taliban and associated forces, in response to the horrific 9/11 attacks," said Harold Koh in his much-quoted speech, and in this context the United States "may use force consistent with its inherent right to self-defense under international law."[105] But Koh makes no mention of *where* the war is. Tacitly implying that geography does not matter, he leaves open the possibility of an everywhere war.

When we think about the law as a traveling phenomenon, it pays to think also of its modes of transportation, its carriers, and its protectors. It is not that (targeted killing) law travels easily or seamlessly but rather that the journeying of law from one place to another is carefully arranged and protected by those who see in it a strategic military value (i.e., lawfare). Inventing and transporting the law of targeted killing was not an easy process, and alongside the lawyers who handled the case, it has been facilitated by the growing use of customary international law in IHL, and also by the involvement of military lawyers in targeting decision—the "lawyering up of the kill chain" that I have written about elsewhere.[106] The two, of course, are connected.

Department of Defense policy requires that "all plans, policies, directives, and rules of engagement issued by the command and its subordinate commands and components are reviewed by legal advisers to ensure their consistency with . . . the law of war."[107] The embedding of lawyers at the operational level and their direct involvement in lethal targeting operations is said to have rendered targeted killing more transparent while also ensuring an unprecedented level of compliance.[108] Yet, as I have argued elsewhere, military lawyers have not become an integral part of the kill chain only by saying "no" to their commanders, and between the strictly prohibited and the clearly permissible there is a gray zone of legal interpretation and inevitably advice often favors military necessity over humanitarian consideration.[109] Customary law—a legal gray zone— is informed by and develops according to state practice and opinion. This means that the behavior of states and the opinion of legal scholars and military lawyers can, through iteration and (re)citation *become* law. Israeli and U.S. lawyers and politicians are well aware that customary international law progresses through violations, and it would appear that their preferred approach is to "update" international law through violence and exceptional action rather than through dialogue and consensus.[110] War and law are no longer separate spheres (if they ever were). Lawfare is not only that which the enemy does. Lawfare does not happen over "there" while rule of law and ethical war happen over "here." The United States and Israel are at the helm of exercising what Eyal Weizman, following Walter Benjamin, has called "legislative violence."[111]

What is novel about the Israel–U.S. approach today is the fact that it has become unthinkable to launch warfare without lawfare. The two have become indistinguishable from one another. Yet Israel–U.S. lawfare is not only about an attempt to legalize and legitimize targeted killing; more significantly, it is also about creating a broad legal architecture within which not only drones and targeted killing but other lethal and nonlethal tactics and weapons may be deployed. The legal architecture that supports targeted killing is also an architecture that enables the deconstruction of the battlefield. If the battlefield is gone—imaginatively or legally—there might be precious space left to escape, evade or stop the violence.

If all of this clarifies anything about the putative "end of the American Century" and the making of a new geopolitical order, it is perhaps that Israel and the United States continue to be at the cutting edge of new forms of imperial lawfare and warfare but also that these strategies and tactics come with intrinsic consequences that signal not strength and vitality but rather the precarity of Israeli and U.S. colonialism. Israel and the United States are responding to and are precipitating changes in the way that war is and will be fought in the twenty-first century. In this regard they have pioneered the way as well as the technology, the know-how and experience, and (of course) the legal architecture for carrying out a way of war that—at the moment, at least—favors their own ways of war. But while these techno-legal architectures favor those who "have" (inter alia) drones and the capacity for "global strike" from those who do not, Israel and the United States possess neither a technological monopoly nor unique access to the legal regimes that secure the "world as battlefield."[112] Indeed, as many as eighty-seven nations possess some form of drone; as the *Washington Post* recently reported, "China uses them to spy on Japan near disputed islands in Asia. Turkey uses them to eyeball Kurdish activity in northern Iraq. Bolivia uses them to spot coca fields in the Andes. Iran reportedly has given them to Syria to monitor opposition rebels."[113] The first drones over Gaza and Afghanistan were also unarmed, and while Israel, the United States, and the United Kingdom may be the only known states to have fired missiles from remotely controlled drones, this will likely not be the case for much longer. And yet it is not only the specter of an increasingly difficult-to-regulate global (drone) arms race and drone industry that threatens this putatively "Western way of war."[114] Its legal architecture does, too, and by way of closing I would like to consider a different geography of traveling law(fare).

On December 1, 1963, Malcolm X was asked to comment on the assassination of President John F. Kennedy. Choosing his words carefully, he characterized it as an instance of the "chickens coming home to roost." It was certainly a controversial comment, but it was not a flippant one. Kennedy, of course, had been in power during the early years of the CIA assassination campaign of the 1960s and 1970s. Malcolm X referred explicitly to Kennedy and the CIA's complicity in the murder of Congolese leader Patrice Lumumba and said that Kennedy had been "twiddling his thumbs" at the assassination of Vietnamese president Ngo Dinh Nhu.[115] In 1975 the monumental Church Committee Report confirmed that the CIA had both direct and indirect involvement in plots to assassinate several foreign leaders. The following year, President Gerald Ford issued a presidential decree banning assassination, and several executive orders since (the most recent of them in 2008) have iterated that "no person employed by or acting on behalf of the United States Government shall engage in or conspire to engage in assassination."[116] But all of this has now been undone, and Malcolm X's metaphorical comment speaks directly to the notion of travelling law and the future that might come to haunt those who have turned the world into a battlefield.

In a letter to President Obama, Kenneth Roth of Human Rights Watch urged Obama in 2010 to avoid setting "dangerous precedents."[117] It might now be too late for that. The very same legal arguments that Israel and the United States (and, most recently, the United Kingdom[118]) have aggressively been pursuing over the last decade and a half apply to and can also be used *against* them. For example, by conducting drone strikes, CIA employees as civilians who are participating in hostilities have become what the United States once classified as "unlawful combatants."[119] As we know, many labeled thus ended up in places like Guantanamo Bay; indeed, many are still in Guantanamo Bay. But even more pointedly, according to the logic of the expansive armed conflict, there is nothing to stop other states and nonstate actors from conducting their own targeted assassinations on Israeli and U.S. military personnel and infrastructure around the world. These could legitimately include Obama himself (as commander in chief of the U.S. military) or the thousands of U.S. and Israeli soldiers and "unlawful combatants" in and off military bases around the world. Possible "legal" strikes could also include the IDF defense compound, the Kirya, located in central Tel Aviv. As I type these closing words, I can see the Kirya through the window of the public library. I wonder whether the civilians around me, and those outside in the bustling cafes might not, according to U.S. and Israeli lawfare, be considered legitimate accidental or incidental "collateral damage" if Hamas or Hezbollah attempted to strike the military compound over the road but missed by a few meters? What happens when other state and nonstate actors begin to use the same legal justification for carrying out assassinations on the streets of London, New York, Ottawa, or Paris? Those chickens have not *yet* come home to roost. As far as the conduct of warfare and lawfare are concerned, the United States and Israel have a huge asymmetric advantage over their enemies: it continues to be a long twentieth century (for now).[120]

Notes

1. Public Committee Against Torture in Israel (PCATI) and LAW—Society for the Protection of Human Rights and the Environment, Assassination Policy Petition (BGZ/02 2002).

2. George Mitchell, Suleyman Demirel, Thorbjoern Jagland, Warren B. Rudman, and Javier Solana, "Sharm El-Sheikh Fact-Finding Committee" (Washington D.C.: U.S. Department of State, April 30, 2001), http://2001-2009.state.gov/p/nea/rls/rpt/3060.htm

3. House of Commons, "Oral Answers to Questions: Foreign and Common-wealth Affairs" (Available from the Palestinian Centre for Human Rights, March 30, 2004), http://pchrgaza.org/files/campaigns/english/almog/jack.pdf.

4. American Embassy in Tel Aviv, "Boucher Says Israeli Action Does Not Contribute to Peace" (US Embassy, July 23, 2002), http://www.usembassy-israel.org/il/publish/peace/archives/2002/july/072406.html.

5. Mitchell et al., "Sharm El-Sheikh Fact-Finding Committee Final Report."

6. Ibid. See also Daniel Reisner, "International Law and Military Operations in Practice—III," *Jerusalem Center for Public Affairs*, June 18, 2009; accessed May 30, 2013, http://jcpa.org/article/international-law-and-military-operations-in-practice-iii/.

7. Quoted in Brian Glyn Williams, "The CIA's Covert Predator Drone War in Pakistan, 2004–2010: The History of an Assassination Campaign," *Studies in Conflict & Terrorism* 33, no. 10 (2010): 873.

8. Quoted in Jeremy Scahill, "The Dangerous US Game in Yemen," *Nation*, March 30, 2011, http://www.thenation.com/article/dangerous-us-game-yemen/.

9. Leonard Small, "Roundtable on Targeted Killing: Lawyering and Targeted Killing," *Jadaliyya*, March 7, 2012, http://www.jadaliyya.com/pages/index/4567/roundtable-on-targeted-killing_lawyering-and-targe.

10. Frédéric Mégret argues that the battlefield is socially constructed, which is not to say that war takes place in a totally undefined imaginary space but rather that the very geography of the battlefield is structured in part by our ideas about the boundaries of war and where it begins and ends: "The battlefield is not a clearly defined space, not even in the most traditional of battles. It is 'an imaginary arena in which the bounds are seen to be the edges of the territory occupied by the two armies during the course of the fight.' But it is space nonetheless, one that has a core and a periphery and whose existence is premised on the ability to distinguish between what occurs within it and what is beyond it. For that space to have any meaning, however, it must be inscribed in a series of understandings about its purpose and its rules. The battlefield is, in other words, as much an idea as it is a space, and only when one understands the assumptions underlying the idea of the battlefield can one understand how the battlefield today has come under threat." Frédéric Mégret, "War and the Vanishing Battlefield," *Loyola University Chicago International Law Review* 9 (2012): 2, citing James H. McRandle, *The Antique Drums of War* (College Station: Texas A&M University Press, 1994).

11. Kenneth Anderson, "Targeted Killing and Drone Warfare: How We Came to Debate Whether There Is a 'Legal Geography of War,'" *Washington College of Law Research Paper No. 2011-16*, April 26, 2011, 2, emphasis added, http://papers.ssrn.com/sol3/papers.cfm?abstract_id=1824783&rec=1&srcabs=1754223.

12. Craig Whitlock, national security and Pentagon correspondent at the *Washington Post* has documented the spread of U.S. drone operations from the Middle East to North and West Africa since 2007: "Since taking office in 2009, President Obama has relied heavily on drones for operations, both declared and covert, in Afghanistan, Iraq, Pakistan, Yemen, Libya and Somalia. U.S. drones also fly from allied bases in Turkey, Italy, Saudi Arabia, Qatar, the United Arab Emirates and

the Philippines. Now, they are becoming a fixture in Africa. The U.S. military has built a major drone hub in Djibouti, on the Horn of Africa, and flies unarmed Reaper drones from Ethiopia. Until recently, it conducted reconnaissance flights over East Africa from the island nation of the Seychelles." Craig Whitlock, "Drone Base in Niger Gives U.S. a Strategic Foothold in West Africa," *Washington Post*, March 21, 2013, https://www.washingtonpost.com/world/national-security /drone-base-in-niger-gives-us-a-strategic-foothold-in-west-africa/2013/03/21 /700ee8d0-9170-11e2-9c4d-798c073d7ec8_story.html. Since the article from which this quote is taken was published, the U.S. military has announced that it will be opening a second drone base in Niger (the third U.S. base in West Africa). Craig Whitlock, "Pentagon Set to Open Second Drone Base in Niger as It Expands Operations in Africa," *Washington Post*, August 31, 2014, https://www .washingtonpost.com/world/national-security/pentagon-set-to-open-second -drone-base-in-niger-as-it-expands-operations-in-africa/2014/08/31/365489c4 -2eb8-11e4-994d-202962a9150c_story.html.

13. Jeremy Scahill, *Dirty Wars: The World Is a Battlefield* (London: Serpent's Tail, 2013).

14. Derek Gregory, "The Everywhere War," *Geographical Journal* 177, no. 3 (2011): 238–50.

15. Gregoire Chamayou, *Theory of the Drone* (New York: New Press, 2014); Christopher Woods, *Sudden Justice: America's Secret Drone Wars* (Oxford University Press, 2015); Andrew Cockburn, *Kill Chain: The Rise of the High-Tech Assassins* (New York: Henry Holt, 2015); Frédéric Mégret, "The Humanitarian Problem with Drones," *Utah Law Review* 2013, no. 5 (2014): 1283–1319; Derek Gregory, "Moving Targets and Violent Geographies" in Merrill, H. and Hoffman, L. M. (Eds.) *Spaces of Danger: Culture and Power in the Everyday* (Athens: University of Georgia Press, 2015); and Bureau of Investigative Journalism, "Covert Drone War," 2015, https://www.thebureauinvestigates.com/category/projects/drones/.

16. See Philip Alston, "The CIA and Targeted Killings beyond Borders," *Harvard National Security Journal* 2 (2011): 283–446; and Markus Gunneflo, "The Life and Times of Targeted Killing" (diss., Lund University, 2014), http://lup.lub.lu .se/record/4316693.

17. B'Tselem, "Statistics," 2014, http://www.btselem.org/statistics; and Kevin Jon Heller, "'One Hell of a Killing Machine' Signature Strikes and International Law," *Journal of International Criminal Justice* 11, no. 1 (2013): 89–119. Heller is quoting an anonymous U.S. intelligence official quoted in Joseph Pugliese, *State Violence and the Execution of Law: Biopolitical Caesurae of Torture, Black Sites, Drones* (Abingdon, U.K.: Routledge, 2013), 933.

18. B'Tselem, "Statistics." B'Tselem split Israeli targeted killings into three time periods: fatalities since the outbreak of the second intifada to the start of Operation Cast Lead on December 26, 2008; Operation Cast Lead, which formally ended on January 18, 2009; and after Operation Cast Lead to July 8, 2014. The statistics quoted use an aggregate of these three periods and represent the total of targeted killings from September 29, 2000 to July 8, 2014. Importantly, these statistics do *not* include targeted killings that took place in Operation Protective Edge (OPE),

the latest Israeli military onslaught on Gaza. The United Nations Office for the Coordination of Humanitarian Affairs (OCHA) in the Occupied Palestinian Territory estimates that 2,131 Palestinians were killed (of which 1,473 were civilians) in OPE though at the time of writing it is not known what percentage of these deaths were the result of a targeted killing operation.

19. Bureau of Investigative Journalism, "Get the Data: Drone Wars," September 21, 2015, https://www.thebureauinvestigates.com/category/projects/drones/drones-graphs/.

20. Amos Harel, "In U.S., Doubts over Targeted Assassinations Are Not as Taboo as in Israel," *Haaretz.com*, February 15, 2013, http://www.haaretz.com/weekend/week-s-end/in-u-s-doubts-over-targeted-assassinations-are-not-as-taboo-as-in-israel.premium-1.503709.

21. I borrow the term—and my title—from Iza Hussin, who writes: "Law is a travelling phenomenon, its logic centred upon the balance between the local and the general." Iza Hussin, "Circulations of Law: Colonial Precedents, Contemporary Questions," *Oñati Socio-Legal Series* 2, no. 7 (2012): 21. Her work draws from colonial theories of law and the globalization of law and legal thought: for example, Duncan Kennedy, "Two Globalizations of Law & Legal Thought: 1850–1968," *Suffolk University Law Review* 36, no. 3 (2003): 631–79, http://www.duncankennedy.net/documents/Two%20Globalizations%20of%20Law%20and%20Legal%20Thought%201850-1968.pdf. Legal anthropologists have also tried to come to terms with the movement and circulation of law, both in the colonial and contemporary context. In analogous work, Franz Benda-Beckmann, Keebet Benda-Beckmann, and Anne Griffiths have proposed the concept of "legal mobility," similarly emphasizing the fact that "law has always been mobile." Franz Von Benda-Beckmann, Keebet Von Benda-Beckmann, and Anne M. O. Griffiths, *Mobile People, Mobile Law: Expanding Legal Relations in a Contracting World* (Aldershot, U.K.: Ashgate, 2005), 7. These theorizations of law challenge conventional comparative law approaches that have tended to think about "legal transplants" and the "diffusion of law" as a simple top-down imperial project: for example, David A. Westbrook, "Theorizing the Diffusion of Law: Conceptual Difficulties, Unstable Imaginations, and the Effort to Think Gracefully Nonetheless," *Harvard International Law Journal* 47 (2006): 489. Circulation, mobility, and travel are thus perhaps more apt metaphors for the phenomenon in question; see, for example, Hussin, "Circulations of Law." Law is no exception with regard to mobility, of course; politics, people, goods, things, ideas, and theory travel too. Edward Said famously wrote of traveling theory and of the potentials and pitfalls in the itineraries of intellectual though (a topic he considered "central to intellectual life in the late twentieth century"). Edward Said, "Travelling Theory Reconsidered," in *Reflections on Exile and Other Essays* (London: Granta Books, 2000), 452. Such movements he noted are "never unimpeded" and necessarily face both overt resistance and conditions of acceptance. Legal anthropology and the current work is indebted to Said's instructive essays on traveling theory. See Said, "Travelling Theory Reconsidered"; Edward Said, "Traveling Theory," in *The World, the Text, and the Critic* (Cambridge, Mass.: Harvard University Press, 1983), 226–47.

22. Edward M. Wise, "The Transplant of Legal Patterns," *American Journal Comparative Law* 38, supplement (1990): 1–22. In a parallel argument (to elaborate on the above note), Said writes that "movement into a new environment is never unimpeded. It necessarily involves processes of representation and institutionalisation different from those of the point of origin. This complicates any account of the translation, transference, circulation, and commerce of theories and ideas." Said, "Travelling Theory Reconsidered," 157.

23. Giovanni Arrighi, *Adam Smith in Beijing: Lineages of the Twenty-First Century* (London; New York: Verso, 2007); cf. Bruce Cumings, *Dominion from Sea to Sea: Pacific Ascendancy and American Power* (New Haven, Conn.: Yale University Press, 2009).

24. Dunlap acknowledges the term is not his own (although he is commonly and mistakenly credited with its coinage; see, e.g., Lisa Hajjar, "Lawfare and Armed Conflict: Comparing Israeli and US Targeted Killing Policies and Challenges against Them" (International Affairs Research Report, American University of Beirut, January 2013), 6, http://www.aub.edu.lb/ifi/international_affairs /Documents/20130129ifi_pc_IA_research_report_lawfare.pdf. The term "lawfare" first appeared in 1975; see John Carlson and Neville Yeomans, "Whither Goeth the Law—Humanity or Barbarity," in *The Way Out: Radical Alternatives in Australia*, ed. Margaret Smith and David J Crossley (Melbourne: Lansdowne, 1975), http://archive.is/cbZ5V. Their use of the term was very different to the way that Dunlap used it because they hoped "lawfare" could be used for pacific ends; they argued that "lawfare replaces warfare and the duel is with words rather than swords", n.p. The term also (nearly) appears in Qiao Liang and Wang Xiangsui, where these two officers in China's People's Liberation Army refer to "law warfare," arguing that powerful states should "seiz[e] the earliest opportunity to set up regulations"; Qiao Liang and Wang Xiangsui, *Unrestricted Warfare: China's Master Plan to Destroy America* (Panama City: Pan American, 2002), 55.

25. Charles J. Dunlap Jr., "Law and Military Interventions: Preserving Humanitarian Values in 21st Century Conflicts," in *Conference on Humanitarian Challenges in Military Intervention* [online]. Washington, D.C.: Carr Center for Human Rights Policy, Kennedy School of Government, Harvard University. November, vol. 29 (Humanitarian Challenges in Military Intervention, Washington D.C., 2001), 5.

26. Department of Defense, "The National Military Strategy of the United States of America: A Strategy for Today; a Vision for Tomorrow," 2004, 5, http:// archive.defense.gov/news/Mar2005/d20050318nms.pdf. David Luban claims "the quoted sentence appeared in the 2002 National Defense Strategy as well"; however, having searched the full document, this doesn't seem to be the case. David Luban, "Lawfare and Legal Ethics in Guantanamo," *Stanford Law Review* 60 (2007): 1981–2026.

27. Fleur Johns, "Guantanamo Bay and the Annihilation of the Exception," *European Journal of International Law* 16, no. 4 (2005): 613–35; D. Gregory, "The Black Flag: Guantánamo Bay and the Space of Exception," *Geografiska Annaler: Series B, Human Geography* 88, no. 4 (2006): 405–27.

28. Michael J. Lebowitz, "The Value of Claiming Torture: An Analysis of Al-Qaeda's Tactical Lawfare Strategy and Efforts to Fight Back," *Case Western Reserve Journal of International Law* 43 (2010): 357–92. See also Tung Yin, "Boumediene and Lawfare," *University of Richmond Law Review* 43 (2009): 865–92.

29. Lebowitz, "Value of Claiming Torture," 359.

30. E. Benvenisti, "The Legal Battle to Define the Law on Transnational Asymmetric Warfare," *Duke Journal of Comparative & International Law* 20 (2010): 348. United Nations, "United Nations Fact Finding Mission on the Gaza Conflict" (United Nations General Assembly, A/HRC/12/48, September 25, 2009), http://www2.ohchr.org/english/bodies/hrcouncil/docs/12session/A-HRC-12-48.pdf. Cf. Craig Jones, "Misrule of Gaza: Israeli Assaults in a Land under Siege" (University of British Columbia, 2010), http://hdl.handle.net/2429/29895; and Hajjar, "Lawfare and Armed Conflict." Hajjar argues that Israel "pioneered" what she calls "state lawfare," and dates its use to 1967. Hajjar offers a useful and encyclopedic account of how the Israeli state has used law as a weapon to justify violence, and her account is an important corrective to those contemporary conversations on lawfare, which focus on Israel and the United States being only victims of lawfare, and not practitioners. I am not sure about Hajjar's claim that Israel pioneered state lawfare, however, because all states practice—indeed, are founded upon—something like lawfare, and, in any case, the history of colonialism is, at least in part, a history of empires seeking to justify their superiority through and with reference to law. See, e.g., Antony Anghie, *Imperialism, Sovereignty and the Making of International Law* (Cambridge: Cambridge University Press, 2007); Anne Orford, *International Law and Its Others* (Cambridge: Cambridge University Press, 2006); Craig A. Jones, "Lawfare and the Juridification of Late Modern War," *Progress in Human Geography* March 16 (2015): 1–19; Helen M. Kinsella, "Gendering Grotius," *Political Theory* 34, no. 2 (April 1, 2006): 161–91, doi:10.1177/0090591705279530; and Helen M. Kinsella, *The Image before the Weapon: A Critical History of the Distinction between Combatant and Civilian* (Ithaca, N.Y.: Cornell University Press, 2011). John Comaroff and Jean Comaroff have written specifically about the colonial origins of lawfare, and their analysis is indebted to Third World Approaches to International Law, the rich intellectual and political movement that emerged in the 1990s with the goal of deconstructing the unequal power relations which are and which have always been constitutive of international law. John L. Comaroff, "Colonialism, Culture, and the Law: A Foreword," *Law & Social Inquiry* 26, no. 2 (2001): 305–14; and Jean Comaroff and John Comaroff, "Law and Disorder in the Postcolony: An Introduction," in *Law and Disorder in the Postcolony*, ed. Jean Comaroff and John L. Comaroff (Chicago: University Of Chicago Press, 2006), 1–56. See also Makau Mutua, "Savages, Victims, and Saviors: The Metaphor of Human Rights," *Harvard International Law Journal* 42, no. 1 (2001): 201–45; and Balakrishnan Rajagopal, *International Law from Below: Development, Social Movements and Third World Resistance* (Cambridge: Cambridge University Press, 2003).

31. David Scheffer points to a similar blindness on behalf of U.S. lawfare commentators: "The popular view of lawfare, put forward by neo-conservative

commentators and some military lawyers, is exceptionally myopic, oblivious to how other nations view inter-national justice, *and disingenuous regarding America's own aggressive use of the law.*" David Scheffer, "Whose Lawfare Is It, Anyway," *Case Western Reserve Journal of International Law* 43, no. 1 (2010): 215; emphasis added.

32. E.g., Laurie R. Blank, "A New Twist on an Old Story: Lawfare and the Mixing of Proportionalities," *Case Western Reserve Journal of International Law* 43, no. 3 (2011): 707–38. For a counterview, see E. Weizman, "Legislative Attack," *Theory, Culture & Society* 27, no. 6 (2010): 11–32; and Eyal Weizman, *The Least of All Possible Evils: Humanitarian Violence from Arendt to Gaza* (London: Verso, 2011).

33. Quoted in Craig Nelson, "Goldstone Report Keeps Israel on Tenterhooks," *National*, January 29, 2010, http://www.thenational.ae/news/world/middle-east /goldstone-report-keeps-israel-on-tenterhooks.

34. Gili Cohen, "Israeli Army Sets up New Unit to Fight Legal Onslaught over Gaza War," *Haaretz.com*, September 3, 2014, http://www.haaretz.com/news /national/.premium-1.613764.

35. For an overview, see William J. Aceves, "Litigating the Arab-Israeli Conflict in U.S. Courts: Critiquing the Lawfare Critique," *Case Western Reserve Journal of International Law* 43, no. 1–2 (March 22, 2010): 313–25; and Hajjar, "Lawfare and Armed Conflict."

36. On the prohibition against torture and indefinite detention, see, e.g., *Hamdi v. Rumsfeld*, 542 US 507; *Hamdan v. Rumsfeld*, 548 US 557; and *PCATI v. The Government of Israel et al.*, HCJ 5100/94. On the legality of targeted killing, see, e.g., *PCATI v. Israel*, HCJ 769/02; *Al-Aulaqi v. Obama et al.*, 10-1469 (JDB); *ACLU v. Dept. of Justice et al.*, 08-cv-1157 (JR); and *Al-Aulaqi v. Panetta*, 12-cv-01192.

37. *Al-Aulaqi v. Obama et al.*, 10-1469 (JDB), 4.

38. Jo Becker and Scott Shane, "Secret 'Kill List' Tests Obama's Principles," *New York Times*, May 29, 2012, http://www.nytimes.com/2012/05/29/world/obamas -leadership-in-war-on-al-qaeda.html.

39. Ken Dilanian, "Congress Zooms in on Drone Killings," *Los Angeles Times*, June 25, 2012, http://www.latimes.com/news/nationworld/world/middleeast/la -na-drone-oversight-20120625,0,6672018.story.

40. Adam Sewer, "Congress Wants to See Obama's 'License to Kill,'" *Mother Jones*, July 31, 2012, http://www.motherjones.com/politics/2012/07/congress- disclose-obama-targeted-killing-memos.

41. Brooke Goldstein and Aaron Eitan Meyer, "Legal Jihad: How Islamist Lawfare Tactics Are Targeting Free Speech," *ILSA Journal of International & Comparative Law* 15, no. 2 (2009): 395–410.

42. The Lawfare Project, "Lawfare: The Use of the Law as a Weapon of War," December 13, 2013, http://www.thelawfareproject.org/what-is-lawfare.html.

43. Blank, "A New Twist on an Old Story," 16.

44. Amitai Etzioni, "Unmanned Aircraft Systems: The Moral and Legal Case," *Joint Forces Quarterly* 57, no. 2 (2010): 66–71. He calls these "abusive civilians."

45. Charles J. Dunlap and Linell A. Letendre, "Military Lawyering and Professional Independence in the War on Terror: A Response to David Luban," *Stanford Law Review* 61 (2009 2008): 422.

46. Patricia Owens, "Accidents Don't Just Happen: The Liberal Politics of High-Technology 'Humanitarian' War," *Millennium–Journal of International Studies* 32, no. 3 (2003): 595–616.

47. Derek Gregory, *The Colonial Present: Afghanistan, Palestine, Iraq* (Malden, Mass.: Wiley-Blackwell, 2004).

48. Michael A. Newton, "Illustrating Illegitimate Lawfare," *Case Western Reserve Journal of International Law* 43 (2011): 255–78; and Dunlap, "Law and Military Interventions."

49. Shane Bilsborough, "Counterlawfare in Counterinsurgency," *Small Wars Journal*, December 14, 2011, http://smallwarsjournal.com/jrnl/art/counterlawfare-in-counterinsurgency; Blank, "A New Twist on an Old Story"; and Laurie Blank, "Finding Facts but Missing the Law: The Goldstone Report, Gaza and Lawfare," *Case Western Reserve Journal of International Law* 43 (2011): 279–305.

50. Gregory, "Everywhere War"; Mégret, "War and the Vanishing Battlefield"; Weizman, *Least of All Possible Evils*; and Craig A. Jones, "Frames of Law: Targeting Advice and Operational Law in the Israeli Military," *Environment and Planning D: Society and Space* 33, no. 4 (2015): 676–96.

51. Charles Dunlap, "Lawfare: A Decisive Element of 21st Century Conflicts?," *Joint Forces Quarterly* 54, no. 3 (2009): 35, emphasis in original.

52. Charles J. Dunlap Jr., "Lawfare Today: A Perspective," *Yale Journal of International Affairs* 3 (2008): 147.

53. D. Gregory, " 'The Rush to the Intimate': Counterinsurgency and the Cultural Turn," *Radical Philosophy*, no. 150 (2010): 8.

54. Dunlap, "Lawfare Today," 146.

55. David Scheffer points to a similar blindness on behalf of U.S. lawfare commentators: "The popular view of lawfare, put forward by neo-conservative commentators and some military lawyers, is exceptionally myopic, oblivious to how other nations view inter-national justice, and disingenuous regarding America's own aggressive use of the law." Scheffer, "Whose Lawfare Is It, Anyway," 215.

56. See, for example, Anghie, *Imperialism, Sovereignty and the Making of International Law*; Costas Douzinas, *Human Rights and Empire: The Political Philosophy of Cosmopolitanism*, new ed. (Abingdon, U.K.: Routledge-Cavendish, 2007); Kinsella, *The Image before the Weapon*; and Samera Esmeir, *Juridical Humanity a Colonial History* (Stanford, Calif.: Stanford University Press, 2012).

57. See Jones, "Lawfare and the Juridification of Late Modern War."

58. Comaroff and Comaroff, "Law and Disorder in the Postcolony," 24.

59. Walter Benjamin, "Critique of Violence," in *Reflections: Essays, Aphorisms, Autobiographical Writing* (London: Schocken Books, 1986), 277–300.

60. Jacques Derrida, "Force of Law: 'The Mystical Foundations of Authority,' " in *Deconstruction and the Possibility of Justice*, ed. Drucilla Cornell, Michel Rosenfeld, and David Gray Carlson (Abington, U.K.: Routledge, 1992), 3–63.

61. Charles J. Dunlap Jr., "Does Lawfare Need an Apologia," *Case Western Reserve Journal of International Law* 43 (2010): 125, emphasis added.

62. Gregory, "Everywhere War"; and Scahill, *Dirty Wars*.

63. E.g., S. Elden, *Terror and Territory: The Spatial Extent of Sovereignty* (Minneapolis: University of Minnesota Press, 2009); and Gregory, *Colonial Present*.

64. On Israel's use of the post-9/11 language of terrorism and the "axis of evil," see Gregory, *Colonial Present*.

65. Craig A. Jones and Michael D. Smith, "War/Law/Space Notes toward a Legal Geography of War," *Environment and Planning D: Society and Space* 33, no. 4 (2015): 581–91.

66. Israeli Ministry of Foreign Affairs, "Press Briefing by Colonel Daniel Reisner," November 15, 2000, http://mfa.gov.il/MFA/PressRoom/2000/Pages/Press%20 Briefing%20by%20Colonel%20Daniel%20Reisner-%20Head%20of.aspx; and Anthony H. Cordesman, *Israel versus the Palestinians: The "Second Intifada" and Asymmetric Warfare* (Center for Strategic and International Studies, 2002), http://csis .org/files/media/csis/pubs/israelvspale_intafada%5B1%5D.pdf.

67. Israeli Ministry of Foreign Affairs, "Press Briefing by Colonel Daniel Reisner."

68. Nils Melzer, *Targeted Killing in International Law* (New York: Oxford University Press, 2009); and Philip Alston, "Report of the Special Rapporteur on Extrajudicial, Summary or Arbitrary Executions," *United Nations Human Rights Council*, 2010, http://www.unhcr.org/refworld/pdfid/4c07635c2.pdf.

69. Daniel Reisner invented the term. Daniel Reisner, interview with author, Tel Aviv, February 21, 2013. It is not, however, a formal legal designation. Rather, it is a deliberately ambiguous term that blurs the boundaries of war and peace. Reisner explains the ambiguity thus:

> From a legal perspective, international law, classical international law, actually only recognizes two situations: peace or war. But life isn't as simple as that, and there are lots of terms running around the concerning the in-between. "Lower intensity conflict", "limited war", etc. . . . So where are we? While we are not at the end of the spectrum, which is war, because war is a conflict between two armies or two states, we are definitely in the area of armed conflict. Call it what you wish, some call it "un-conflict", some call it "active hostilities"—whatever the term you wish to use that's fine with us, but please understand that for us, we have reached the decision . . . that the current situation has more of a *semblance of war than of peace.*

Quoted in Israeli Ministry of Foreign Affairs, "Press Briefing by Colonel Daniel Reisner."

70. David Kennedy, *Of War and Law* (Princeton N.J.: Princeton University Press, 2006); Weizman, *Least of All Possible Evils*; and Katia Snukal and Emily Gilbert, "War, Law, Jurisdiction, and Juridical Othering: Private Military Security Contractors and the Nisour Square Massacre," *Environment and Planning D: Society and Space* 33, no. 4 (2015): 660–75.

71. *Thabet v. Sharon et al.*, HCJ 192/01.

72. *Barakeh v. Sharon et al.*, HCJ 5872/01.

73. *PCATI v. Israel*, HCJ 769/02, sec.3.9, cites the dismissal of the prior two petitions: "the choice of means of war employed by respondents in order to prevent

murderous terrorist attacks before they happen, is not among the subjects in which this Court will see fit to intervene."

74. B'Tselem, "Statistics."

75. Gideon Alon and Amos Harel, "IDF Lawyers Set 'Conditions' for Assassination Policy," *Haaretz.com*, February 4, 2002, http://www.haaretz.com/print -edition/news/idf-lawyers-set-conditions-for-assassination-policy-1.53911. Cf. Yuval Yoaz, "High Court: International Law Does Not Forbid Targeted Killings," *Haaretz.com*, accessed December 12, 2013, http://www.haaretz.com/news/high -court-international-law-does-not-forbid-targeted-killings-1.207185.

76. Cordesman, *Israel versus the Palestinians*, 1.

77. Anthony Dworkin, "Israel's High Court on Targeted Killing: A Model for the War on Terror?," *Crimes of War Project*, 2006, On file with Author.

78. There is an irony here that I return to below, but is also worth signposting here. General Counsel to the Department of Defense Jeh Charles Johnson recently rejected the label of assassination for his administration's drone-led killing spree, calling the term "one of the most repugnant in our vocabulary." Jeh Charles Johnson, "Jeh Johnson's Speech on 'National Security Law, Lawyers and Lawyering in the Obama Administration,'" February 22, 2012, http://www.cfr.org/national -security-and-defense/jeh-johnsons-speech-national-security-law-lawyers -lawyering-obama-administration/p27448. Despite this, the CIA has a long history of assassination that seems to have vanished from view in contemporary discussions of U.S. drone warfare. As early as the 1950s the CIA issued a training manual to its agents and operatives at the time of the agency's covert coup d'état to topple the Guatemala government and depose the democratically elected president, Jacobo Arbenz-Guzman. In 1975 when the U.S. Senate investigated a string of CIA assassination plots ranging from Guatemala to the Congo (Patrice Lumumba) and Cuba (Fidel and Raul Castro), the Church Committee found that although "assassination is not a subject on which one would expect many records or documents to be made or retained, there were, in fact, more relevant contemporaneous documents than expected." U.S. Congress Senate Select Committee to Study Governmental Operations with Respect to Intelligence Activities, "Alleged Assassination Plots Involving Foreign Leaders : An Interim Report of the Select Committee to Study Governmental Operations with Respect to Intelligence Activities, United States Senate : Together with Additional, Supplemental and Separate Views" (Washington, D.C.: U.S. Government Printing Office, 1975), http:// archive.org/details/allegedassassinaooounit.The 350-page report finds that the United States was directly and indirectly involved in several assassinations and assassination attempts. Since the report was published, several CIA documents relating to assassination have been declassified, and U.S. assassination has been the subject critical scholarship: e.g., Philip Agee, *Inside the Company: CIA Diary* (New York: Stonehill, 1975); Jonathan Kwinty, *The Crimes of Patriots: A True Tale of Dope, Dirty Money, and the CIA* (New York: W. W. Norton, 1987); Michael McClintock, *The American Connection: State Terror and Popular Resistance in Guatemala* (London: Zed Books, 1985); and William Blum, *Killing Hope: U.S. Military and CIA Interventions since World War II* (London: Zed Books, 2003).

79. Reisner, "International Law and Military Operations in Practice—III."

80. Reisner, Interview with author. He was tempted to say, "I told you so," but he refrained.

81. Ori Nir, "Bush Seeks Israeli Advice on 'Targeted Killings,'" *Electronic Intifada/The Forward*, February 7, 2003, http://electronicintifada.net/content/bush-seeks-israeli-advice-targeted-killings/4391.

82. Hussin, "Circulations of Law," 21.

83. Ibid.

84. David Delaney, *The Spatial, the Legal and the Pragmatics of World-Making: Nomospheric Investigations* (Abington, U.K.: Taylor & Francis, 2010).

85. Wise, "The Transplant of Legal Patterns," 21.

86. Jones, "Frames of Law."

87. Alston, "CIA and Targeted Killings beyond Borders," 408–9. The works cited by Alston in order are Amos N. Guiora, "License to Kill," *Foreign Policy*, July 14, 2009, http://www.foreignpolicy.com/articles/2009/07/13/licence_to_kill#sthash.zCjE83OL.dpbs; and G. Blum and P. Heymann, "Law and Policy of Targeted Killing," *Harvard National Security Journal* 1, no. 167,169 (2010), http://papers.ssrn.com/sol3/papers.cfm?abstract_id=1631342.

88. Afsheen Radsan and Richard Murphy, "Due Process and Targeted Killing of Terrorists," *Cardozo Law Review* 31 (2009): 1234.

89. Alston, "CIA and Targeted Killings beyond Borders," 410–18.

90. Department of Justice White Paper, "Lawfulness of a Lethal Operation Directed against a U.S. Citizen Who Is a Senior Operational Leader of Al-Qa'ida or an Associated Force," April 2, 2013, http://msnbcmedia.msn.com/i/msnbc/sections/news/020413_DOJ_White_Paper.pdf; and Jameel Jaffer, "The Justice Department's White Paper on Targeted Killing," *American Civil Liberties Union*, April 2, 2013, https://www.aclu.org/blog/national-security/justice-departments-white-paper-targeted-killing.

91. Guiora, "License to Kill"; Amos Guiora, "Drone Policy: A Proposal Moving Forward," *Jurist Forum*, March 4, 2013, http://www.jurist.org/forum/2013/03/amos-guiora-drone-policy.php, noting: "broad definitions of imminence combined with new technological capabilities drastically affect the implementation of targeted killing predicated on legal and moral principles. The recently released U.S. Department of Justice white paper regarding the Obama administration's drone policy defines "imminence" so expansively that there need not be clear evidence of a specific attack to justify the killing of an individual, including U.S. citizens.

92. Kenneth Anderson, "The Shift from Proportionality to Necessity and an Indirect Comment on Gaby Blum's Article," *Opinio Juris*, February 5, 2011, http://opiniojuris.org/2011/02/12/the-shift-from-proportionality-to-necessity-and-an-indirect-comment-on-gaby-blums-article/.

93. On Lebanon, see IDF Spokesperson Unit, "In Response to Rocket Fire, IAF Targets a Terror Site in Lebanon," *Official Blog of the Israel Defense Forces*, August 23, 2013, http://www.idfblog.com/2013/08/23/in-response-to-rocket-fire-iaf-targets-a-terror-site-in-lebanon/. On Syria, see "IDF Strikes Syrian Target in Response to Shelling," *Times of Israel*, October 9, 2013, http://www.timesofisrael

.com/idf-strikes-syrian-target-in-response-to-shelling/. See also Gregory, "Every-where War."

94. Michael N. Schmitt, *Tallinn Manual on the International Law Applicable to Cyber Warfare* (Cambridge: Cambridge University Press, 2013).

95. Mégret, "War and the Vanishing Battlefield," 15.

96. Gregory, "Everywhere War."

97. Jennifer C. Daskal, "The Geography of the Battlefield: A Framework for Detention and Targeting Outside the 'Hot' Conflict Zone," *University of Pennsylvania Law Review* 161 (2013): 1165–1409; and Anderson, "Targeted Killing and Drone Warfare."

98. George Bush, Authorization for Use of Military Force, Pub. L. No. 107-40, 115 Stat. 224 (2001).

99. Scahill, *Dirty Wars.*

100. Quoted in Noam Lubell, *Extraterritorial Use of Force against Non-State Actors* (Oxford: Oxford University Press, 2010), 121.

101. David Wippman and Matthew Evangelista, eds., *New Wars, New Laws? Applying the Laws of War in 21st Century Conflicts* (Leiden: Transnational Publishers, Hotei Publishing, 2005).

102. L. R. Blank, "Defining the Battlefield in Contemporary Conflict and Counterterrorism: Understanding the Parameters of the Zone of Combat," *Georgia Journal of International and Comparative Law* 39, no. 1 (2010): 4.

103. Natasha Balendra, "Defining Armed Conflict," *Cardozo Law Review* 29, no. 6 (2008): 2467; quoted in Blank, "Defining the Battlefield," 4.

104. Anderson, "Targeted Killing and Drone Warfare," 16.

105. Harold Kongju Koh, "The Obama Administration and International Law," Speech at the Annual Meeting of the American Society of International Law Washington, DC, March 25, 2010, U.S. Department of State, http://www.state.gov /s/l/releases/remarks/139119.htm.

106. Jones, "Frames of Law."

107. "Department of Defense Directive: DoD Law of War Program," U.S. Department of Defense, May 9, 2006, https://www.aclu.org/files/dronefoia/dod /drone_dod_231101e.pdf.

108. Jack M. Beard, "Law and War in the Virtual Era," *American Journal of International Law* 103 (2009): 409–45.

109. Jones, "Frames of Law."

110. Ibid.

111. Weizman, "Legislative Attack."

112. Hu Yumin, "U.S. Building 'Global First Strike Capacity' against Russia and China," *Global Research*, January 13, 2013, http://www.globalresearch.ca/u-s -building-global-first-strike-capacity-against-russia-and-china/5318728. See Yumin, *Global First Strike Capacity.*

113. Guy Taylor, "U.S. Intelligence Warily Watches for Threats to U.S. Now That 87 Nations Possess Drones," *Washington Times*, November 10, 2013, http:// www.washingtontimes.com/news/2013/nov/10/skys-the-limit-for-wide-wild-world-of-drones/.

114. "Killer Drones Report: UK Complicity in Israel's Crimes against the Palestinian People" (London: War on Want, December 2013), http://www .waronwant.org/campaigns/corporations-and-conflict/private-armies/action/18 038-killer-drones-report; and Carrie Giunta, "Blood Coltan: Remote-Controlled Warfare and the Demand for Strategic Minerals," *Pambazuka News*, no. 655, (November 21, 2013), http://www.pambazuka.org/en/category/features/89735.

115. "Malcolm X Scores U.S. and Kennedy," *New York Times*, December 2, 1963.

116. George Bush, Executive Order 12333 United States Intelligence Activities, as amended by Executive Orders 13284 (2003), 13355 (2004) and 13470 (2008), 2008.

117. Human Rights Watch and Kenneth Roth, "Letter to Obama on Targeted Killings and Drones," December 7, 2010, http://www.hrw.org/en/node/94791.

118. Ewen MacAskill Defence, "Drone Killing of British Citizens in Syria Marks Major Departure for UK," Guardian, September 7, 2015, http://www.theguardian .com/world/2015/sep/07/drone-british-citizens-syria-uk-david-cameron.

119. Gary Solis, "CIA Drone Attacks Produce America's Own Unlawful Combatants," *Washington Post*, March 12, 2010, http://www.washingtonpost.com/wp -dyn/content/article/2010/03/11/AR2010031103653.html.

120. Arrighi, *Adam Smith in Beijing*.

Drone Executions, Urban Surveillance, and the Imperial Gaze

ASHLEY DAWSON

In 2012 the U.S. Air Force began deploying a new airborne surveillance technology to Afghanistan called the Gorgon Stare. Unlike most current Air Force drones, which capture images using a single camera with a relatively narrow-angle lens capable of focusing on an area the size of a building or two, the Gorgon has nine video cameras mounted on a remotely piloted aircraft, allowing it to transmit live images of a wide sweep of terrain to soldiers on the ground or to intelligence analysts stateside. As Maj. Gen. James Poss, the Air Force's assistant deputy chief of staff for intelligence, surveillance, and reconnaissance, puts it, "Gorgon Stare will be looking at a whole city, so there will be no way for the adversary to know what we're looking at, and we can see everything."[1] Seated in an air-conditioned building at Creech Air Force Base near Las Vegas, the pilots of the Gorgon Stare survey the territory in countries such as Afghanistan, ready to mete out fiery death to those halfway across the world whom the empire deems its enemies.

The Gorgon's panoptical power is perhaps so appealing precisely because of the dubious effectiveness of drone strikes. We need to be very clear about this: *drone strikes do not work*. They may be effective on a tactical level by facilitating the United States' policy of summary execution against enemy insurgents, but they are not and cannot be successful on a broader strategic level. This is because, like previous forms of aerial bombardment, they alienate significant segments of the populations among whom insurgents dwell, making it far harder to put down insurgencies in the long term.[2] The evidence of this is not hard to find; for example, Gen. Stanley McChrystal, commander of U.S. forces in Afghanistan, opined that "preoccupied with protection of our own forces, we have operated in a manner that distances us—physically and psychologically—from the people we seek to protect. In addition, we run the risk of strategic defeat by pursuing tactical wins that cause civilian casualties or unnecessary collateral damage."[3]

Despite such testimony concerning the flaws of the drone strategy, important organs of public opinion in the United States are constitutively unable to see the contradictions in their reasoning on the topic. An article in the *New York Times*, "Lull in Strikes by U.S. Drones Aids Militants in Pakistan," offers evidence of this contradictory attitude: the article openly admits that the campaign of bombing in Pakistan has been a public relations disaster, leading U.S. forces to cut back attacks dramatically over the last year.[4] But the article then goes on to say that this lull in drone strikes has allowed insurgents to regroup, implying that the United States should once against step up its campaign—as if this would not produce the identical strategic disaster that led to the cut in attacks in the first place. What explains these contradictions and the broader acquiescence of the U.S. public to the drone assassination campaign?

One of the undeniable factors is the Obama administration's retooling of U.S. empire. When Obama came into office, Western military forces were stretched thin by protracted ground wars in Iraq and Afghanistan. Equally important, public antipathy to the U.S. occupation of these countries was growing, both domestically and internationally. Rather than dismantle U.S. empire, as some of his more naïve supporters had hoped he would, Obama simply renamed the project, shifting from Bush's unabashedly bellicose "war on terror" to the more Orwellian and obfuscatory "overseas contingency operations."[5] In tandem with this shift in nomenclature, Obama amped up the Bush administration's program of drone attacks. Although this policy has killed hundreds and perhaps thousands of civilians in Pakistan, Afghanistan, and Yemen and has flouted international laws against extrajudicial killings in the process, it has allowed the United States to reduce the numbers of soldiers being sent into combat and thus diffused domestic political pressure against warfare.[6] Analysts of Obama's drone assassination program such as Caren Kaplan have pointed to the program's chilling and heretofore unmatched ability to inflict military violence from a distance.[7] The modalities through which U.S. empire under Obama wages war from afar is undoubtedly novel, but the capacity to wage war over a distance has a long genealogy and is mobilized through a surprisingly continuous set of cultural imaginaries.

We can find some clues to this genealogy in previous campaigns of aerial reconnaissance and bombing. In *Spies in Arabia*, for instance, Priya Satia discusses the Royal Air Force's campaign in Iraq during the 1920s, arguing that the Orientalist lens through which British forces viewed the populations of the region had a dramatic impact on what the imperial state saw and how it acted on such perceptions.[8] Reasoning that colonial populations were particularly susceptible to the terror provoked by aerial bombardment because of their purportedly primitive mentality, the Royal Air Force killed tens of thousands of Iraqis through bombing sorties while arguing that such slaughter was more humane than traditional "pacification" measures.[9]

But the increasing appeal of drones lies not just in what they do to the populations whom the United States has declared suspects in the war on terror. The vertiginously increasing deployment of drone strikes in recent years is also explained by what drone vision does for the imperial self. Underlying such policies is the fantasy that a new technology such as the Gorgon Stare will fix previous "mistakes" through a heightening of precisely the technologies of remote visual surveillance that are responsible for mass killings in the first place. The fantasy animating aerial bombardment, in other words, is embedded in deeply inscribed cultural perceptions that I call the imperial gaze—the irresistible desire to look at the colonized. My argument is that empire is characterized by the drive to surveil its subjects visually and, through this culturally inscribed visual and cognitive mastery, to try to cement its domination of the colonized.

In this chapter, I explore this drive to "see everything" in three sites, underlining the similar modes of imperial visuality deployed in nineteenth-century Calcutta during the British Raj, in early twentieth-century Algiers under the French, and in contemporary American video games, including those in which U.S. combat in Iraq is featured. Through this exploration I shed light on the broader genealogy of contemporary U.S. forms of the imperial gaze. The increasingly sophisticated scopophilic representational technologies of empire, I argue, paradoxically lay bare the overextension and internal contradictions of U.S. empire.

Historical discourses concerning the colonial city are important today because of the perception among U.S. military planners that overwhelming American firepower has driven insurgents in the Middle East and Central Asia into urban-based, asymmetric forms of combat.[10] This helps explain why drones are imagined by planners such as General Poss as the ultimate technology for urban warfare. In understanding the appeal and increasing pervasiveness of drone technology, I draw on contemporary theorists of visuality such as those articulated by Nick Mirzoeff and

Derek Gregory. Unlike the former, however, whose *The Right to Look* provides a compelling colonial genealogy of visuality, I locate the imperial gaze in a very specific geographical space: the city.[11] Mirzoeff's magisterial overview of visuality and countervisuality tends to emphasize rural geographical sites such as the plantation. As I demonstrate in the following, the spatial politics of urban sites are very different from those of the plantation or even the Napoleonic battlefield that Mirzoeff discusses precisely because comprehensive visuality is constitutively impossible in labyrinthine cities. In addition, while I find Gregory's discussions of U.S. imperial urban visuality and the cultural turn in the war in Iraq exceptionally illuminating, my project here is to offer a longer genealogy of the imperial gaze and the city.[12]

Drone technology is the latest instance in the invention of a vertical axis of vision through which urban space can be viewed and ultimately catalogued, a key component in legitimating and facilitating imperial urban politics during the nineteenth century. By lifting the viewer above the incessantly mutable hurly-burly of everyday life in the colonial city, new representational technologies such as the demographic map sought to quantify and freeze urban space into a decipherable and actionable set of discrete segments. Yet this vertical axis of the urban visual economy always existed in tension with the horizontal axis, through which the often opaque but always titillating flow of city life could be recorded. Nonetheless, technological changes of the late nineteenth and early twentieth century added to the potency of the vertical axis as first photography and then cinema allowed the imperial gaze to adopt a bird's-eye perspective. Today, new technologies such as the video game and the drone intensify the underlying epistemological orientation—and deadly effects—of the imperial gaze.

The imperial gaze is, at bottom, about implementing and maintaining various states of insecurity. As Michael Dillon has argued in his expansion of Michel Foucault's comments about security in the context of European urban life during the plague, "You cannot secure anything unless you know what it is," suggesting that "integral to the problematizations of security are the ways in which people, territory and things are transformed into epistemic objects."[13] If, drawing on Foucault, Dillon equates geopolitics with territory and population with biopolitics, as does Derek Gregory, I argue that the imperial gaze brings together these various apparatuses of power.[14] Understanding the long genealogy of this gaze makes the interwoven character of biopower and geopolitics impossible to ignore. In surveying urban space, the imperial gaze mobilizes forms of biopolitical power that adjudicate in the starkest terms who is to die and who is to live. The ultimate aim of this paper is to intervene in this necropolitics by helping to build the campaign against current U.S. policies of summary robotic execution in the Middle East and Central Asia.

AS IS SUGGESTED by the high visibility of urban environments in U.S. Joint Forces Command's strategic document, *Joint Operation Environment (JOE) 2010*, the military is highly aware of the urbanization of warfare over the last three decades. If the paradigmatic image of the Vietnam War was the burning village, today's key icon of war is the riotous city. It was not supposed to be this way. In the late 1980s Pentagon theorists began discussing a so-called revolution in military affairs that would endow the United States with unparalleled "full-spectrum dominance."[15] In many ways this was a reaction to the protests catalyzed by Vietnam; in fact, U.S. Cdr. Gen. William Westmoreland famously predicted the future automation of warfare in reaction to the guerrilla tactics of anticolonial insurgents in the late 1960s, saying, "We are on the threshold of an entirely new battlefield concept, one that will replace forever the man with the machine."[16] By the 1980s military theorists were doing their best to realize Westmoreland's vision, arguing that the United States could use cutting-edge networked information technology to vault beyond all potential military antagonists in the same manner that the Germans' use of coordinated air and armored assaults had handed them primacy in the blitzkrieg against continental Europe at the onset of World War II. As James Der Derian has remarked, the ferocious destructive potential of U.S. military technology as it developed in the 1990s had the paradoxical effect of strengthening the belief in virtuous warfare by allowing civilian and military leaders to unleash violence from a distance and by remote control—with few American casualties.[17] The satellite-controlled destruction that rained down on Iraqi forces retreating from Kuwait during the first Gulf War seemed to confirm the hype associated with the revolution in military affairs, helping to exorcise the ghost of Vietnam by banishing fears about U.S. casualties in a protracted ground war.

Yet these visions of god-like military supremacy quickly dissolved as war went urban. For much of the military, the urbanization of war was a product of the United States' overwhelming hegemony in traditional combat. In order to explain Operation Urban Resolve, a Joint Forces

Command war gaming "experiment," for example, military communiqués cite U.S. superiority as a primary factor for insurgents' move to urban terrain: "The explosive growth of the world's major urban centers, changes in enemy strategies, and the global war on terror have made the urban battlespace potentially decisive and virtually unavoidable. Some of our most advanced military systems do not work as well in urban areas as they do in open terrain. Therefore, joint and coalition forces should expect that future opponents will choose to operate in urban environments to try to level the huge disparity between our military and technological capabilities and theirs."[18] Given the military's renewed interest in urban warfare and the shift to targeted assassinations by drones in such areas by U.S. intelligence agencies, it is worth looking back at colonial representations of urban space to see how the imperial gaze constructs city culture. Keeping in mind Henri Lefebvre's seminal arguments about the way in which the city does not simply express social relations but rather shapes and produces them, we will want to pay particular attention to the ways in which the imperial gaze navigates the social relations played out in the colonial city, seeking not simply to lay bare these social relations to its inquisitive eye but also to transform those relations through processes of representing, surveying, and cataloguing.[19] To what extent, we will want to consider, does such colonial urban scopophilia anticipate the technologies of representation deployed in the new urban wars?

I initiate this discussion of the visual economy of empire in Calcutta under the British Raj, where representations of colonial urban space gained important early articulations. British artists in Bengal in the late eighteenth and early nineteenth centuries were confronted by a terrain that lacked the ideally variegated topography inherited from the Italian landscape tradition; Bengal was, after all, mainly flat swampland. In place of sublime mountains and lakes, however, British artists such as William Hodges and William Daniell added luster to their depictions of Bengal by focusing on the picturesque decaying remains of the Mughal Empire in the region. These crumbling, vine-strewn mosques piqued the European fascination with lost civilizations and sparked a craze for Oriental architecture in late-eighteenth-century Britain. At the same time, though, such images legitimated the expansionist designs of the East India Company in Bengal by suggesting that Indian civilization was in a phase of decadence, unable to develop the land adequately and incapable of ruling itself.

When they turned to representations of Bengali cities such as Calcutta, British artists redeployed such pictorial codes, creating a panorama that mixed vibrant commerce with what looked to an aristocratic European eye to be brutish squalor and decay. In James Baillie Fraser's "A View of the Bazaar Leading to Chitpore Road" of 1819, for example, we see precisely this combination of desire and dread in the European colonial gaze. Fraser's painting catalogues the tremendous variety of wares for sale in the Calcutta bazaar but also depicts decaying buildings and native bodies in various states. This ambivalent visual economy was paralleled by accounts of urban space in contemporary travel narratives such as that of Bessie Knox Fenton, who described a visit to the bazaars of Calcutta in the following terms: "The lanes are dark, narrow and filthy, filled with the effluvia issuing from the dens (for I cannot call them houses) of the natives, and they too look barbarous, half-naked, and as if on the watch to take hold of you. There is a kind of market-place covered over and dividing into separate stands; they are perfectly wonderful to a European. There are heaped on one board all sorts of shoes, slippers, sandals to suit the native taste."[20] Representations of the European portions of Calcutta could not have been more starkly different. Here, artists such as Thomas Daniell depicted a neoclassical idyll in which the orderly symmetry of the administrative buildings of the East India Company lends visual and moral authority to British rule in Bengal. In James Baillie Fraser's "Views of Calcutta and Its Environs" (1826), for example, we see Government House, the seat of East India Company rule. In the distance, just in front of the massive neoclassical company headquarters, we catch a glimpse of Gov. Gen. Lord Hastings about to set off for a drive, with his carriage and bodyguard awaiting. The segregationist intentions of colonial urbanism are made quite evident by the separation of the well-trafficked roadway in the foreground of Fraser's painting from the grounds of Government House, which is set off by an iron railing on a plinth that is interrupted by four triumphal gateways at both ends of the carriageways running across the north and south facades of the building.

As these images of Calcutta under the Raj suggest, the visual economy of urban empire was underpinned by a broader representational politics that suggested that Europeans alone had the right to occupy the key institutional sites of city space.[21] In her discussion of representations of Calcutta, Swati Chattopadhyay argues that Orientalist discourses represented authentic India as grounded in village life, cultural antiquity, and defective theocracy.[22] Similarly, in discussing colonial rule in Africa, Mahmood Mamdani makes an analogous point, arguing that the colonial state in Africa was "bifurcated, with different modes of power in rural and urban areas. Urban power spoke the language of civil society and civil rights, rural power of community and culture. Civil power claimed to protect rights, customary power pledged to enforce tradition."[23] If, in other words, colonial rural areas were the space of authentic colonial subjects, the city was the space of the European citizen, transplanted from Britain or France, as the case may be, in order to administer the extraction of natural wealth and labor that was the underlying rationale of empire.

This neat Manichean division of colonial space was a convenient fiction of empire, one that had little to do with the quotidian realities of colonial power. As James Baillie Fraser's representations of early-nineteenth-century Calcutta suggest, everyday life in Indian cities for European colonials involved inevitable propinquity to Indian officials, merchants, concubines, and servants of many different kinds. Moreover, as Chattopadhyay convincingly shows, the myth of "dual cities" divided into segregated "white" and "black" towns is based on imperial narratives of difference and superiority that were belied in Calcutta by the constant blurring of spatial boundaries as heterogeneous populations moved in and out of particular portions of the city and as specific buildings were put to heterogeneous uses.[24]

These regulatory fictions of spatialized racial difference were nonetheless extremely powerful and continued to overwrite empirical realities that demonstrated precisely the opposite. By 1847, for example, James Snow had discovered the water-borne nature of the cholera epidemic that decimated Britain after traveling across the Eurasian continent from Bengal in the early nineteenth century. But colonial medicine in India retained its belief in a miasmic theory of disease that emphasized the danger of noxious airborne contaminants, which were in turn connected in texts such as James Ranald Martin's seminal *Notes on the Medical Topography of Calcutta* of 1836 to the notion that disease was produced by a combination of the insalubrious tropical climate and the lax morals of the indigenous inhabitants of the city. By the mid-nineteenth century, colonial medical discourse had shifted from the notion of "seasoning" Europeans to the tropical climate that had prevailed in earlier centuries to sanitary paradigms based on mapping disease onto a biopolitical grid of race, religion, and caste difference in order to establish a cordon

sanitaire around the aptly named European civil lines and military can-
tonments, as maps of cholera outbreaks in Calcutta show. Cholera maps
such as those produced in Calcutta during the late nineteenth century
represented the native precincts of the city as a pathological space, their
unsanitary conditions linked to superstitious, premodern beliefs. The
epidemiological mapping of colonial urban space was linked to broader
biopolitical and cultural practices of urban segregation. As Anthony
King put it in his study of colonial urbanism, "above all else, the [Euro-
pean] compound was a *culture area*, an area modified to express the value-
system of the metropolitan society as interpreted by colonial community.
In conditions of exile, creation of this environment was instrumental in
maintaining a sense of identity."[25] The aim was to create a rigidly differentiated, systematically hierarchized, and therefore thoroughly sa-
lubrious space of imperial urban spectacle, a goal that necessitated the
transfer of the Raj's capital to Delhi and, ultimately, the construction of
New Delhi.

The invention of a vertical axis of vision through which urban space
could be catalogued was an important component in legitimating and facilitating this politics of the imperial cordon sanitaire. By lifting the
viewer above the hybrid realities life in the colonial city, representations
such as the cholera map constituted a powerful representational technology that could quantify and freeze urban space into a decipherable and
actionable set of discrete segments. Yet this vertical axis of the urban visual economy always existed in tension with the horizontal axis, through
which the often opaque but titillating flow of city life could be recorded.
Nonetheless, technological changes of the late nineteenth and early
twentieth century added to the potency of the vertical axis, as first photography and then cinema allowed the imperial gaze to adopt a bird's-
eye perspective. As we shall see, the bird's-eye ultimately became a
bombardier's point of view. These transformations in the visual economy of urban empire are particularly evident in the Maghreb, where
the invention of aerial bombardment took place in 1911.

Just as in India under the British Raj, the primary dynamic driving
the production of urban space following the French colonization of
Algeria in the mid-nineteenth century was the engineering of racial
segregation. One of the first comprehensive designs for Algiers, Charles
Fréderick Chassériau's plan of the 1860s, carried out the effective division of the city into a European zone, the Marine Quarter, which was
firmly separated from the indigenous casbah on the densely populated

hills above by a broad boulevard.[26] This principle of segregation remained of cardinal importance into the modern period, as the influential experimental plans of Le Corbusier for the city's development in the 1930s demonstrate: Le Corbusier planned to create an overpass that would allow European officials to transit from the suburbs to a massive office tower on the waterfront without ever coming into contact with the denizens of the casbah. As in other colonial cities, French urban planners in Algiers evinced a lively concern with the creation of clean, well-ventilated spaces.[27] Located outside the cordon sanitaire that putatively insulated European colonial society, the casbah during the colonial era exemplified the original dynamic that Foucault identified within biopower: a race war in which the tag "society must be defended" comes to legitimate the deployment of forms of power that blur the boundary between regulation and warfare. Indeed, the colonial city demonstrates the fallacy of assuming that regulation and warfare are antinomies; only by ignoring the Manichean spaces of the colony can these two apparatuses of power be seen as opposed to one another.[28]

Despite its association with racial alterity and contamination, the Algerian casbah always exerted a strong pull on the French colonial imaginary. European writers and painters alike found the casbah's sweeping wall of whitewashed houses with their rooftop terraces irresistibly picturesque. The fascination of the casbah for the Orientalist gaze lay not simply in its dramatic vertical architectonic qualities, however, but also in the specific interplay of public and private space that characterized the area. While she is critical of sweeping stereotypes concerning "the Muslim city," urban historian Janet Abu-Lughod nonetheless argues that Islam did shape social, political, and legal institutions in the cities of the Maghreb and that gender segregation was perhaps the foremost concern molding the urban fabric in the region.[29] As a result of this emphasis, public spaces such as streets in Algiers tended to be the domain of men while women primarily occupied the domestic spaces of traditional houses. Because of these gendered codes and the climatic qualities of the region, areas such as the Algiers casbah were composed of narrow, twisting alleys bordered by high, nearly uninterrupted building facades. Inside these blank walls, however, traditional houses opened out onto courtyards surrounded by arcades. In addition, the serried rooftop terraces of the casbah provided a common living space that allowed women in different buildings to communicate with one another. The frisson of difference and mystery generated by this architecture of gendered seclusion proved endlessly provocative for French urbanists and colonial policymakers.

The lure of the casbah, represented in metonymic form as a feminized other, was rampant in French colonial culture. The prototypical image in this regard is, of course, Eugène Delacroix's 1834 painting *Femmes d'Alger dans leur appartement*. Delacroix's painting gained its appeal not simply by laying bare the exotic garb and proscribed flesh of a group of Algerian women but also through the fantasy it unfolds of effortless entry into the hidden sanctum of the Algerian house.[30] These themes of voyeuristic penetration into proscribed spaces and the objectification of women that went along with such male fantasies are repeatedly obsessively throughout the late nineteenth and into the twentieth century. The seductive character of these representations of Oriental mystery and sexuality in academic art became even more prurient after the invention of photography catalyzed a lively trade in pornographic postcards of Northern African women.[31]

Such imperial urban scopophilia reached a crescendo as cinema turned to the colonies for subject matter in the early to mid-twentieth century. Julien Duvivier's film *Pépé le moko* of 1937 offers cinemagoers the tale of a French gangster who evades the police by hiding out in the casbah, represented in the film as an impenetrable space of multiracial, polyglot, feminized alterity. Introducing the casbah to viewers, one of the local police officers explains to a visitor from Paris why they are unable to capture Pépé:

> From the air the casbah looks like a teeming anthill, a vast staircase where terraces descend stepwise to the sea. Between these steps are dark, winding alleys like so many pitfalls. They overlap, intersect, twist in and out to form a jumble of mazes. Some of them are narrow, some vaulted like caves; wherever you look, stairways climb steeply like ladders or descend into putrid chasms and slimy porticos, dank and lice-infested. Dark, overcrowded cafes. Streets with obscure names: Impotence Street, Soum Soum Street, Honey Hotel Street, Man with a Pearl Street. There are 40,000 people in a space meant for 10,000: Kabyles, Chinese, Gypsies, Slavs, Sicilians . . . and girls of all nations, shapes, and sizes, tall, fat, short, ageless, formless. Chasms of fat no one would dare approach.[32]

For the gendered imperial gaze, the casbah represents a kind of polyglot bordello, a space that is at once alluring and terrifying, offering endless titillation but also the fear of dissolution and unmanning. Above all, however, it is a space that is ultimately unknowable, its teeming alleys creating a labyrinth that defeats all efforts to establish visual and cognitive mastery. Indeed, in Duvivier's film, the dashing gangster Pépé, hiding out in the impenetrable casbah, is ultimately undone by his desire for a Parisian woman who penetrates into his lair, suggesting that he has become unmanned despite his tough-guy exterior by his sojourn in the bowels of the Orient.

If the imperial gaze is both lured and repelled by the casbah, the increasingly powerful technologies of representation through which that gaze came to be deployed during the late colonial era present the titillating fantasy of penetrating the casbah's labyrinthine streets in ever more realistic ways. Yet this realism was of course a construction, as the Orientalistic excess of *Pépé le moko* underlines. Film, as Walter Benjamin suggested, might have been able to carve up reality like a surgeon, yet it hardly did so in a sanitized and objective manner. Indeed, the scopophilic imperial gaze often substituted fantasies of technological penetration for the far less seemly modes of power assumed by colonial urban conquest and counterinsurgency. Gillo Pontecorvo's great docudrama of the Algerian revolution, *The Battle of Algiers*, consciously juxtaposes these conflicting modes of urban biopower. The film opens with a torture scene in which the French paratroopers force a captive Algerian civilian to confess the hiding place of the last remaining leaders of the liberation movement. Pontecorvo's film then cuts to the opening credits, which unfold over scenes of the paras swarming through the streets and across the rooftops of the casbah. The French ability to move effortlessly across the proscribed rooftops of the casbah and to penetrate into the private spaces of Algerian homes, the rest of the film demonstrates, is gradually developed and ultimately won through systematic practices of torture and summary execution that polarized French society and threatened the liberal regime of parliamentary rule that obtained in the metropole with the forms of authoritarian power articulated in the colony.[33] Such blowback, *Battle of Algiers* implies, is the ineluctable outcome of imperial urban scopophilic fantasy.

How do representations of contemporary urban warfare compare with these colonial-era texts? Contemporary video games are a particularly important cultural site for the unfolding of imperial scopophilia today. Many such games are manufactured through explicit collaborative arrangements between the U.S. military and private entertainment corporations, and the products of these collaborative agreements are used in training military personnel.[34] Moreover, as Nick Mirzoeff shows in his essay "War Is Culture," video games have become part of the cultural surround through which U.S. war planners such as Gen. David Petraeus, author of the new U.S. military counterinsurgency manual, seek to produce full-spectrum dominance of the battlefield.[35] Counterinsurgency commanders are explicitly counseled by Petraeus to inhabit the first-person-shooter perspective of the video gamer as they seek to gain visual control of the battlefield.

It would be wrong to see video games as antagonistic to previous scopic technologies, however, since they build on and incorporate many of the key tropes of Hollywood representation. This should not be so surprising given the fact that, through outfits such as the University of Southern California's Institute for Creative Technologies, what James Der Derian calls MIME—the military-industrial-media-entertainment complex—has consolidated notable synergies between academia, Hollywood, and the military. Importantly, these video games vastly augment cinema's claims to realism by allowing players not simply to look at a spectacle but to perform acts within the imaginary world conjured up through digital aesthetics.[36] In fact, claims to fidelity of representation seem to be central aspects of the appeal of such games. During an era in which "embedding" prevented most members of the American press corps from gaining access to uncensored battle zones in Iraq and Afghanistan, video games produced either by the U.S. military or through the many cooperative agreements that characterize the burgeoning military-entertainment complex offered the U.S. public privileged glimpses of the predominantly urban battlefields of the war on terror.

One of the most successful of these video games is *America's Army*. Developed using $7 million of taxpayer money, the game was made available for free on an Army website and was downloaded 2.5 million times during the two months following its release.[37] The game theoretically takes players through strenuously accurate versions of the Army's basic training program that include training in military operations in urban terrain, allowing successful players to graduate eventually to Special Forces operations in combat zones—most of which are situated in some generic version of a Middle Eastern city. Promotional material for the game, which also serves quite openly as an Army recruitment drive, stresses the verisimilitude of the game by ironically blurring the dividing line between reality and the game, suggesting that warfare has become a totally cybernetic experience.

Despite these gestures to heightened realism, the game still plays out on a relatively deterritorialized and Orientalized "Middle Eastern" urban space. Unlike the imperial gaze manifested in the work of James Baillie Fraser's or Eugène Delacroix, that is, contemporary video games generate a generic urban battle zone not unlike the artificial Arab villages set up by the U.S. military on training bases around the world following the invasion of Iraq.[38] This generic quality underlines the region- and even globe-sweeping ambitions of the Obama administration's drone war, which Derek Gregory aptly calls "the everywhere war."[39] As critics such as Caren Kaplan have emphasized, new technologies such as drones do facilitate unparalleled forms of long-distance domination across multiple different geographic regions. U.S. drones currently operate out of multiple countries across the Middle East and Central Asia, for example, but also on the U.S.–Mexico border, in the Philippines, and, most recently, in the Sub-Saharan countries of Mali and Niger.[40] While it is important to note and offer critique of the globe-spanning character of U.S. imperialism under Obama, it would be a mistake to ignore the significant continuities with previous modalities of empire. Underlying new technologies such as the drone are enduring forms of the imperial gaze; to emphasize these continuities is to underline not simply the long-standing pernicious power of U.S. empire but also to highlight its contradictions.

As was true in colonial-era cinema, for example, the imperial cybernetic technology on display in contemporary video games interpolates subjects in a particular manner. The first-person-shooter format of the game reduces urban spaces to free fire zones. Game players are always positioned as American or British troops. When groups of networked players battle one another, each team sees their antagonists through a form of cybernetic Orientalism, their opponents' skin tone magically rendered more swarthy and their upper lips sporting Saddam-style mustaches. The feeling of interactivity and somatic immersion programmed into the game thus creates an illusory experience of realism since the game always reproduces the dominant ideological orientation of the current policy establishment. No consideration is given to the broader ethical questions raised by warfare in the name of fostering democracy, and there is little opportunity within the space of the game to consider the impact of war on civilians or on the long-term psychological health of combatants. The more such games emphasize contextual detail, the more glaring is the discrepancy between such gestures toward verisimilitude and the streamlined and endlessly reproducible character of the first-person-shooter game on which they are all modeled.

While screening out the contradictions of urban warfare, post-9/11 video war games emphasize bonding through combat in a manner analogous to and perhaps more powerful than that of cinematic relations of theirs such as *Black Hawk Down*.[41] The game *Full Spectrum Warrior*, whose title archly refers to Joint Forces Command's doctrine of supremacy on multiple different levels of the battle zone, hinges on precisely such male bonding. The game begins with two squads—Alpha and Bravo companies—dropped off like the Rangers in *Black Hawk Down* in the midst of a city filled with hostile fighters. Cut off from squad commanders by the static of war, players must leapfrog their teams through the dangerous streets of yet another generic Middle Eastern city. What unfolds in the game is an intense homosocial fantasy, one in which the soft flesh of the enemy is the medium through which video war gamers achieve immortality by bonding with a band of brothers and by freezing time in the eternal present of the gaming battle zone.[42]

None of this crop of video games attempt to hide the bloody character of urban war; instead, the thanatopoetic performance of the war gamer is an extension of the erotomaniac gaze of the colonial scopophiliac. There are few women present in these games, civilian or otherwise, and none of the eroticized objects that attracted the colonial gaze. Instead, the city itself is turned into a plastic, feminized body, to be swarmed over and penetrated at will by the cybernetic warrior. There is, I would argue, a strong link between the repetition compulsion of cybernetic death-dealing in games like *Full Spectrum Warrior* and the desire for eternal life that characterizes the ambivalent drives of the imperial gaze across the colonial/postcolonial divide. War games literally provide an intoxicating opportunity for players to live out the perennial imperial fantasy of fully automated warfare, creating a space in which death can be overcome through the cybernetic extension of the self into an eternal future.

Although *Full Spectrum Warrior* locates its players in the chaotic spaces of global cities of the Middle East, the vertical axis of the imperial gaze always beckons. When either of the squads gets particularly badly pinned down by enemy fire, for example, team leaders / players can use GPS to survey the area and, when things get really hectic, can call in helicopter reconnaissance and bombardment. At these moments in the game, as the vertical axis of imperial vision reasserts itself, players adopt the perspective of what Jordan Crandall calls "a militarized, machinic surround," an angle of vision involved in "positioning, tracking, identifying, predicting, targeting, and intercepting/containing."[43] The fantasy here is of a militarized cyborg identity in which the horizontal and vertical axes of imperial vision blend seamlessly together. The libidinal tug of this form of what Crandall calls "armed vision" is strong. As he puts it, "One cannot underestimate the extent to which representation, cognition, and vision are embedded within this circuit. The drive is bound up in an erotic imaginary of technology-body-artillery fusion, fueled under the conditions of war."[44]

Yet the dreams of technological mastery that animate video games and robotic technologies such as the Gorgon drone are, despite the apparent paradox, a symptom of U.S. imperial weakness.[45] First, we should recall that the world's first campaign of aerial bombardment was ordered by Winston Churchill in Iraq in 1915.[46] The newly formed Royal Air Force was supposed to replace fifty-one battalions of soldiers in a campaign of "control without occupation." This step was necessary because the British could no longer afford a massive occupation of Mesopotamia.[47] The parallel with the United States' own state of imperial fiscal and political overextension today is not so hard to make out. It is this crisis of imperial hegemony that lies behind increasing calls for the use of drones in humanitarian monitoring missions in countries such as Syria.[48] Yet, as Sven Lindqvist shows so brilliantly in his *History of Bombing*, the godlike feelings of power evident in early memoirs of European colonial bombing campaigns such as Bruno Mussolini's *Power*, which describes the Italian fascist campaign in Ethiopia, soon gave way to European nightmares of being bombed themselves.[49] In novels like Edward Shanks's *People of the Ruins* (1920), London is bombed back to the stone ages by colonial forces who have successfully hijacked European technologies of aerial warfare. Fears about drone blowback are likely to feature increasingly prominently in the imperial imaginary.

Indeed, if drone technology offers the imperial gaze the tantalizing dream of precision robotic aerial killing, like previous bombing campaigns, it also threatens to proliferate the space of war to the ends of the earth, unleashing unpredictable forms of blowback. In 2011, for example, the Obama administration's legal team engaged in a heated debate about the latitude the United States has to kill people whom it deems to be Islamicist militants in countries such as Yemen and Somalia, where it is not directly engaged in warfare. The administration's extension of lethal drone attacks against low-level militants and civilians to such countries greatly expands its policy of summary execution by drone strike, erasing virtually all borders in the war on terror.[50] Total war has now expanded to much of the region. But technologies of robotic destruction such as drones are relatively easy to hack and hijack. In August 2010 Sayyed Hassan Nasrallah, Hezbollah's secretary-general, revealed that in the mid-1990s the party had found a way to intercept and download the video feed from Israeli drones, allowing it to track these drones and then attack Israeli troops deployed in the area surveyed by the drones.[51] In fact, Nasrallah claimed that Hezbollah's ambush of a team of Israeli naval commandos in 1997 near the village of Ansariyah in southern Lebanon was precipitated by precisely such tactics. The recent capture of a CIA-flown RQ-170 Sentinel drone by Iran supports claims that such technology is increasingly vulnerable to electronic hijacking.[52] Now that drones have been captured by Iran and, perhaps, Hezbollah, it is only a matter of time before they are deployed against U.S. and allied forces in battle zones throughout the Middle East and Central Asia.

If the prospect of drone proliferation throughout the Middle East is on the horizon, the hijacking of warfare-based video games has already taken place. Hezbollah's "Special Force 2" allows players to reenact conflicts with the Israeli Defense Forces in southern Lebanon, firing Katyusha rockets at Israeli towns, battling tanks in the rocky valleys of southern Lebanon, and raiding Israel to capture soldiers.[53] Such redeployment of video game technology is part of a far broader, highly sophisticated use of new media of various sorts by groups classified as "terrorist" by the United States. As the Retort Collective argued some time ago, Islamist vanguard groups were driven by state censorship to establish sophisticated means of conjuring a transnational Arab multitude into being using electronic communications, including satellite TV stations, listservs, chat rooms, text messaging, traffic in CDs and DVDs, and, most recently, the use of the so-called deep web by groups like the Islamic State of Iraq and al-Sham, or ISIS.[54]

Unless the desire for technological mastery that characterizes the vertical axis of the imperial urban gaze is checked, robotic weapons such as drones are likely to become as ubiquitous and deadly as landmines for everyone in—and even outside—combat zones. One of the main attractions of drones such as the Predator is that they are relatively inexpensive and easy to manufacture. Yet, as happens so often with imperial technologies, moves are already afoot to deploy drone technologies against domestic "enemies" within the United States, including at the U.S.-Mexico border.[55] Following the passage of a federal law that compels the Federal Aviation Administration to allow drones to be used for all sorts of law-enforcement and commercial schemes, drones are set to become a staple of budget-squeezed domestic police forces in cities such as Los Angeles and New York, not to mention snooping paparazzi, raising significant questions for domestic civil liberties—although such concerns pale in comparison with the high number of civilian deaths caused by U.S. drone strikes in countries such as Pakistan.[56]

Finally, as armed robots become increasingly autonomous in order to cope with the deluge of information they generate, issues concerning agency, responsibility, and violence arise. The philosopher Peter Asaro asks particularly thorny questions about who is to be held responsible when a robotic drone carries out a summary execution that decimates civilian populations, allied troops, or U.S. combatants.[57] At the very least, we must develop new legal regimes banning the deployment of autonomous military robots since it is impossible to determine ultimate responsibility for war crimes committed by such weapons. Equally, if not more urgently, though, critics of U.S. empire need to militate against campaigns of summary execution carried out through drone strikes, both through effective political organizing and through continuing efforts to deconstruct the imperial scopophilia that animates such strikes. Drones are part of a long history of sanitizing imperial violence, whether it is through labeling such violence "constabulary action" against unruly imperial subjects rather than warfare against another nation or through the precision surveillance and killing technologies of the latest unmanned aerial vehicles.[58] The sooner we understand the dangers of this tempting Gorgon Stare, the better.

Notes

1. Quoted in Ellen Nakashima and Craig Whitlock. "With Air Force's Gorgon Drone, 'We Can See Everything,'" *Washington Post*, January 2, 2011, accessed January 7, 2012, http://www.washingtonpost.com/wp-dyn/content/article/2011/01/01/AR2011010102690.html.

2. Copious evidence of the ineffectiveness of bombing campaigns is offered, among other places, in Sven Lindqvist, *A History of Bombing*, trans. Linda Haverty Rugg (New York: New Press, 2001).

3. Quoted in Nathan Hodge, "McCrystal: Afghan War Needs More Troops, Strategy Shift," *Wired Magazine*, September 21, 2009, http://www.wired.com/dangerroom/2009/09/mcchrystal-its-make-or-break-time-in-afghanistan/.

4. Eric Schmitt, "Lull in Strikes by U.S. Drones Aids Militants in Pakistan," *New York Times*, January 7, 2012.

5. Scott Wilson and Al Kamen, "Global 'War on Terror' Is Given New Name," *Washington Post*, March 25, 2009, accessed November 17, 2013, http://articles.washingtonpost.com/2009-03-25/politics/36918330_1_congressional-testimony-obama-administration-memo.

6. For analysis of the civilian death toll of the U.S. drone campaign, see Amnesty International, "Will I Be Next? U.S. Drone Strikes in Pakistan" (2013), accessed December 21, 2015, http://www.amnestyusa.org/research/reports/will-i-be-next-us-drone-strikes-in-pakistan; Human Rights Watch, *Between a Drone and Al-Qaeda: The Civilian Cost of U.S. Targeted Killings in Yemen* (2013), accessed November 17, 2013, http://www.hrw.org/reports/2013/10/22/between-drone-and-al-qaeda-0; and Stanford International Human Rights and Conflict Resolution Clinic, Living Under Drones: The Aftermath of Drone Attacks, accessed December 21, 2015, http://chrgj.org/wp-content/uploads/2012/10/Living-Under-Drones.pdf /

7. Caren Kaplan, "Sensing Distance: The Time and Space of Contemporary War," Social Text Online, accessed November 17, 2013, http://socialtextjournal.org/periscope_article/sensing-distance-the-time-and-space-of-contemporary-war/.

8. Priya Satia, *Spies in Arabia: The Great War and the Cultural Foundations of Britain's Covert Empire in the Middle East* (New York: Oxford University Press, 2008).

9. Ibid., 245.

10. For a fuller discussion of this dynamic, see Ashley Dawson, "Combat in Hell: Cities at the Achilles Heel of U.S. Counter-Insurgency," *Social Text* 91 (2007), 169–80.

11. Nick Mirzoeff, *The Right to Look: A Counter-History of Visuality* (Durham, N.C.: Duke University Press, 2011).

12. See, for instance, Derek Gregory, "'In another time-zone, the bombs fall unsafely . . .': Targets, Civilians, and Late Modern War," *Arab World Geographer* 9, no. 2 (Summer 2006), 88–111; and Derek Gregory, "American Military Imaginaries and Iraqi Cities: The Visual Economies of Globalizing War," in *Globalization, Violence and the Visual Culture of Cities*, ed. Christoph Lindner, (New York: Routledge, 2009) 67–84.

13. Michael Dillon, "Governing Terror: The State of Emergency of Biopolitical Emergence," International Political Sociology 1 (2007): 7–28, at 12, 18. See also Michel Foucault, *Security, Territory, Population: Lectures at the College de France* (New York: Palgrave Macmillan, 2007).

14. Derek Gregory, "The Biopolitics of Baghdad: Counterinsurgency and the Counter-City," *Human Geography* 1, no. 1 (2008), accessed February 2, 2012, http://www.hugeog.com/index.php?option=com_content&view=article&id=86:polbagh&catid=34:hgissues1&Itemid=64.

15. The doyen of U.S. military theorists, Andrew Marshall of the Pentagon's Office of Net Assessment, notes that the Soviets were the first to begin speculating about the impact of information technology on warfare, although it was his legendary memorandum of 1993, "Some Thoughts on Military Revolutions," that triggered the full blown discourse on a revolution in military affairs within the United States. See James Der Derian, *Virtuous War: Mapping the Military-Industrial-Media-Entertainment Network* (Boulder, Colo.: Westview, 2001), 28.

16. Gen. William Westmoreland, quoted in David Cortright, *Soldiers in Revolt: G.I. Resistance during the Vietnam War* (New York: Anchor/Doubleday, 1975), 160.

17. Der Derian, *Virtuous War*, xv.

18. Sharon Anderson, "Urban Resolve 2015," *CHIPS: The Department of the Navy's Information Technology Magazine* (October–December 2006), accessed February 1, 2012, http://www.doncio.navy.mil/CHIPS/ArticleDetails.aspx?ID=3051.

19. Henri Lefebvre, *The Production of Space* (New York: Wiley-Blackwell, 1992).

20. Bessie Knox Fenton, *The Journal of Mrs. Fenton* (London: Edward Arnold, 1901), 253.

21. Compare with accounts of colonial urban space and identity in Sub-Saharan Africa and North Africa in the work, respectively, of Mahmood Mamdani in *Citizen and Subject: Contemporary Africa and the Legacy of Late Colonialism* (Princeton, N.J.: Princeton University Press, 1996) and Timothy Mitchell in *Rule of Experts: Egypt, Techno-Politics, Modernity* (Berkeley: University of California Press, 2002).

22. Swati Chattopadhyay, *Representing Calcutta: Modernity, Nationalism, and the Colonial Uncanny* (New York: Routledge, 2006), 9.

23. Mamdani, *Citizen and Subject*, 18.

24. Chattopadhyay, *Representing Calcutta*, 77.

25. Anthony D. King, *Colonial Urban Development: Culture, Social Power and Environment* (London: Routledge, 1976), 142.

26. Zeynep Çelik, *Urban Forms and Colonial Confrontations: Algiers under French Rule* (Berkeley: University of California Press, 1997).

27. On the miasmic theory of disease, see Sheldon Watts, *Epidemics and History: Disease, Power, and Imperialism* (New Haven, Conn.: Yale University Press, 1999). For discussion of the role of the miasmic theory of disease in the colonial urban development of New Delhi, see King, *Colonial Urban Development*, 108–22.

28. For a discussion of Foucault's notions of biopower, neoliberalism, and warfare, see Leerom Medovoi, "Global Society Must Be Defended: Biopolitics without Boundaries," *Social Text* 25, no. 2 (Winter 2008): 53–79.

29. Cited in Çelik, *Urban Forms and Colonial Confrontations*, 15.

30. For more extensive discussion of Delacroix's painting, see Assia Djebar, *Women of Algiers in their Apartment* (Charlottesville: University of Virginia Press, 1999).

31. See Malek Alloula, *The Colonial Harem* (Minneapolis: University of Minnesota, 1986).

32. Julien Duvivier, dir., *Pépé le moko* (Paris Film, 1941).

33. Alistair Horne, *A Savage War of Peace: Algeria 1954–1962* (New York: New York Review Books, 2006).

34. On video game sales, see Ed Halter, *From Sun Tzu to Xbox: War and Videogames* (New York: Thunder's Mouth, 2006), xviii.

35. Mirzoeff, Nick. "War Is Culture: Global Counterinsurgency, Visuality, and the Petraeus Doctrine," *PMLA* 124, no. 5 (2009): 1–18.

36. On the realist aesthetic in video games, see Alexander Galloway, "Social Realism in Gaming," *Game Studies* 4, no. 1 (November 2004), accessed September 25, 2009, http://gamestudies.org/0401/galloway/.

37. Halter, *From Sun Tzu to Xbox*, xviii.

38. See, for example, Christian Fuchs, "Typecasting for Iraq: U.S. Army Hires Arabs as 'Iraqi' Extras for War Games in Germany," *Spiegel Online International*, February 9, 2007, accessed November 17, 2013, http://www.spiegel.de/international/typecasting-for-iraq-us-army-hires-arabs-as-iraqi-extras-for-war-games-in-germany-a-465402.html.

39. Gregory, Derek. "The Everywhere War," *Geography Journal* 177, no. 3 (September 2011): 238–50.

40. Eric Schmitt, "Drones in Niger Reflect New U.S. Tack on Terrorism," *New York Times*, July 10, 2013, accessed November 17, 2013, http://www.nytimes.com/2013/07/11/world/africa/drones-in-niger-reflect-new-us-approach-in-terror-fight.html.

41. For a more extensive discussion of *Black Hawk Down* and the semiotics of the U.S. urban imperial imaginary, see Ashley Dawson, "New World Disorder: *Black Hawk Down* and the Eclipse of US Military Humanism in Africa," *African Studies Review* 54, no. 2 (Summer 2011): 177–94.

42. On *Full Spectrum Warrior* in particular and imperial video gaming in general, see Nick Dyer-Witheford and Greig de Peuter, *Games of Empire: Global Capitalism and Video Games* (Minneapolis: University of Minnesota Press, 2009), 97–123.

43. Jordan Crandall, "Armed Vision," *Multitudes* 15 (May 2004), accessed February 1, 2012, http://jordancrandall.com/main/+writings/_htmls/ArmedVision.pdf.

44. Ibid.

45. Stephen Graham, *Cities under Siege: The New Military Urbanism* (New York: Verso, 2010); and P.W. Singer, *Wired for War: The Robotic Revolution and Conflict in the 21st Century* (New York: Penguin, 2009).

46. Lindqvist, *History of Bombing*.

47. Ibid., 101.

48. See, for example, Anne-Marie Slaughter, "How to Halt the Butchery in Syria," *New York Times*, February 23, 2012, accessed April 16, 2012, http://www.nytimes.com/2012/02/24/opinion/how-to-halt-the-butchery-in-syria.html.

49. Lindqvist, *History of Bombing*, 151, 7.

50. Charlie Savage, "At White House, Weighing Limits of Terror Fight," *New York Times* (September 15, 2011), accessed January 7, 2012, http://www.nytimes.com/2011/09/16/us/white-house-weighs-limits-of-terror-fight.html.

51. Nicholas Blanford, "Speculation Continues over Hezbollah's Ability to Disable Israeli Drones," *Daily Star*, November 9, 2011, accessed February 1, 2012, http://www.dailystar.com.lb/News/Lebanon-News/2011/Nov-09/153450-speculation-continues-over-hezbollahs-ability-to-disable-israeli-drones.ashx.

52. Frank Gardner, "Why Iran's Capture of US Drone Will Shake CIA," *BBC News*, December 8, 2011, accessed February 1, 2012, http://www.bbc.co.uk/news/world-us-canada-16095823/.

53. "Hezbollah Video Game: War with Israel," *CNN*, August 16, 2007, accessed September 2, 2014, http://edition.cnn.com/2007/WORLD/meast/08/16/hez bollah.game.reut/.

54. Retort Collective, *Afflicted Powers* (New York: Verso, 2005). On ISIS and the "deep web," see Vocativ, "ISIS: We Are Operating in Gaza," July 15, 2014, accessed 2 September 2014, http://www.vocativ.com/world/israel-world/isis -operating-gaza/#!bOvxtm. For discussion of videogame development in the Middle East in general, see Vit Sisler, "Videogame Development in the Middle East: Iran, the Arab World, and Beyond," in *Gaming Globally: Production, Play, and Place*, ed. Nina B. Huntemann and Ben Aslinger, 251–72 (New York: Palgrave Macmillan, 2013).

55. Peter Finn, "Domestic Use of Aerial Drones by Law Enforcement Likely to Prompt Privacy Debate," *Washington Post*, January 23, 2011, accessed January 7, 2012, http://washingtonpost.com/.

56. Nick Wingfield and Somini Sengupta. "Drones Set Sights on US Skies," *New York Times*, February 17, 2012, accessed April 16, 2012, http://www.nytimes .com/2012/02/18/technology/drones-with-an-eye-on-the-public-cleared-to-fly .html.

57. Peter Asaro and G. Dabringer, "Military Robotics and Just War Theory," in *Ethica Themen: Ethical and Legal Aspects of Unmanned Systems, Interviews*, ed. Gerhard Dabringer (Vienna, Austria: Austrian Ministry of Defence and Sports, 2010).

58. Elizabeth Bumiller and Thom Shanker, "War Evolves with Drones, Some Tiny as Bugs," *New York Times*, June 19, 2011, accessed April 16, 2012, http://www .nytimes.com/2011/06/20/world/20drones.html.

Technology's Borders

The United States, Palestine, and Egypt's Digital Connections

HELGA TAWIL-SOURI

> A U.S.–Egypt free trade agreement, when combined with
> free trade agreements with Israel, the Palestinians, and Jordan,
> would form the basis for a Middle East Free Trade Region. . . .
> Regional economic integration will be a key to lasting peace and
> stability in the region.
>
> —U.S. Congress, Letter to President Clinton, November 1, 2000

Much is made of the relationship between technology and political
change: Have states become impotent in the face of social media? Are
particular kinds of regimes a threat because of YouTube, Twitter, or cell
phones? Have territory and our sense of place become irrelevant because
of our ability to digitally connect across international borders? Taking the
examples of Palestine and Egypt, my contention in this chapter is that the
power of any technology must be understood within a historical and
geopolitical framework. Specifically, in the context of Egypt and Palestine, technology has not been devoid of larger geopolitical processes
because in both alike, technology has come hand-in-hand with "free
trade" and "peace." The reason for this tripartite matrix has to do with the
United States' role as the global driver of technological developments and
its critical—if often contradictory—role in the politics of the Middle East.

In Egypt and Palestine, the United States has been the primary driver
of technology development, whether through nonprofit assistance programs and for-profit investment projects or through its influence in su-
pranational institutions such as the World Bank. Over the past two or
three decades both the Egyptian and Palestinian technological landscape
have become "Americanized" in the influx of American capital, technology, ideology, and expertise. In fact, one can think of both Palestine and
Egypt as having been "opened" by the push toward liberalization and
privatization driven by U.S. and international forces in conjunction with

national elites who have amassed great wealth in the process. Moreover, given the United States' influential role in technology development in Egypt and Palestine and the United States' relationship with Israel, this has meant that technology has come hand-in-hand with various "peace" agreements. As such, when attempting to understand the role of technology in political change—whether in fostering revolution or eradicating borders—one must equally invoke "peace" and "free trade" in the mix.

This chapter analyzes the contradictory role technology plays in the spatiality of Palestine and Egypt, particularly as these relate to borders and thus also question what "openness" has come to mean. Technology has played an important role as a driver of "borderlessness" in the sense of "opening" Palestine and Egypt to external influences, investments, capital flows, expertise, and much more. Technology has certainly problematized and altered a state's borders—whether the United States' reach outward or Egypt's and Palestine's opening of them. But it has not eradicated them all together. In fact, technology brings about new forms of spatialities and new forms of bordering mechanisms while often keeping intact "older" forms of borders.

The unshakable bond that the United States has with Israel has also largely defined the initial development of technology investment, in the case of Egypt, or the ways in which technology investments work, in the case of Palestine. The combination of a politically motivated relationship and neoliberal economic approaches has often meant trilateral agreements with Israel such as the establishment of free trade zones, for example. In fact, a political economy approach demonstrates that the promises of technology to equalize (global) economic relations, modernize society, empower women, or digitally connect youth have not challenged the underlying structures of oppression—whether Israeli colonialism, Egyptian corruption, the uneven hand of neoliberal capital accumulation or internal (economic) inequalities. In the Palestinian case, technology has been constrained by territorial borders imposed by Israel, which the United States has done nothing on the ground to counter—thus making the United States implicit in Israel's own colonial project. In the Egyptian case, the state's borders have been "transgressed" since Egypt's trajectory toward liberalization in 1974 and U.S.-administered Israeli–Egyptian peace in 1979, which have nonetheless gone hand-in-hand with dictatorial control. The Egyptian uprising in 2011 further demonstrated the continued importance of territoriality no matter the role of technology—thus the limited "power" of technology. Twitter, Facebook, and satellite TV have not provided a migration of politics to a virtual realm; in fact, what the uprising demonstrated quite explicitly is the importance of being in place.

In short, the matrix of technology, neoliberal free trade, and peace has come with a set of constraints—very often uneven in their manifestation. My point is not to judge the success of the Egyptian uprising or to question the role of technology in Palestinian resistance but to place the politics of Palestine and Egypt in a technological materiality. The analysis of technology's development—particularly on the infrastructural level—in both Palestine and Egypt demonstrates the paradoxical role of technology in a world in which territory is of continued importance.

In what follows, I approach the technological landscape of Palestine and Egypt through a largely political economy lens, and I approach the relationship between technology and place(s) through a critical geography one. I argue the following: first, technology infrastructures are integral aspects of states' territoriality; second, territoriality continues to matter in an increasingly technological world; and third, the relationships between technology and places bring about different forms of borders. I begin with a focus on Palestine's technology infrastructure territorial confines, then look at the role of the United States in technology investment within Palestine. In the second half, I turn to Egypt's longer-standing relationship with the United States and the development of information technology (IT) and the former's strategies of liberalization as paving the way for openness. I then turn my analysis inward to the importance of a different form of territoriality during the Egyptian uprisings. The examples of Palestine and Egypt are of course unique, despite similarities. But I am approaching them as case studies along a spectrum that problematize our assumptions about globalization, territory, borders, communication, and, ultimately, political change—in the Middle East and beyond.

Digital Occupation

The agreements of 1993–95 Oslo Accords established the Palestinian Authority (PA) and enabled state-building and gave Palestinians permission to establish their own infrastructures for the first time in history. The accords also meant to demarcate Palestinian self-administered territory and hand the PA responsibilities over civilian life and its related infrastructures. This resulted in the reorganization of Israeli power over Palestinians rather than its withdrawal.[1] The supremacy of Israeli security combined with Palestinian territorial fragmentation into Areas A, B, and C, combined with the expansion of settlements and the establishment of checkpoints, by-pass roads, and eventually the security barrier, would delineate the territorial extent of any possible "Palestine."[2] Area A, 18 percent of the West Bank, was in theory under full PA civil and security control. Area B, 20 percent of the West Bank, was meant to be under Palestinian civil control and joint Israeli and Palestinian security control. Area C, 62 percent of the West Bank, was under full Israeli civil and security control.

Oslo II specified that "Israel recognizes that the Palestinian side has the right to build and operate separate and independent communication systems and infrastructures including telecommunication networks."[3] However, as with other infrastructures (e.g., broadcasting, sewage, population registries, water, transportation), Palestinians were subject to Israeli constraints that would counter their right—or simply their ability—to build separate and independent systems. With regard to telecommunications, Israel continues to determine the allocation of frequencies, where Palestinians are permitted to build infrastructure and install equipment, and much else that shapes the field. The territorial fragmentation would serve to constrict technology infrastructure (as all Palestinian infrastructure) by only permitting the PA to build or control infrastructure within Areas A, seldom in Areas B, and never in Areas C. In addition, Israel prohibited Palestinians from installing infrastructures all along the security barrier/wall and in Israeli-defined buffer zones. Just as the geographies of the West Bank and Gaza Strip were increasingly fragmented and contained during the Oslo and post-Oslo "peace" years, the space of infrastructure was also confined to follow territorial boundaries. Some new borders were created.

Israel handed over responsibility for telecommunications in 1995 to the PA. What little there existed of a technically debilitated fixed-line infrastructure in permissible areas was handed over; in the remainder of Palestinian territory, the PA would be responsible for building it from the ground-up. I start with and focus mostly on the example of cellular telephony as it is has been the fastest-expanding IT market, it has much larger penetration and use in the territories, and it highlights important tensions between ideals of "mobility," movement, and territoriality.

The first and largest Palestinian cellular provider, Jawwal, was established in 1994 as a subsidiary of the Palestinian telecommunications monopoly, Paltel. From its inception, Jawwal has been limited and constrained by Israeli-defined and Israeli-imposed policies that have been territorially bordered. First, where Paltel and Jawwal can build their infrastructure (whether underground cables, cellular towers, or exchange stations) is determined by Israeli authorities. Second, what kinds of equipment Palestinian operators are permitted to import, install, and use are also constrained by Israeli decisions—whether in simply preventing certain technologies, in confiscating them for years on end, or in instituting a policy of preferential treatment toward Israeli manufacturers rather than foreign ones. The equipment needed to build and maintain the infrastructure is also controlled so that, for example, Jawwal is still struggling to enhance its network to 2G (while much of the rest of the world is already moving from 3G to 4G). The strength, capability, and range of cellular signals are also determined by the Israeli Ministry of Communication—how much overall spectrum Palestinian providers are permitted and at what megahertz, and even what direction broadcasting towers can face. Jawwal was also given its own area code by Israeli authorities—which has meant that calling from one area code to another has either been forbidden or is extremely expensive. A cell phone user in the West Bank on a Palestinian cellular network cannot connect to a cell phone user, for example, in Jerusalem on an Israeli network—as agreements between Palestinian and Israeli providers to connect calls are wrapped in contentious political decisions. What this means "on the ground" for Palestinian users is that signals are weak, the network is overburdened, and in many areas there is simply no network access. There are too many other limitations to enumerate; what is important to recognize is the extent to which Israeli policies and practices territorially constrain Palestinian cellular communications. By the end of 2011 Jawwal boasted more than two million subscribers; each and every one of them pays for substandard service because Jawwal's network has not been permitted to expand beyond the initial requirements—to support a total of 120,000 subscribers in both the Gaza Strip *and* the West Bank.

A second Palestinian cellular provider, Wataniya, established service in the West Bank in 2009. In large part the policy to introduce competition into the cellular market was one driven by external players. Wataniya had to wait upward of three years for the Israeli Ministry of Communications to award it frequency—and eventually it was permitted less frequency spectrum than any other commercial provider in the world. As of late 2014 Wataniya is still not permitted to operate in the Gaza Strip and is limited by the same Israeli-imposed controls mentioned above.

Palestinian technological development, however, cannot be understood as separate from Israel's own technological development. In 1986 the Israeli national telecommunications company, Bezeq, launched its cellular subsidiary, Pelephone, which offered mobile service inside Israel and to Israeli settlements in the West Bank and the Gaza Strip. Since market liberalization in 1994, another three private cellular companies provide service: Cellcom, which launched in 1994; MIRS, in 1998; and Orange, in 1999. The four Israeli cellular providers contend that they operate in the territories to provide service to settlers, to Israelis traveling on by-pass roads, and, of course, to the military. The four companies generally have the liberty to install their equipment wherever they want, together boast 2,000 times more frequency spectrum than Palestinian providers, and turn a blind eye to the profitability they gain from the hundreds of thousands of Palestinians who purchase phones, chips, and time cards for use on Israeli networks. A large number of Palestinians in the territories use Israeli cellular providers since signals are stronger, more available throughout Palestine-Israel, and cheaper.

Cellular signals by their nature do not "know" to stop at political boundaries; thus, given settlements' locations, Israeli cellular signals can be enjoyed in many parts of the West Bank. These must be paid for even though they are illegal by Israeli, Palestinian, and Oslo Accords standards. The result is that even in the depths of the West Bank, Israeli digital flows are largely unencumbered, highlighting the paradoxes of (uneven) borders in the landscape of technology infrastructures. In other words, Israeli infrastructure, networks, and signals are, in relation to Palestinian ones, unfettered. This highlights a contradiction between the supposed liberatory aspects of high-tech networks and the continued determinativeness of territoriality and borders; the spaces of communications networks and infrastructures for Palestinians follows Israeli-imposed territorial boundaries. But only for Palestinians.

Such constraints are not unique to cellular telephony. The majority of aspects related to *all* high-tech infrastructures are controlled by Israel. All Palestinian bandwidth use—whether for cellular telephony, television, radio, Internet, ambulance and police communications, and the like—is determined by Israel. All infrastructure building—the decisions about where to install, what kinds of equipment, among others—face the same kinds of limitations as Jawwal.

Take, for example, the Palestinian landline telephone infrastructure—necessary not only for telephone networks but Internet as well—all of which falls under the management of the Paltel monopoly. All of Paltel's international calls, whether incoming or outgoing, are routed through Israeli providers because Paltel is not permitted its own international gateway. All of Paltel's Gaza–West Bank calls are switched inside Israel because Paltel cannot dig under Israeli land to install a fiber-optic cable, nor has it been allocated enough spectrum bandwidth to use microwave technologies. Paltel calls *within* the West Bank and *within* the Gaza Strip are also frequently routed through Israeli providers because of the limitations of where and what kinds of equipment Paltel can install. All such phone calls are also double-billed because Israeli providers—that Paltel and thus also Jawwal have no choice but to rely on—add termination charges and connection fees.

The sole Palestinian Internet service provider, Hadara (also a subsidiary of Paltel), faces many of the same constraints. It is still waiting for Israeli permission for an Internet trunk-switching system to allow Internet traffic to circumvent Israeli providers. Thus, Palestinian Internet traffic is routed through switches located *outside* the Gaza Strip and the majority of the West Bank. And as with cellular telephony, bandwidth allocation is limited by the Israeli Ministry of Communication so that no Palestinian end user can have an Internet connection faster than 2mb per second. Strict limitations are also imposed on the kinds of technologies permitted—whether Wi-Fi, encryption, or GPS-enabled devices.

Palestinian users and the infrastructure as a whole are territorially (and otherwise) bound by area codes; the landline infrastructure; the range of television signals; the kinds of equipment permitted; the range, strength and direction of signals; among other policies, all of which tend to follow the narrow and fragmented territorial boundaries of Palestinian land enclosures. Technology infrastructure in Palestine-Israel is not a metaphor for the Palestinian–Israeli conflict. It is the conflict in built form. The limitations imposed on the realm technology infrastructures within the Palestinian Territories demonstrate that the "bordering" of Palestinians is as much technological as it is territorial or physical. Palestinian flows are largely contained according to Israeli-defined *territorial* boundaries that prevent, limit, or thwart intra-Palestinian and international connections. These very same "borders" are largely irrelevant to

Israeli flows. Palestinians live under a regime, which I have elsewhere described as one of digital occupation.[4] Borders are a dialectical process in that they are created by various social actors, interacting with historical, geographical, political, and economic conditions. They are also dialectical in that they also result in contradictory processes; if Palestinians are on the one hand "bordered," there are also inevitably "debordering" processes going on simultaneously.

"Opening" Palestine

The development of information communication and technology (ICT) and telecommunications infrastructure in the territories have to be understood in the context of a conjuncture of events. The early 1990s witnessed the global growth of the high-tech sector, state-building, and international development efforts that would place primacy on privatization and liberalization (often called the Washington Consensus) and the fervor over what came to simply be called globalization. That Israel became a successful hub in this new global economy would itself impact Palestinians as development of a Palestinian high-tech sector would either be naively framed as a means to compete with Israel's or, at the least, able to build upon it by becoming its (cheap) labor supplier. Within this matrix, much state-building efforts focused on new technologies as means for economic growth but also problematically assumed to be able to bring about all kinds of societal changes such as peace, democratization, and women's empowerment, to name only some.[5]

The 1993–95 Oslo Accords have also been formative. The agreements gave birth to the PA and the influx of international development and private investment into the territories, which would make infrastructural development possible. As such, telecommunications and ICT sectors are very much products of Oslo and the "opening" of Palestine. The processes of high-tech globalization and the peace accords networked Palestinians into channels of international capital flows, neoliberal state-building efforts, and high-tech firms. Some "borders" were thus shattered. As such, technology infrastructures highlight how Palestinians are incorporated into a global network (of technology, international development, capital, media flows, etc.)—even if simultaneously contained through a combination of Israeli policies.

One cannot wholly assess the development of a technology industry or infrastructure, international trade relations, or policy matters without taking consideration the formidable position of the United States and American multinational high-tech firms (globally as well as within the specific context of Palestine). ICT development has been under U.S. tutelage. This influence includes the U.S. premier government aid arm, the U.S. Agency for International Development (USAID), private high-tech firms (namely, Cisco, Microsoft, Intel, and Hewlett-Packard) as well as U.S. influence in multinational aid agencies such as the World Bank. Between 1995 and 2013, the United States has provided more than US$4.5 billion for ICT projects alone in the Palestinian Territories. Moreover, U.S. subsidiary firms inside Israel—Intel, Oracle, and Microsoft—have been major engines of ICT growth for Palestine. The United States generally supports private-sector growth within the territories through industry-related outcomes or those that provide support for commercializing private-sector ventures. These firms have often been even more important players than any of the nonprofit institutions. Cisco, for example, is often billed as an exemplary partner for the Palestinian economy, investing more than US$15 million between 2008 and 2013 alone in Palestinian start-ups and training programs.

ICT also came with the added obfuscation of promises of job creation, modernization, democratization, empowerment, and assurances about economic viability fostered by a technologically determinist perspective. U.S. funders emphasized and preferred projects such as technology incubators to create and support ICT entrepreneurship, computer science departments and labs in universities, for-profit training programs such as Cisco and Microsoft Academies, and Internet youth centers and refugee camp computer labs. Collectively such programs help produce future economic partners and markets for U.S.-based corporations, demonstrating the explicitly stated purposes of furthering U.S. foreign policy interests in "expanding free markets." As the Palestinian minister of telecommunications and information technology complained in 2005 in a personal interview about ICT projects: "I don't like to work with US-AID projects because I know it benefits them more than us. . . . But we must utilize whatever comes our way. . . . There is no other choice."[6]

The growth of technology (and the financial investment that made its expansion possible) echoed the language of "modernization" and "integration into the global economy." The Internet accommodated the interests of neoliberal actors and their tacit goal of engineering the Palestinian economy according to free-market values. For example, the Palestinian Ministry of Planning and International Cooperation echoed the discourse that ICT is necessary because today's world makes it so: "A modern and competitive Palestinian economy must be information-based—or risk being neither modern nor competitive.... We Palestinians must be part of the global 'new economy' or we're nowhere."[7] As one researcher observed in 2004, "ICT represents one of the very few hopeful developments in an otherwise hopeless situation.... ICT is deeply, and probably irreversibly, integrated into Palestinian life." But he also warned that, "like so much about Palestinian nation-building, the ICT experiment is driven by desperation."[8] The latter observation is much closer to reality.

Many projects are focused on private-industry growth but also on bilateral (United States–Palestine) or more often trilateral (United States-Palestine-Israel) outputs. These largely result in economic profits for U.S. and Israeli firms and Palestinian elites and help give an impression of opening borders between the three players. These projects complicate the borders of Israel and the United States, expanding their reach well beyond their state's territorial borders. All of these, however, do not address the structural inequalities and constraints imposed by Israel.

The United States' involvement here demonstrates a number of important limitations. First, U.S. projects do not affect or change the "macro" structure of unevenness such as Israeli occupation, territorial expansion, and technological and economic superiority, on the one hand, and Palestinian containment and de-development, on the other hand. This has been a standing issue since the beginnings of the Oslo Accords and is very much tied to promises, contradictorily, of "peace." Equally important was the Paris Economic Protocol, which established a "customs union" resulting in an absence of any economic borders, thus preserving the uneven economic relations that had already existed. Subsequent funding projects would therefore never challenge a weak Palestinian economy integrated in and dependent on the Israeli economy. Both political and economic agreements ignored issues of Palestinian economic, political, or territorial sovereignty and left Palestinians unable to control their own development strategy—echoing the notion that ICT is driven by "desperation."

Particularly in the realm of ICTs, American donors and nongovernmental organizations have been so enthused with the promise of peace-building that they have underestimated (or overlooked) the political and economic difficulties that lay ahead: Israeli closures and control of the territories and the various limiting mechanisms "legalized" in the accords—such as control of spectrum and what kinds of technologies would be permitted into the territories, among many other issues. This has meant that most international support does little to change these underlying structures but at best mitigates some of their effects. The role for Palestinians is then preemptively confined to providing various forms of support to the Israeli (and U.S.) markets and industries in an off-shore structure that relies (and must maintain for the sake of being competitive) the much cheaper labor price of Palestinians.

Thus, one of the impacts of ICT in the Palestine-Israel-U.S. matrix is that it makes permanent the originally temporary conditions of the Oslo Accords, further rooting the accords' inequalities and limitations into the territory of Palestine-Israel. It also means that there is no resolution to the conflict—either through ICTs or otherwise. The gamut of ICT projects serve different interests and may touch different parts of society, but none are able—either individually or collectively with other projects— to tackle the underlying problem that is Israeli occupation. Israel's territorial control seeps into all concomitant spatial aspects, from borders to infrastructures, from economic sovereignty to trade agreements. Following that, the United States is incriminated in Israel's continued control over Palestinians in the various ways the latter are "bordered" and the United States' inability (or unwillingness) to eradicate those borders. What this suggests vis-à-vis borders is that the United States' borders are expanded in the sense of the enlargement of the zone of trade and influence across a region well outside its own territory at the same time that Israel expands its reach over Palestine.

In summary, technology infrastructures in Palestine demonstrate how spatialities of inclusion and exclusion operate across logics and processes of neoliberal restructuring, legal frameworks, military violence, technology architecture, and modes of manipulation and exploitation at different scales. New technologies create (and are part of) a matrix in which Palestine's borders are constrained, Israel's are expansive, and the United States' are fuzzy. Some of these borders are old, some new, some territorial, some technological, but all invariably highlight the complex spatiality of the role of ICTs within and between states and regions. What is true for Palestine-Israel may be extreme but not unique: everywhere else in our global network age borders and their related processes are shifting and dynamic. Borders are enforced, experienced, and circumvented in different ways and across different spaces, continually reformulated, reinforced, and negotiated. If, as in the case of Palestine, borders are erected for some and trespassable for others, their uneven processes in Egypt seemed to have resulted in a relatively more "open" space.

An Already-Opened Egypt

Major breakthroughs in Egypt's drive to use IT in the service of economic and human development began in 1999, when in September of that year, President Hosni Mubarak announced the National Project for Technology Renaissance. Since then, building an information society for economic and social development has been a central goal of government, demonstrated by the establishment of a new Ministry of Information and Communication Technology. Part of the mission of the new ministry was to articulate the government's ICT strategy for Egyptian society. The ministry's projects ranged from computer clubs for low-income youth to training for small- and medium-sized business managers; from linking professional communities like physicians to enhancing knowledge flows in Egypt to off-shore software development and training schemes. As with Palestine, the promise of technology was framed as something the state had to do, or otherwise be left behind: "Computers and the internet will help Egypt to progress into the 21st century. We must be quick to take advantage of the forces of globalization," claimed one official.[9]

The U.S. involvement in Egypt in ICT and the larger geopolitical realm is extensive and stems from much deeper historical events and relations that ICT is a manifestation of Sadat's 1974 Open Door Policy (also referred to as *infitah*) and the 1979 Camp David Accords. These renewed Egyptian–U.S. diplomatic relations and prompted the resumption of what has become a substantial amount of foreign assistance. With the Camp David Accord, Egypt began to reap approximately $2 billion per year in U.S. aid, the second-largest allocation after Israel. Egypt's incorporation into the American domain was perceived to be essential for Middle East peace. Aid to Egypt was at its core "a political symbol of evenhanded economic support," as one U.S. government report put it, especially as the large sums Egypt received were beyond its capacity to effectively absorb.[10] For the United States, the benefits of foreign aid to Egypt were strategic, diplomatic, and political.[11] Egypt was often a meeting point for U.S. peacemaking efforts between Arab states, Israel, and the Palestinians. The United States hoped that peace with Egypt would create a domino effect in the region. The United States wanted to ensure, above all, Egyptian regime stability. U.S. foreign aid, it was believed, would undercut the ability of Islamic extremists to attain power while increasing the popularity of the Egyptian regime. As such, U.S. economic assistance would also allow the regime to delay implementing political liberalization by quelling the urban masses through government subsidies—particularly in the realm of food aid. In short, foreign aid to Egypt fulfilled U.S. strategic, diplomatic, and political objectives while it was also intended to be a conduit for future economic liberalization.

U.S. hope for the region was that Egyptian–Israeli peace would serve as an example for other (moderate) Arab states to emulate. After peace, the suggestion was, U.S. capital flows would follow. Jordan's peace treaty with Israel in 1994, for example, also "opened" Jordan to increased military and economic assistance as well as trilateral "free trade" agreements.

As with Palestine and the Oslo funding structures, investment in and assistance to Egypt also had to make "peace dividends" obvious in order to garner support from Egyptian citizens. A "peace funding" matrix presses for high-visibility projects with shorter implementation time in order to demonstrate peace's tangible effects grew. Consequently, USAID implemented projects that were more symbolic in nature than economically sound. USAID found itself promoting projects that clearly showed Egyptians that the project had been paid for by the United States. "As a result, overly large and expensive projects were implemented merely because they were highly visible to both the Egyptian regime and Egyptian people."[12]

In 1994 a new relationship was formally called the U.S.-Egypt Partnership for Economic Growth and Development. The purpose of the initiative was to foster American private investment in Egypt as an alternative to official U.S. government aid, ushering in a new model for U.S.-Egyptian relations. The structure of the partnership consisted of various committees in charge of promoting private-sector development. The Presidents' Council consisted of fifteen American and fifteen Egyptian corporate representatives, among them telecommunications/ICT firms. The relationship between the Egyptian government and U.S. technology firms has resulted in various kinds of projects such as training partnerships with IBM, Oracle, Lucent, and Microsoft (supported in part by USAID); the Regional Information Technology Institute and Information Technology Institute as local institutions established with government and private-sector funds; training and certification for young IT professionals; and training university students in database development, among many others.

USAID has continued to be an active player, as has the American Chamber of Commerce in Egypt. American interest in Egypt's IT development stems from USAID's Aid to Trade policy, which is a defining principle of USAID's Egypt 2000–9 Strategic Plan. USAID projects focus on establishing a "cashless society" in Egypt and computerizing banking services (to help increase consumer spending), enacting cyber laws, and protecting intellectual property (to protect American interests). Other USAID projects include legal and regulatory reform, increased e-government and e-business initiatives, expanded use of ICT, and administration grants to nongovernmental organizations to enable the implementation of IT strategies for development work at the grassroots.

As in the Palestinian case, many programs failed to address underlying problems. Similarly, many projects seemed so enthused with technological determinist promises that it seemed it was that enthusiasm (or perhaps capital investment) rather than realistic goals that were pursued. One well-funded program sponsored by USAID attempted to provide expensive state-of-the art computer laboratories in the Ministry of Education and universities while failing to account for the complex social environments that would be required for such laboratories to actually function, let alone make an educational difference. As a result, hardware and software purchased for the laboratories remained locked up and unused for more than a year, losing a good portion of their value.[13] As Mark Warschauer notes, both USAID and the government have devoted huge amounts of resources to integrating new technologies in schools without addressing the broader problems of illiteracy, poverty, and rural/urban inequalities, among others. He analyzes this approach as an effort to overcome two great divides, one international and one domestic:

> At the international level, technology in education is seen as a way to leapfrog ahead and catch up with the West. . . . At the domestic level, educational technology is seen as narrowing the gap between the country's elite, almost all of whom live in the principal cities of Cairo and Alexandria, and its poor, who are spread out in urban and rural areas across the nation, especially in more remote communities of Upper (i.e., southern) Egypt. This is to be accomplished through the use of the Internet and satellite television for distance education.[14]

The realm of education is not unique; the same is largely the case in projects toward e-government or software training. While the monies and the realities on the ground are very different, on the level of discourse and "failure" there is not much different between these projects in Palestine or in Egypt.

The state policy toward economic liberalization first instituted by President Anwar Sadat in 1974 and continued by Hosni Mubarak in the ensuing decades, *infitah*, paradoxically came hand-in-hand with policies directed at social and political oppression—not an uncommon result of dictatorial regimes mixing economic openness and political control.[15] Accompanying these neoliberal measures was a natural corollary: the concentration and centralization of wealth in the hands of a tiny layer of the country's elite and the immiserization of a vast majority. The neoliberal policies of "opening" in Egypt ought not to be understood as an aberration to a neoliberal system but a key feature of capital accumulation. Technology generates economic (and political) distinctions and differentiations, such as the uneven developments of and within cities, regions, and countries.[16] The social shaping of technology is intimately tied up with broader issues of class and power. "For the government to engage in high-visibility technology efforts without meaningful reform is thus not necessarily a contradiction at all, but rather a projection of state control," rightly claims Warschauer.[17] In other words, technology, neoliberal policies, "peace," uneven development, and political oppression can go hand-in-hand. However, *infitah* was not simply significant because of the privatization and poverty that became widespread but in the way that it also opened the floodgates for media and technology, which I return to below.

Egypt has experienced substantial growth, even if technological penetration is low compared to other countries and the majority of users are in urban areas. Due to the successful implementation of a free Internet strategy in 2002, Egypt now has the largest Internet market in Africa with more than 5 million users in early 2006. Egypt's Internet users as percent of total population was 16 percent in 2009 and 35.5 percent in 2012; its cellular penetration rate is 34.7 percent.[18] On an infrastructural level, all landlines are owned by Telecom Egypt (a pseudo private–government entity). There are three cellular providers: Vodafone Egypt, Mobil, and Etisalat. Although many boast that there are around 220 Internet service providers in Egypt, that number is skewed by omitting the fact that all of these are resellers of bandwidth from one of the 5 infrastructure providers. In fact, all class 1 tier Internet service providers are owned by the major telecommunications companies operating in the country.

In short, despite the Mubarak regime's stringent media policies, by January 2011 the Egyptian media and technology landscape was varied, even if not fully pluralistic. This was a process that had been materializing since the 1980s, tied to *infitah*.

Territorial Presence

After *infitah*, the regime, on a symbolic level at least, became less (territorially) self-contained and exclusive. It continued trying to control the kinds of information people received, and certainly did so through its state-run media, but as the media and technological landscape expanded, the state increasingly lost control over its own image and over its citizens. What shifted in the past decades, then, was the regime's need to project itself in a landscape that was increasingly beyond-the-national.

The result is an uneven spatial landscape in which we witness a diffusion and expansion (of technology flows, of influences, of citizens' access, etc.) and simultaneously a disintegration and shrinking of the regime's national power (echoing long-standing discussions of globalization as a threat to a national regime). The result is a fragmentation of a regime's authority and an increase in the points (or spaces) that contribute to anti-regime opposition, both locally (inside the state) and globally (outside the state). This shifting spatiality shrinks regimes' room for maneuverability. In other words, the conjuncture of technology and mediated events end up "collapsing" the spatial reach of the regime. The collapse is metaphorical and material: political weakening, changing economic flows, and a shifting geographic manifestation of power.

To put it simplistically, *infitah* and globalization were serious challenges to the regime's hegemony. The government was still a powerful site of values, ideals, and information but in an increasingly competitive landscape. Under "open skies," Egypt was gradually open to foreign media (e.g., increased numbers of foreign journalists, foreign media investors, technologies imported from elsewhere), while the Egyptian population simultaneously enjoyed the proliferation of media outlets and technologies (e.g., Sheikh Yusuf al-Qaradawi's televised speeches, satellite dishes, cellular phones, and so on). For example, Alexandria and Sharm el-Sheikh have been important hubs in fiber-optic connections for the entire Mediterranean region, making Egypt part of a high-tech network very much unlike the Palestinian Territories; Egypt was the first Arab nation to launch satellite networks and eventually permit satellite signals in; its largely dominant and powerful media-content-producing abilities over the years has also relied on foreigners, not just Egyptians. These processes are deeply spatial as well as political.

The uprising highlighted this shifting spatiality of politics in the ways the regime attempted to prevent both local and global connections: the regime's response to jam Al Jazeera signals, its shut-down of the Internet and telephone connections, and its heightened propaganda on state-run television and newspapers. But it is important to recognize that this process of collapse had long preceded January 2011, whether in the regime's decision to permit Al Jazeera in and out of Egypt, to allow Internet and telephone services, or to loosen its media policies vis-à-vis television and the press.

Technologies help expand spatiality. While of course the process of globalization is unevenly dialectical, the regime's desperation to manage—if not even back track—these shifts was highlighted during the initial days of the uprising. The five-day shut down of the Internet and mobile telephony, combined with the interception of Al Jazeera signals and the jailing and threatening of journalists (both national and international), and the regime's sending of its own propagantistic text messages, among other examples, communicated important facts. First, it demonstrated the regime's panic and desperation to contain and suppress the uprising. Second, it highlights infrastructure's importance. One scholar suggests that "forces of globalization and technological change have diminished the capacity of sovereign nation states and media content producers to directly control information flows. This loss of control over content and the failure of laws and markets to regain this control have redirected political and economic battles into the realm of infrastructure."[19]

Governments responding to technological dissent with technological repression is not at all unprecedented.[20] Third, by mobilizing even more anti-regime fervor and essentially forcing people out onto the streets to know what was going on, it also demonstrated that the uprising was never simply a virtual one. The media shut-down highlighted the way in which *other* media were integrally important, thus challenging the notion that this was simply a social media revolution. In the face of no or limited Internet and mobile telephony access, protesters across Egypt relied on older media and communicative forms. During the uprising, the demonstrators organized themselves through landline calls and face-to-face meetings in safe houses that had been predetermined before the uprising (only in part because organizers knew that phones, Twitter, and Facebook were under surveillance). Moreover, it also demonstrates the extent to which Egypt was already "networked." Egypt and its citizens have not been, in other words, technologically bordered and contained in the way Palestinians are. Although references were made during the days of the shut-down that people had woken up to the blackout and thought themselves in North Korea, it was never really the case. Egypt had already been one of the region's largest media producers and consumers, a country networked through satellites and fiber-optic cables, open to foreign journalists and technologies, with an already vibrant—even if not completely democratic and pluralistic—media and technology landscape. Egypt was quite *maftuha* (open).

The condition described here is not placeless, however. Place does not disappear in favor of a "city of bits."[21] On the contrary, place is as important as ever. First, it is important to reiterate the materiality of technology. Technology infrastructures exist in place. They are territorially etched and are themselves actively involved in the production of space. Television stations, mobile networks, Internet routers, underwater fiber-optic cables, landlines, and broadcasting towers are built and immobilized in space. And that fixity is integral to that specific place's development. They produce privileged places.[22] As processes in space and as spatial processes themselves, they are indicative and embedded in a host of political, economic, and ideological factors. Second, technology networks have a perfectly identifiable territorial geography in which their routes and locations largely replicate the structure of patterns of earlier modes of communication and transportation networks. Thus, even from the network perspective, place does not disappear into the ether; in fact, place is as important as ever. Third, technology is not simply made up of technical and instrumental choices but is also about the form of social and political life we seek to build. Some technologies sui generis have political properties, and others are strongly compatible with particular kinds of political relationships.[23] In short, there exists in the connection between technology and politics a dialectic that is manifested on multiple levels, from the decisions made outside of technology to those made within it. Fourth, physical presence matters. Physical distance matters too. One's distance from a telecommunication provider's central exchange determines the maximum speed of a DSL line; one's distance from a broadcast transmission tower determines the clarity of the signal.

More importantly here is how the uprisings have foregrounded a different form of "real" place as related to technology. From the perspective of the Mubarak regime, there long existed a tension between the forces of localization and globalization, and thus a tension about the relevance of *place*. Place matters: revolutions do not happen in the virtual realm; they are rooted in specific local contexts and must take place on the streets and squares. Freedom of expression continues to be contingent on the freedom of assembly.

What was most formidable about the events in Tahrir was what was most "placed": displaying the extent to which political dissent became the politics of settlement. Being present day and night became itself a form of political expression. It was that refusal to leave, to stay steadfast on the ground, that posed the largest challenge to the regime. (The comparisons here with Palestine are contradictory and multifold: on the one hand, Palestinians' longest-standing form of resistance has been *sumud*—the idea of remaining steadfast on the ground. On the other hand, Israeli settlement of territory and concomitant shrinking of Palestinian living spaces also demonstrate the extent to which territorial control and presence is of continued importance.)

The primary channels of mobilization were not (only or necessarily) mass/high-tech but those that were physically and territorially local. As such, the politics of *tahrir* (both the square and freedom) is also a reflection of the Mubarak regime's actions that attempted to limit citizens' access to public spaces—precisely preventing them from coming together the way they did in January 2011. The emergency law established in 1981 restricted the organization of public rallies and distribution of posters in streets; a handful of adults in a public space constituted cause for arrest. But what the regime sought to physically do in place also mattered: state-led urban planning and zoning laws made parts of the square inaccessible, whether by erecting parking lots, allowing parts of it to degenerate, or closing sections of it off to build a metro station. Despite attempts to prevent citizens from congregating in Tahrir Square, people would still find the means to gather in real places. For example, when the Mubarak regime imposed even stricter security measures to control and prevent street rallies in the aftermath of the Spring 2006 sit-in, street cafes, youth centers, mosques, and "safe houses" became the venues for political dissent. It was also at that time that the regime began to arrest bloggers. Thus, the regime's policies on the ground were part of the reason for the growth of the Egyptian blogosphere as a tool for political communication and the phenomenon of (re)publishing blogs in the more mainstream media throughout Egypt and beyond. In that sense, new media was a space of navigation, even circumnavigation around policies erected on the ground, not a space that replaced real place. In short, the Egyptian activists of the Kefaya movement and the April 6 movement gained experience in online journalism, blogging, and linking with media in and outside of Egypt but also, crucially, in local street tactics.[24]

Whether in 1972, 2003, or 2011, social encounters in and on the street became the political event. Indeed, the gatherings in Tahrir Square draw from a classic repertoire of contention used by social and political movements to flood into public spaces and fill them with an active presence.[25]

What became clear in the days leading up to Mubarak's downfall—and has continued since—is that presence in and taking over of physical (and in this case largely urban) space was crucial to the success and continuity of the uprising. Tahrir Square was and represented one of the "placed" means of citizens staging their right to public assembly. The transformation was a physical, territorial, and embodied manifestation of democratic possibility: citizens could meet, walk around, be flaneurs, gather, discuss, share, protest, take photographs, put on musical performances, display their posters, and so on. In other words, citizens need to congregate in real places in order to interact, to stage political demands, to be seen and heard, to be present in the face of any kind of oppression—and no amount of Facebooking, tweeting, or social media networking can replace (and re-place) that.

Technological Territoriality and Borders/Borderlessness

No space is ever void of social and political relations. In our drive to understand the networked globalized age, and the attraction of an idea of an unfettered world, we end up rendering invisible the very infrastructures that simultaneously keep us grounded and mobile. The examples of Israel–Palestine and Egypt speak to a spatial, multifaceted strategy by different players that reshapes flows, whether in the context of political occupation or dictatorial repression as they coexist with the confines of a capitalist-driven economy. They are both processes and products of an active "relandscaping" of different kinds of spaces that highlight important factors about the connection between media/technology and territoriality.

First, technology infrastructures are politicized assemblages and thoroughly political constructions that embody often congealed interests. These processes are part and parcel of economic and political processes themselves situated in particular histories: technology infrastructures are a *spatial* actor important in the shaping of digital, virtual, physical, territorial, economic, and political spatialities. Thus, technology development in Palestine and in Egypt is as much about the growth of particular forms of tools and communication as it is about the formation and extension of U.S. influence, Israeli interests, capital accumulation, and even "peace." The example of Egypt highlights how territorial borders themselves can be trespassed, ruptured through communicative platforms. But these media and technology platforms are both the result of political processes that have "opened" the Egyptian territory to external flows and are also deeply etched in specific places.

Second, and as importantly, is the recognition that high-tech networks are integral instruments in the production of a new spatiality that is not unfettered and mobile in a virtual dream-space but a result of political, ideological, and territorial processes. Consequently, the borders of the technological may seem less visible than the walls, gates, fences, and checkpoints of the physical world, but they are no less real or politically insignificant. Arrangements of technical architecture are also arrangements of power. They can also function as territorial borders themselves, even if they can also function to rupture those same borders. High-tech and media networks and infrastructures demonstrate the continued importance of territoriality and place.

Third, one of the immediate results of global interconnections and movements is a proliferation of borders, security systems, and physical and virtual frontiers. Any careful study of our surroundings indeed reveals a multiplicity of borders, walls, fences, thresholds, sign-posted areas, checkpoints, virtual frontiers, specialized zones, protected areas, and areas under control. Nowhere is this more obvious than in Palestine-Israel.

Finally, the 2011 Arab uprisings confirmed that places, presence, and actions in places continue to matter in these days of flows. When, where, and for how long people gather, what they choose to do in their immediate and shared presence in a specific location continues to be a fundamental requirement for political expression and change. Politics are embodied and territorial. But the events of the Egyptian uprising also demonstrate the continued importance of people's actions in real place, ranging from a state's urban planning and spatial decisions and policies, to citizens' decisions to take to and remain on the streets.

The examples of Egypt and Palestine demonstrate the extent to which technology is political and the extent to which the political is also technological. What they also clearly demonstrate is that there is a shifting spatiality in our world in which the role of technology is integral. Space becomes more important exactly as it becomes less important. In other words, our technology-globalization-network age is premised on the continued importance of place, not its disappearance.

Notes

1. Adi Ophir, Michal Givoni, and Sari Hanafi, eds. *The Power of Inclusive Exclusion: Anatomy of Israeli Rule in the Occupied Palestinian Territories* (New York: Zone Books, 2009).

2. Eyal Weizman, *Hollow Land: Israel's Architecture of Occupation* (New York: Verso, 2007).

3. "The Israeli-Palestinian Interim Agreement—Annex 3," September 28, 1995. Accessed on September 7, 2015. http://www.mfa.gov.il/mfa/foreignpolicy/peace /guide/pages/the%20israeli-palestinian%20interim%20agreement%20-%20 annex%20iii.aspx.

4. Helga Tawil-Souri, "Digital Occupation: Gaza's High-Tech Enclosure," *Journal of Palestine Studies* 41, no. 2 (2012): 27–43.

5. Tawil-Souri, Helga. "Move over Bangalore. Here Comes . . . Palestine? Western Funding and 'Internet Development' in the Shrinking Palestinian State," in *Global Communications: Toward a Transcultural Political Economy*, ed. Paula Chakravartty and Yuezhi Zhao, 263–84 (Lanham, Md.: Rowman & Littlefield, 2007).

6. Personal interview, July 2005. MTIT Minister, Sabru Saidam. Ramallah

7. Quoted in *UNDP Focus*, 2001, 6. http://www.undp.ps/en/newsroom /publications/pdf/focus/o1v2.pdf.

8. Iain Guest, "The Communications Revolution in the Palestinian Territories," *Humanitarian Exchange Magazine* 28 (2004), http://odihpn.org/magazine/the -communications-revolution-in-the-palestinian-territories/.

9. Quoted in Deborah L. Wheeler, "Egypt: Building an Information Society for International Development." *Review of African Political Economy* 30, no. 98 (2003): 627–42, at 628.

10. Quoted in Bessma Momani, "Promoting Economic Liberalization in Egypt: From U.S. Foreign Aid to Trade and Investment," *Middle East Review of International Affairs* 7, no. 3 (2003): 88–101.

11. For background information, see Duncan Clark, "Us Security Assistance to Egypt and Israel: Politically Untouchable?" Middle East Journal 51(2): 200–214.

12. Momani, "Promoting Economic Liberalization in Egypt," 90.

13. Mark Warschauer, "Dissecting the 'Digital Divide': A Case Study in Egypt," *Information Society* 19, no. 4 (2003): 297–304.

14. Ibid., 299.

15. Timothy Mitchell, "Dreamland: The Neoliberalism of Your Desires," *Middle East Report* no. 210 (Spring 1999): 28–33, doi:10.2307/3012500.

16. Saskia Sassen, *The Global City: New York, London, Tokyo* (Princeton, N.J.: Princeton University Press, 2001).

17. Warschauer, "Dissecting the 'Digital Divide,'" 302.

18. ITU, http://www.itu.int/en/ITU-D/Statistics/Pages/stat/default.aspx (last accessed June 14, 2015).

19. Laura DeNardis, "Hidden Levers of Internet Control: An Infrastructure-Based Theory of Internet Governance," *Information, Communication & Society* 15, no. 5 (2012): 720–38, at 721.

20. Ronald Deibert, John G. Palfrey, Rafal Rohozinski and Jonathan Zittrain, eds. *Access Controlled: The Shaping of Power, Rights, and Rule in Cyberspace* (Cambridge, Mass.: MIT Press, 2010).

21. William J. Mitchell, *City of Bits: Space, Place, and the Infobahn* (Cambridge, Mass.: MIT Press, 1995).

22. Sassen, *The Global City*, 2001.

23. Langdon Winner, *The Whale and the Reactor: The Search for Limits in an Age of High-Technology* (Chicago: University of Chicago Press, 1988).

24. Wael Salah Fahmi, "Bloggers' Street Movement and the Right to the City: (Re)Claiming Cairo's Real and Virtual 'Spaces of Freedom.'" *Environment and urbanization* 21, no. 1 (2009): 89–107.

25. Alberto Melucci, *Challenging Codes: Collective Action in the Information Age* (New York: Cambridge University Press, 1996); and Asef Bayat, *Life as Politics: How Ordinary People Change the Middle East* (Stanford, Calif.: Stanford University Press, 2010).

The Counterrevolutionary Year

The Arab Spring, the Gulf Cooperation Council, and U.S. Foreign Policy in the Middle East

OSAMAH KHALIL

In late March 2012 Secretary of State Hillary Clinton traveled to Saudi Arabia. Clinton was in Riyadh for the inaugural session of the United States' Strategic Cooperation Forum with the Gulf Cooperation Council (GCC). The meeting was convened fifteen months after revolutions swept across the Arab states and unseated or challenged the long-standing rule of different autocratic regimes. Composed of Bahrain, Kuwait, Oman, Qatar, Saudi Arabia, and the United Arab Emirates (UAE), the GCC's conservative rulers have been an important part of Washington's strategy to contain Iran. They have also been at the forefront of attempts to influence and undermine the Arab Spring.[1]

America's sponsorship of the Strategic Cooperation Forum contrasted sharply with Washington's rhetorical support for the Arab uprisings. Yet academics with ties to the Obama administration claimed that U.S. foreign policy was undergoing a "revolution" under Clinton's leadership. Princeton scholar and former State Department official Anne Marie Slaughter declared that Clinton was implementing a new diplomatic strategy, which she dubbed "pivoting to the people." According to Slaughter, Clinton's State Department "introduced policies, programs and institutional reforms designed to support government-to-society and society-to-society diplomacy, alongside traditional government-to-government relations."[2] Yet the new emphasis was lost on the UAE, which shuttered the Dubai offices of the National Democratic Institute (NDI). The NDI's focus on improving governmental accountability and transparency and ties to the Democratic Party should have placed it at the forefront of Clinton's new strategy, if it was actually a priority.

This chapter examines Washington's response to the Arab Spring. In spite of its public rhetoric, I argue that the Obama administration sought to contain and undermine the Arab revolutions either directly or through local allies. This approach is similar to that adopted by the Dwight D. Eisenhower administration in 1958—another revolutionary year in the

Arab world. The comparison between 1958 and 2011, I contend, offers an insight into Washington's perceptions of the Arab world as well as how America and its allies respond to real or perceived threats to their interests in the Middle East. I demonstrate that these perceptions were reinforced by leading academics in the press and reproduced in official policy statements. While the Arab revolutions have received significant attention, I assert that the counterrevolutions have been more successful in maintaining the status quo in the region.[3]

Recontaining Arab Nationalism?

Announced before a joint session of Congress on January 5, 1957, the Eisenhower Doctrine was the first presidential doctrine specifically targeting the area known as the "Middle East."[4] Developed after the 1956 Suez War, the Eisenhower administration claimed that the policy was intended to protect the nations in the "general area of the Middle East" from the aggressive threats of "International Communism." In reality, President Dwight D. Eisenhower and Secretary of State John Foster Dulles sought to contain the influence of Egyptian president Gamal Abdel Nasser across the region and beyond. Although it was clear that Nasser was not a Communist, the Eisenhower administration feared that his policies of pan-Arabism and Arab socialism would invariably assist Soviet ambitions in the region. Nasser's position within the Non-Aligned Movement caused even greater consternation in Washington. According to historian Salim Yaqub, Eisenhower and Dulles were convinced that Nasser's "positive neutrality" in the Cold War competition between Washington and Moscow was neither positive nor neutral. In short, Nasser's policies were either deliberately or unwittingly serving the interests of the Kremlin. In implementing the Eisenhower Doctrine, the administration sought out conservative allies in the region. Washington believed that Saudi Arabia, Jordan, and Iraq would serve as bulwarks to Nasser's perceived "radicalism."[5]

The Eisenhower administration viewed Jordan as the state most vulnerable to Nasser's influence. This was due to the prevalence of pro-Nasserist officers within the Jordanian Arab Army, the country's reliance on British aid, and King Hussein's youth and inexperience. Eisenhower and Dulles believed that the Hashemite regime was unlikely to survive the combination of internal and external threats. After the Eisenhower Doctrine instigated a confrontation within Jordan and Hussein emerged victorious, his regime became increasingly allied with and dependent upon Washington for economic and military aid.[6]

The U.S.–Saudi alliance began during the Second World War. Saudi Arabia's vast oil reserves led Washington to deem it a vital national security interest. In its efforts to combat Nasser's growing prestige, the Eisenhower administration attempted to promote Saudi Arabia's King Saud as a leader of the Arab and Muslim worlds. Because the kingdom was the site of Islam's holy cities in Mecca and Medina, Eisenhower believed—incorrectly—that Saud could become the equivalent of a Muslim pope. As Nasser's popularity eclipsed that of the Saudi royal family, Saud was unwilling to openly confront him or to fully endorse the Eisenhower Doctrine. Instead, in what would set the trend for the next half century in dealing with radical political leaders and movements in the region—or merely those that were not in line with its interests—Riyadh publicly embraced Nasser while working covertly with Washington and other Arab leaders to undermine him. Saudi Arabia also welcomed members of the Muslim Brotherhood who fled persecution by Nasser's regime. The split between Riyadh and Cairo became more pronounced in the early 1960s and the second phase of the Arab Cold War.[7]

American troops intervened in Lebanon in July 1958. However, Eisenhower's decision was driven by events in Iraq rather than in Lebanon. Although the bloody coup that overthrew Iraq's Hashemite monarchy was inspired by Nasser's example, the plot to topple King Faisal II was homegrown. Indeed, the new Iraqi revolutionary government led by Gen. 'Abd al-Karim Qasim remained independent of Cairo. Qasim backed out of joining the United Arab Republic with Egypt and Syria and purged Nasserists from his cabinet and arrested others. A distinct chill in relations between Baghdad and Cairo followed, and Nasser sided with the conservative Arab regimes against the even more "radical" Iraqi government. Even before the Marines were dispatched to Lebanon, the White House was already reevaluating its Middle East policy and attempting to come to terms with Nasser. By the end of 1959 the Eisenhower Doctrine was shelved and Washington and Cairo began a brief public rapprochement that continued into the Kennedy administration.[8]

One consequence of the 1958 revolutions was that the United States decided to rely more heavily on the "Northern Tier."[9] The Northern Tier was composed of Turkey, Iran, and Pakistan. It was intended to serve as a defense pact along the Soviet Union's southern border that coordinated with the U.S.-led North Atlantic Treaty Organization. Thus, the Northern Tier was Washington's first line of defense for the Persian Gulf *and* a barrier to contain the spill-over effects of pan-Arabism.[10] Yet the ability of the Northern Tier to act as a tripwire for a potential Soviet invasion or a barricade to Arab radicalism was limited.[11] The end of the Eisenhower Doctrine also marked the beginning of a new stage in the Arab Cold War, in which Nasserism was to be weakened or defeated outright.

CENTCOM and the GCC

Four years before the Eisenhower Doctrine was announced, the United States and United Kingdom orchestrated a coup that overthrew Iranian prime minister Mohammad Mossadegh. Under the rule of Mohammad Reza Shah Pahlavi, Iran became a staunch Cold War ally of the United States. Richard Nixon served as Eisenhower's vice president and developed a personal relationship with the shah. After Nixon was elected president in 1968, the United States faced a very different international landscape. The combination of a failing war in Vietnam, domestic strife, and Britain's decision to withdraw from the Persian Gulf region created an opportunity for greater coordination between Washington and Tehran.[12]

Iran became a key pillar of the Nixon Doctrine. Nixon's policy reflected America's decreased influence and capabilities due to the Vietnam War. Instead of direct American intervention, the Nixon administration empowered local allies to secure its interests around the globe. In the Middle East, Iran was joined by Israel and Saudi Arabia. However, the Nixon Doctrine was abandoned after the shah was overthrown.[13]

The Iranian revolution forced Washington to reevaluate America's military presence in the Persian Gulf. While the new strategy was under development, President Jimmy Carter decided to allow the ailing shah into the United States in October 1979 for medical treatment. In response, student protesters stormed the U.S. Embassy in Tehran and seized over fifty Americans. The Soviet invasion of Afghanistan in late December further tested the Carter administration. During his State of the Union Address a month later, Carter warned Moscow. "An attempt by any outside force to gain control of the Persian Gulf region will be regarded as an assault on the vital interests of the United States of

America," he declared, "and such an assault will be repelled by any means necessary, including military force." In April 1980 a mission to free the hostages held in Iran failed and undermined Carter's firm stance with the Kremlin. The Carter administration established the Rapid Deployment Joint Task Force, which marked the beginning of greater American military involvement in the region.[14]

The Reagan administration expanded on Carter's policies. By 1983 the Rapid Deployment Joint Task Force was replaced by the U.S. Central Command (CENTCOM).[15] Originally based in Saudi Arabia, CENTCOM's initial "area of responsibility" ranged from Kenya to Pakistan.[16] In the post–Cold War era, the United States dramatically increased the number and size of its military bases in the Persian Gulf. CENTCOM's area of responsibility also expanded and currently stretches from Egypt to Kazakhstan.[17]

The GCC was established two years before CENTCOM and was driven by the same regional concerns. It was created in response to the Iranian revolution and the outbreak of the Iran-Iraq War. The GCC was supposed to be a regional economic, political, and military alliance that supported Iraq and served as a barrier to Iranian influence in the region.[18] However, economic coordination took priority over military cooperation. Yet this has not stopped the individual GCC states, particularly Saudi Arabia, from acquiring massive quantities of advanced American weapons systems and equipment.[19]

Back to the Future

In December 2011 American forces completed their withdrawal from Iraq. Troops were redeployed around the region and Washington sought expanded ties with the GCC. The U.S. military also began planning for the post-Iraq era drawing on prior deployment plans. Maj. Gen. Karl R. Horst, CENTCOM's chief of staff, described the new approach as "back to the future."[20]

The emphasis on the GCC coincides with increased American weapons sales to countries in the region. Both the George W. Bush and Barack Obama administrations sold unprecedented amounts of advanced weapons systems to the GCC countries. In January 2008 the Bush administration announced that the GCC states would buy $20 billion worth of arms.[21] Two years later Saudi Arabia agreed to purchase $67 billion in weapons systems.[22] The following year, the UAE bought an advanced antimissile defense system for $3.5 billion.[23] These arms sales are just the beginning, with defense industry analysts predicting that the GCC states will spend "$385 billion toward defense and security through 2016."[24] Although far smaller in size, Washington's decision to continue selling arms to Bahrain after its crackdown on civilian protesters reveals the limits of the Obama administration's support for the Arab revolutions.[25]

Washington's strategic concerns remain paramount. In December 2012 retired Air Force lieutenant general Thomas McInerney explained to the *Washington Times* that weapons sales to the Gulf states were "designed to help them cope" with the threat from Iran, which he described as "a general destabilizing force in their neighborhood." According to McInerney, "the Sunni Arabs are very concerned about [Shiites] sweeping across the Arabian Peninsula into Lebanon, Syria and Gaza, fueled by Iran's leadership and resources."[26]

Like the Northern Tier during the Cold War, the GCC extends American hegemony in the region. Rather than containing and countering the Soviet Union or Egypt, the goal is to contain Iran and any real or perceived influence it may have among Shi'a minority and majority populations. Once again, Saudi Arabia is at the center of the conservative response. The massive amount of weapons sales demonstrates Washington's real policy and dwarfs democracy promotion initiatives and outreach to activists in the region.

Good Revolutions versus Bad Revolutions

The Saudi-led GCC invasion of Bahrain in March 2011 drew only a muted response from Washington. This was repeated in Jordan, Yemen, Algeria, and Morocco. It also contrasted with the vocal criticisms of the regimes in Syria, Tehran, and the intervention in Libya. Indeed, the Obama administration's view of the Arab revolutions appears to be one of "good revolutions" versus "bad revolutions." Like Libya, the "good revolutions" were deemed deserving of American support—if not overt intervention—to ensure their success. Moreover, following the apparent success of the intervention in Libya by America and its North Atlantic Treaty Organization allies, pressure built on the Obama administration for a similar action in Syria. However, the administration decided to pursue a policy of overt and covert funding and training of "moderate" opposition forces rather than a direct intervention.[27]

In contrast, the "bad revolutions" have largely been ignored or down-played by the U.S. media and policymakers. For example, in a February 2011 interview U.S. senator (and current secretary of state) John Kerry claimed that he was not concerned that protests in Jordan could lead to regime change. Kerry, then chairman of the Senate Foreign Relations Committee, stated that "King Abdullah of Jordan is extraordinarily intelligent, thoughtful, sensitive, in touch with his people. The monarchy there is very well-respected, even revered."[28] Kerry's comments ignore the overwhelming evidence of Jordan's repressive state security forces, electoral fraud, and endemic political corruption. Similarly, protests in Yemen have received scant coverage in the U.S. press—especially in comparison to Syria and Libya—even though Yemeni human rights advocate Tawakkol Karman was one of three women awarded the 2011 Nobel Peace Prize for nonviolent activism.

This dynamic reflects discussions within the Obama administration. As the Arab revolutions unfolded, key officials advocated for continued support of America's regional allies regardless of their history of repression and corruption. Secretary of State Clinton, Vice President Joe Biden, Secretary of Defense Robert Gates, and National Security Advisor Tom Donilon argued against abandoning Egypt's Hosni Mubarak. However, some of Obama's younger aides sided with the protesters. In *Hard Choices*, Clinton writes that the fear of another Iranian revolution hung over the deliberations. President Obama attempted to accommodate both sides by calling for Omar Suleiman, head of Egyptian intelligence, to replace Mubarak. Protesters in Cairo's Tahrir Square and across Egypt were angered by Washington's attempt to stage-manage Mubarak's transition from power. In contrast to their position on Egypt, Clinton and Biden recommended regime change in Syria, including arming the opposition.[29]

Influential American academics shared the Obama administration's reticence toward the Arab revolutions. In a February 2011 interview with the *Jerusalem Post*, retired Princeton scholar Bernard Lewis argued that the region-wide protests grew out of the Arabs' "widespread sense of injustice." Lewis was one of the intellectual architects of George W. Bush's "Freedom Agenda." However, he cautioned that a rush toward Western-style elections in the Arab states would lead to victories by Islamist parties. Lewis explained that Islamist movements have a network of communications that other parties could not match and used familiar language to appeal to broad segments of the population. "The language of Western democracy," he cautioned, "is for the most part newly translated and not intelligible to the great masses." Lewis explained that most of the Arab world was "not ready for free and fair elections" and that the consequence of such elections would possibly be the victory of the Muslim Brotherhood and similar organizations. Therefore, the region would "gradually sink back into medieval squalor."[30]

A similar warning was issued by Harvard's Niall Ferguson. Ferguson asserted that one possible outcome of the revolutions was a restored Islamic caliphate stretching from Iran across North Africa by 2021.[31] He also chastised Americans for their support of "revolution" from the French to the Russian to the Chinese as well as the Arab revolutions without understanding the possible outcomes. "Only the hopelessly naive imagine that 30-something Google executives will emerge as the new leaders of the Arab world, aided by their social network of Facebook friends," Ferguson wrote; the "far more likely outcome—as in past revolutions—is that power will pass to the best organized, most radical, and most ruthless elements in the revolution, which in this case means Islamists like the Muslim Brotherhood." Ferguson also decried the lack of a strategy by the Obama administration to deal with the aging autocrats. He cautioned that the revolutions could turn violent and lead to a regional war the outcome of which "could emerge an enemy as formidable as Napoleon's France, Stalin's Soviet Union, or Mao's China."[32]

Nor were these criticisms limited to intellectuals tied to the neoconservative wing of the Republican Party. Leslie Gelb, the former president of the Council on Foreign Relations, took these critiques even further. Gelb argued that the revolutions were not only bad for the United States and Israel but ultimately for the protesters. This was because the uprisings were unlikely to result in systemic change. Instead Gelb claimed that the unrest would lead to increased economic burdens and hardship, including rising oil prices that would have a negative impact worldwide.[33]

Washington initially tolerated the post–Arab Spring electoral victories of some Islamist parties. This was in part because it had limited alternatives and the status quo was untenable. But it was only a brief flirtation, especially in Egypt. The September 2012 protests against the U.S. Embassy in Cairo and the attack on the U.S. consulate in Benghazi were initially believed to be related to a film released on YouTube. Four Americans were killed, including the U.S. ambassador to Libya, Christopher Stevens. Afterward President Obama publicly hinted at a reassessment in U.S.–Egyptian relations.[34]

The Benghazi attack also led to a round of recriminations in the U.S. press disguised as analysis. The culprit was clear: Islam. For example, CNN's *The Situation Room* declared that the Arab Spring had turned into an "Arab Winter."[35] Accompanying the coverage were maps of the protests ranging across North Africa to insular Southeast Asia—far beyond the Arab states (and even the most extensive boundaries of the "Middle East"). Meanwhile, CNN's resident curmudgeon, Jack Cafferty, asked "Was the Arab Spring Worth it?"[36] Less than a week later the cover of *Newsweek* infamously declared "MUSLIM RAGE."[37]

Nor were scholars immune from such assessments. In January 2012 the Hoover Institution's Fouad Ajami broke with fellow neoconservatives and debunked the "five myths about the Arab Spring."[38] Yet in the wake of the Benghazi attack, Ajami resorted to myth making of his own. "Modernity," he wrote, "requires the willingness to be offended. And as anti-American violence across the Middle East and beyond shows, that willingness is something the Arab world, the heartland of Islam, still lacks." What explains this lack of modernity and the accompanying grievances that frequently spirals into homicidal violence? First, Ajami claimed, was the sense of "divine providence" that accompanied Islam's rise and rapid expansion. He asserted that "if Islam's rise was spectacular, its fall was swift and unsparing." With the sacking of Baghdad by the Mongols and the rise of the Ottoman Empire, Ajami declared, "The blessing of God, seen at work in the ascent of the Muslims, now appeared to desert them." "After the Ottoman Turks overran Arab countries to their south in the 16th century, the Arabs seemed to exit history; they were now subjects of others," he wrote.[39]

While the September 2012 protests were far ranging, they were also remarkably small. Indeed, they were far too small for such sweeping and inaccurate assertions about Arabs and Islam. Moreover, the revelations that the Benghazi attack was a coordinated and premeditated operation tied to the anniversary of the September 11, 2001, attacks further exposed the pseudo-psychological and tortured historical analysis of American pundits and national security academics.

Only ten months later, however, a coup by the Egyptian military provided another opportunity for suspect commentary and analysis. Following the overthrow of Egyptian president Mohamed Morsi and widespread crackdown on the Muslim Brotherhood, *New York Times* columnist David Brooks explained, "It's not that Egypt doesn't have a recipe for a democratic transition. It seems to lack even the basic mental ingredients." Brooks also understated Washington's role in the events, claiming "the U.S. has no ability to influence political events in Egypt in any important way."[40] Yet the Egyptian military maintains close ties to Washington and since the Camp David Accords has been the second largest recipient of U.S. military aid after Israel, which raises the question: What was the United States' role in orchestrating or approving the coup?

Prior to the coup, the Obama administration mediated between Morsi's government and the Egyptian military. Conversations between Obama and Morsi were reportedly tense as the Egyptian president insisted on his elected legitimacy. Obama, however, countered that "democracy is about more than elections." Washington refused to classify Morsi's removal as a coup d'état, and Secretary of State John Kerry defended the actions of the Egyptian military.[41] Shortly after the coup; Saudi Arabia, Kuwait, and the UAE pledged $12 billion in aid to the new Egyptian government.[42] Less than a year later, former defense minister Field Marshall Abdel Fattah el-Sisi was elected president. Although there were clearly issues surrounding the election, Washington did not raise any substantial concerns or criticisms.

American Hegemony in the Age of Obama

Unlike his predecessor, Barack Obama's policy declarations have not been easily definable. Indeed, the Bush Doctrine's emphasis on preemption and democracy promotion does not have a direct equivalent in the Obama administration. While significant attention has been paid to Obama's June 2009 Cairo speech and his May 2011 speech in response to the Arab revolutions, far less discussed are his administration's official policy pronouncements. Although the line between interests and values was blurred by the Bush administration, the Obama administration has sought to draw a distinction between the two.

This is demonstrated by the 2010 National Security Strategy (NSS). Published seven months before the Tunisian revolution, the NSS's "Strategic Interests" section asserted that in the area of the "Greater Middle East," U.S. engagement "should extend beyond near-term threats by appealing to peoples' aspirations for justice, education and opportunity and by pursuing a positive and sustainable vision of U.S. partnership with the region."[43] The NSS's emphasis on "appealing" rather than "ensuring" or "achieving" rights is telling. In addition, it is unclear how Washington's continued embrace of the conservative monarchies in the GCC as evidenced by the Strategic Cooperation Forum and ongoing arms sales corresponds with the goal of a "positive and sustainable" partnership with the region. The NSS's "Values" section stated that the United States recognized the legitimacy of all peaceful democratic movements. "America respects the right of all peaceful, law-abiding, and nonviolent voices to be heard around the world," the document explained, "even if we disagree with them." "Support for democracy must not be about support for specific candidates or movement," it added.[44]

Yet, as evidenced by how Washington responded to the Arab revolutions, it has belatedly and inconsistently sought to ensure that this particular value was upheld. In Tunisia, American support for the revolution came only after Ben Ali fled the country. More troubling was the Obama administration's support of Omar Suleiman to replace Mubarak. As the head of Egyptian intelligence, Suleiman was complicit in the Mubarak regime's corruption and repression. Egyptian intelligence actively participated in the United States' rendition and torture program as well as Israel's siege of Gaza. Even more troubling still has been the double standard toward the different revolutionary movements: Syria and Libya versus Bahrain, Yemen, and Jordan.

This gulf between interests and values was further enshrined in the Pentagon's Strategic Review. Published in January 2012, the Strategic Review articulated America's defense policies for the next century. The review stated that the Arab revolutions presented "both strategic opportunities and challenges" to the United States. It noted the possibility that more representative governments could emerge that were "more responsive to the legitimate aspirations of their people, and are more stable and reliable partners of the United States." The review emphasized the importance of Gulf security and countering Iranian influence in collaboration with the GCC. Most importantly, it stressed that, "to support these objectives, the United States will continue to place a premium on U.S. and allied military presence in—and support of—partner nations in and around this region."[45] Which raises the question: How will Washington respond when allied nations which repress their own people are faced with popular movements for change? If the events of the past three years are any indication, these movements will find support from Washington lacking, if at all.

The announcement of the 2012 Defense Strategic Review led at least one prominent journalist to announce that it was the end of the September 11 era. *Washington Post* columnist David Ignatius explained that Obama administration officials were now pivoting toward China and the Pacific region.[46] In a January 5 speech at the Pentagon to announce the Strategic Review, President Obama declared that the United States was "turning the page on a decade of war." Although Obama did not mention China specifically, he explained that "we will be strengthening our presence in the Asia Pacific [region]."[47] Ignatius noted that administration officials "keep repeating that this won't mean a policy of 'containment' and that the United States accepts a rising China as a 21st-century inevitability." However, he cautioned that "a period of rivalry and tension is ahead in the Pacific."[48] What is the role of the area called the "Middle East" in the coming competition between Beijing and Washington? The close economic ties and linkages between China and the United States and Europe make a new Cold War seem unlikely.

Yet hegemony has its own logic. The Middle East's strategic location and resources will ensure greater competition. Indeed, Washington's emphasis on and support for an expanded and emboldened GCC demonstrates that America's Middle East policy will continue to be driven by maintaining hegemony over the flow of oil from the region—and denying the emergence of a rival—either regional (like Iran) or global (like China). However, these policies and plans have their limits. The emergence of the Islamic State in Iraq and al-Sham (ISIS) is a blowback from America's promotion of the GCC states. Less than three years after withdrawing from Iraq, American fighter jets and Special Forces have returned in order to counter ISIS. Meanwhile, those struggling for freedom across the region will find little more than rhetorical support, if that, from Washington.

Conclusion

The Arab revolutions brought into sharp relief the disparity between American interests and values in the Middle East. When forced to choose, the Obama administration adopted policies that aligned with America's interests rather than its values. Yet at the end of 2010 few would have imagined the rapid changes that would be unleashed within a few weeks. Three years after the Arab revolutions began, the changes and challenges continue. Like the 1958 revolutions, the Arab Spring has been undermined by the same combination of external and internal pressures, rivalries, and competing interests. However, the future remains unwritten, and it is still too early to write a final epitaph on the Arab Spring.

Notes

1. For more on the GCC meeting, see Vijay Prashad "Washington Bets on the Gulf Royals," *Counterpunch* April 26, 2012, accessed November 10, 2013, http://www.counterpunch.org/2012/04/26/washington-bets-on-the-gulf-royals/.

2. Ann Marie Slaughter, "Pivoting to the People," *Al Jazeera English* March 26, 2012, accessed April 6, 2012, http://www.aljazeera.com/indepth/opinion/2012/03/201232112591968789.html; and Steven L. Meyers, "United Arab Emirates Shutters U.S. Backed Group," *New York Times*, March 31, 2012.

3. Several scholars have also commented on the counterrevolutions, including Hussein Agha and Robert Malley, "The Arab Counterrevolution," *New York Review of Books*, September 29, 2011; Toby C. Jones, "Saudi Arabia's Regional Reaction," *Nation*, August 24, 2011; and Kristian Coates Ulrichsen, "Counterrevolution in the Gulf," *Foreign Policy*, May 6, 2011.

4. See Osamah Khalil, "The Crossroads of the World: U.S. and British Foreign Policy Doctrines and the Construct of the Middle East, 1902–2007," *Diplomatic History* 38, no. 2 (April 2014).

5. Salim Yaqub, *Containing Arab Nationalism: The Eisenhower Doctrine and the Middle East* (Chapel Hill: University of North Carolina Press, 2004), 2.

6. Ibid., 119–45.

7. Ibid., 44–49, 102–6; Robert Vitalis, *America's Kingdom: Mythmaking on the Saudi Oil Frontier* (Stanford, Calif.: Stanford University Press, 2007), 184–93; and Juan Cole, *Engaging the Muslim World* (New York: Palgrave Macmillan, 2009).

8. Yaqub, *Containing Arab Nationalism*, 237–67; and Juan Romero, *The Iraqi Revolution of 1958: A Revolutionary Quest for Unity and Security* (Lanham, Md.: University Press of America, 2011), 205–8.

9. See Diane B. Kunz, "The Emergence of the United States as a Middle Eastern Power, 1956–1958," in *A Revolutionary Year: The Middle East in 1958*, ed. William Roger Louis and Roger Owen (New York: I. B. Tauris, 2002), 97; and Michael J. Cohen, *Strategy and Politics in the Middle East, 1954–1960* (London: Frank Cass, 2005): 198–217.

10. See Lloyd C. Gardener, *Three Kings: The Rise of an American Empire in the Middle East after World War II* (New York: New Press, 2009), 149–51.

11. Romero, *Iraqi Revolution of 1958*, 158–60. Turkey, Pakistan, and Jordan sought approval and logistical support from Washington and London to intervene in Iraq and overturn the coup. However, American and British officials were skeptical that that the countries had the ability to restore the Hashemite regime without overt military assistance.

12. See Ervand Abrahamian, *The Coup: 1953, The CIA, and the Roots of Modern U.S.–Iranian Relations* (New York: New Press, 2013); and Rohan Alvandi, *Nixon, Kissinger, and the Shah: The United States and Iran in the Cold War* (New York: Oxford University Press, 2014).

13. See Khalil, "The Crossroads of the World," 331–33.

14. Michael A. Palmer, *Guardians of the Gulf: A History of America's Expanding Role in the Persian Gulf, 1833–1992* (New York: Free Press, 1992), 106–10.

15. Ibid., 112–17.

16. Jeffrey T. Richelson, *The U.S. Intelligence Community* (Boulder, Colo.: Westview Press, 1999), 108.

17. A map of CENTCOM's current area of responsibility can be found at http://www.centcom.mil/, accessed November 11, 2013.

18. Matteo Legrenzi, *The GCC and the International Relations of the Gulf: Diplomacy, Security, and Economic Coordination in a Changing Middle East* (London: I. B. Tauris, 2011), 27–33.

19. Thomas L. McNaugher, *Arms and Oil: U.S. Military Strategy and the Persian Gulf* (Washington. D.C.: Brookings Institution, 1985), 55–56n13. McNaugher provides an assessment of the military capabilities of the GCC countries within U.S. strategic planning during the late Cold War period. He notes that Saudi Arabia purchased maintenance equipment to support four times as many F-15 fighter jets as were deployed by the Royal Saudi Air Force. McNaugher adds that according to a report prepared for the U.S. Senate Foreign Relations Committee on the sale of advanced aircraft to Saudi Arabia that "some U.S. Air Force officers 'anticipate that the Saudis would go so far as to allow U.S. pilots to fly Saudi F-15s to meet a threat.'"

20. Quoted in Thom Shanker and Steven Lee Myers, "U.S. Planning Troop Buildup in Gulf after Exit from Iraq," *New York Times*, October 29, 2011.

21. Sean L. Yom, "Washington's New Arms Bazaar," *Middle East Report and Information Project*, Spring 2008, accessed November 10, 2013, http://www.merip.org/mer/mer246/washingtons-new-arms-bazaar. Yom states that since the end of the first Gulf War (1990–91) through the rest of the decade, "Saudi Arabia allocated a rough average of 40 percent of central state expenditures to its defense sector, Oman and the Emirates 40 to 45 percent, and Kuwait, Bahrain and Qatar 20 to 25 percent." He adds that in historical terms, "Saudi Arabia purchased almost $62 billion in U.S. armaments by 2005, Kuwait nearly $7.8 billion, the UAE over $2 billion and Bahrain over $1.8 billion." Yom notes that the majority of these sales were after the first Gulf War.

22. "Gulf Arms Sales Vital for U.S. Companies," *United Press International*, November 15, 2011.

23. "U.S. in $3.5 Billion Arms Sale to UAE amid Iran Tensions," *Reuters*, December 31, 2011.

24. "Amidst Regional Changes, the Middle East 'Arms Bazaar' Remains Open," *Defense Web*, February 7, 2012, accessed November 10, 2013, http://www.defenceweb.co.za/index.php?option=com_content&view=article&id=23278:amidst-regional-changes-the-middle-east-arms-bazaar-remains-open-&catid=7:Industry&Itemid=116.

25. Paul Koring, "U.S. Arms Sale to Bahrain Raises Eyebrows," *Globe and Mail*, February 9, 2012; and Joel Beinin, "Arms Sales to Bahrain under the Scanner," *Al Jazeera English*, November 6, 2011, http://www.aljazeera.com/indepth

/opinion/2011/11/2011111101357837629.html. Washington was originally slated to sell $53 million in weapons to Bahrain, however, the sale was suspended pending the release of a final report into human rights abuses during the crackdown on protesters. Koring reports that the Obama administration deliberately reduced the size of the amount to under $1 million in order to avoid Congressional scrutiny.

26. Quoted in Rowan Scarborough, "U.S. Arms to Gulf Allies Hint of Strategy," *Washington Times*, December 16, 2012.

27. For example, see Daniel Byman, "Finish Him," *Foreign Policy*, February 2, 2012; Steven Cook, "It's Time to Think Seriously about Intervening in Syria," *Atlantic*, January 17, 2012; Shadi Hamid, "Why We Have a Responsibility to Protect Syria," *Atlantic*, January 26, 2012; Ann Marie Slaughter, "How the World Could—and Maybe Should—Intervene in Syria," *Atlantic*, January 23, 2012; Ann Marie Slaughter, "How to Halt the Butchery in Syria," *New York Times*, February 23, 2012; and "Should the U.S. Intervene in Syria with Military Action," U.S. News And World Report—Debate Club, February 14, 2012, accessed November 9, 2013, http://www.usnews.com/debate-club/should-the-us-intervene-in-syria-with -military-action. It should be noted that leading commentators were split over whether the United States should attack Syria in September 2013. See Max Fisher, "Should the U.S. Strike Syria? These Are the Five Smartest Arguments," *Washington Post*, September 3, 2013.

28. John Kerry, interview by Ray Suarez, *NewsHour*, PBS, February 1, 2011 http://www.pbs.org/newshour/bb/politics/jan-june11/johnkerry_02-01.html.

29. Hillary Rodham Clinton, *Hard Choices* (New York: Simon & Schuster, 2014), 339–41.

30. Quoted in David Horovitz, "A Mass Expression of Outrage against Injustice," *Jerusalem Post*, February 25, 2011, accessed February 25, 2012, http://www .jpost.com/Opinion/Columnists/Article.aspx?id=209770.

31. Niall Ferguson, "In 2021 We'll Be Amazed How Much the World Has Changed," *Telegraph*, March 14, 2011, accessed February 25, 2012, http://www .telegraph.co.uk/finance/financevideo/8367183/Niall-Ferguson-In-2021-well-be -amazed-how-much-the-world-has-changed.html.

32. Niall Ferguson, "Un-American Revolutions," *DailyBeast.com*, February 27, 2011, accessed November 29, 2015, http://www.thedailybeast.com/articles/2011/02 /27/why-americans-should-fear-the-middle-east-and-north-africa-revolutions .html.

33. Leslie Gelb, "Meet the Losers," *DailyBeast.com*, March 9, 2011, accessed February 25, 2012, http://www.thedailybeast.com/articles/2011/03/09/mideast -revolution-people-lose-oil-companies-win.html.

34. Devin Dwyer, "Obama Says Egypt neither Ally nor Enemy," ABC News, September 13, 2012, accessed December 9, 2014, http://abcnews.go.com/blogs /politics/2012/09/obama-says-egypt-neither-ally-nor-enemy/.

35. CNN, *The Situation Room with Wolf Blitzer*, September 14, 2012.

36. CNN, *The Cafferty File*, "Was the Arab Spring Worth It?" September 12, 2013, accessed November 9, 2013, http://caffertyfile.blogs.cnn.com/2012/09/12/ was-the-arab-spring-worth-it/.

37. See *Newsweek*, September 17, 2012.

38. Fouad Ajami, "Five Myths about the Arab Spring," *Washington Post*, January 12, 2012. The myths Ajami identified included the role of social media, the invasion of Iraq, and Obama's Cairo Speech.

39. Fouad Ajami, "Why Is the Arab World so Easily Offended?" *Washington Post*, September 14, 2012.

40. David Brooks, "Defending the Coup," *New York Times*, July 5, 2013.

41. Michael Gordon and Kareem Fahim, "Kerry Says Egypt's Military Was 'Restoring Democracy' in Ousting Morsi," *New York Times*, August 1, 2013; and Mark Landler, "Aid to Egypt can Keep Flowing, Despite Overthrow, White House Decides," *New York Times*, July 25, 2013.

42. Jeremy Ravinsky, "Friends Again? Saudi Arabia, UAE jump in to Aid Egypt," *Christian Science Monitor*, July 10, 2013.

43. Barack Obama, 2010 National Security Strategy, May 2010, accessed November 10, 2013, http://www.whitehouse.gov/sites/default/files/rss_viewer/national_security_strategy.pdf.

44. Ibid, 38.

45. United States Department of Defense, "Sustaining U.S. Global Leadership: Priorities for 21st Century Defense," accessed February 25, 2012, http://www.defense.gov/news/Defense_Strategic_Guidance.pdf.

46. David Ignatius, "Obama Closes the Book on the 9/11 Era," *Washington Post*, January 7, 2012.

47. Barack Obama, "Remarks by the President on the Defense Strategic Review," January 5, 2012. Accessed April 7, 2012, http://www.whitehouse.gov/the-press-office/2012/01/05/remarks-president-defense-strategic-review.

48. Ignatius, "Obama Closes the Book on the 9/11 Era."

Contributors

CRISTINA MORENO ALMEIDA completed her Ph.D. dissertation (2015), titled "Critical Reflections on Rap Music in Contemporary Morocco: Urban Youth Culture Between and Beyond State's Co-optation and Dissent," in Cultural Studies at SOAS (School of Oriental and African Studies). Her research interests cover popular youth cultures, urban cultures, transnational identities, music, hip-hop culture, nationalism, gender, race, and postcolonial and cultural studies. During the past years Cristina has established her residence in Morocco, where she is committed to develop strategies of cultural intervention that stimulate ongoing collaborations between young artists, institutions, and academia.

ASHLEY DAWSON is professor of English at the City University of New York's Graduate Center and at the College of Staten Island/CUNY. He is the author of *Capitalism and Extinction* (forthcoming from O/R Press), *The Routledge Concise History of Twentieth-Century British Literature* (Routledge, 2013) and *Mongrel Nation: Diasporic Culture and the Making of Postcolonial Britain* (University of Michigan Press, 2007). He is also coeditor of four essay collections: *Against Apartheid: The Case for Boycotting Israeli Universities* (Haymarket Books, 2015), *Democracy, the State, and the Struggle for Global Justice* (Routledge, 2009); *Dangerous Professors: Academic Freedom and the National Security Campus* (University of Michigan Press, 2009); and *Exceptional State: Contemporary U.S. Culture and the New Imperialism* (Duke University Press, 2007). A former editor of *Social Text Online* and of the AAUP's *Journal of Academic Freedom*, he is currently completing work on a book entitled *Extreme City: Climate Change and the Urban Future* for Verso Press.

BRIAN T. EDWARDS is professor of English and comparative literary studies and Crown Professor in Middle East Studies at Northwestern University, where he is the founding director of the Program in Middle East and North African Studies. He is the author of *After the American Century: The Ends of U.S. Culture in the Middle East* (Columbia University Press, 2016), which examines the circulation of American culture in the contemporary Middle East and North Africa. He is also the author of *Morocco Bound: Disorienting America's Maghreb, from Casablanca to the Marrakech Express* (Duke University Press, 2005), and editor or coeditor of *Globalizing American Studies* (University of Chicago Press, 2010) and *On the Ground: New Directions in Middle East and North African Studies* (Northwestern University in Qatar, 2013). His essays and articles have been published in such publications as *Public Culture, American Literary History, Journal of North African Studies, Chicago Tribune, NOVEL, The Believer, Foreign Policy,* and many others.

303

RAYYA EL ZEIN is a Ph.D. candidate in theater at the Graduate Center, City University of New York. Her dissertation focuses on material and affective aspects of hip-hop and rap concerts in Beirut, Ramallah, and Amman over the past decade. Her research so far has been generally concerned with popular culture, affect, and theories of spectatorship in Arab urban contexts shaped by neoliberalism.

WALEED HAZBUN teaches international relations at the American University of Beirut, where he directs the Center for Arab and Middle Eastern Studies. He holds a Ph.D. in political science from MIT and previously taught at the Johns Hopkins University. Dr. Hazbun is author of *Beaches, Ruins, Resorts: The Politics of Tourism in the Arab World* (University of Minnesota Press, 2008) and several studies of U.S. policy in the Middle East. His current research explores the global politics of aviation in the Middle East.

CRAIG JONES is a postdoctoral fellow in the Department of Geography at the University of British Columbia. His doctoral dissertation, entitled "The War Lawyers: US, Israel and Spaces of Targeting," examined the role of military lawyers in targeting operations conducted by the U.S. and Israeli militaries. His current research focuses on casualty evacuation and medical care of soldiers and civilians in Iraq, Syria, and Palestine.

OSAMAH KHALIL is assistant professor of U.S. and Middle East history at Syracuse University's Maxwell School of Citizenship and Public Affairs. He received his Ph.D. from the University of California, Berkeley. Khalil is finalizing his book on the relationship between U.S. foreign policy and Middle East studies and expertise from 1902 to 2012.

MARWAN M. KRAIDY is the Anthony Shadid Chair in Global Media, Politics and Culture and Director of the Project for Advanced Research in Global Communication at the Annenberg School, University of Pennsylvania. He has been the Edward Said Chair in American Studies at the American University of Beirut, the Dupront Chair at CELSA Université-Sorbonne, and the Bonnier Professor at Stockholm University. The recipient of Guggenheim, ACLS, NEH, Woodrow Wilson, and NIAS fellowships, Kraidy has published more than one hundred essays and six books, including *Hybridity, or the Cultural Logic of Globalization* (Temple University Press, 2005), and *Reality Television and Arab Politics* (Cambridge University Press, 2010), which won three major prizes. Kraidy's *The Naked Blogger of Cairo: Creative Insurgency in the Arab World* is forthcoming from Harvard University Press in 2016. He tweets at @MKraidy.

ALEX LUBIN is professor and Chair of the American Studies Department at the University of New Mexico. From 2011 to 2013 he served as the director of the Center for American Studies and Research at the American University of Beirut. Lubin's scholarship engages global histories of race, the African Diaspora, and America in the world, with a particular focus on U.S.–Middle East relations. He is the author of *Geographies of Liberation: the Making of an Afro-Arab Political Imaginary* (University of North Carolina Press, 2014) and *Romance and Rights: the Politics of Interracial Intimacy, 1945–1954* (University Press of Mississippi, 2005). He is the editor of *Revising the Blueprint: Ann Petry and the Literary Left* (University Press of Mississippi, 2007); and "Settler Colonialism," a *South Atlantic Quarterly* special issue (with Alyosha Goldstein).

MOUNIRA SOLIMAN is an associate professor of comparative literature at Cairo University and is currently a visiting professor at the American University in Cairo (2012–). She also served as the associate director of the Center for American Studies and Research at AUC (2014–15). Her research interests include American studies, Middle East studies, and popular culture. She is the coeditor of *Popular Culture in the Middle East and North Africa: A Postcolonial Outlook* (Routledge, 2013). She also cotranslated into Arabic *The Political Writings of Thomas Jefferson* (Saqi Books, 2011). Her other publications include *Egyptian Women Artists* (Women and Memory Forum, 2008) as well as some recent articles, including "The History of Arab National Songs: A Popular Culture Approach" (2015); "Between Art and Activism: Egyptian Women and the Revolution" (2014); "The (Un)wanted American: A Visual Reading of Arab and Muslim Americans" (2011); and "Palestine ← America → Israel: A Reading of America's Role through Political Cartoons" (Second International Conference Proceedings, American University in Beirut, 2011). Dr. Soliman was a Fulbright Senior Specialist at Yale in 2008 and a Fulbright Visiting Scholar at New York University in 2005.

HELGA TAWIL-SOURI is a media scholar, photographer, and documentary filmmaker whose work focuses on issues of spatiality, technology, and politics in the Middle East. The bulk of her scholarship analyzes culture and technology in everyday life in Palestine-Israel, theorizing how media technologies and infrastructures function as control and bordering mechanisms, and studying how territorial/physical boundaries function as cultural spaces. She writes on contemporary Palestinian cultural politics, Internet, telecommunications, television, cinema, and videogames as well as physical markers such as identification cards, checkpoints, and buffer/border zones. She is associate professor of media, culture, and communication and director of the Hagop Kevorkian Center for Near Eastern Studies at New York University.

JUDITH E. TUCKER (Ph.D., history and Middle Eastern studies, Harvard University, 1981) is professor of history at Georgetown University and former editor of the *International Journal of Middle East Studies* (2004–2009). She is the author of many publications on the history of women and gender in the Arab world, including *Women in 19th Century Egypt* (Cambridge University Press, 1985), *In the House of the Law: Gender and Islamic Law in Ottoman Syria and Palestine* (University of California Press, 1998), *Women, Family, and Gender in Islamic Law* (Cambridge University Press, 2008), and coauthor of *Women in the Middle East and North Africa: Restoring Women to History* (Indiana University Press, 1999). She has authored numerous articles for professional journals, edited volumes, and encyclopedias. Her research interests focus on the Arab world in the Ottoman period, women and gender in Middle East history, Islamic law, women, and gender, and most recently the Arab World and global connections in the eighteenth century.

ADAM JOHN WATERMAN is assistant professor of American literature and culture in the Department of English at the American University of Beirut. A former Fulbright scholar, he received his Ph.D. from the Department of Social and Cultural Analysis at New York University, where he was a MacCracken Fellow in the American Studies Program. His research focuses upon the relationship between literature, historiography, and the culture of American settler colonialism. His manuscript "The Corpse in the Kitchen: History, Necropolitics, and the Afterlives of the Black Hawk War" is currently under review with Duke University Press.

Index

corporations compared, 167; overview, 7–10; post-American world and, 14–22. *See also* American University of Beirut (AUB); knowledge production

American Studies Association, 160–61

American Studies in a Moment of Danger (Lipsitz), 15

American University of Beirut (AUB), 159, 197, 199, 201

Amkoullel (Mali hip-hop group), 121, 124, 126–27, 127–28

Amor, Hamada Ben (Tunisian hip-hop artist), 106

Andalus, al-, conquest of, 37, 65

Anderson, Kenneth, 222, 225

Anthony, David, 34, 41

Antiphony (call and response), 108, 109–14, 115, 117–18, 125–27, 129

Anti-Semitism, 36–37, 41, 54–55, 113. *See also* "the Jew"

Appadurai, Arjun, 162

Après l'empire: Essai sur la décomposition du système américain (Todd), 16

Arab American identity, 121

Arab Cold War, 288

Arab Human Development Report, 196

Arabic (language), 87, 130 (n. 4)

Arab identity, 81–82

Arab-Israeli conflict, 204 (n. 65)

Arab-Israeli war (1967), 189

Arablish (language), 132 (n. 30)

"Arab Meat (Lahme) Song," 132 (n. 28)

Arab Spring: American Autumn and, 163–71; American studies and, 159–63, 168–69, 170–71; cultural production and, 129–30, 168–69; media and, 169–70, 171 (n. 2); U.S. undermining of, 254–55, 286–98. *See also* Arab uprisings; Egyptian revolution (2011), U.S. reception and

Arab uprisings: American studies and, 14, 287, 292–93; borders and, 9–10; Eisenhower Doctrine and, 288–89;

end of American Century and, 198; globalization and, 126; information technology and, 264–65, 279–80, 280–81; Obama and, 291–95; rap/hip-hop and, 121–22; spatiality and, 265, 279, 283–84; U.S. hegemony and, 18, 19–20. *See also* Arab Spring; nationalism, Arab; rap/hip-hop

Arbenz-Guzman, Jacobo, 237 (n. 78)

Arbitrary choice, 45–46, 50

Arrighi, Giovanni, 15, 16, 164, 166, 167

Asaro, Peter, 258

Asia, 16. *See also* China

Assassinations, 198–99, 227, 228, 237 (n. 78). *See also* drones and targeted killing

Aswan High Dam, 181, 188

Aulaki v. Obama et al. (U.S. D.C. District Court), 213

Authenticity, 1, 36, 42, 95, 98, 123, 124, 247–48

authoritarian regimes and oppression: France and, 137, 252; modernization and, 176, 177, 191, 192, 195; technological, 279–80; U.S. support for, 143, 144, 194, 296. *See also* Arab uprisings; *specific authoritarian regimes*

Awlaki, Anwar al-, 222

'Azzy, 87, 102 (n. 47)

Badeau, John S., 187, 189–91

Badran, Ahmed, 111

Baghdad Pact, 182

Bahrain, 8, 19, 291, 299 (n. 21), 300 (n. 25)

Baker, Jennifer, 35

Balendra, Natasha, 225

Bambaataa, Afrika, 81

Baradei, Mohamed El, 144–45, 148–49

Barbary pirates, 38–39

Barkawi, Tarak, 200

Barret, Roby, 191

Battlefield deconstruction, 208, 209, 211, 219, 223–28, 229 (n. 10), 244, 245, 255

Battle of Algiers, The (docudrama), 252

Bayoumi, Moustafa, 117

"Beginnings of Modernization in the Middle East" (Polk), 184

Beirut school, 200

Beit Sahour attack, 207

Ben Ali, Zine El Abidine, 20

Benda-Beckmann, Franz and Keebet, 231 (n. 21)

Benghazi attack, 293–95

Benjamin, Walter, 216, 226, 252

Benvenisti, Eyal, 211

Berman, Jacob Rama, 32–33

Bezeq (cellular company), 268

Bhangra (music), 123

Biden, Joe, 147, 292

Bigg, Don, 83, 85, 92

Biopolitics and biopower, 245, 250, 252

Birmingham cultural studies scholars, 6–7

Black, Cofer, 208

Black female rappers, 115

Blackmer, Donald M., 183

Black Morocco (El Hamel), 87

Blackness, 84–88. *See also* race and racism; skin color

Black Panthers, 84

Black soldiers (Morocco), 62–63

Blackwashing, 120, 127

Blank, Laurie, 214, 224–25

Blum, Gabriella, 221

Bombardment, invention of, 249

Borders: Arab uprisings and, 9–10; drones and, 254; global capitalism and, 14; information technology and, 264, 265–74. *See also* nationalism, Arab; spatiality (territoriality) (place)

Boucher, Richard, 207g

Boulainvillier, Henri de, 67

Bourgeois hegemony, 33

Bowles, Chester, 188

Braudel, Fernand, 164

Brazil, 17, 88

Bretton Woods agreement, 13, 194

BRICS countries (Brazil, Russia, India, China, South Africa), 17

Britain, England and United Kingdom: capitalism and, 165; circulation of law and, 220; definition of war and, 214; dictators and, 137; drones and, 227; Egypt and, 141; 18th century commentators and, 33; finance and, 38; India and, 246–49; Iran and, 289; Iraq and, 241–42, 242–43, 256; lawfare and, 228; military power and, 193; Reisner and, 219; Suez canal and, 181–82; UNESCO and, 22

Brookings report, 121, 134 (n. 41)

Brooklyn Academy of Music, 119, 124, 128

Brooklyn concert, 113

Brooks, David, 294–95

Brown, Wendy, 127

B'Tselem, 230 (n. 18)

Bulliet, Richard, 192

Bush, George W.: Arab uprisings and, 292; drone strikes and, 208; lawfare and, 219; modernization and, 21, 175, 195–96; perceptions of U.S. and, 18, 19, 142, 151, 170; UNESCO and, 22; U.S. hegemony and, 14, 166; weapon sales and, 290–91. *See also* Project for the New American Century

Business as Usual: The Roots of the Global Financial Meltdown (Silver and Arrighi), 164, 166

Cairo: My City, Our Revolution (Soueif), 152

Calcutta, 246–49

Call and response (antiphony), 108, 109–14, 115, 117–18, 125–27, 129

Camp David Accords (1979), 147, 274, 295

Capital (Marx), 165

Capitalism and free markets: American studies and, 165–66; anti-Semitism and, 36–37; Cold War and, 12–13; early American literature and, 37–38; economic development *versus*, 194; expansion of, 164–65, 167, 178; freedom and, 11; global, 14–17; information technology and, 271–72. *See also* finance, fictitious; free trade; neoliberalism

Captain Majid, 105 (n. 95)

Carlson, John, 232 (n. 24)

Carolinas, 68

Cartoons, 143–44, 147, 149, 153

Casablanca, 83, 90

"Casanegra" (Biggs), 85

Casbah, 250–52

Castro, Fidel and Raul, 237 (n. 78)

"Cazafonia" (Dizzy DROS), 89–90

Cellcom (cellular company), 268

Cellular telephony, 266–68, 277, 278

Censorship, 108, 127

CENTCOM, 290, 299 (n. 17)

Center for American Studies and Research (CASAR) , 159, 160–62

Center for American Sut, 159

Chassériau, Charles Frédérick, 249–50

Chattopadhyay, Swati, 247–48

"Checkmate" (Modydick), 96–97, 97–98

Chile, 13

China, 17, 227, 232 (n. 24), 293, 297

Chomsky, Noam, 137, 139, 146

Christianity and Islam, 44, 65–69. *See also* conversion

Churchill, Winston, 256

CIA, 178, 208, 227, 228, 237 (n. 78), 257

Cinema, 244, 249, 251, 254, 255

Circulation of culture: American exceptionalism and, 162; Arab Spring and, 170–71; capitalism and, 169; empowerment and, 199; of hip-hop, 81–82, 107–8; lawfare and, 210–11, 220; Said on, 232 (n. 22)

Classes, social-economic, 122–23

Clayton, Jace (DJ/rupture), 125

Clinton, Bill, 166, 207–8

Clinton, Hillary, 120, 136–37, 145, 170, 286, 292

Cold War: American studies and, 10, 21, 22, 167, 184; Arab Spring and, 170; capitalism and, 12–13, 16; consent of governed and, 16; GCC countries and, 299 (n. 19); Middle East and, 181; modernization theory and, 178, 180; Nasser and, 287; Nixon Doctrine and, 189. *See also* American Century

Collateral damage, 208–9, 209–10, 214, 218–19, 228, 241

Colonialism, 181, 200, 215–16, 220, 226, 233 (n. 30). *See also* Algeria; imperialism, American; India

Comaroff, Jean and John, 215–16, 233 (n. 30)

Comic books, 169

Commodity relations, 36, 90

Common interests, 175

Communication and Cultural Domination (Schiller), 22

Communication studies, 20–21, 21–22

Communism, 12, 13, 180, 182, 188, 287

Community, 107, 109–19. *See also* multitude; radical belonging

Contrast, The (play), 45

Conversion, 44–51, 57 (n. 36), 66, 69, 75

Corsairs, 57 (n. 22), 65, 66, 69, 70

Cosmopolitanism, 66, 70, 169, 170–71

Counterinsurgency efforts, 178, 253

Covering Islam: How the Media and the Experts Determine How We See the Rest of the World (Said), 31

"Cowboy Dynamo" (Haddad), 148

Cowboy photos, 3 (ill.)

Crain, Caleb, 45

Crandall, Jordan, 256

Credit. *See* finance, fictitious

Crips, the, 90

Early American society, 32, 37–38.
See also The Algerine Captive (Tyler);
The Algerine Spy in Pennsylvania
(Markoe); *Tales of the Alhambra*
(Irving)
Eastern European movements, 153
"Eastern tales," 71–72
Eazy E, 92
Education: *Algerine Captive* and, 47;
conflicts of interest and, 201–2;
information technology in, 276–77;
Iraq and, 186; modernization theory
and, 176; Moroccan urban youth
and, 83; neomodernization and, 177;
rap and, 95; Salim and, 74–76. *See
also* American University of Beirut
(AUB)
Edwards, Brian T., 199
Egypt: Benghazi attack and, 293–94;
end of American Century and, 198;
Gaza and, 296; information technology and, 263–65, 264–65, 274–82,
282–83; Israel and, 146, 181; Lerner's
study and, 21; media and, 294–95;
Middle East studies and, 199–200;
modernization theory and, 193;
1970s and, 194; U.S. hegemony
decline and, 138; U.S. relations and,
137–38. *See also* Egyptian revolution
(2011); El Deeb; Nasser, Gamal
Abdel *and other Egyptians*
Egyptian-Israeli conflicts, 275
Egyptian revolution (2011), U.S.
reception and: background, 136–40;
Egyptian response to U.S., 137,
140–42, 147–53; January activity
described, 145–47; Obama and, 292;
pseudo-democracy and, 142–45;
year later, 154–55. *See also* Arab
Spring; Arab Spring
Eisenhower, Dwight, 119, 137, 181, 182,
183, 184, 185, 286–87, 287–89
Ekbladh, David, 178
Embodiment, call and response and,
113, 115–16, 118–19, 126–27

Emcees, Arabic hip-hop, 109, 121–29
*Emerging Nations: Their Growth and
United States Policy, The* (Millikan
and Blackmer, eds.), 183
Empathy, 21
Empire. *See* imperial gaze; imperial-
ism, American
Empowerment. *See* agency, empower-
ment and disempowerment
England. *See* Britain, England and
United Kingdom
Enlightenment, 33, 35, 47–48
Epistemes and knowledge production,
15, 166–68, 197–202, 244. *See also*
education; imperial gaze; Islami-
cism; Orientalism
Eslam Jawaad (Anglo-Syrian rap
group), 110
Essai sur les moeurs et l'esprit des nations
(Voltaire), 67
Ethiopia, 230 (n. 12)
Etisalat (cellular company), 277
Europe: American studies and, 7–8;
Arab world and, 19; capitalism/
anti-Semitism and, 36–37; conver-
sion and, 44; enslaved Europeans,
45, 47, 49–51, 69; Muslim youth
discourse and, 84; neoliberalism
and, 82; Orientalism and, 34;
post-WWII, 13; Salim and, 66–67.
See also Britain *and other countries*
Exceptionalism, American, 25 (n. 2),
159, 167, 168, 195
Exoticism, 123, 127

Fahmy, Ziad, 141
Faisal bin Abdulaziz Al Saud, 193, 205
(n. 77)
Faisal II, 288
Faith, 50
Fatwas, 66
Federalists, 40, 45, 58 (n. 39)
Feinstein, Dianne, 213
Femmes d'Alger dans leur appartement
(Delacroix), 251

Fenton, Bessie Knox, 247
Ferguson, Niall, 293
Finance, fictitious: early American literature and, 35, 37–38, 40, 41–42, 50–51, 52–56; identity and, 41–43; Irving and, 53–54; Lukács on, 35–36
First Gulf War, 245
Fischer-Lichte, Erika, 114
Fisk, Robert, 144
Flash Kicker, 105 (n. 95)
Fnaïre (rap group), 87
"Food for Peace" program, 188
Ford, Gerald, 227
Foucault, Michel, 244, 250
France, 137, 181–82, 249–52
Fraser, James Baillie, 247, 248
Freedom, global, 11, 14
Freedom of assembly, 282
Freedom of press, 22
Freedom of religion, 67
Free trade, 263, 264, 265–66, 275. See also capitalism and free markets; neoliberalism
Fribgane, Brahim, 124
Friedman, Thomas, 196
Frith, Simon, 123
Fuchs, Georg, 113
Full Spectrum Warrior (video game), 255–56
Funk, 109

Gaddafi, Muammar, 20, 96–97
Gaonkar, Dilip, 169
Garda, Imran, 149
Gates, Robert, 292
Gaye, Marvin, 94
Gaza and West Bank: definition of war and, 217–18, 222; drones/targeted killing and, 227, 231 (n. 18); Egyptian intelligence and, 296; hip-hop and, 110, 111, 117; information technology and, 266, 267, 268, 269; invasions of, 19, 110; lawfare and, 212, 217–18; Nasser and, 181;

Occupy Wall Street and, 131 (n. 17); weapons sales and, 291. See also DARG; Palestinian/Israeli conflict
Gelb, Leslie, 293
Gender, 95, 250–52
Général, El (hip-hop artist), 106, 121, 124, 127
Geneva Conventions, 224
Germany, 16. See also National Socialism
Gibbs, Robert, 146, 149–50
Gilroy, Paul, 7
Givens, Samuel, 64
Globalization: American studies and, 160; Arab uprisings and, 126; CASAR and, 162; Egyptian literature and, 169; information technology and, 270, 273–74, 279, 283; nationalism and, 278. See also cosmopolitanism
Global war on terror (GWOT): battlefield deconstruction and, 209, 223; capitalism and, 14–17; Cold War geopolitics and, 170; cultural production and, 120; drones and, 208; end of American Century and, 16; lawfare and, 214–16, 217, 219; video games and, 253–54
Gnawa tradition, 86–87
Gold reserves, U.S., 13
Goldstein, Brooke, 213
Goldstone, Richard, 212
Gomaa (cartoonist), 143–44
Goodman, Amy, 139
Graffiti, 153
Gramsci, Antonio, 16, 122–23
Green Zone, 215
Gregory, Derek, 209, 214, 215, 223, 244, 254
Griffiths, Anne, 231 (n. 21)
Gross, Eyal, 221
Guantanamo Bay, 211
Guatemala, 237 (n. 78)
Guerrilla warfare, 245
Guiora, Amos, 221

Gulf Cooperation Council (GCC) , 19, 286, 289–90, 291, 295–96, 297, 299 (n. 19)
GWOT. *See* global war on terror

Haddad, Amin, 151–52
Haddad, Fouad, 148
Hajjar, Lisa, 232 (n. 24)
Hall, Stuart, 7, 122–23, 141
Halpern, Manfred, 191–92
Hamas, 212
Hamel, Chouki El, 86, 87
Hamid, Shadi, 150–51
Harb, Mona, 201
Hard Choices (H. Clinton), 292
Hardt, Hanno, 21
Hardt, Michael, 110
Harel, Amos, 210
Harethi, Qaed Salim Sinan al-, 208
Harlem concert, 115, 116
Harvey, David, 135 (n. 60), 166
Hasan Salaam (African-American rap group), 110
"Hauntology," 161
"Hegemony Unravelling," (Arrighi), 166
Heller, Kevin John, 209
Heyman, Phillip, 221
Hezbollah, 4, 196–97, 201, 228, 257
Hichkas (Iranian rap group), 110, 111
High Court of Justice (HCJ) (Israel), 212–13, 218–19, 221, 236 (n. 73)
Hip-hop. *See* rap/hip-hop
History of Bombing (Lindqvist), 256
H-Kayne (rap group), 83
Hoban, Stephen, 149
Hodges, William, 246
Holland, 164, 165
Hooks, bell, 84, 88
Horst, Karl R., 290
Humanitarianism, 211
Humanitarianism, U.S., 12. *See also* empathy
Human Rights Watch, 228
Hunt, Michael, 178

Huntington, Samuel, 194
Hussein of Jordan, 287–88
Hussin, Iza, 220, 231 (n. 21)

Ibn Battuta, 62
Ibn Khaldun (d. 1406), 62
Identity: Afghanistan war and, 117; African urban space and, 260 (n. 21); *Algerine Captive* and, 46–47; *Algerine Spy* and, 38–43; American, 162; American music and, 120; American Revolution and, 35; Arab American, 121; conversion and, 49, 50; Egyptian revolution and, 141–42; fictitious finance and, 41–43; Gnawa tradition (Morocco) and, 86–87; hybrid, 107, 122, 123–25, 127; Islamic, 38–43; Mansour and, 116, 119; "Moorish," 65; multiracial, 61, 81, 88, 251; multitude and, 110–11; 9/11 and, 138; rap/hip-hop and, 81–82, 83, 89, 107, 115, 121–29; "Rhythm Road" initiative and, 109. *See also* race and racism; Salim the Algerine
IDF (Israeli Defense Force), 207, 208, 212, 217–19, 221, 222, 228
Ignatius, David, 297
I Love Hip Hop in Morocco (Fnaïre), 87
Imam, Sheikh, 148
Imperial gaze: British, 242–43, 246–49; drones and, 241, 243, 256–58; French, 249–52; history of, 243–45; media and, 242; urban warfare and, 243–44, 246; video games and, 252–56
Imperialism, American: American studies and, 160, 166–67; Cold War and, 12; cultural, 25 (n. 2), 81, 99, 107; Lerner and, 20–21; Obama and, 242, 254; Orientalism and, 33–34, 56. *See also* colonialism; imperial gaze
India, 17, 243, 246–49
Indyk, Martin, 194–95

Information communication and
technology (ICT) , 271. *See also*
technology, information
Insanity, 72–73, 80 (n. 46)
Intellectual activity, 122–23
International Humanitarian Law
(IHL) (Laws of Armed Conflict) ,
207, 218, 224, 225
International Monetary Fund, 13, 135
(n. 60)
Internet service, 269–70, 271–72,
277–78, 279, 280
Intik (Cool), 81, 107
Iran: "destabilization" and, 146;
drones and, 257; GCC and, 286;
Gulf Cooperation Council and, 296;
Lerner's study and, 21; modernization theory and, 193; 1970s and, 194;
Nixon/Carter and, 289–90; Obama
and, 19, 143; Saudis and, 291;
weapons sales and, 291. *See also*
Northern Tier
Iraq and Iraq war: Arab Americans
and, 117; Britain and, 241–42, 256;
coup (1958) and, 183, 184, 185–86,
288–89, 298 (n. 11); definition of
war and, 214, 222; drones and, 229
(n. 12); Egyptian democracy
movement compared, 151; Eisenhower Doctrine and, 287; GCC and,
290; Kennedy era and, 188; lawfare
and, 215; modernization theory and,
175, 195–96; Nasser and, 288;
nationalism and, 184, 185; neomodernization and, 177; Obama and, 143,
242; regime change and, 14; targeted
killing and, 210; video games and,
243; war (1991) and, 194–95
Iraqi Communist Party, 185
Irving, Washington. *See Tales of the
Alhambra* (Irving)
ISIS (Islamic State in Iraq and
al-Sham), 210, 257, 297
Islam and U.S.: Benghazi attack and,
294; Christianity and, 44, 65–69;

Eisenhower Doctrine and, 288;
extremists/fundamentalists and, 128,
275; Maghreb and, 250; Middle East
studies and, 195; modernization
theory and, 180, 184–85, 192–93;
Morocco and, 87; overview, 31–32;
racism and, 99; *Tales of Alhambra*
and, 54. *See also* conversion; Orientalism; Salim the Algerine *and other
Muslims; Tales of the Alhambra*
(Irving)
Islamic identity, 38–43
Islamicism, 32
Islamic State in Iraq and al-Sham
(ISIS), 210, 257, 297
Islamist movements, 194; language
and, 292–93; post-revolution,
292–93. *See also* Hezbollah *and
others*
Ismai'il, Mawlay, 62–63
Israel: American Studies and, 8;
American Studies Association and,
160–61; colonialism and, 226; Egypt
and, 146, 181; Eisenhower and, 185;
global war on terror and, 217;
Hezbolla and, 196–97; Jordan and,
275; Kennedy/Nixon era and, 189;
kuffiyeh and, 132 (n. 26); modern-
ization theory and, 190, 191; Nixon
Doctrine and, 289; targeted killing
and, 207–8, 208–9, 221–22; U.S. support for, 4, 18, 20. *See also* anti-
Semitism; lawfare; Palestinian/Israeli
conflict
Israeli Defense Force (IDF), 207, 208,
212, 217–19, 221, 222, 228
Istanbul, 66, 69, 70
Italian states, 164, 165
Italy, 229 (n. 12)

Jackson, Michael, 94
Jacobs, Matthew, 180–81
"#Jan25" (Offendum), 121–22
Japan, 13, 16
Jazz Ambassador tours, 119–20

Meade, William, 69
Media: Arab Spring and, 169–70, 171
(n. 2); Arab uprisings and, 292;
CASAR and, 161–62; common
interests and, 175; drones and, 242;
Egypt and, 141, 278, 280, 294–95;
Egyptian, 279; on Obama, 296–97;
Turkey and, 179. *See also* technol-
ogy, information
Medieval period, 33, 36–37
Mégret, Frédéric, 223, 229 (n. 10)
Mexico, 254
Meyer, Aaron Eitan, 213
Mic Check (BAM festival), 120–21,
124–29, 135 (n. 57)
Micro Brise le Silence, le ("The
microphone breaks the silence")
(MBS), 81
Middle East studies, 159, 184, 195,
199–200
"Mideast Policy Must Look Beyond
This Crisis" (Rostow), 182–83, 191
Migrants to Morocco, 86, 87, 93
Migrations into Europe, 82
Military power: American studies and,
8–9; capitalism and, 165; Carter and,
289; diminishment of, 198–99; Egypt
and, 154, 295; Eisenhower Doctrine
and, 182; GCC countries and, 299
(n. 19); information technology and,
273; Iraq coup (1958) and, 298 (n. 11);
Iraqi nationalism and, 186; lawfare
and, 213, 216; Lebanon and, 4, 288;
Middle East studies and, 195;
modernization theory and, 176,
190–92, 193, 196; 1980s-90s and, 194;
Nixon/Carter and, 289–90; Obama
and, 296; terrorism and, 198–99; 21st
century, 17; urban war and, 245–46;
video games and, 253. *See also*
American Century; battlefield
deconstruction; drones and targeted
killing; global war on terror
(GWOT); Palestinian/Israeli
conflict *and other conflicts*

Millikan, Max F., 178, 183
MIME (military-industrial-media-
entertainment complex), 253
MIRS (cellular company), 268
Mirzoeff, Nick, 243–44, 253
MIT Center for International Studies,
178–79, 180, 182–83, 185
Mitchell, George, 207–8
Mobil (cellular company), 277
Mobydick, 82, 85, 89, 93–98, 96, 105
(n. 86)
Modernity, 33, 294
Modernization theory: American
studies and, 201; Arab nationalism
and, 184–86, 189–90; Cold War
and, 180–83; eclipse of, 193–96;
failures of, 189–95; information
technology and, 271–72; Islam and,
180, 184–85, 192–93; Kennedy/
Nixon eras and, 186–89; military
force and, 190–92, 193; nationalism
and, 184–86, 189–90, 205 (n. 79);
neo-Orientalism and, 195–96; rise
of, 175–80. *See also* technology,
information
Mohamed Mahmoud events, 153
Mohammadi, Hay, 83
Mohammed VI, 86
Mohyeldin, Ayman, 121–22
Moors, 76
Morality, 71–72
Morocco, 62–63, 86, 291
Morsi, Mohamed, 20, 295
Mossadegh, Mohammad, 289
Mubarak, Hosni: cartoons and, 149;
coercive lending and, 27 (n. 25);
information technology and, 274;
Mohyeldin on, 122; Obama and, 19,
20, 145, 149–50, 152, 153, 154, 170,
292; public perceptions of, 136, 140,
141, 146–47, 149, 154; spatiality and,
281–82; Wisner and, 147, 148
Multinational corporations, 165, 167,
271
Multitude, 108, 110–11, 112, 113–14, 257

Munasifi, Remy, 116, 133 (n. 30)
Murphy, Richard, 221
Muslim Brotherhood, 20, 288, 293, 294
Muslim hegemony, 44
Muslims. *See* Egyptian revolution;
Islam and U.S.; Palestinian/Israeli
conflict *and other conflicts;* rap/
hip-hop
Mussolini, Bruno, 256

Nafar, Suhell and Tamer, 110
Nafisi, Azar, 169
Narcicyst, the (Iraqi Canadian rap
group), 110, 113, 123, 124
Nasrallah, Sayyed Hassan, 257
Nass El Ghiwane (music group),
83, 86
Nasser, Gamal Abdel, 181–82, 185, 187,
188, 189, 287–88
National Democratic Institute (NDI)
(U.S.), 286
Nationalism, Arab: Eisenhower and,
287–89; globalization and, 278;
information technology and, 279;
Kennedy and, 186–87, 188; military
force and, 186; modernization
theory and, 184–86, 189–90, 205
(n. 79); 1970s and, 194; Obama and,
296. *See also* borders; Nasser, Gamal
Abdel
National Security Council (NSC),
11–12, 137
National Security Strategy (NSS),
295–96
National Socialism, 37
Native Americans, 5 (ill.)
NATO, 178
Nazism, 37
Near East Foundation, 187
Negm, Ahmed Fouad, 148
Negri, Antonio, 110
Neimneh, Shadi, 139
Neocolonialism, 200
Neoconservatism, 196, 233 (n. 31).
See also Lawfare Project

Neoliberalism: American studies and,
160; Arab elites and, 198; cultural
production and, 107; Egypt and,
277; hybrid identities and, 122;
information technology and, 22,
270, 271–72, 273; rap/hip-hop and,
82, 125, 127, 128–29; U.S. decline
and, 17, 19; U.S. foreign policy and,
135 (n. 60), 194; World Bank
lending and, 18. *See also* capitalism
and free markets; free trade
Neomodernization, 177, 195–96, 201
Neo-Orientalism, 195–96, 201
Netanyahu, Binyamin, 212
New American Century, 14
"New International Economic
Order," 194
New World Information Order, 22
New York City, 52–53, 115, 116, 117,
131 (n. 17)
Nhu, Ngo Dinh, 227
Nicaragua, 14
Niger, 230 (n. 12), 254
"Nigga," 88
9/11: American studies and, 166–67;
Arab identity and, 138; battlefield
deconstruction and, 223, 224, 225;
drones and, 208; global war on
terror and, 217; lawfare and, 214,
219; modernization theory and, 175,
177, 195–96
Nixon, Richard and Nixon Doctrine,
13, 148, 189, 194, 289
Nolte, Richard H., 184
Non-Aligned Movement, 287
Nongovernmental organizations, 128,
135 (n. 60), 154, 272–73, 276
"North African" (Malien musician),
128
North Africans (Moors), 64–65
North Atlantic Treaty Organization,
20, 291
Northern Tier, 288–89
*Notes on the Medical Topography of
Calcutta* (Martin), 248

278–84. *See also* cellular telephony; Internet; media; social media; text messaging

Telecom Egypt (cellular company), 277

TelQuel (magazine), 92–93

Tenet, George, 208

Territoriality. *See* spatiality

Terrorism: drones and, 221; lawfare as, 211; military power and, 198–99; protests *versus,* 208; targeted killing and, 209, 221; video games and, 257. *See also* global war on terror; 9/11; al-Qaeda

Text messaging, 169

Thabet killing, 218

"Theorizing the Diffusion of Law: Conceptual Difficulties, Unstable Imaginations, and the Effort to Think Gracefully Nonetheless" (Westbrook), 231 (n. 21)

Third World, 13, 22; modernization theory and, 178, 189–95; nationalism and, 181

Third World Approaches to International Law, 233 (n. 30)

Thob, 115

Thompson, Robert Farris, 109

1001 Arabian Nights, 71

3alam (Dizzy DROS), 104 (n. 76)

3azzy, 87–90, 92

3azzy 3ando Stylo (Dizzy DROS), 92–93

Thug Gang (rap group), 83, 85

Tiananmen Square, 153

Tilimsānī, Muḥammad ibn Muḥammad al-, 65–66

Todd, Emmanuel, 16

Tolerance, 127

Torture, 211, 212, 296

Totem pole, 2 (ill.)

"Toward a Policy for the Middle East" (Nolte and Polk), 184

Traditional society, 20–21, 179, 180, 248. *See also* modernization theory

Tragedy of American Diplomacy, the (Williams), 12–13, 14

Trance and music, 132 (n. 18)

Transformative Power of Performance, the (Fischer-Lichte), 114

Transnational alliances, 109

Traveling law, 210, 231 (n. 21)

"Travelling Theory Reconsidered" (Said), 231 (n. 21)

Tristan, Pierre, 153

True Nature of Imposture Fully Displayed in the Life of Mahome, The (Prideaux), 67

Truman Doctrine, 181

Tucker, St. George, 63–64, 71, 78 (n. 8)

Tunisia: Arab Spring and, 163; digital revolution and, 170; France and, 137; Haddad and, 152; media and, 106, 171 (n. 2); 1970s and, 194; U.S. attitudes toward, 20, 296

Tunisian crew, 121

Turkey, 21, 179, 196, 198, 229 (n. 12), 298 (n. 11). *See also* Northern Tier

2008 financial meltdown, 164, 166

TXT messaging, 169

Tyler, Royall, 34, 45. *See also The Algerine Captive*

Ulama, 62–63

UNESCO (United Nations Educational, Scientific and Cultural Organization), 22

"Unexampled Time of Prosperity, An: The Great Mississippi Bubble" (Irving), 52

United Arab Emirates (UAE), 229 (n. 12), 286, 290–91, 295, 299 (n. 21)

United Arab Republic, 288

United Kingdom. *See* Britain, England and United Kingdom

United Nations, 14, 22, 231 (n. 18)

United States: Arab world and, 9; culture of, 20, 22; western frontier and, 1–6, 64. *See also* American

Century; American Studies; early American society; media; U.S. foreign policy

U.S. Agency for International Development (USAID), 271, 275, 276

U.S. Air Force, 241

U.S. Department of Defense, 225–26

U.S. dollar, 13

U.S.-Egypt Partnership for Economic Growth and Development, 275–76

U.S. foreign aid, 183, 187–88, 274–75

U.S. foreign debt, 166

U.S. foreign policy, 11–12, 18. *See also* American Century; authoritarian regimes and oppression; imperialism, American; Israel; military power; modernization theory; neoliberalism; Obama, Barack *and other Americans;* USAID *and other programs*

U.S. hegemony: Arab uprisings and, 19–20; Arab world and, 18–21; decline of, 14–17, 82, 138, 166; Obama and, 295–97. *See also* American Century; Arab Spring

United States Information Agency (USIA), 7–8

U.S. Pentagon, 296–97

U.S. State Department, 9, 11–12, 161, 187, 207. *See also* "Rhythm Road"

University of Bahrain, 8

Unrestricted Warfare: China's Master Plan to Destroy America (Liang and Xiangsui), 232 (n. 24)

Urban battlefields, 241–58, 248–49, 260 (n. 21)

USS *Cole*, 208

Video games, 243, 252–56, 254–55

Vietnam war, 13, 227, 245

"View of the Bazaar Leading to Chitpore Road, A" (Fraser), 247

"Views of Calcutta and Its Environs" (Fraser), 247

Vindication of the Rights of Woman (Wollstonecraft), 33

Virginia (U.S. state), 68, 71

Virno, Paolo, 113

"Vision of Selim, The" (Tucker), 71–72

Vitalis, Robert, 193, 199–200

Vodafone Egypt (cellular company), 277

Voltaire, 67

Waleed, Jihad, 147

Wallerstein, Immanuel, 15–16

Walt, Stephen, 16–17

Wansharisi, Ahmad al-, 66

War: democracy and, 254–55; expanding definition of, 208, 209, 214, 217–18, 222–23, 224, 236 (n. 69); regulation and, 250. *See also* battlefield deconstruction; lawfare; Palestinian/Israeli conflict *and others*

War crimes, 258

"War Is Culture" (Mirzoeff), 253

War on terror. *See* global war on terror (GWOT)

Warschauer, Mark, 276, 277

Washington Consensus, 198, 270

Waterbury, John, 200, 201–2

Weapons, 153, 181, 290–91, 296

"We Are the Kentucky Dudes," 150

Weberian sociology, 178

Weizman, Eyal, 226

Welcome Father Nixon ("Shara ya Nixon Baba") (Negm and Sheikh Imam), 148

West Bank. *See* Gaza and West Bank

Westbrook, David A., 231 (n. 21)

West Coast U.S., 90

Westmoreland, William, 245

White, Ed, 58 (n. 39)

White nationalist fantasy, 95

"Whither Goeth the Law—Humanity or Barbarity" (Carlson and Yeomans), 232 (n. 24)

Whitlock, Craig, 229 (n. 12)

WikiLeaks, 20
Williams, William Appleman, 12–13, 14, 15
Williamsburg society, 63–64, 67
Wise, Edward, 220
Wisner, Frank, 147–48
"Wolfert Webber; or, Golden Dreams" (Irving), 52–53
Wolfowitz, Paul, 208
Wollstonecraft, Mary, 33
World Bank, 13, 18, 83, 135 (n. 60), 181, 263, 271
"World Music," 123–24
Worlds-systems analysis, 165–66
World War II, 11, 12

Xiangsui, Wang, 232 (n. 24)

Yaqub, Salim, 287
Yemen: definition of war and, 222; drones and, 208, 209, 229 (n. 12), 241, 242, 257; Nasser and, 188; Saudis and, 291; targeted killing and, 209–10; U.S. media and, 292
Yeomans, Neville, 232 (n. 24)
"Yesterday I had a dream" (Biggs), 85
Yom, Sean L., 299 (n. 21)

Zakaria, Fareed, 15
Zamane, 86
"Zenga Zenga" (Street, Street) (Mobydick), 97
Zucotti Park march. See Occupy movement
Zulu Nation, 81, 99 (n. 4), 115